Catholics and Jews
in Twentieth-Century America

Catholics and Jews in Twentieth-Century America

EGAL FELDMAN

UNIVERSITY OF ILLINOIS PRESS
Urbana and Chicago

Library of Congress Cataloging-in-Publication Data
Feldman, Egal, 1925–
Catholics and Jews in twentieth-century America /
Egal Feldman.
p. cm.
Includes bibliographical references and index.
ISBN 0-252-02684-5 (cloth)
1. Judaism—Relations—Catholic Church. 2. Catholic
Church—Relations—Judaism. 3. Judaism—United
States—History—20th century. 4. Catholic Church—
United States—History—20th century. 5. Christianity
and antisemitism—History. 6. United States—Ethnic
relations. I. Title.
BM535.F43   2001
261.2'6'09730904—dc21   2001001174

To my wife, Joan Bischoff,
whose vision and support made this book possible

Lizkor ve lo lishkoach
(Remember and do not forget)

—motto of Yad Vashem

Contents

Preface

One of the most remarkable transformations which occurred during the twentieth century involved the relationship of Roman Catholics and Jews in the United States. Yet American historians have paid only scant attention to it. Despite the importance of the interfaith movement in American religious life, its historiography remains small. The task of examining and evaluating the interfaith movement, upon which much public praise has been showered, has been relegated mostly to theologians.

Years ago, I concluded that a history of Jewish-Christian relations in the United States would profit by separating the numerous Protestant denominations from the Roman Catholic Church. I dealt with the former in *Dual Destinies: The Jewish Encounter with Protestant America* (1990). Yet, in a certain sense, Roman Catholics and Jews appear more compatible than do Protestants and Jews. Both were for many years lumped by the Protestant majority with recent newcomers, the religiously suspect, and questionable citizens. Yet both groups could claim representatives in the New World whose arrival preceded that of the Pilgrims. Both groups represented ancient religions whose origins were as old or older than Western civilization, in the case of the Jews by two millennia. Both groups dispatched their greatest numbers to the New World during the nineteenth and twentieth centuries. Yet both groups—Catholics and Jews—were divided by religious beliefs and practices coupled with bitter historical memories which continued to fester in the free environment of their adopted land. How Jews and Roman Catholics learned to accommodate each other and live more comfortably with their differences is the subject of this book.

Unlike their Protestant neighbors, Jews and Catholics are linked more firmly with their coreligionists abroad. The Jewish people, few in number (more than 15 million the world over in 1939), surrounded by a threatening mass of non-Jews but united by deep religious ties, have been forever conscious and protective of their widely scattered brethren. For their part, Roman Catholics, 800 million members of what they see as a universal church at whose head sits the bishop of Rome, can also not isolate themselves from the rest of the world. Neither can a study of Jews and Catholics in the United States ignore the importance of these international links. Thus, this book must cross national frontiers.

□ □ □

In the course of this work, a number of individuals have shared their views with me. I am grateful to each of them. It would be impossible to name them all. Those who come to mind include Rabbi Jack Bemporad, who shared with me his knowledge of Jewish relationships with the Holy See; Professor Steven Bayme of the American Jewish Committee, who took time to discuss with me the plan for this book; Rabbi Laurence J. Silberstein, who shared his teaching experience at the Pontifical Gregorian University in Rome; Henry Feingold, whose conversation about the papacy of Pius XII remains memorable; the late Professor A. Roy Eckardt, who provided invaluable insights; Father John T. Pawlikowski, who discussed with me his views about the work of Elie Wiesel. None of these individuals should be held responsible for my conclusions.

I must also note the support that I have received from librarians and university administrators. Despite our age of electronic information, librarians remain indispensable to the historian. Accordingly, I thank Beverly Lahti and Eileen Wasyliszyn of the staff of the Jim Dan Hill Library of the University of Wisconsin–Superior. I also extend my appreciation to the staffs of the Memorial Library of the University of Wisconsin, the Wilson Library of the University of Minnesota, and the library of the College of St. Scholastica. David Lull of the Duluth Public Library could always be relied upon to check references and track down an obscure source. Professor Roger Forseth supplied me with relevant newspaper clippings which I might have otherwise missed. The administration of the University of Wisconsin–Superior generously granted me a number of travel and research grants which enabled me to complete this book and, when I retired from teaching, supplied me with an office and secretarial service. I also wish to thank Wayne State University Press for permission to quote from my previously published book *The Dreyfus Affair and the American Conscience, 1895–1906*. The greatest debt of all, however, I owe to my wife, Professor Joan Bischoff, for her cooperation, encouragement, and constant assurance that it was all worth while. It is to her that I dedicate this book.

Catholics and Jews
in Twentieth-Century America

Introduction:
Two Communities

Roman Catholics and Jews did not possess mutually entwined interests at the opening of the twentieth century. On the contrary, each community was deeply engrossed with its peculiar problems of adjusting to the realities of an American environment. Both Roman Catholics and Jews were immigrant people. Their numbers grew substantially at the end of the nineteenth century, although, due to small migrations from England, Portugal, and Spain, both groups could claim a representation in the New World even before the arrival of the Pilgrims. Unlike what was witnessed in American Catholicism, Jewish population growth was more modest. During the first three-quarters of the nineteenth century, Jewish numbers in the United States grew very slowly, from about 3,000 people in 1790 to nearly 250,000 in 1877. Jews were scattered across America at this later date and constituted only .5 percent of the population. Sixty years later, in 1937, they were 3.7 percent of the American population. By the opening of the twentieth century, the sources of Jewish immigration had also undergone change from predominantly Central European and German-speaking origins to Eastern European. Most immigrants spoke the Yiddish language.[1] At a time when most Americans lived on farms and in small towns, both religious groups, Catholics and Jews, preferred settling in the cities of the Northeast and Midwest.

Those Jews who were first to cross the ocean were chiefly preoccupied with the arrival of hundreds of thousands of their brethren from the hamlets of eastern Europe (two million between 1880 and 1920). Under the aegis of the czar, they had been subjected to economic deprivation and government-sponsored mob violence: pogroms. Ideologically, the new arrivals did not comprise a homogeneous group. Some had led a deeply pious existence in the Old World, a life of study of sacred texts and obedience to the laws of the Torah. They hoped to continue their lives unmolested in America. Others were attracted more to a secular form of Judaism—a few to socialism or Marxism. Still others were captivated by the rising spirit of Jewish nationalism: Zionism. Most were penniless when they arrived in America and contrasted conspicuously as they took their place beside the smaller but well-established earlier arrivals of German-speaking Jews from Central Europe.

At the opening of the twentieth century, Jewish religious life was far from uniform. Newcomers from more traditional backgrounds soon learned that the Reform, or Liberal, movement dominated Jewish religious practice at the expense of more traditional behavior. Religious splintering was characteristic of American cultural voluntarism. Sociologists of American religion, such as Will Herberg and Andrew M. Greeley, have documented the pluralistic character of American religion. Greeley's assertion "that denominationalism is a central characteristic of American religion" and Will Herberg's comment that "the unity of American life is indeed a unity of multiplicity" recognize the importance of this principle in American culture.[2] It was a deeply embedded liberal ideal with which most Jews were able to live comfortably.

Judaism had never been a monolithic system of belief, even though, as in Protestantism, a few of its adherents would have liked to make it so. The Reform, or Liberal, movement in American Judaism matured during the last quarter of the nineteenth century. Under the leadership of Isaac M. Wise, an organizational structure had been erected that stood the test of time and guaranteed permanency to the movement. It included the founding in 1873 of what would shortly become its national organization, the Union of American Hebrew Congregations. Two years later, to prepare a pool of Liberal rabbis, the Hebrew Union College was established in Cincinnati. To provide a forum for the movement's leadership, the Central Conference of American Rabbis was founded in 1889.

Throughout the latter years of the nineteenth century, Reform Judaism continued to conform to the religious conditions imposed upon it by its upwardly mobile, rapidly Americanized membership. With the Jewish community numbering nearly one quarter of a million by 1880, and growing numbers dispersed throughout the smaller cities of the Midwest, zealous adherence to traditional religious requirements declined. At the same time, almost paradoxically, Reform rabbis became increasingly conscious of what they believed was their appointed mission: to transmit to the world the moral and ethical values of monotheism. The dispersion of Israel, long considered a heavenly burden to be patiently borne, was now inverted into a providential opportunity, a blessing to Israel for the sake of humankind.

No document expressed more succinctly the ideology that guided Liberal Judaism during the late nineteenth century than the one produced by eighteen American rabbis who gathered near Pittsburgh in November 1885. For the next fifty years, their eight-point declaration, known as the Pittsburgh Platform, was considered the most authoritative statement of the theology and practice of Reform Judaism.[3]

Kaufman Kohler, rabbi of New York's Temple Beth El and a leading theoretician of Reform Judaism, was the chief engineer of the conference. Kohler arrived at the meeting determined to persuade his colleagues that only through drastic adjustments would Judaism continue to thrive on American soil. His dissatisfaction with the state of late nineteenth-century Judaism was evident in his opening declaration: "Every one who has watched the condition of the affairs of Judaism in general and in our country in particular, must have been impressed with the urgent need of decisive action in view of the appalling indifference which has taken hold of the masses."[4]

Following his jeremiad, Kohler presented a series of proposals, which were shortly adopted. These included such radical suggestions as the one that the authors of supernatural biblical accounts be discarded, together with the binding nature of ceremonial laws, "except those that elevate the sanctity of our lives."[5] Jewish dietary laws were dismissed as outmoded, for, as the rabbis put it, they failed "to impress the modern Jew with a spirit of priestly holiness." Since the rabbis had welcomed the dispersion of Israel as a heavenly gift, they also rejected the notion of Zionism.[6]

The Reform movement's reaction against ancestral religious practices, however, did not withstand the test of time. Within a few decades, there were indications that Reform was sliding slowly backwards to tradition. The rejection of Zionism was one of the first of the newer concepts to wither. A century later, almost every one of the principles of the Pittsburgh Platform had been repudiated. Reform rabbis donned skullcaps and prayer shawls, increased the use of the Hebrew language during religious services, and urged their congregants to follow the Mitzvot (Commandments) of the Torah (Hebrew Pentateuch).[7]

Even after the adoption of the Pittsburgh Platform in 1887, these radical suggestions were not universally welcomed. The theology of the platform was particularly distasteful to the newer arrivals, who had been conditioned by a more traditional upbringing. Reform Judaism's radical break with tradition represented a dangerous breach with the past too drastic for their comfort. Even the more modernized among recent immigrants, although prepared for religious change, preferred to move more cautiously. They sought, at least, some continuity with the past. Caught between their loyalty to traditional practices and the social requirements of the new era, they found more comfort in what was shortly to be known as the Conservative movement, or the Historical School, in American Judaism.

The formalized structure of the Conservative movement was established in 1886 when a group of traditionalist leaders joined by a number of disillusioned Reformers created the Jewish Theological Seminary. Located in New York City, the school was designed to offset the influence of Hebrew Union College by training rabbis and teachers in the more traditional learning of Judaism. With the founding of the movement's lay organization in 1913, the United Synagogue of America, and its professional organization, the Rabbinical Assembly, in 1918, a new and separate bureaucracy had emerged within American Judaism.

Beyond New York and Philadelphia, Orthodox congregations with an Eastern European orientation were inconspicuous during the earlier years of the nineteenth century. The founding of Beth Hamidrash Hagadol in New York City in 1852 by a small group of Russian Jews represented one of the early triumphs of American Orthodoxy. By 1900, however, three hundred Eastern European Orthodox synagogues were in existence in New York City alone, although many had only a handful of members.[8] Orthodox immigrants brought with them traditions and customs, including the Yiddish language, which had been part of their evolving culture for a number of centuries. Their religious and theological outlook differed profoundly from that seen in Reform and Conservatism.

Orthodox Judaism, the third branch of American Judaism, although it had existed earlier in the century as did Conservatism, came into its own during the 1880s. Like their rivals, Orthodox Jews developed an institutional structure that maintained a semblance of ecclesiastical order. In 1902, American Orthodox rabbis formed their own professional organization, the Union of Orthodox Rabbis of the United States and Canada. After 1912, the ultra-Orthodox organization Agudath Israel branched out from Poland, where it was founded, to the United States, where it quickly divided the Orthodox movement.[9] By 1915, Yeshiva University, the chief center of higher learning for American Jewish Orthodoxy, had been founded.

Of the three divisions in American Judaism, Orthodoxy found it most difficult to accept the reality of American life. It tried desperately, at first, to insulate itself from the openness, voluntarism, and religious laxity with which it found itself surrounded. The first Orthodox rabbis who arrived in the United States from Eastern Europe were repelled by the thought of having to make religious compromise, preferring rather to isolate themselves from the world around them. The renowned scholar Rabbi Jacob Joseph, who was brought to New York from Vilna in 1887 by a group of traditionalists, found it almost impossible to adjust to American conditions.[10] With time, by the 1920s, Orthodoxy learned to make the required adjustments that enabled it to grow into an acceptable branch of American Judaism.[11] Robert Gordis's succinct distinction among the three branches of Judaism is illuminating: "Reform declared that Judaism has changed throughout time and that Jewish law is no longer binding. Orthodoxy denies both propositions, insisting upon the binding character of Jewish law and negating the view that Judaism has evolved. Conservative Judaism agrees with Orthodoxy in maintaining the authority of Jewish Law and with Reform that Judaism has grown and evolved through time."[12]

◘ ◘ ◘

The dramatic growth of American Catholicism during the final quarter of the nineteenth century was one of the great religious achievements of the age. Between 1880 and 1900, the American Catholic population doubled in size, increasing from six to twelve million, primarily as a result of a huge influx of European Catholics. Adjusting comfortably to an environment permeated by a Protestant lifestyle and religious values, Catholics could nevertheless boast by the end of the century thousands of churches, chapels, priests, and seminary students; about a hundred colleges; and four thousand parochial schools and academies. By the end of the twentieth century, there were about fifty million Roman Catholics in the United States.[13] Catholic institutions materialized in the face of enormous financial hardships.[14] Like Jews, Catholic immigrants from Italy, Poland, Germany, Ireland, and elsewhere arrived poor and, like Jews, came from different cultural backgrounds held together by a common faith.

Yet, unlike in the case of the Jewish people, the principle of church "authority" was of primary importance to Catholic arrivals and served as an additional bond.[15] As William Cardinal O'Connell explained to a women's group in Boston in 1909, "This unity was essential; without it there would be no universality. The Catholicity of the Church is but the expansion of its unity. Without unity of doctrine there would be as many opinions as there were individuals; without unity of government, the one Church would soon be divided into a multiplicity of sects and a Church rent into fragments at war with one another could no more be considered a universal Church."[16] The principle of authority continued to be a cornerstone of the church throughout the twentieth century. For example, Joseph Cardinal Ratzinger, who, during the last two decades of the twentieth century served as president of the Congregation for the Doctrine of the Faith, was seen as the "Church's guardian of Orthodoxy." The *National Catholic Reporter* described the cardinal in 1999 as one who "has drawn lines in the sand and [wields] the tools of his office on those who cross them."[17]

More specifically, for immigrant Catholics, religious authority was vested in the priests of the church, the bishops, but most preeminently in the bishop of Rome, the pope. Papal supremacy in matters of faith was the cornerstone of Catholicism.[18] The Third Baltimore Council of 1884 reaffirmed for American Catholics the principle of obedience to church authority and its leaders as mediators between God and human.[19]

This is not to suggest that American Roman Catholics agreed with each other on all matters.[20] Like Jews and, for that matter, all Americans, Catholics were found on all sides of the political and social spectrum. A more rigorous discipline was applied on theological matters and issues of doctrine. Despite Catholics' substantial numbers and diverse cultural backgrounds, therefore, ecclesiastical divisions into "movements," as was experienced by the Jewish community, did not materialize. Even so, not all American Catholics adhered rigidly to church rulings. Living in a democratic and open society imposed limitations upon the degree of authority that could be exercised by the church. As in Judaism, laxity prevailed among the rank and file of American Catholics.[21]

While in American Judaism, efforts to conform to American customs inspired religious divisions, Catholics' efforts to accommodate their religion to a democratic society drew charges of heresy from abroad.[22] The ability of the American Catholic church to fit into and thrive in the democratic polity of the New World raised eyebrows in European clerical circles. Old World religious leaders, many of whom were conservative in theological matters, found it disconcerting to see such spectacular strides made largely at the expense of Europe's Catholic population.[23] In 1898, a charge of heresy was flung at the American church by a group of ultramontane French priests, particularly at such liberal leaders as John Ireland, archbishop of St. Paul; John J. Keane, bishop of Richmond; John Lancaster Spalding, bishop of Peoria; and James Cardinal Gibbons, archbishop of Baltimore. These charges were "conjured up," as a contemporary put it, "by men who detest every form of free government." American Catholic leaders considered the charge uninformed and insulting, particularly when it was followed by a papal rebuke, in 1898, in the form of an encyclical, *Testem Benevolentiae*.[24] Although mild in its tone, it was the way of Pope Leo XIII (1878–1903) to caution the church in the United States against capitulating to the temptations of modern culture.[25] That the papal scolding was resented is understandable when measured against the enormous progress the church had made in its efforts to win government support for the education of Catholic children despite popular resistance.

American opinion was rigorously opposed to the expenditure of public money on private religious educational needs. For their part, many American Roman Catholics, unlike most Jews, objected to sending their children to public schools, which they believed were dominated by Protestant religious values. On the other hand, public school officials considered their curriculum nonsectarian. This issue became particularly critical for Catholics at a time when millions of them were entering American ports from southern and eastern Europe, a condition which demanded the creation of hundreds of new parochial schools.[26]

Clearly, at the turn of the twentieth century, Catholics and Jews were grappling with different, unrelated issues. To be sure, both groups were immigrant people who resided near one another, while their synagogues and churches stood in close proximity. While the Catholic population was much larger and growing more rapidly, both communities were viewed by the Protestant majority as minorities (even though American Roman Catholics were by 1900 the largest single Christian denomination in the United States). Actually, compared to Jews, Catholics could hardly be considered a minority worldwide, while Jews were a minority around the globe (with the exception of the small state of Israel after 1948). Catholics constitute a majority in many countries, a number of which persecuted Jews. It is not surprising, therefore, that as they arrived in the United States, many Jews brought their suspicions of Roman Catholicism with them.[27]

A Protestant country splintered into numerous denominations, America had inherited a deep hostility toward and fear of the growing power of the Roman Catholic Church, which added to Catholic tribulations at the turn of the twentieth century. Both the Know Nothing Party of the mid-nineteenth century and the American Protective Association (APA), founded in Iowa in 1887, were short-lived but represented dangerous political anti-Catholic sentiments.[28]

The anti-Catholicism of the nineteenth century, however, did not contain the deeply rooted intensity of antisemitism of the Catholic community. The foundations of this antisemitism, forged over nearly two thousand years and transported to the New World, lingered as an incurable theological virus. At least for the foreseeable future, it created an impassable frontier between Catholics and Jews.

I

Theology of Contempt

Undergirding the chasm which separated Catholics and Jews was a deeply embedded legacy of Catholic principles and teachings of anti-Judaism which had been transported to the United States.[1] These ideas, which for centuries had been part of European Catholic culture, produced much more than a dislike of Jews, although that was an inevitable outcome: they generated a deeply embedded visceral hostility.

The baggage of inherited notions about Jews could be designated as the "theology of contempt," as suggested by Jules Isaac's phrase, "the teaching of contempt." This popular theology rested on the conviction that Jewish spiritual blindness prevented the Jews from recognizing Christ, the Son of God, as their promised messiah. In so doing, Jews had mortally sinned against God. Jewish spiritual blindness, according to the theology of contempt, was compounded by the Jews' hatred of Christ. This theology included the belief that the Jewish people had conspired with the Roman authorities to crucify Jesus. It also included the Catholic conviction that the Jewish people collectively—past, present, and future—bore the primary responsibility and guilt for the murder of the Christian Savior. This deadly myth, which was perpetuated through the centuries and caused Jews incalculable suffering, concerned not a terrible event which occurred in the distant past but one relived by pious Catholics daily.[2]

In the European world, this highly charged belief motivated mob violence, pogroms, and false accusations of ritual murder (to obtain Christian blood for ceremonial purposes).[3] Jewish suffering was seen as divine retribution, the price exacted for Jews' collective culpability and denial of the divinity of the Christian Messiah.[4] Likewise, the ejection of the Jewish people from their Holy Land, destruction of their holy temple in Jerusalem in 70 C.E., and their dispersion among the nations of the world were also viewed as God's punishment for their notorious sin.[5] For the next nineteen hundred years, the Roman Catholic Church saw the Jews as an accursed and reprobate people. Only through conversion to Christianity would they be forgiven for their heinous crimes and restored to God's grace. Meanwhile, the story of their misdeeds was told and retold.

A popular vehicle for the transmission of knowledge of Jewish crimes was the Passion Play, a dramatic depiction of the story of Jesus, culminating in his suffering and death. Christianity's world-famous center for this reenactment was the town of Oberammergau, a Bavarian village at the foothills of the Alps. For more than three centuries, beginning in the 1630s, the drama was performed there every decade before an increasingly large and international audience who gathered in the open air outside a local church to witness the tragic and spiritually uplifting story of their Savior. American Catholics were interested in the Oberammergau event; one American Catholic journal, *Catholic World,* described it in considerable detail in 1880. The drama offered an important religious experience, but it was one which also helped disseminate the purported negative Jewish role in the Christian drama.[6]

What were American Catholics to think when they read the emotional account of a play which portrayed a fanatical mob of Jews trailing the procession which followed Jesus to his death, shouting, "Away with him! He must die!"? The Jewish fanatics, according to a *Catholic World* correspondent, "kept up the cry with hideous persistence." On the side of the stage, one Jew lurked, half hidden in the shadow: "How he mocks and grimaces and gleefully rubs his hands, as the terrible *cortège* approaches. How he enjoys the tortures of the captive."[7]

It must have been plain to American Catholic readers that the sinister, shadowy figure represented the Jewish people. They also devoured vivid descriptions of an ugly mob of Jews who milled around the cross, where they formed "a veritable blood thirsty rabble" around the meek and helpless victim, with all their "fiendish malignancy, born of ignorance and brutal passion."[8]

The villagers of Oberammergau, who went to enormous expense and spent much time to prepare their presentation, were a "good and pious people," according to this account; "May they continue to perform their cherished passion play which all must regard as the most marvelous dramatic exhibition of our epoch."[9]

Elaborate productions of this kind were not as prominent in America, but church leaders reminded American Catholics of these events during the holy season, apparently without any consciousness of the possible damage they could produce in interreligious affairs.[10] When Kaufman Kohler, by then president of Hebrew Union College, published his study *Jewish Theology* in 1918, he was reprimanded by a Catholic reviewer for challenging the Christian mythology. *Catholic World* noted that Kohler's book was "interesting merely as an instance of how far prejudice will warp the minds of those who undertake to discuss a religion they hate but do not understand."[11]

Clearly, the gulf between the communities remained as wide as ever.

□ □ □

Included in the lexicon of derision transported to the New World was the Catholic description of the Jewish group known in ancient Palestine as the Pharisees. They represented in Jewish history a movement of innovative Jewish religious leaders and scholars (rabbis, as they would shortly be called) who inspired among the Jewish people a shift of religious focus from temple cult activities to synagogue prayer and study during the Second Temple period.[12] The Pharisees held an exalted place within the Jewish community, comparable, in some respects, to that held by the church fathers in Catholic history and upon whom adulation was bestowed. Christians not only considered the theology of the Pharisees inferior to the teachings of Jesus (who was believed to have sprung from a Pharisaic group) but painted the Pharisees in dark and evil colors. In accordance with church teachings, the Pharisaic movement epitomized for the Catholic believer the very essence of what Catholicism opposed.[13] Pharisees were viewed as representatives of the worst of Jewish teaching. Enslavement to the Law of Moses was a chief accusation against them. Obsessed with petty details in the study of the Law, Pharisees found it scandalous, wrote one Catholic at the close of the nineteenth century, "that Jesus chose simple, unlettered men as his associates."[14] From another American Catholic sermon came the assertion that the Pharisees were jealous of the church's influence on the people, for it was they who aspired to popular leadership. Such comments as these, which denigrate the Pharisees, both demean and distort the views of one of the most respected and influential groups in Jewish history.

Catholic writers were fond of harping on what they alleged to be the narrow legalistic thinking which dominated the life of the "corrupt Pharisaism" and the "mask of hypocrisy" of the Jewish leadership.[15] Indeed, the charge of "hypocrisy" aimed at the Pharisees was a common refrain, because, it was charged, they did not live in accordance with their religious beliefs. Even their pretensions to vast learning were considered inadequate. American Catholics were informed, for example, that the teaching of Rabbi Hillel, probably the leading Talmudic scholar of his generation shortly before the time of Jesus, was vastly inferior intellectually to that of the Christian Savior. Hillel, it was alleged, simply did not have the depth of understanding of the law of love contained in Christ's message. Hillel, like other Jews of his time, was enslaved to the ceremonial laws and ritual of the Torah; Christ was not. Hillel was a disciple of rabbinic teaching; Jesus was a disciple of no one. Hillel had no compassion for the poor and ignorant; Jesus did. Although the author of these statements hesitated to include Hillel among the "hypocritical" Pharisees, he made strenuous effort to whittle him down to a satisfactory size.[16]

□ □ □

The description of the Jewish Pharisees in Roman Catholic teaching at the turn of the century conveyed a distorted image of Judaism during the time of Jesus. It did little to bridge the gulf between the two communities, and it kept alive the misunderstandings that existed between them. The conveyed distortion was aggravated, as we have seen in the examples of Hillel and the Pharisees, by Catholic disapproval of the role that the "Law" ("Torah" would be a better term) plays in Jewish religious life. American Catholics were told early in the century, for example, that the Jews of Jesus' time had "fallen away from the path of truth, and while constantly exacting a more strict observance of the letter of the law were at the same time losing every vestige of respect for its spirit."[17] That the Pharisees were enslaved to the "letter of the Law" but were ignorant of its "spirit" was a frequent charge directed at the Jews during the turn of the twentieth century, as it had been in the early years of the Christian era.[18] Jewish "Law" was constantly juxtaposed against the faith, love, and charity of Jesus Christ. There was little of love but much of "terror" in these laws.[19] An example of the "terror" was a reference to the misunderstood and distorted biblical injunction to render, in cases of criminal behavior, "eye for eye, tooth for tooth, even between friends," in the 1920 comments of the English author of *The Christian Faith*.[20] The narrow, harsh legalism and "shallow piety" attributed by Christians to the Pharisees of the Second Temple period "symbolizes," as the Catholic scholar Father John T. Pawlikowski has observed, "the general ignorance of Second Temple Judaism in the Church."[21]

What escaped the church's attention during these years was an appreciation of the Jewish mission to abide by the Commandments, or *Mitzvot* (a more precise translation than "Law"). For those Jews who chose to do so—that is, to abide by the Commandments of the Torah—it constituted no enslavement to "narrow legalism" or "false piety" but opened a path to freedom and fulfillment. From a Jewish perspective, as the Jewish theologian Rabbi Jacob Bernard Agus observes, "The Law is God-given but it is obligatory for Jews only because they accepted it voluntarily." Even so, despite Catholicism's own elaborate and complex structure of canon law and emphasis upon personal sin and fear of heavenly punishment, it could not accept the special "legal" requirements of the Torah imposed by God upon the Jews.[22]

◻ ◻ ◻

It could be said that anti-Judaism went far beyond a Catholic dislike of Jews but was an "expression of Christian self-affirmation."[23] Even more damaging to the image of the Jewish people and a cornerstone of Christian belief transported to America is the theology of displacement, or supersessionism.[24] The idea suggests that with the emergence of Christianity, the Old Israel was displaced, or superseded, by the New. This miraculous transcendence of Christianity over Judaism, morally and religiously, alleges that Israel's mantle of chosenness was shifted to Christianity, that its transformation was absolute. The belief was that it would so remain, at least until the end of time or until the conversion of the Jews to Christianity. This Christian conviction constituted the ultimate negation of Judaism. One American Catholic writer expressed it this way: "With the coming of Jesus, the promulgation of a universal religion which appropriated and subjected to its dominion and utility all the results of previous preparation" superseded the entire Jewish past in one swoop.[25] The Jews, Catholics were taught, because of their stubborn refusal to acknowledge the divinity of Christ and their collaboration in his execution, must assume total responsibility for their displacement and its consequences of an uncertain future. Because of the theology of displacement, the Christian world relegated Jews to a status of permanent inferiority.[26]

From a Christian perspective, the consequences of supersessionism were very serious. For the Jews' rejection of the Son of God, the Jews lost their place as the "people of God." No more would they serve as the instruments of salvation for the world. That task was now relegated to the church. The destruction of Jerusalem, the church alleged, symbolized the eclipse of Judaism, which was now displaced because of the crimes of the Jews. The destruction of the holy city was interpreted by the church as the destruction of moral evil, the demise of the once–chosen people, banished into exile and humiliation.[27]

At the same time, the values of Jewish past achievements were diminished. The teachings of the Torah "did not go forth from Jerusalem to the whole world," as Jews would have liked to believe. The Old Testament laws only prepared the way for the "New Law," which supplanted the laws of the Jews. With the coming of Jesus, Catholics argued, Jewish law was at once both demolished and fulfilled.[28] Therefore, not only were the Jewish people displaced but also their sacred Torah was demoted in significance. Even a sympathetic writer declared early in the century that "the Old Testament by itself is not a safe guide in morals; it does seem to sanction much that is imperfect, crude, low and cruel. It has ever been a commonplace with Catholic writers that the ordinary man is quite likely to gather out of it false moral ideas, and so the Church has reserved its interpretation to herself."[29] Still, the theologian Father John Fenton advised his Catholic readers to examine the Old Testament, assuring them that they need not fear being contaminated: "Most of us stand in little danger of desiring to emulate the warlike deeds and spirit of the Hebrews or of believing we have a divine call to preach such a gospel in this day."[30]

Turn-of-the-century sermons did not always conceal their efforts to foster disdain for the Jews. A leading church prelate from Boston, who ordinarily spoke of Jews and their religious traditions respectfully, reminded his listeners that from their isolation in Judea, the Jews "held all other nations in contempt," while they held on stubbornly to their ancient ways. They opposed the new religion of Christianity with a "dreadful opposition carried out with the most cruel heartlessness."[31]

All this is not to suggest that this anti-Judaic theology was associated exclusively with the American Catholic church or with all of its adherents. Nevertheless, one cannot gainsay that many such principles of anti-Jewish hostility, the theology of contempt, can be traced, if not to the New Testament itself, then certainly to the teachings of the church fathers who fashioned the foundations of the church and who contributed many anti-Jewish tracts in the early centuries of Christianity. The American Catholic theologian Rosemary Radford Ruether expressed it this way: "At its root, anti-Semitism in Christian civilization springs directly from Christian theological anti-Judaism. It was Christian theology which developed the thesis of the eternal reprobate status of the Jews in history, and laid the foundation for the demonic view of the Jews which fanned the flames of popular hatred."[32]

2

Medievalism and Modernity, 1890–1930

The Christian displacement of the Jewish people from meaningful future human events did not eradicate them physically from the Western world. On the contrary, their continued existence, Christians postulated, was ordained by Providence for a very special purpose. The church, which held supreme power, was to tolerate the continued existence of the Jewish people, who were to remain in a perpetual state of degradation as an example of those who rejected the Christian Messiah as well as the hope of their future conversion. It is understandable that because of this belief, throughout the centuries, conversion of the Jews received a high priority. Those Jews who stubbornly refused to accept Jesus as their Savior (and this would be an overwhelming majority) were to be kept in a state of misery, so that all could witness the humiliating condition of the non-believers.[1] To put it mildly, it was a theology that would hamper severely the progress of Jewish history. It was also a religious recipe that would, especially in the early years of historical writing, make it difficult for any Catholic historian with deep orthodox tendencies to examine the record of the Jewish past with any degree of discernment or sensitivity.

Coupled with this theological impediment with regard to historical writing was the general condition of Catholic historiography which prevailed in the United States during the early twentieth century. The Catholic writer Patrick Allitt's thoughtful book *Catholic Intellectuals and Conservative Politics in America, 1950–1985,* clarifies this issue when he contends that Catholic historiography before 1950 was dominated by the orthodox theological views of priests and bishops. What is more, their historical writings rarely extended beyond the boundaries of the institutions of the church and its interests. Neither did these historians seek out sources and writings which lay beyond the threshold of the church. Only material (usually written by church officials) which did not stray from accepted ecclesiastical doctrine provided the main sources for Catholic history.[2]

Jews made only an occasional appearance on the stage of American Catholic historical writing. If one discounts the role of the Jewish people in the beginning of the Christian era, then the medieval period was the subject of choice. Catholic scholars have maintained a special attachment to the early centuries of Christian history. Orthodox Catholic observers especially looked backward to the age of heroic chivalry, to the medieval world when the church enjoyed a measure of hegemony. Catholics have usually looked upon this age as one whose values were morally and intellectually superior to those of modern America. Catholic intellectuals, for example, thought of the twelfth and thirteenth centuries as an age of clear thought and moral vigor, creative imagination and deep religiosity, a time which had been lost and had yet to be recaptured. They would have liked to inject the spirit of medievalism into contemporary American democratic culture. Even the liberal Catholic George N. Shuster expressed his desire in the early twentieth century for the "spiritualization of democracy."[3] According to Allitt, "It was common in the early twentieth century for Catholic scholars to laud the Middle Ages with special fervor as the culmination of Catholic Christendom."[4] To another Catholic historian, Phillip Gleason, thoughtful Catholics of the early twentieth century viewed the Middle Ages as an "era of luminous clarity and intellectual brilliance under the benign governance of the Universal Catholic Church." Gleason recalls that during the first third of the twentieth century, Roman Catholics regarded the Middle Ages as a religious and cultural golden age.[5]

As American Catholics looked back at the Middle Ages, they perceived a time of saintliness. Gleason contends that American Catholics' attraction to medievalism came about because it represented to them the religious and moral values which American modernity lacked. They believed, or wished to believe, that the period of the Middle Ages was profoundly religious and "spiritual," while American society was secular and materialistic. They saw the medieval world as unified religiously, while American civilization was divided. The medieval world was aesthetically pleasing; America was coarse. In short, to Catholics, medievalism represented a time for which American Catholic intellectuals longed. They were repelled by the atomization and social experimentalization of the early twentieth century. They preferred the religious unity and social harmony which they believed had existed in medieval society. They saw in the Middle Ages a model for their own times.[6]

▢ ▢ ▢

All this is well and good. But Jews also existed in the Middle Ages. Looking back from the vantage point of the early twentieth century, what were Jews to make of the "luminous clarity" and exalted moral standards, said to be the blessings of religious unity of this "Golden Age"?

One need not look far or search deeply for the answer. It was in 1930, a culminating point of American Catholicism's love affair with medievalism, that the prominent Jewish historian Abram Leon Sachar published the first edition of his classic work *A History of the Jews*. What emerges clearly in that book is that from a Jewish perspective, the European Middle Ages was hardly a golden age of religion and culture. On the contrary, the Middle Ages constituted in many respects a nightmare era to which few Jews would wish to return.

The Middle Ages were a time in which the threat to Jewish life increased in direct proportion to the ever strengthening power and influence of the clergy.[7] With the coronation of Pope Gregory VII (1073–85), one of the most influential pontiffs in the Middle Ages, social and economic restrictions were imposed on the Jews of Europe. With the launching of the First Crusade, the first of several religious wars beginning in 1096 which were endorsed by church authorities, the Jews of Central Europe were subjected to an unprecedented reign of terror. These religious wars, propelled by deeply spiritual motives, lasted almost two hundred years, well into the fourteenth century. Designed to wrest Palestine, Jerusalem, and the Holy Sepulchre from the control of the Arabs, the Crusades degenerated into orgies of burning and plundering of synagogues and the massacre and forced baptism of Jews. Although such Christian fanaticism was not endorsed by the church, the zeal that activated it was inspired by its preachings.[8]

The thirteenth century, so important to early twentieth-century medievalists, was an age ruled first by Innocent III (1198–1216) and later by Gregory IX (1227–41). Both pontiffs were obsessed with Christian unity and were determined to root out heretics. Under the reign of Innocent III, the Jews were forced to wear a distinguishing yellow circle on their garments, "the badge of shame," and, later in the century, a pointed hat. Both measures were designed to isolate Jews from their Christian neighbors. Under Gregory, all Talmudic writings were confiscated and burned. For Jews, the thirteenth century was an age of horror.[9]

The total isolation and demonization of the Jews of Europe was an outgrowth of the Crusading generations. Expelled from various European countries where they had resided for centuries, Jews were charged with poisoning the water supply; creating epidemics, such as the Black Death; and performing unspeakable anti-Christian acts, including ritual murder. Under these circumstances, Jews did not object to their isolation; it provided them a measure of safety. Being herded into ghettos was not the most terrible thing that could happen to them. But it was the degradation, mob violence, and false accusations that made the long centuries of the Middle Ages abhorrent.[10]

Captivated by the Middle Ages, American Catholics were not completely impervious to the church's historical relationship with the Jews of Europe. But they preferred to see it far more benignly than the record would justify. In this regard, and with some justification, Catholic historians preferred to accentuate the positive. They preferred to underscore the protective role which the pontiffs of medieval Europe played in regard to the Jews. For example, the *Southern Cross* of December 7, 1927, lauded Innocent III, who, during the Crusades, the writer recalls, urged Catholics to refrain from "exterminating" Jews, demolishing their synagogues, or interfering with their synagogue worship. Jews, Innocent III explained to Catholic zealots, should be allowed to survive, not because they deserved to, but because it would provide them with an example of Christian witness.[11] Catholic writers, in a somewhat inflated fashion, were fond of observing the candid and even benevolent relationship that the Jews of Rome maintained with the medieval popes. Evidence of their physical security is indicated by the growth of the Jewish population of Rome, which climbed to about thirteen thousand at the end of the Middle Ages.[12]

These writers were correct in their observations that some Jews found refuge within the walls of Rome during the Middle Ages (as they did during the Nazi era) and that in numerous instances the papacy offered the Jews protection against the fury of unruly mobs.[13] Catholic historians have also been correct in their assertion that since the thirteenth century, a number of popes have countered the pernicious and popular belief that the Jews practice "ritual murder." Popes Innocent IV (1243–54), Gregory IX, and Martin V (1417–31), to name a few, have been cited among medieval pontiffs who rejected the blasphemous rumor that Jews utilized in rituals the blood of murdered Christian children, a falsehood which caused immeasurable pain and suffering for medieval Jewry. Pope Innocent IV, for example, warned Catholics that it was a sinful slander designed by evil men to attack Jews and despoil them of their possessions.[14]

No doubt, the popes of the Middle Ages served at times as safety valves for Jews threatened by mob violence. What is striking, however, is the limited attention devoted by Catholic historians of the early twentieth century to the plight of the Jews during an age with which they were particularly captivated. Neither does the papal protective shield conceal the papal custodianship of the church's teachings that inspired the dark experiences of their elder brothers.

The tendency, however, among Catholic writers was either to minimize, or reject, or ignore altogether any church responsibility for Jewish tribulations during the Middle Ages. Expulsions from European Catholic countries, for example, were justified, and their impact upon Jewish lives was minimized. The essence of expulsion serves as a case in point. The ejection of the Jews from Catholic England at the end of the thirteenth century was regarded by one writer as a culmination of popular hostility toward Jews, which in no way should be attributed to the church. The church was "rarely actively hostile to the Jews." It was the English people who believed Jews to be not only economic competitors but enemies of God.[15] The author of these comments absolves the church for the mistreatment, violence, and subsequent expulsion of the Jews from England: "The Church sanctified feudal institutions but did not demand them, and cannot be held responsible for any misfits. She neither preached nor practiced violence . . . and considering the value the Middle Ages placed upon Christianity, the medieval attitude toward Judaism was understandable. . . . Jews and Catholics . . . must consider the general setting of their *drama* [italics mine] and in addition look for the *comic relief* [italics mine] which accompanies the tragedy."[16]

Expulsion of the Jews from European countries during the later Middle Ages was not uncommon, but the expulsion that embedded itself most strongly on the Jewish collective memory was that from Spain in 1492. Because Jews had lived in Spain for a number of centuries in relative security in greater numbers and had earned a greater degree of social acceptance there than elsewhere, their expulsion proved particularly shocking. Yet even here the reader is confronted with American Catholic insensitivity.

The Jewish expulsion from Spain was not a subject ordinarily discussed by Catholic scholars. Interest in the event peaked, however, around 1892, the four hundredth anniversary of the expulsion. But Catholic writers were reluctant to paint Spain in negative colors. The reader is reminded in one case that the Jews, after all, were not typical or reliable citizens of Spain. In three invited essays provided to *Catholic World* by the prominent Spanish historian Manuel Perez Villamil, a member of Spain's prestigious National Academy, the Jews are painted in particularly dark colors. Here the American reader learns that during Spain's war against the Arabs, the Jews were consistently disloyal to Spain. They aided and abetted the Arabs in their effort to hold Spanish territories.[17] What is more, Jewish disloyalty to Spain did not prevent them from winning protection from the church, while they continued to live as "a nation within a nation."[18]

Villamil acknowledges to his American readers that such accusations engendered violence against Spanish Jewish communities during the late fourteenth century.[19] But, he hastens to add, they "were not so bad as afterwards claimed by the Jewish historians." After all, observes the Spanish historian, Jews continued to reside in Spain for another century before the decree of expulsion was issued by King Ferdinand and Queen Isabella, "during which time the Jews—thanks to the uprighteousness of our sovereigns and the generous disposition of our nation—applied themselves anew to repair the losses suffered through the immense disasters."[20]

Most important, Villamil argues, the expulsion was the fault of the Jews, not that of the Spanish monarchs. It was a tragedy which admittedly brought about the annihilation of the Hebrew population in Spain, but it was brought about by its own vices and errors.[21] He rejects the oft-repeated view that the Jews were expelled because their wealth was coveted. On the contrary, most were of very humble origins and poor. Contrary to the assertion of Jewish historians, the expulsion of the Jews did not include the learned and wealthy, Villamil argues.[22]

The Jews were ejected, according to Villamil, because they were too politically and socially ambitious, too inclined to fish in politically troubled waters for their own advantage. The Jews of Spain, many of whom had converted to Christianity, aspired to control the kingdom, much to the anger of church officials.[23] Spaniards still lamented the bloody years of the reconquest from the Muslims, and they saw Jewish ambitions as a reminder of another alien conquest. The Catholic monarchs, Ferdinand and Isabella, rescued Spain from such a dreadful possibility.[24]

It was because of the rulers' decision to rid Spain of its Jews that the country underwent a religious purification marked by "an explosion of energy" which resulted in "the most brilliant chapter in all history." Because Jews were considered unreliable, an unstable element in the overwhelmingly Catholic population, constituting a threat to Spanish national stability, their elimination was imperative.[25]

Unlike Villamil, Jewish historians see little that is noteworthy about the expulsion of Spanish Jewry in 1492. They agree that Ferdinand and

Isabella desired the expulsion in order to unify and purify Christian Spain. The Spanish monarchs viewed the Jews as a "source of annoyance," a dangerous influence, a contamination of Catholic society.[26] The historians note, however, that the edict of expulsion signed by the Spanish monarchs on March 31, 1492, did not receive the sanction of the papacy. The reigning pope found the terms of the expulsion too harsh. Nonetheless, with the stroke of a pen, in the name of Christian unity, Ferdinand and Isabella destroyed the largest and most successful Jewish community in European history of the past fifteen hundred years.[27]

As a rule, Jewish historians have included the Spanish Inquisition within the parameters of the Jewish medieval experience. To be sure, the Spanish inquisitorial courts established in 1479 by church authorities before the expulsion were designed to punish heresy among baptized Jews. For a while, such Jewish converts were fully accepted by Spanish society, into which the *conversos* seemed completely integrated. Increasingly, however, these new Christians were looked upon suspiciously, denied normal civil privileges, and treated as a class of unreliable Christians. Not surprisingly, more and more new Christians returned to the practice of their ancestral faith. They did so clandestinely, since such a practice was deemed heretical. Those suspected of this heresy were forced to face inquisitorial courts, sanctioned by the church, and if guilty were subject to severe penalties, at times torture and burning. Once implanted, the Inquisition was difficult to uproot. The Inquisition continued for almost four hundred years, during which time thousands of former Jews, many of them innocent of heresy, fell prey to its horrors. No new Christian remained above suspicion for long, and religious commendations were offered to anyone who voluntarily exposed backsliders, that is, those who continued to practice Judaism secretly.[28]

While the Spanish Inquisition was difficult to eradicate from Jewish historical memory, as has been seen, it did not technically belong to Jewish history. Roman Catholic writers, although captivated by the Middle Ages, paid little attention to it. Yet here also, when they considered the Spanish Inquisition, they minimized its importance or even justified it. Catholics did not conceal its brutality but belittled its terrible consequences or uniqueness. Other peoples and other ages, they said, had their Inquisitions too. One commentator observed that "the Inquisition, established to judge heretics, is an institution whose severity and cruelty are explained by the manners of the age." Even while the church behaved vengefully toward suspected heretics, "She never ceased to respect the conscience of those outside her fold."[29]

◻ ◻ ◻

Catholic thinking about Jews remained relatively constant through the centuries. This is reflected in American Catholic writing about Jews during the late nineteenth and early twentieth centuries. For example, the statement of Pope Leo XIII (1878–1903) about Jews at the opening of the twentieth century did little to enhance Jewish-Catholic relations. After all, when one of the most admired pontiffs of the nineteenth century instructs the "men of Israel" to accept the dogma of the church, an ancient anti-Jewish signal is sounded in American Catholic circles.[30] Neither did the pope's efforts to reconcile the faith of Catholicism with the rational thought of modernity open a path for civil discourse between Catholics and Jews. Indeed, his actions only aggravated their relations. Leo XIII concluded that the obstacles to reconciling revealed religion and modern thought were the fault of Jewish and Arab intellectuals of the Middle Ages. It was they who had elevated reason at the expense of religious faith, which Catholics must once again restore.[31]

American Catholics were not impervious to the Jews who lived next door. What they thought about their neighbors is difficult to say with precision. But glimpses of their attitudes toward Jews can be gained from periodicals, such as *Catholic World* and diocesan newspapers. Outbreaks of violence against Jews by Irish toughs at the turn of the century in New York City's Lower East Side have been documented. One of the most egregious outbursts occurred on July 30, 1902, when the funeral cortège of New York's chief Orthodox rabbi, Jacob Joseph, was disrupted and pelted with missiles from apartments above, culminating in the beating of Jews by Irish police.[32]

This is not to suggest that Catholic teaching should be held responsible for this attack on New York's Jews, but that possibility cannot be completely discounted. In a perceptive study of the attitudes of German and Irish Catholics toward Jews in Baltimore during the turn of the last century, Till Van Rahden relates the following event:

In 1925 Avrum Rifman, son of Eastern European Jewish immigrants, served as umpire in the final game of Baltimore's Catholic baseball championship. Of 15 candidates he, the only non-Christian, had been chosen by the Catholic managers of both teams. It was an honor that brought anything but· joy to Rifman. "Each team and the managers disagreed on all matters except one," Rifman recalls. "When a critical decision was given in favor of one team, invariably, the other team, and all the fans in the stand as one, would yell out in screaming and piercing unison, 'Kill that Jew!'" Was this expression of anti-Semitism consistent with a tradition of anti-Semitic prejudice within Catholic images of Jews in Baltimore?[33]

Rahden's study, based upon a good sampling of Baltimore's Catholic newspapers between 1890 and 1920, documents an unmistakable tendency among Baltimore's Catholics toward various degrees of antisemitism. Quite common were the economic stereotypes with which Catholics smeared their Jewish neighbors. Such hostile rhetoric toward Jews as found among the Irish and German residents of Baltimore cannot be attributed solely to economic competitiveness or envy of some Jewish success. Catholics viewed Jewish economic success as sinister, since Jews were involved in unproductive occupations. It was believed that they were obsessed with a drive for money and employed any means to acquire it. Catholics accused the Rothschild banking house of fleecing Europe and undermining its stability.[34] Such charges were quite common among American Western antisemites, the Populists. Clearly, Baltimore Catholics were not immune from making them either.[35]

◻ ◻ ◻

Hostility toward Jews in Baltimore or in the United States did not spring from American soil. It was, as indicated, deeply rooted in Catholic teaching. It was enhanced by the antisemitism of the Old World and was transported from Europe's soil to America. When German Catholics relocated to America, for example, they continued to be inspired by the anti-Judaism of the German-Catholic press on both sides of the Atlantic.[36] Reading these newspapers reveals that they reflected on the growing antisemitic tendencies in Europe and wondered if the Jews themselves had not brought such bigotry upon their own heads. "It is hard to say," reasoned one writer, Charles C. Starbuck, "whether the anti-Semites or the pro-Semites are the more unreasonable." He also contends that defining "an anti-Semite makes sense if it is defined as a man who believes the Jews to be in Christendom a disintegrating and dangerous force." Starbuck also writes: "The Jew differs from Christianity only in two points, but they are vital. One is: Jesus is not the Messiah. The other: the law of Moses is permanently binding on all who claim to be Israelites. Christianity differs from Judaism in the reverse order. . . . Therefore, in the eyes of every orthodox Jew [Christianity] is a gigantic heresy."[37]

According to this reasoning, the Jewish people have earned the opprobrium cast upon them. What is more, the Jewish rejection of Christianity is compounded by their behavior. They segregate themselves from Christian society. They live, unlike Christians, self-contained, materialistic lives. They know little of love in the Christian sense. "Talmudic Judaism is concerned [only] with this world." Jews care only about their own welfare and are indifferent to the needs of Christianity. Even more ominously, according to Starbuck, the Jews of Europe are "laying a web which entangles all gentile business and prosperity in a subordination to itself."[38]

Resentment toward Jews in Germany, Starbuck tells his Catholic readers, is understandable, given the Jews' antipathy toward the Gospel and the "notorious grip they have upon the national press, especially in Berlin." The Jews, the writer informs us, use the press "to pour scorn on Christian enterprises" and "on foreign missions." Jews "use the press not only to revile Christians but Christianity in general." Starbuck was blunt in his resentment of Jews: "Nowhere for doctrinal and for historical reasons, in the memory of the deepest wrongs suffered and inflicted, does it seem possible that there should be such an immitigable hatred in the breast of any other human being towards the Redeemer as may be conceivably gathered in the breast of a Jew."[39]

Such shameful distortions about and hostility toward the Jewish people, published in *Catholic World,* one of the most respected Catholic journals of the modern age, may also explain an indifference—even a degree of callousness—displayed by American Catholic intellectuals toward the crises which Jews faced at the turn of the century and later.

◻ ◻ ◻

To illustrate this, one can turn to the Catholic reaction to the Dreyfus affair, an event which startled the European world at the close of the nineteenth century. It offers an illustration of how American Catholics reacted toward a critical Jewish concern, one in which European Catholics were deeply involved.

The arrest of Alfred Dreyfus, an obscure artillery captain in France, late in 1894 on the charge of transferring French military secrets to Germany, was at first not a major concern in the United States. It was a foreign event which had no direct bearing on American interests. Gradually, however, after Dreyfus had been sent to live in an isolated cage for life on Devil's Island and the French writer Emile Zola publicly accused the French military of engineering the arrest in 1898, it became clear that Dreyfus had been falsely accused because he was a Jew. The event divided France, where it generated an upsurge of anti-Jewish hatred, and affected other European countries as well. American newspapers and magazines also took an interest in this celebrated event.

Most American newspapers and periodicals were sympathetic to the cause of Dreyfus and were severely critical of France's false accusations against an innocent army officer and of the antisemitic implications of the case. American newspapers were at times critical and infuriated at the intense anti-Jewish hostility which resulted from it. Understandably, for the most part, American Jews, especially the recent immigrants, were particularly disturbed by the event in France, a country known for its liberalism.[40] They detected in this occurrence a possible replication of the horrors they had just left behind in Eastern Europe. Many American Catholics, however, especially those of Irish heritage who detected England's hand behind the critics of France, saw things differently.[41]

To be sure, because France was a Roman Catholic country, American Catholics were especially sensitive about an assault upon its behavior, especially by a predominantly Protestant society that was generally unfriendly to its Roman Catholic citizens. Still, given the facts of the Dreyfus case, none of this could justify the bitter resentment that Catholic writers directed at American critics of France. The Boston *Pilot* expressed this resentment as follows: "It requires only some crime of the Dreyfus character in one of the unhappy lands where English is not spoken to call forth an exhibition of that complacent self-righteousness, Pharisaism and cant, which seems to be all of the inheritance of Puritanism."[42]

Although Catholics did not express a unified point of view about the affair, there was nevertheless an unusual amount of hostility directed toward Jews because of it, which was also difficult to justify. The ostensible indifference of Pope Leo XIII to the fate of Dreyfus and the pleas of the prisoner's wife and friends disturbed American Jews. The pope's declared devotion to social amelioration, it was observed, did not extend to any attempt to stem the mounting tide of Jew-hatred in France. His silence provided a source of comfort, even inspiration, to antisemites, who interpreted Vatican neutrality as a tacit endorsement of their behavior.[43]

Even so, American Catholics were eager to divest their church of any charge that it encouraged antisemitism. Repeated questions about the pope's significant silence on the Dreyfus matter disturbed them, though they tried to dismiss the issue as a fantasy of the yellow press, typical of its irresponsible and sensational reporting. They accused their critics of demanding a higher standard of moral behavior from Catholics than from other religious groups:

> How about the other Princes and Potentates? We have not observed that the Czar of Russia, Head of the Greek Church; the Queen of England, Head of the Episcopal [sic] Church; the President of the United States, the Sultan of Zanzibar, or any other of the great ones of earth took pains to interfere

in a matter which did not concern them directly. The Pope, with the generous spirit which governs all his acts, interceded for clemency—politely, because he is a gentleman; but knowing his place, as a gentleman does, he demanded nothing.[44]

Efforts were made to disassociate the actions of the Holy Office from antisemitism. The popes were pictured as the lone protectors of the European Jew throughout the centuries. Jewish survival itself was attributed to papal tolerance. Writing in *Catholic World,* Elizabeth Raymond-Barker acknowledged that "it is true that at Rome as elsewhere the Jews were despised, obliged to live in their quarter of the city, and as a rule, compelled to wear a distinctive badge or color." "Still," she argued, "to the student of history, there is no doubt that amidst the intolerance and barbarities of the Middle Ages and the times succeeding them, Rome set a great example of moderation."[45]

It is doubtful whether the Vatican was directly involved in France's outburst against the Jews, but it was not completely blameless. *L'Osservatore Romano,* a newspaper reflecting Vatican views, did little to allay French fury when it observed that Jews had little right to complain about their condition, because of their inbred sinfulness. They "must always be outcasts," said one writer, "a scattered and homeless race." They must perpetually bear "the blame for the Crucifixion" and for their efforts to debase the spiritual values of Western society. Consequently, they have no right to complain of the hatred and violence directed toward them.[46] Even though Pope Leo XIII notably did not approve of such sentiments, there was a fanatical group of clergy who did. What is clear, however, is the pope's lack of effort to stem the growing anti-Jewish hatred. It was difficult for American Catholics to avoid the conclusion that the eradication of Jew-hatred did not receive the highest priority at the Vatican.

More than non-Catholics, American Catholics preferred to minimize their criticism of France. Justifications of French behavior, generally absent in non-Catholic circles, were common in the Catholic community. Even the liberal voices of what was a predominantly conservative institution preferred to withhold judgment about the matter. Until the end of the affair, Bishop John J. Keane, James Cardinal Gibbons, and Archbishop John Ireland, who were far more ecumenically minded than their European and American counterparts and who were eager to participate in a dialogue with Jews, hesitated to condemn the behavior of French Catholics.[47]

This is not to say that American Catholics refused to admit that injustices against Jews were committed in France. Liberal voices did express their annoyance. For example, the *Pittsburgh Catholic* in the winter of 1898 called the attack on the Jews of Paris "a repetition of a blackened page in the world's history." The *Iowa Catholic Messenger* and the Boston *Pilot* joined other Americans in denouncing irregular French proceedings against Dreyfus.[48] Such anger, however, was not typical of American Catholic utterances. In keeping with the rhetoric of anti-Judaism, Catholic writers were more likely to maintain a hostile stand toward Jews. They charged them with manipulating the American press so that no favorable image of France would be displayed.[49] The Catholic press made every effort to minimize the importance of the crime committed against Dreyfus. One journal declared: "Before jumping at the rash conclusion that it was, as some call it, 'the monumental crime of the century,' let us see if France is alone in her ignominy."[50] While many Americans were condemning France and her judicial institutions, American Catholics were commending France and her achievements, heaping praise on her church and on priests who vilified Dreyfus and his supporters.[51]

American Catholics, as we have seen, not only displayed less sympathy for the cause of Dreyfus than did any other identifiable group of Americans, with perhaps the exception of American radicals, but were even perturbed at the degree of support shown for the victim in other quarters. It is difficult to find in American Catholic periodicals of the late nineteenth century a wholehearted endorsement of liberal trends in Europe. Jewish and socialist influences were suspected behind every threat to the ancient monarchies and their strong Catholic traditions. At the same time the rising wave of antisemitism in eastern and western Europe was virtually ignored, and one might almost conclude that the assaults upon the Jews of Paris in 1898 had never occurred.[52]

In the wake of the embarrassment that the Dreyfus affair caused the church, there was a tendency in some conservative circles to accuse the Jewish people of collective treachery toward France. The *Catholic Columbian and Record* characterized the Jews as the "historic enemies of France," who had been paid by Germany to engineer the downfall of the French empire in 1870. "Behind the advancing armies of France's enemies," explained the popular Catholic journalist James R. Randall in 1900, "was a procession of men with long beards and gabardines representing Hebrew money lenders, who were about to settle the financial affairs of the fallen French Empire after the two Christian nations had ceased killing each other in battle."[53]

When American Jews objected to these infamous allegations, Randall assured them that his intention was "not to impugn the Jewish race or religion but only its commercial methods. It was common knowledge," he wrote, that Jews hold "most of the coined gold in the world. . . . I have not attacked the Jew on his spiritual or religious side or his race issue. . . . I regret that the Israelite . . . cannot make proper distinctions on this subject." Randall added a reminder that Jews maintained a potent and insidious grasp upon the American economy as well.[54]

It is difficult to measure precisely the intensity of antisemitism in the American Catholic community, although its presence was unmistakable. It varied from city to city, from editor to editor, even from week to week in the same periodical. Although the church did not endorse the ancient aberration, there is little evidence that its leaders—not even the most popular and venerated prelate of his time, Archbishop John Ireland— tried to curb it. American Jewish support for Dreyfus annoyed Archbishop Ireland. After returning from a trip to Paris in 1899, he declared that American Jewish criticism of France had unnecessarily injured the pride of the French army and had aggravated the situation of the Jews of France.[55]

On the other hand, James Cardinal Gibbons of Baltimore, who shared with Archbishop Ireland many views and was an equally prominent cleric, was more outspoken in attacking antisemitism. His condemnation of Russian persecution of Jews was the strongest which came from an American prelate: "For my part," Gibbons wrote, "I cannot well conceive how Christians can entertain other than kind sentiments toward the Hebrew role when I consider how much we are indebted to them."[56] For such views, Gibbons was condemned by France's Catholic conservative prelates, who found little comfort in his liberal attitudes. One French priest, Father Henry Delassus, accused Gibbons of working with the Jews to "hasten the overthrow of the Catholic Church and the triumph of the anti-Christ." Even the *Catholic Mirror* of Baltimore, which as a rule endorsed Gibbons's position on public and religious issues, offered little support for the cause of Dreyfus or sympathy for the plight of French Jewry.[57]

In 1906, Dreyfus was finally cleared of charges and reinstated in the French army. Yet the Jesuit monthly *Catholic Mind*, recalling the anti-Catholic assault that had been mounted against the church in France, where it was divested of state support, continued to assert in its pages that the hand of the Jew lay behind the catastrophe.[58] Catholic thinking about Jews or Judaism, either against the backdrop of the Middle Ages or that of crises of more modern times, contained an ominous consistency.

3

Holy Land and Homeland, 1900–1939

The Dreyfus affair had a subsidiary significance: it inspired Theodore Herzl, a well-known Jewish Viennese journalist, novelist, and playwright, to publish *Der Judenstaat* (The Jewish State) in 1896. This small book changed the course of Jewish history by triggering the political Zionist movement. Herzl, who was at the time the Paris correspondent for Austria's largest newspaper, was in attendance at Dreyfus's public military degradation on January 5, 1895. Herzl had been thinking for a number of years of the growing tide of European antisemitism and groping for solutions. For a while he toyed with the idea of advocating a mass Jewish conversion to Christianity, but what he witnessed on January 5 dispelled that notion forever. The spectacle appalled him. He was stunned by the shouts of "Death to the Jew!" coupled with other obscene vituperations flung at the prisoner by the Parisian mob while he was paraded around the military courtyard. Citizens of a country reputed to be among the most progressive in the world behaving like barbarians altered Herzl's thinking and activities forever.[1]

The idea to establish a homeland for the Jews was not born with Herzl. The Jews' hope of a return to their ancestral home had existed in Jewish thought since the destruction of the Second Temple and expulsion from Judea in 70 C.E. The desire, however, was not transformed into a political concept until the latter half of the nineteenth century. It was only in the late 1870s that Jewish youth residing in the Russian "Pale," a large territory in western Russia set apart for Jews, organized small Zionist groups called Choveve Zion, "lovers of Zion." In 1884, these groups joined into a federation of Lovers of Zion. By the 1890s, Lovers of Zion was represented in almost every country in Europe and in the United States. American chapters were especially popular among immigrant Russian Jews. Three prominent rabbis, Reform and Conservative, offered the fledgling American Zionist movement leadership: Gustav Gottheil, Benjamin Szold, and Marcus Jastrow. The loosely held amalgamation of Zionist chapters was tied together by one idea: a desire to build for Jews a homeland with a government of its own in Palestine. But it was Theodore Herzl who provided the charismatic leadership that brought this avant-garde movement to world attention.[2]

Roman Catholics had difficulty reconciling their Christian teachings about Jews with contemporary exclusive Jewish claims upon the Holy Land. Neither did they see Jewish national aspirations as totally compatible with their own religious affection for the land of the Bible. To be sure, this Christian attachment, which declined following the seventh century, after the Islamic victories in the Middle East, was not reactivated until the Christian invasion during the Crusading era of the Middle Ages, but the Christian memory of the Holy Land before or after that time was not obliterated. Robert L. Wilken, the Catholic scholar who is a leading authority of the patristic era and author of *The Land Called Holy*, observes that "it is evident to any visitor to the Middle East that Christianity has a peculiar relation to the lands embraced by the State of Israel, the West Bank and Jordan."[3] Wilken reminds his readers that "few realize that Christianity's role in the land of the Bible is not restricted to the time of Jesus and Christian origins. The Christian religion has a long history in Palestine."[4] It is a land which has remained holy for Christians as well as Jews throughout the centuries. For Western Catholics, the "Holy Land," in its origin a Hebrew biblical term, was a territory which lacked the cultural and political dynamic associated with modern political Zionism. For Catholics, the term "Holy Land" had predominantly a religious association linked to the Bible: a selected group of shrines, such as the Church of the Holy Sepulchre, the Church of the Nativity, and the Church of the Ascension; and, most important, the birthplace of Jesus and the origin of the Christian faith. For Catholics, the Holy Land continued to be primarily a land of holiness first and foremost, only secondarily a land to reside in.[5]

Notwithstanding their religious recollections and attachment to the birthplace of Christianity, late nineteenth-century Western Roman Catholics registered no desire to establish a national homeland in Palestine. Consequently, the links that Catholics and Jews shared with the Holy Land were very different. This is not to suggest that Jews lacked a deep religious feeling for the Holy Land; on the contrary, the religious view of the "Land" lay at the very heart of Jewish belief and fueled the modern political Zionist movement. As Howard M. Sachar observes,

> Among the most cherished features of the Russian Jewish cultural heritage, surely, was the memory of the ancestral homeland, the lost and lamented Zion that was enshrined in the ceremony and folklore of virtually every believing Jew. The truth was that throughout all the centuries of Jewish dispersion until modern times, Zion, hardly less than the Deity, functioned as a binding integument of the Jewish religious and social experience. Rabbinic and midrashic literature, the prayerbook, medieval literary treatises, all displayed a uniform preoccupation with the Holy Land.[6]

□ □ □

Somewhat less than other American Christians, Catholics joined in the renewed interest in Palestine which occurred in the nineteenth century. The rediscovery of the Holy Land was fueled by a rising European imperialism, faster and safer ships and trains, and a growing interest in the Middle East as a geopolitical region of concern for the Western world. Neither did missionary opportunities escape the interests of the Christian faithful.

Before 1917, however, American Protestants evinced a more intense curiosity, even attachment, to the land of the Bible.[7] The American Catholic historian Robert D. Cross concludes an essay on this subject with the following observation: "American Catholics did not speak very much about the Holy Land before 1917. They were much more likely to use the term 'Holy Places'; they did not clearly distinguish between the Holy Places in Palestine and many other Holy Places around the world; and when they *thought* [italics mine] of Palestine, the presence of Jews there, actual or potential, did not seem very important."[8]

Before the second decade of the twentieth century, preoccupation of American Catholics with the Holy Land was very limited. The care of millions of European immigrants, most of whom were poor and deprived of adequate education, was the church's chief responsibility. Little else beyond the condition and safety of the "Holy Places" commanded any attention.[9] During these early years, unlike a number of Protestant denominations, the American Catholic church did not dispatch missionaries to the Holy Land. Cross observes that recent Catholic immigrants were still emotionally and religiously attached to the shrines and "Holy Places" which they had recently left behind in various European countries.[10]

Although Catholic interest in the Holy Land before 1917 did not measure up to that which was displayed by American Protestants, it did very much exist and ought not to be overlooked. American Roman Catholics were not impervious to the increasing rate of travel to the Holy Land during the latter half of the nineteenth century.[11] *Catholic World* featured articles about the Holy Land and recommended books about it for Christmas reading.[12] "The present state of the world," Eugene Vetromile, one of the early Catholic pilgrims to Palestine, announced in 1871, "in which the most distant parts are brought comparatively close together by the application of steam and electricity," offers encouragement for Catholic pilgrims.[13] The writer also explains the need for Catholic travel and Catholic descriptions of such travels, so that they will not be misrepresented by Protestant writers. The holy places of the Holy Land would be best served if left to Catholic writers to describe, says Vetromile, for it is the church that best understands their religious mystery and meaning.[14]

Pilgrimages to the Holy Land were undertaken by American Catholics as early as 1867. In that year, James Roosevelt Bayley, the bishop of New York and later the archbishop of Baltimore, traveled to the Holy Land. His undertaking was not a typical one for American Catholics, most of whom were Irish and German immigrants. Bayley, raised in New England and educated in that region's academies, converted to Catholicism from Episcopalianism. He had the interest in the land of the Bible so typical of New England Protestants. Like non-Catholic travelers at this time, he yearned to tread on holy soil, but he was repelled by the discomforts of the neglected land and the coarseness of its inhabitants. Like other travelers to the Middle East, upon his return to the United States, he lectured to other Catholics, who, it seemed, were eager to share vicariously in his experiences.[15]

In the following years, other Catholic travelers to Palestine followed him. In 1883, John J. Keane, bishop of Richmond, Virginia, sailed to Palestine in order to purchase a cornerstone for a cathedral which he was planning to build in Richmond. He acquired his cornerstone from the Franciscans in Jerusalem, who were the custodians of the holy places in the Holy Land.[16]

Early Catholic pilgrims were moved religiously as they viewed the sites about which they had read in the Scriptures. Gershom Greenberg, a historian and the author of *The Holy Land in American Religious Thought,* reports the experience of William H. Bergan, a Catholic from Philadelphia who left for the Holy Land in 1874. Bergan wrote, "It is useless to attempt to describe the feeling of my heart when in the presence of these sacred and dear localities, especially the Holy Sepulchre and the place of the Crucifixion. It is impossible to enter the Tomb without a feeling of holy awe and holy reverence. What passed within my heart while I was present in them, God only knows."[17]

□ □ □

Catholic interest in the Holy Land was permeated with Christian anti-semitism. This is best illustrated in the case of the Franciscan order. In 1880, Charles Vissani, a Franciscan ordained in Rome in 1854, was appointed the first commissary of the Holy Land Commissariat in the United States, established in that year by Pope Leo XIII. This custodial relationship which the Franciscans maintained with the holy places had originated during the Crusading years when Pope Clement V (1305–14) entrusted the order with the care of the shrines of the Holy Land. Vissani led the first group of one hundred American Catholic pilgrims to the Holy Land in 1889.[18] Upon their return, the Franciscan father inspired other Catholic pilgrims. These visitors' piety and dedication to the Holy Land did not alter their traditional views of Judaism. Unlike evangelical Protestant travelers to the Holy Land who assigned to the Jewish people a distinct role in Christian eschatology, Catholic pilgrims viewed the Jews as an irritant and a sinful annoyance.[19]

To Eugene Vetromile, for example, a missionary to Indians in Maine as well as a Catholic traveler to the Holy Land, the Jews were an unfortunate people with a "propensity to superstition. . . . Deceived by diabolic fraud and hardened in their hearts, they feel so humiliated . . . they never attempt to enter the Church of the Holy Sepulchre."[20] Vetromile's contempt for the Jews of the Holy Land was also reflected in his tacit endorsement of Jewish guilt because of their alleged practice of ritual murder.[21]

Vetromile's attitude was matched by that of Andrew E. Breen, another early Catholic pilgrim and biblical scholar who traveled to the Holy Land in 1890.[22] Breen held a great affection for the biblical Jews, for it was from them that the Christian Savior came. This empathy, however, did not extend to the Jews of the Holy Land whom he met in 1890. He noted in his diary, which he kept throughout his pilgrimage, that they were "despised by all men. . . . They are a most wretched race. They have a strange unnatural expression."[23] Breen found the Jews of the Holy Land uncouth and insensitive. Writing of Jews' behavior at a Jewish funeral he attended, he reported that "while the grave was being dug, they smoked, talked, and joked with one another, manifesting no thought of the solemnity of the occasion. . . . It was the weirdest burial that I ever saw."[24] A pious man, a student of Jewish antiquity and religious practices, Breen was still unable to conceal a deeply embedded disdain for Palestinian Jewry.[25]

□ □ □

No city in the Holy Land commanded greater attention and veneration from Catholic travelers than did Jerusalem.[26] That the Jewish presence in the Holy City was also increasing by the close of the nineteenth century did not escape the notice of Catholic visitors. But Christians were only vaguely aware that Jerusalem represented for Jews the central territorial focus of their faith and nationhood, both of which were indispensable for meaningful Jewish existence. With the early stirrings of Zionism at the end of the nineteenth century, a small stream of Jewish settlers began to return to the land and to Jerusalem. Here they joined the earlier residents whose presence, though small, had never disappeared since the destruction of the Second Temple in 70 C.E. Catholic visitors, however, found it difficult to reconcile their religious beliefs with an increasing Jewish presence in the Holy City. After all, they had been taught that the Jews had rejected and murdered the Christians' Savior, for which they had earned eternal damnation. One Catholic traveler remarked after visiting the Holy City in 1898 that the Jews would never possess enough gold to purchase Jerusalem because of the curse they had brought upon their own heads.[27]

The problem is that Catholic pilgrims to Jerusalem were unable to think of Jews there except as the crucifiers of Christ, which for Christians was one of the two most significant occurrences that transpired in Jerusalem. The tragedy was linked in the Christian mind with the alleged complicity of the Jewish population. Consequently, almost in retaliation, Catholic travelers described the Jews of Jerusalem at the end of the nineteenth century in the most unflattering language as pathetic and their religious behavior as peculiar, if not ludicrous.

James Pfeiffer, a priest who joined the Franciscan pilgrims of 1889, found Jewish religious exercises at the Western Wall, a surviving remnant of the Second Temple complex, "touching and painful." Another participant of the 1889 pilgrimage characterized the Western Wall as a "place where Jews come to weep." And they will continue to weep, he prophesied: "Thus they have wept since the coming of Christ and thus they will weep . . . as long as this world will exist."[28]

John T. Durward, an intensely religious man, traveled twice to the Holy Land. His first pilgrimage was as a member of the Franciscan journey. In 1910, he returned to Palestine. He wrote two books about his trav-

els, one in 1890 and the other in 1913. His writing about the Holy Land
was motivated by his conviction that no account had yet been written
from a Catholic perspective, with glimpses of contemporary life in the
Holy Land.[29]

However, Durward's visit to Jerusalem also elicited distinctly negative
views about the role of its Jewish inhabitants. He did not consider Jerusalem a city appropriate for Jews to return to. To Durward, Jerusalem
had lost its meaning for Jews. He acknowledged his great veneration for
the city, but, he admitted, "We love the land for what it *has been*."[30]
Besides, Durward noted, the Jewish dream for restoration had been transferred to the church. Durward was a good student of the theology of
displacement. Biblical promises made to the Jews, he observed, had not
been directed to the Jewish people "but rather to those who are the chosen and faithful . . . who by obedience to God are the spiritual descen-
dants of Abraham [and] . . . the Church."[31]

Writing on the eve of the First World War, a time when the Jewish
population of Jerusalem was rising rapidly, surpassing ninety thousand,
Durward refused to admit that there might be any positive future for the
city: "Jerusalem is one huge burial ground. . . . How can one be jovial
in Jerusalem? . . . In fact, no one laughs in Jerusalem."[32]

To Durward, the city of Jerusalem was "wretched and squalid." The
people's dwellings, he tells us, are dirty, "including their places of worship." Jews there are ashamed to look you in the eye; and "they are still
the money-changers," as in the days of Jesus. Clearly, "the malediction
they called down on themselves has been fulfilled." They have been
cursed for rejecting and slaying the Messiah.[33] Otherwise a great admirer
of Jews and their religious traditions, Durward was unable to escape the
chains of scorn he held for the living Jew.[34]

It is the kind of ambivalence found in other Catholic travelers to Jerusalem. William A. Bergan, who revisited the holy city a few years before the outbreak of World War I, writes movingly: "The first view of
Jerusalem made an impression upon my mind never to be effaced . . . and
almost daily since has the Holy City come up before me with the same
distinctness and with as strong emotions as at that time. The brightest
day-dream of my heart for years was fully realized. I could scarcely believe it. I thought it was all a dream. . . . The glowing descriptions came
to my mind with a beauty and force never before felt." But all this
changed when Bergan entered the city: "The vision was dissipated; narrow, dirty, ill paved streets, dilapidated buildings, poverty, a wretched
population . . . are all that first meet the eye. You look about and wonder is this a reality or is it a dream; can this be Jerusalem the Holy City,

the Zion of the Living God? . . . The desolation foretold centuries ago has been fearfully accomplished—all her glory is departed."[35]

Similarly, Andrew E. Breen, who spoke of the city of Jerusalem in the most pious terms, viewed its Jewish population contemptuously. Observing Jews worshiping at the Western Wall, the holiest shrine in Judaism, Breen found the worshipers "repulsive." In his diary, he wrote that the Jews "embrace the stones, kiss them and weep over them. The expression on their countenances is most repulsive." Jews can be readily identified in Jerusalem, observed Breen, by their "peculiar" expressions, "mysterious, hopelessly sad. . . . They are a people apart, a mystery of the human race."[36] In keeping with the theology of contempt, Breen explains the neglect and poverty of Jerusalem and the isolation and repugnance of its misled Jews as a consequence of God's punishment for their rejection of the true Christ and his teachings. For this error, they have earned God's eternal hate.[37]

Not all Catholic travelers described the Jews of Jerusalem in as stark terms as did Durward or Breen. Indeed, even the latter and others who pictured the Jewish people as doomed because of their sins reverted to moments of admiration and awe of the long history and religious traditions of the Jewish people.[38] But the religious contempt, coupled with social insults, suppressed more positive observations found in print during the first two decades of the twentieth century.

□ □ □

Catholic pilgrims to the Holy Land at the turn of the century rarely indicated any awareness of Zionist stirring within the Jewish community. The Jews' desire to restore their homeland in Palestine was not an issue which preoccupied American Catholics. Indeed, on the highest levels of the church, Jewish national aspirations were dismissed as chimerical and inappropriate. According to the Roman newspaper *L'Osservatore Romano,* the Vatican was displeased when it heard of Jewish intentions of "occupying" Palestine.[39] Commenting on Jewish national aspirations articulated at the First World Zionist Congress, convened in Basel, Switzerland, in 1897, the official Vatican periodical *Civiltà Cattolica* remarked: "1827 years have passed since the prediction of Jesus of Nazareth was fulfilled, namely, that Jerusalem would be destroyed . . . that the Jews would be led away to be slaves among the nations and that they would remain in the dispersion until the end of the world."[40]

When in 1904 Theodore Herzl met with Pope Pius X (1903–14), hoping to receive the pontiff's cooperation for Jewish nationalism, the pope declared: "We are unable to favor this movement. We cannot prevent the Jews from going to Jerusalem—but we could never sanction it. The ground of Jerusalem has been sanctified by the Life of Jesus Christ . . . The Jews have not recognized our Lord. Therefore we cannot recognize the Jewish people."[41]

Throughout his Zionist campaign, Herzl tried to obtain the cooperation of the Holy See for his Jewish national ideas. Through the pope's subordinates, Herzl attempted to keep the pope informed about the progress of the Zionist movement.[42] Shortly before his death in 1904, Herzl acknowledged his inability to elicit any cooperation from the Vatican for his Zionist schemes. According to Pius X, the Vatican would be better served if the land remained under Turkish Muslim control rather than in Jewish hands.[43]

The pope was quite emphatic in his refusal to endorse Jewish national aspirations. In a twenty-five-minute audience with Herzl, Pius X declared:

> I, as the head of the Church, cannot do this. There are two possibilities. Either the Jews will cling to their faith and continue to await the Messiah, which, for us, has already appeared. In that case, they will be denying the divinity of Jesus, and we cannot help them. Or else they will go there without any religion, and then we can be even less favorable to them.
>
> The Jewish religion was the foundation of our own; but it was superseded by the teachings of Christ, and we cannot concede it any further validity.[44]

A clearer case of religious contempt for Judaism, coupled with a ringing pronouncement of a displacement theology, uttered by a leader of world Catholicism, would be hard to find.

◻ ◻ ◻

World War I erupted in Europe unexpectedly in the summer of 1914. Because of this conflict, the course of Jewish history in Palestine was drastically changed. The results of this war also induced the Catholic world to focus more attentively upon the Holy Land.

Early in November 1917, in part to attract world and American-Jewish support for the Allied cause and hopefully through American-Jewish influence to draw the United States as an ally into the conflict, Great Britain issued an important declaration. It originated as a letter from the British foreign secretary, Lord Arthur James Balfour, to Lord Walter Rothschild and would henceforth be remembered as the Balfour Declaration. The letter announced Britain's readiness to support the Jewish desire to create a national homeland in Palestine.[45] The British government hoped that such an announcement would inspire American Jews to persuade their own government to enter the war as Britain's ally. It goes without saying that American Jews were elated with the declaration, which had an electrifying impact on the Zionist movement. Finally, the idea of a national home for the Jewish people had won the backing of a major world power, England. It was hoped that the United States would shortly follow with its own endorsement.

America's non-Jewish secular press as well as the religious newspapers expressed great satisfaction at the news. But, as was seen in the American reaction to the Dreyfus affair, and as Esther Feldblum observes in her pathbreaking study, "A notable exception to the favorable response accorded to the Balfour Declaration . . . in America was the chilly silence maintained by the nation's Catholic press."[46]

This was somewhat surprising, since Pope Benedict XV (1914–22), who met with Nahum Sokolow, a ranking member of the Zionist movement, on May 10, 1917, gave him encouragement and promised more support.[47] At least for the first year following the Balfour Declaration, the American Catholic hierarchy hesitated to take a clear position on it. In response to a request by the Zionist Organization of America in November 1918, one of the most liberal members of the American hierarchy, James Cardinal Gibbons of Baltimore, told American Jews that he was in favor of the declaration.[48]

Such Catholic endorsement of the Balfour Declaration was relatively rare in the United States. Feldblum observes that the American diocesan press viewed the ejection of Turkey's army from Jerusalem on December 10, 1917, as a victory for Catholicism rather than for the Jews. American Catholics saw General Edmund Allenby's victory as the beginning of Christian, not Jewish, restoration in the Holy Land. Allenby's armies were compared by the American Catholic press to the Crusaders, "Crusaders in khaki," who had retrieved Jerusalem from Muslim hands so that once again it would become a Christian enclave.[49] That such events as the Balfour Declaration and the conquest of Palestine by British forces might have contributed some benefits for Jewish nation building seemed to have escaped the American Catholic mind. Indeed, any suggestion of the possibility of Zionist success in colonizing Palestine that might result from these events was dismissed as illusory. Jews, Catholic editorials argued, could not attain the population growth, the governing skills, or the necessary authority to establish a Jewish homeland. The skills needed for governing, Catholics asserted, belonged to the Christians; and it would be they, not the Jews, who would eventually build a Christian society in Palestine.[50]

Even Pope Benedict, who had at first voiced approval of the Balfour Declaration, quickly reversed himself after Allenby's conquest of Jerusalem. The Jews, he now feared, might prove a threat to Catholic interests. One of the pope's major concerns was whether Catholic holy places in Jerusalem and elsewhere would be safe in British and Jewish hands. During the years following World War I, the Vatican preferred that all its shrines be placed under international supervision.[51]

Such concerns suggest that by 1918, a Catholic awareness of Zionism and its realities began to emerge. Unlike evangelical Protestants, however, who were thrilled at the sight of a Jewish return, Catholics remained either indifferent, ambivalent, or even hostile to such a prospect. While for evangelical Protestants, Jewish ingathering in their ancestral home was seen as a clear sign for the preparation of Christ's return to earth, for Catholics, the Zionist movement was a threat to the church's security.[52]

◻ ◻ ◻

None of this is to suggest that all American Jews were drawn toward or approved of the cause of Jewish nationalism, certainly not during Zionism's formative years of the early twentieth century. Assimilated American Jews, mostly members of Reform congregations, looked with consternation upon any event that might retard the progress of their acceptance as equal partners in their adopted land.

The emergence of political Zionism collided with the Reform movement's efforts to universalize the image of Judaism and to divest Judaism of its national character. Some American Jews were concerned that Zionism might cast suspicion on the Reform movement despite its efforts to make Judaism an "American" religion, to strip away all remnants of its ancient particularity. Judaism's current mission, argued some Jews, to bring "truth, justice, and peace" to all of mankind, transcended its national past, a past which Reformers believed they had outgrown. "We consider ourselves no longer a nation but a religious community and therefore expect neither a return to Palestine . . . nor the restoration of any of the laws concerning the Jewish state," declared a group of Reform leaders late in the nineteenth century.[53]

Liberal Jews were distressed at the suggestion that they should think of the Holy Land as a political haven. Isaac M. Wise, a leading voice of the Reform movement, characterized modern Zionism as an unfortunate mutation, an outgrowth of European antisemitism, which he insisted was a transient tendency. Wise considered the frequently repeated prayer for the restoration of a Jewish kingdom sinful.[54] "To my mind," wrote David Philipson, a leading voice for Reform Judaism, "political Zionism and true Americanism have always seemed mutually exclusive. No man can be a member of two nationalities."[55] Zionism, other assimilated Jews believed, would obstruct the Americanization of immigrant Jews and would generate public suspicion about their loyalty.[56]

The appearance of Theodore Herzl's *Der Judenstaat* and the convening of the First Zionist Congress in Basel were disquieting events for many Liberal American Jews. Reform leaders denounced Herzl's program, proclaiming that "the object of Judaism is not political nor national, but spiritual."[57] A number of Reform rabbis declared, "We are unalterably opposed to political Zionism. The Jews are not a nation but a religious community. . . . America is our Zion." Such sentiments were even accepted by some Jews of the Conservative movement.[58]

Still, not all Jewish leaders of either the Liberal or Conservative branches adopted an anti-Zionist stand. Indeed, many of the leaders of American Zionism, such as Stephen S. Wise, Judah Leon Magnes, Bernhard Felsenthal, Gustav Gottheil, and Joseph Krauskopf, were provided by the ranks of Liberal and Conservative Judaism. Felsenthal tried to reconcile the idea of Zionism with Reform's idea of a universal mission. Gottheil, senior rabbi of Temple Emanuel in New York City, made no effort to conceal his Zionism from his well-to-do congregants. Gotthard Deutsch, a professor at the anti-Zionist Hebrew Union College, frequently lectured his colleagues on the spiritual meaning of a Jewish national rebirth.[59]

However, it was a short-lived opposition. During the early decades of the twentieth century, an increasingly large section of Americanized Jewish opinion began to shift away from anti-Zionism. These Jews moved to positions of either pro-Zionism or non-Zionism. The pro-Zionists became supporters; the non-Zionists were willing to offer the fledgling Jewish homeland fiscal and diplomatic counsel, not for their own benefit or spiritual comfort but for those Jews who chose to reside there.[60] No doubt, the change of heart which occurred was due in part to Great Britain's Balfour Declaration and Allenby's victory in Palestine. American endorsement of England's accomplishments also conferred political legitimacy on Zionism.[61] What is more, by the end of the second decade of the twentieth century, the rising number and growing influence of the mass of Eastern European Jewish immigrants could hardly be ignored. It was these individuals who contributed the bulk of American support to the Jewish national movement. In matters of Zionism, it was these newcomers, not the earlier immigrants, well-integrated and well-heeled, who would carry the day.

Even so, the anti-Zionism which lingered among a shrinking circle of American Jews differed radically from that of American Roman Catholics. While the first was born out of a desperate desire for acceptance in a Christian world, the latter emanated from a theological resentment of Jews and Judaism, a theology of contempt.

◦ ◦ ◦

While support for the Zionist movement increased among Jews during the years following the First World War, criticism and suspicion of Jewish nationalism continued unabated in American Catholic circles. The theological roots for this resentment were buried deep in the history of Christianity, nurtured by patristic polemics and kept alive by Christian supersessionism, the idea that the Jews had been ejected and displaced by the New Israel.[62] What is more, the Vatican's anxiety about the security of its holy places—the fear that they might fall under Jewish control—added fuel to this Catholic anti-Zionism.

It was the Vatican's hope in the years after the conquest of Jerusalem that Jewish settlements would be confined to areas outside the jurisdiction of international control of the holy places in Jerusalem, Nazareth, Tiberias, and Bethlehem.[63] The *Chalutziut* (pioneering) practices which the early Jewish settlers introduced to Palestine caused the Catholic Church additional anxiety. For Rome, the collective lifestyle and secular practices of the Jewish pioneers organized in kibbutzim (collective settlements) seemed to suggest that Bolshevism was being introduced into the Holy Land.

The Vatican's suspicion of Zionism was further exacerbated by the privileged position that it believed Zionism was attaining in the international community. Especially annoying was Britain's appointment of a Jew, Sir Herbert Sammuel, as the first high commissioner of Palestine in 1922.[64] The Vatican anxiety about Palestine was expressed in a 1922 memorandum. Sergio Minerbi, a student of Vatican affairs in Palestine, observed that the Vatican was concerned about the role that the Jews might play there, which the Council of the League of Nations had now placed under British mandate. The Vatican sought a revision of some of the mandate articles, "because they accorded the Jews a privileged position over the Catholics and because . . . the rights of the Christians were not adequately protected."[65]

American Jesuits noted that Vatican resistance to the rise of Zionism and the building of Jewish settlements in Palestine also stemmed from its desire to cooperate with the Arabs, whose resistance to Zionism was in turn inspired by the support they received from the Vatican.[66] The notion that the Arab population would be unable to live with the Jewish settlers and that Arabs had the right to decide which and how many immigrants should be admitted to Palestine was reflected in the comments of American Catholics.[67] The Latin patriarch of Jerusalem, whose hatred of Jews knew few bounds, believed that "the Zionists were not religious and were even antireligious. . . . Zionist immigration would sweep the Christians out of Palestine and would destroy the country's Christian character."[68]

These anti-Zionist polemics voiced by a leading Catholic prelate must have influenced Vatican policy toward Zionism during the 1920s. Such views, coupled with the traditional anti-Jewish attitudes of the church and its concern about the security of its holy sites, helped shape a long-range Catholic anti-Zionist policy which lasted until the decade following the Second World War. Throughout the 1920s, the Jews of Palestine were accused of desecrating Jerusalem, of introducing prostitution and pornography into the Zionist "Jewish republic," of "holding dancing parties in front of Calvary." In 1930, a Catholic writer, Vincent Sheean, pronounced Zionism a disaster and predicted its failure.[69]

Another American Catholic writer declared that the concessions made to the Jews in Palestine were a serious blunder "and full of peril." The author, Cyprien Jourdin, stated his position as follows: "Without being in any sense of the term an anti-Semite, it is only necessary to open one's eyes to see that the formation of a national Jewish home in Palestine, such as now appears in reality and practice, encroaches on the legitimate rights of Catholics of the entire world and creates a new center of disturbance in the Moslem world."[70]

Interestingly, Jourdin's greatest fear was that the Zionists, having attained some influence in their homeland, would persecute the Christian residents of Palestine just as the Christians had for centuries turned against the Jews. Jourdin wrote: "A people who have been consistently told that they have been persecuted, mocked and jeered at for centuries by the Christians, who have been accustomed to mix instincts of revenge with zeal for their own interests, will these people maintain their balance in the midst of their joy and hope renewed? Must Jewry not passionately hope to humiliate Christianity in its turn to revenge itself? Noble and lofty souls are not more numerous here than elsewhere."[71]

Jourdin told his Catholic readers that the Zionist ambitions included a desire to subjugate the Arab population and to assume total mastery over Palestine. According to him, even the British appeared unaware of Zionism's sinister ambitions. The Catholic writer argued that the Christian population would inevitably be reduced to a condition of inferiority. The churches of Palestine, Jourdin declared in 1922, had already declined below the conditions they had assumed under Turkish rule before 1917. He accused the Jews of Palestine of employing people to secularize Christian holy places, "transforming them for worldly usage." The Zionists, he wrote, are desecrating the city of Jerusalem. But what can one expect of Jews, asked Jourdin, "a people marked with a sign more terrible than that of Cain: 'Deiciders'?"[72]

If American Catholic anti-Zionism did not always show the intensity of Jourdin, it nevertheless existed in a more moderate form during these years. Throughout the 1920s, a time when Catholics themselves were attacked as an un-American minority by Protestant hate groups, they hesitated to assault American Jewish interests too harshly. Even so, from a theological perspective, American Catholics were unable to accept fully the Jews' return to their ancestral home. Carlton J. H. Hayes, a liberal Catholic professor of history at Columbia University, declared that the Jewish national movement did not conform to the biblical idea of Judaism. Jewish nationalism, he announced, was a "tribal" religion of the "Chosen People" which contradicted the highest values of Christianity.[73] Christian doctrine in the years before World War II regarded the Zionist movement ambiguously. "On the one hand," as the Catholic theologian Eugene J. Fisher explains, "the interpretation of the diaspora as divine punishment on the Jews led some Catholics to view a reborn state of Israel as virtually a theological impossibility, unless the Jews first repented their 'rejection' of Jesus, converted, and were thus reconciled with God, who would then no longer impede their return to the land of promise. Such a return, however, would be seen . . . as a sign of the End Time. This latter potential quite naturally made people very cautious about the whole question."[74]

This kind of ambivalence continued unabated into the late thirties, a time of desperation for world Jewry. American Catholics rejected a Jewish claim to the Holy Land, as an American Catholic explained in 1936 when he declared: "[The] Holy Land is neither Jewish nor Islamic. It is Christian. And as its soil was trodden by the Incarnate Word Who founded His Church there, the welfare of Palestine is inextricably bound up with the Catholic and Apostolic Church of Christ."[75]

When in 1939, on the eve of the *Shoah* (Holocaust),[76] Jews tried to persuade Great Britain to open the doors of Palestine more widely for Jewish immigrants, the editor of the Jesuit magazine *America* griped of "the force and vehemence of the attack of international Jewry," adding that "the union of sentiment, the similarity of method, the use of propaganda, the moral pressure of Jews in every nation, particularly in the British Commonwealth and the United States, all manifest that Jewry is an international power."[77]

Indeed, as the 1930s drew to a close, and Arab restlessness intensified, and world conflict loomed on the horizon, and the fate of Jews reached its darkest point, Catholic ambivalence toward the *Yishuv* (the Homeland) turned increasingly hostile.[78]

4

Darkening Horizons, 1920–40

Notwithstanding the theological underpinnings of the Catholic view of Judaism, suspicious attitudes did not surface all the time. At least for a short while during the 1920s, Catholic and Jewish interests converged. Both faith communities shared concerns about a rising tide of racism, anti-Catholicism, antisemitism, and immigration restriction.[1] A common front was necessary to meet these threats. This cooperation was shattered during the following decade, however, as Catholic and Jewish anxieties about domestic and foreign events drove the groups toward different paths.

In part, the domestic difficulties that Catholics and Jews shared during the 1920s stemmed from disillusionment with the results of World War I. As the world conflict ended, Americans became fearful that the virus of European Bolshevism would infect American institutions and endanger the stability of the government and Constitution. The violent and unexpected overthrow of the czarist monarchy and the outbreak of Communist rebellion in Hungary and Germany made Americans concerned about their own future.

This national paranoia generated suspicion of immigrants in general and Jews in particular. The latter were accused of importing Bolshevik ideas that would corrupt American traditions and institutions. Many Americans demanded a restriction of immigrants, especially those from Eastern Europe, whose values were purported to be at variance with those of Americans. In 1924, a restrictive immigrant quota system was legislated by the Congress and approved by the president, which reduced further Jewish immigration to a trickle. Meanwhile, American Jews faced increased discrimination at home. They were prohibited from residing in certain neighborhoods and denied access to country clubs, vacation resorts, employment, and the professions. They were also restricted from entrance into colleges and professional schools and universities.[2]

One of the most vicious antisemitic tracts of the century was published by Henry Ford during the 1920s in his own newspaper, the *Dearborn Independent*. Entitled "The International Jew," the tract was originally published as the *Protocols of the Elders of Zion* by czarist agents. It accused the Jews of conspiring to overthrow Christian civilization.[3] The *Protocols* lingered throughout the 1920s, becoming a bible of the revived Ku Klux Klan.

Like Jews, Catholics were also beneficiaries of the vast immigration of the early twentieth century. Like Jews, whose additions came largely from Eastern Europe, Catholics also augmented their numbers with newcomers from Italy, Poland, Hungary, and other Catholic centers.

Like Jews, Catholic leaders defended the value of immigration to American society, and they rejected the nativist arguments employed by immigration restrictionists. As Frederick Siedenburg, a Jesuit priest and professor of sociology at Loyola University in Chicago, wrote in 1916: "Objections now used against the Italians, the Jews and the Slavs were once used with equal violence against the Germans and the Irish. They have since proved to be false."[4] It was not an unusual reaction. The church urged its adherents to accept immigrants, regardless of their ethnic origins. The Jesuit periodical *Catholic Mind* pointed with pride to "two universities in this country that have eighty-five percent of Jews of recent arrival among their students. That is an eloquent testimony of the self-assertiveness of our Jewish fellow-citizens."[5] Many Catholic writers were among the most outspoken voices of opposition to the restrictive immigration laws of the 1920s.[6] And like American Jews, many Catholics found the racist doctrines which circulated in the United States during the 1920s unacceptable, even alarming.

George N. Shuster is a case in point. A member of the editorial staff of *Commonweal,* Shuster shared with a certain number of other Catholics a warm interest in their Jewish fellow citizens. Shuster, a leading Catholic intellectual during the decades preceding the Second World War, became disillusioned with American Protestantism. He found the Protestants overly concerned with "sin" and "hell." He advised Protestants to adopt a page from Judaism, specifically "its concern for ideals that transcend the here and now." Catholics, Shuster reminded his coreligionists, would profit by knowing good Jews better.[7] Shuster also challenged with eloquence the racial doctrines which prevailed during conflict, followed in 1919 by the National Catholic Welfare Council (NCWC), considerable uniformity and discipline were brought to a previously fragmented church. One researcher argued that there was a considerable degree of unity in respect to religious, social, and political issues among American Catholics during the administration of Franklin D. Roosevelt.[20]

Hitler had already assumed power in Germany when John F. X. Murphy addressed the American Jesuit Philosophical Association on August 28, 1934, on the topic "The Problem of International Judaism." The key question the priest raised was, "What is the problem that the International Jew is causing to the rest of the world, and especially to our world?"[21] Clearly, by 1934, the very posing of such a question by a Catholic scholar to an intellectual Catholic audience was not only provocative but inflammatory.

The explanations Murphy offered for the "problems of Judaism" were also intemperate. While he found many American Jews—Orthodox, Conservative, or Liberal—friendly to "Gentiles," he discovered that some Jews "maintain the fiercest spirit of hostility towards the Goyim." The writer seemed surprised that the Jews had any animosity at all toward Christians. "The concept of the Jew as an innocent victim" of "Christian malice down through the ages," intones Murphy, "is an untrue and unhistorical one." What is more, "The Jews have done much to draw down upon themselves Christian opposition and distrust."[22] He accuses Jews of possessing an "uncanny ability for accumulating coin" and viewing "all Gentiles" as "lesser breeds without the Law" and themselves evidencing "religious and racial haughtiness and exclusiveness." The American Jesuit philosopher's most chilling warning for Jews is that Adolph Hitler might be justified in his persecution of them. Murphy declares, "In defense of Hitler, in Germany though the Jews are only one percent of the population . . . they fill fifteen percent of the professoriats, the medical and legal professions, and the lucrative government offices. Clearly, under these circumstances, Hitler's anger against the Jews is understandable."[23] It is a danger that could overtake America as well. Following the Nazi lure even further, Murphy contends that because of their warped morals, "Jews do an immense amount of harm . . . in their influence upon the stage, the movies, the radio, and above all the daily press. . . . Everywhere we see the uninhibited lust for a gain inducing them to prostitute agencies . . . into instruments for debasing the taste if not the morals of the multitude."[24]

The Catholic Church, readers of *Catholic World* were assured in 1937 by Gerald Wynne Rushton, a well-known English writer on Catholic

the 1920s. He found particularly annoying the popular notion of "Nordic racial superiority." He described it as "a theory projected into American society by a powerful group bent upon establishing its sense of superiority."[8]

Most frustrating for American Catholics was the revival of anti-Catholicism during the 1920s. Public animosity against the Church of Rome was underscored during the election campaign of 1928. The vicious attacks directed at the candidacy of the popular New York governor, Irish Catholic Alfred E. Smith, illustrated the long journey that Roman Catholics had yet to follow for full acceptance in their native land. Throughout the decade, Catholics were viewed suspiciously. Even some liberal Americans charged them with a lack of patriotism and subservience to the will of a foreign leader: the pope in Rome.[9]

Neither were some American Jews free of misconceptions and suspicion of Catholicism. Shuster complained in 1927 that Jews shared with Americans in general a perplexity about the Catholic Church. "Even educated and sensitive Jews," he wrote in 1927, "like Ludwig Lewishon and Irwin Edman have set down in sober print certain impressions of Catholic services which one respects but which one cannot help considering lumberingly amateurish."[10] That Catholics and Jews shared an ignorance of the religious ways of the other does not mitigate the distress felt by each of them.

The American Catholic church's most implacable enemy was the Ku Klux Klan, which *Catholic World* described in 1923 as "the most curious combination of comedy and tragedy, of melodrama and burlesque, of buffoonery and villainy that has appeared in America."[11] The Ku Klux Klan had exerted vigorous effort to bring about the defeat of Al Smith in 1928 and to win the presidency of Herbert Hoover. The Klan opposed Smith's candidacy simply because he was a Roman Catholic. To the Klan, Roman Catholicism was incompatible with Americanism.

In the process of attacking the Klan for its fanatical intolerance, American Catholics not only were serving their own interests but were joining with Jews in a war against bigotry.[12] Jews, more vulnerable than American Catholics, welcomed these overtures. Nevertheless, this situation should not be viewed as a permanent change of heart on the part of Catholics toward Jews. Catholic reaction to Zionism was ample evidence of the tenuousness of such gestures. The convergence of interests in the 1920s was little more than an acknowledgment that on a pragmatic level, antisemitism, like anti-Catholicism, did not conform to the pluralistic values of American civilization. But the theology of contempt was still very much in place.

◻ ◻ ◻

Whatever unity materialized on domestic issues between Catholics and Jews during the 1920s, it disintegrated under the enormous stresses placed upon it in the following decade. Shaken by domestic economic collapse and unprecedented international chaos, the decade turned out to be one of the most traumatic ever experienced in peacetime. It was also a critical one in the relationship of Catholics and Jews. With the appointment of Adolf Hitler as chancellor of Germany in 1933 and with him the dictatorship of the Nazi Party, American Jews witnessed the most frightening assault launched against their German and European brethren in recorded history. German Nazism inspired American antisemitic imitators. The number of anti-Jewish groups continued to climb throughout the decade, reaching a peak shortly after Japan's attack on Pearl Harbor on December 7, 1941. Before that date, hundreds of anti-Jewish hate groups had been actively spreading their message throughout the United States.[13]

The persecution of the Jews of Germany did not seriously move American public opinion. Polls conducted during the late thirties indicate that the majority of the American public perceived Jews as possessing objectionable traits—dishonesty, greed, aggressiveness—and constituting a greater menace to American society than any other single ethnic group. A small minority, 20 percent of the respondents in one poll, recommended that Jews be expelled from the United States. In a poll taken shortly before World War II, data showed that almost half of the respondents believed that Jews "partly" deserved what they were receiving from Hitler.[14]

American Jewish Defense agencies—the American Jewish Committee, B'nai B'rith Anti-Defamation League—were kept busy monitoring the direction of the domestic hate campaign. The 1935 report of the secretary of the Anti-Defamation League indicated that some of the hate groups about which the league was collecting information included the Silver Shirts, Black Shirts, Khaki Shirts, and others whose names suggest Nazi influence. The American Jewish Committee estimated that by 1939, five hundred antisemitic organizations, encouraged by the success of German Nazism, were active in the United States. Nazi antisemitic propaganda distributed through German consulates provided continuous outreach for American extremists.[15]

As the Nazi noose tightened around Europe's Jews, American Jews found themselves desperately alone, surrounded by an uncaring gentile world. Neither did they find much comfort in the official actions of the nation's policymakers. Paralyzed by immigration restriction laws and,

as Richard Breitman and Alan M. Kraut document, a State Department bureaucracy petrified by an unimaginative interpretation of its responsibilities, compounded by the reluctance of a president to assume risks on behalf of European Jews, the future of world Jewry appeared bleak.[16]

Obviously, one could not know if Germany's desire to humiliate and crush its Jews might have been stemmed by early American intervention, since even relatively minor signals of disapproval from Washington to the Third Reich were nonexistent. To what degree antisemitism had permeated America's Department of State and the foreign service has been debated by American historians. Certainly immigration laws formed in the preceding decade were welcomed by those who wished to prevent the entrance of refugees from Nazism. David Wyman's study *The Abandonment of the Jews* substantiates the thesis that the strong anti-Jewish sentiment among American policymakers inhibited more creative rescue efforts.[17]

Neither can one discount the indifference that prevailed in the halls of Congress on the eve of the Second World War. It was a sentiment motivated in part by a fear that Jewish anti-Nazi agitation might draw the United States into the conflict with Germany. In this sense, Congress was echoing the public's reluctance to exert any special effort to save Europe's Jews. Deborah Lipstadt in her study of American press opinion, *Beyond Belief,* finds that throughout the thirties, much of the nation's press opposed any relaxation of immigration laws.[18]

The hostile attitude toward Jews in the United States is documented by Leonard Dinnerstein, the historian of American antisemitism. He observes its "devastating psychological" effect on many American Jews. Dinnerstein writes:

American Jews knew of existing antisemitism. . . . But in the 1930s the intensity of antisemitism, the appeal of hate organizations and the popularity of demagogues, combined with an escalation of serious physical abuse especially in the cities of the northeast and midwest where more than 85 percent of American Jews dwelled to have an absolutely chilling effect. And the worst thing was that the hatred seemed to be accelerating. For the first time in America's history Jews feared that their attackers might acquire the kind of political influence and respectability that antisemites had in Europe.[19]

Catholics shared with other Americans in the 1930s a dislike of Jews. It is, of course, difficult to generalize about all American Catholics; still a unified voice on issues important to American Catholics was much more likely in the 1930s than in the years preceding the First World War. But with the formation of the National Catholic War Council during the

themes, bore no responsibility for the mounting Jew-hatred throughout the world. It is wrong, writes Rushton, to believe that the church was ever guilty of persecuting the Jews. On the contrary, the Church of Rome has always been the greatest defender of the Jews.[25] There is some validity to Rushton's argument, at least with respect to the Middle Ages. Jewish survival in the hostile Christian atmosphere of the Middle Ages was indeed due in part to the church's insistence that Jews continue to survive. "An analysis of the Papal Bulls affecting the Jews," argues Rushton, "reveals more clearly than anything else the fine work of the Church for them."[26]

The American church, it seemed, as it had during the Dreyfus scandal, made repeated efforts in the 1930s to divest its past from the stigma of anti-Judaism. As late as 1941, at a time when German death squads were busy killing Jews and gas chambers were about to be erected, Catholic readers were reminded that medieval popes denounced accusations of Jewish "ritual murder," that the yellow "badge of shame," though supported by the popes, was not at all as bad as it seemed. "The insignia were made by the civil authorities," explains a Catholic writer, "and sold to the Jews much as bicycle or auto tags are sold today."[27] It was a benign description of an experience enforced by the church but remembered by Jews as a lamentable imposition and embarrassment.

How can one account for American Catholic ambivalence, even hostility, toward Jews, as we have witnessed in the case of John Murphy and other Catholic writers? No doubt, racist antisemitism which spread throughout the Western world infected many American Catholics, as it did other Americans. But it is unlikely that the majority of Catholic opinion makers, leaders of the church, succumbed to Nazi doctrines. The chief source of anti-Judaism remained as it had in previous decades: the theological foundations of Christianity in general and Catholicism in particular.

Despite his anti-Judaism, even Murphy admitted there was help for the Jews. Full acceptance was theirs for the asking, if they turned to Jesus. "Down the ages," writes Murphy, "Jews have made the most magnificent converts. . . . Conversion to Christianity would be ideal!"[28] Obviously, the theology of contempt continued to hover in the skies of the 1930s like a dark cloud that would not dissipate. For example, Catholics were reminded that the New Covenant had displaced or superseded the Old. "Israel's failure to observe the Covenant," Catholics were told, resulted in its "loss of all the rich possibilities which it contained." But for "the faithful few another Covenant [was] established which would more securely unite man with God."[29]

Catholic theologians in the 1930s were not unconcerned about the impact of displacement theology on Jewish-Catholic relations. William Newton insisted in 1934 that "the old relation between God and Man *is put aside* [italics mine], and in its place a more perfect one established."[30] Newton juxtaposed the Old Covenant against the New in this way: "The new is individual, the old was national; . . . the new is permanent, the old was but temporary; it is absolute, the old was conditional; it is the end, the old was but the means to it."[31]

What is more, Newton reminds his readers that the Jews were too taken with ceremonial practices and ritual and obsessed with the petty details of the Law rather than its spirit. This was "ecclesiastical materialism," declared another Catholic writer in describing the religion of the Pharisees. For the Catholic, such Pharisaic practice was "a fundamental perversion of values."[32] Indeed, according to E. I. Watkin, a Catholic writer, "In the sphere of religion, legalism," so characteristic of Jewish practice, "is peculiarly repulsive."[33]

Such an attack on the Pharisees and their achievements by the popular Catholic writer in 1939 displays both a misunderstanding of the work of the early rabbis and a contempt for the Jews of the Second Temple period and the Torah. It certainly did little to create bonds of civility between the two faith communities.

□ □ □

Events in central and eastern Europe did little to mitigate misunderstanding between Catholics and Jews during the 1930s. The growing power and ideological influences of Communism and Nazism increased anxiety in both faith communities. While Catholics detected a growing partiality toward Bolshevik authoritarianism among American Jews, Jews detected on the part of Catholics a greater fear of Soviet influence than of Adolf Hitler's Germany.

As did the majority of Americans, most Roman Catholic leaders despised the Nazi regime of Germany. They recognized the danger it held for the Western democracies. Likewise, most American Jewish spokespersons suspected the danger of Russian Bolshevism. In the light of Germany's virulent antisemitism, it goes without saying that Jews saw that country as the far greater of the two evils. In the light of history, their fear was justified. So was their suspicion that many American Catholics feared Communist atheism as the principal evil of the 1930s.

The concern of American Jews was not Catholic opposition to Bolshevism. Most Jews, as Catholic readers were occasionally informed in

Catholic periodicals, had little use for its authoritarian rule and its collective ideology.[34] The concern Jews had was twofold. First, because a small number of Jews were actively involved in the growing Communist movement, there was a custom among Catholic writers to accuse *all* Jews of being supporters of Communism. Second, and more important, as the decade progressed, Jews detected on the part of American Roman Catholics a tendency to equate the evils of Soviet Communism with those of Nazism, in some instances pointing to Soviet Communism as the greater problem of the two.

American Catholics were at the forefront in opposing American diplomatic recognition of the Soviet Union in 1934.[35] As late as November 1941, a statement issued by the administrative board of the NCWC denounced Soviet Communism, equating it with Nazism as a threat to Christian values. Both of their dictators "assume a power which belongs to God."[36] The equation, pronounced by the most distinguished group of American bishops while the ovens of Auschwitz were being activated, betrayed a callousness toward the plight of Europe's Jews.

That the Holy See considered Soviet Communism the chief enemy of civilization was not lost on the leaders of the American church. The condemnation of Communism issued by Pope Pius XI (1922–39), who served as bishop of the Universal Catholic Church until the outbreak of World War II, was taken very seriously by America's bishops. Pius XI had undertaken his anti-Communist mission from the beginning of the 1930s.[37] It was the deplorable plight of the Catholic Church in the Soviet Union that grieved Pius XI and his successor Pope Pius XII (1939–58). The nightmare of atheistic Bolshevism sweeping over the European continent haunted both pontiffs.

The Vatican's profound dread of the spread of Communism and atheistic ideology, which allowed no room for the Catholic Church, made its behavior toward Nazism suspect. On July 20, 1933, the Vatican negotiated a concordat with the Nazi government. It stipulated that in return for the church's promise to stay out of Nazi politics, the Nazi government would grant the church freedom of religious practice. The concordat was signed on behalf of the pope by his secretary of state, Eugenio Cardinal Pacelli, who became Pope Pius XII in March 1939 and whose anti-Communism and relations with Nazi Germany remained matters of speculation and debate at the close of the twentieth century.[38] It was only after the German government failed to abide by the terms of the concordat and turned against the German Catholic Church that the Holy See altered its own attitude toward the Nazi regime. Pius XI's famous anti-Nazi encyclical of 1937, *Mit brennender Sorge* ("With

Burning Concerns"), denounced Nazi racial laws and Germany's failure to live up to its agreement with the Vatican but did not mention Nazi
antisemitism or Nazi atrocities committed against Jews.[39]

In this light, one can only conclude that had the Hitler regime adhered
to the agreement and permitted the German Catholic Church to exist
freely and quietly in the Third Reich, the plight of Germany's Jews would
have been ignored by the church.

□ □ □

The divisions between American Jews and Catholics deepened further
with the outbreak of the Spanish civil war on July 17, 1936, when General Francisco Franco led a revolt against the Republican government
of Spain. The war that ensued was bloody and brutal, ending in 1939
with Franco's triumph. The civil war was more than just a domestic
conflict. It soon became intertwined in a complex web of international
and ideological issues. Since each of the belligerents allied itself with
foreign powers—Franco with Nazi Germany and Fascist Italy and the
Loyalists with the Soviet Union and friends of its international appara-
tus—the conflict left a popular impression that it was a war between
totalitarianism and democracy. The Republican government had impris-
oned and tortured priests, events which American Catholics viewed with
horror. Catholic support for Franco, however, disturbed the Jewish community, which saw his alliance with Nazism as a threat to Jewish survival. It turned out, as the war progressed, that except for American
antisemites, Catholic support for the *Caudillo* did not result in his great
popularity among Americans. Most thinking Americans—among them
journalists, professors, and artists—sympathized with the more Liberal-
minded Loyalists of the Republic.[40]

To be sure, as J. David Valaik explains, there were a few notable exceptions to the support of Franco among American Catholics, people
who voiced support for the Loyalists of Spain. They too believed that
Franco represented a serious threat to democratic institutions. Even a
few American Jesuits, whose society bore the brunt of the Republican
anti-clericalism, were somewhat ambivalent.[41] Some, admirers of the
French Catholic theologian Jacques Maritain, took seriously his admonition not to canonize the reactionary ideology of Francisco Franco. It
was a view that most American Catholics were advised by faithful believers to ignore. The reaction was similar to that of the few other dissenters. Whether editors of *Commonweal* or young Catholic college

professors, they were either ignored or showered with calumny by pro-Franco American Catholic voices.[42]

As a general rule, the American Left—Socialists, anarchists, and Communists—hoped for a decisive defeat of the "reactionary" forces of Franco. The position of this group, from a Catholic perspective, put them squarely in the camp of Joseph Stalin and his Communist opposition to Franco. However, many American Liberals and intellectuals who were not fellow travelers were also flung into the same camp. Guttmann names a few: "Ruth Benedict, Franz Boas, George Counts, John Dewey, Mark Van Doren, Harry Emerson Fosdick, Robert Lynd, Reinhold Niebuhr . . . John Herman Randall, James T. Shotwell, and Harry F. Ward—[were] all signers of statements in support of the Republic."[43]

Neither could college presidents of Amherst, Smith, Mount Holyoke, Yale—all supporters of the Spanish Republican Loyalist cause—be accused of being fellow travelers of Stalin's Third International. All of these individuals believed that the Spanish Republic represented a democratic and liberal cause that the forces opposed to it were rejecting for the darkness of totalitarianism.[44] It was the kind of idealism which compelled American youth to volunteer for the Abraham Lincoln Brigade, which left for Spain to fight for the survival of the democratic republic.

Not surprisingly, Jews were found in the ranks of the Lincoln Brigade. The memory of medieval Spain was not a pleasant one for Jews. The expulsion instigated by church and crown loomed large in the collective Jewish memory. Ever since then, Jews had felt unwelcome in Spain. But Franco's Nationalist movement's link with Adolf Hitler was a trumpet call of looming danger. The Republic which overthrew the monarchy in 1931 and was now in danger deserved their support. For the first time in more than four hundred years, Jews were welcomed into Spain. Jewish periodicals such as the *American Hebrew* and the *Contemporary Record* praised the Republican government of Spain for its new attitude toward Jews. As one American Jewish volunteer wrote home from the battlefield of Spain: "Today Jews are returning welcomed by the entire Spanish people to fight the modern inquisition. . . . I am sure we are fighting in the best Maccabean tradition."[45]

The assault of Hitler's Jew-hating army on the Spanish Republic in support of Franco's Fascist forces made a victory for the Republic Loyalists a personal imperative. Possibly a thousand of the three thousand volunteers for the Abraham Lincoln Brigade who went to Spain to fight for the Loyalist cause were Jews. About one-third of them never returned home.[46]

American Catholic leaders saw things quite differently. To them, Franco's legions were defending the Catholic church and its sacred traditions. They were also battling the Red menace of Bolshevism, then infecting Spain with its poisonous atheism. For American Catholic leaders, Hitler's support for Franco was either ignored or minimized. Their focus was on the scourge of Bolshevism.[47]

A case study of Boston's Catholic community confirms the reaction to the Spanish crisis. Donald F. Crosby concludes a discussion by suggesting that "the attitude which stands out most sharply is Catholic preoccupation with Communism." The Catholics evaluated every aspect of the war in its relationship to the Soviet threat. Boston's Catholics believed that the Loyalists were Communists and that their American supporters were working with them to destroy the church in Spain. Only Franco and his supporters could reverse the Spanish nightmare.[48]

American Catholics had reason to be concerned about the security of the Spanish church. Shortly after the overthrow of the Spanish monarchy in 1931, the Republican government disestablished Catholic institutions and confiscated church property. Vatican concern filtered down to the American hierarchy, which assured its Spanish counterparts of its sympathy and support.[49]

All American Catholics were especially disturbed by news of the brutality directed by Loyalist forces against Spanish clergy. They attributed it to the satanic inspiration of Stalinism.[50] That savagery had engulfed the church of Spain was obvious to American Catholics: it was due to the aggressive forces of Stalinism. The Holy Father had already made that clear and warned that other countries, even the United States, could follow. After all, the *Daily Worker* had declared the church the enemy of the Spanish people. The Soviets were exerting enormous effort to break the unity of the Universal Church by alienating American Catholics from their counterparts in Spain.[51]

Church leaders lauded the heroic efforts of General Franco. He had gathered under his banner thousands of Spaniards who, like him, dreaded the insidious incursions of the Reds and desired to save the Catholic Church. An American Jesuit scholar described Franco as "the Man who was the inspiration of the revolt and is the soul of the Nationalist movement . . . of the Spanish faith of the Spanish character."[52]

Praise and adulation were showered upon Franco. The accolades came from leading American Catholics, who did not hesitate to compare him to George Washington and Thomas Jefferson, who, like Franco, fought for liberty and freedom of conscience. Franco was seen as called to save the church of Spain. The popular prelate Fulton J. Sheen compared

General Franco's war against the Popular Front of Spain to the American rebellion against England.[53]

Not all American Catholic leaders spoke with one voice on Spanish issues. A few, such as George Shuster of *Commonweal*, felt a nagging uncertainty about the righteousness of either side. Even the editor of *Catholic World* revealed skepticism at times about some of the anti-Loyalist propaganda that he received. Still, the American hierarchy maintained a consistent pro-Franco position.[54] As on other public issues, there sometimes was a difference of opinion on Spain between prelates and priests on the one hand and lay Catholics on the other. As J. David Valaik notes,

> No doubt the leaders of the Catholic Church in America made every effort to persuade the faithful of the rectitude of Franco's cause and the wickedness of his opponent's. There is, however, considerable doubt that they succeeded. The circulation of such magazines and newspapers as *Columbia*, the publication of the Knights of Columbus, the Brooklyn *Tablet*, the Denver *Catholic Register* and *Our Sunday Visitor* was extensive, and any survey of the Catholic press, including the magazines of the pro-Franco and anti-Loyalist theme, was drummed into Catholic senses with great zeal and regularity. This same message was also to be heard in Catholic schools, in the meeting places of Holy Name Societies, and in the councils of Catholic men and women.[55]

Yet, Catholic ambivalence can be detected in a Gallup poll taken in 1939. It indicated that 53 percent of American Catholics sympathized with neither side in the Civil War, and only 38 percent favored Francisco Franco's cause.[56]

However, whatever uncertainty might have prevailed among Catholic laity, there was much more uniformity of views among Catholic editors, priests, and bishops. These individuals did not seem overly disturbed by the Nazi and Fascist support that flowed to the *Caudillo*. His crusade to save the church of Spain was much too important to allow quibbling over his means to the worthy end. Indeed, the American Jewish tendency to side with other liberals in criticizing Franco's attack on Spain's liberal government was severely and insensitively attacked by Catholic writers. When Jews joined in protesting Franco's brutal behavior toward Loyalists, Catholic writers wondered why they failed to protest similar attacks of Loyalist atrocities. "Nazis from Germany," argued one Catholic editor, "were no worse than intruders from Russia."[57]

Both secular and religious Jewish journalists were attacked by Catholic writers for their criticism of Franco and his cause. Newspapers owned by Jews and known for their pro-Loyalist views, such as the *New*

York Times and the *New York Post,* were seen by Catholics as "Jewish newspapers" and fair game.[58] Jews, Catholics griped, were always reminding newspaper readers about the horrors their brethren were experiencing in Berlin but never mentioned the torture of priests in Madrid. Catholics asserted that because of Jewish-dominated media, the Catholic position on Spain rarely received public exposure. Since Jews had aligned themselves with the forces of "slaughter and anarchy," Catholics were advised to ignore any future Jewish complaints about gentile persecution of them. The bishop of Erie, Pennsylvania, John Marc Gannon, told Catholics not to read Jewish-dominated newspapers but to seek the truth about Spain in the Catholic press.[59]

Rabbis who defended the Republic, as did Rabbi Harry Halpern of Brooklyn, New York, were attacked by the Catholic press. The *Tablet,* a Catholic newspaper, warned its readers "against the Halperns of America. . . . It is rather galling to find vociferous and misrepresentative Hebrews championing Stalin and his caballeros while they denounce Hitler."[60] Rabbi Stephen S. Wise, one of the most prominent Reform rabbis in the United States, was severely criticized by the Catholic press for his remonstrance to Patrick Cardinal Hayes "for offering a prayer for Franco's victory." At the same time, the Catholic press struck out at Rabbi Wise's pro-Loyalist resolution presented at a meeting of the Central Conference of American Rabbis.[61] Indeed, to many Catholic leaders, all Jews who lent their support to the Loyalist cause were seen as enemies of Catholicism.[62]

Following Franco's victory in 1939, American Catholics showed little regret for their alignment with Fascist and Nazi powers. Searching for some lessons that could be derived from the tragic years, the editors of *Catholic World* determined that only one conclusion was significant: Russian Bolsheviks must assume full responsibility for the savagery. "Jack the Ripper would not have slashed a corpse. But the savages from Moscow were guilty of that. . . . Spaniards . . . learned very quickly from this."[63] Other than that, they drew no memorable lessons from Franco's nationalist crusade.

◻ ◻ ◻

A self-proclaimed defender of Christianity against Jews and international Communism, Canadian-born Father Charles Edward Coughlin erupted on the American scene in the 1930s. His hatred of Jews fitted better into the mold of non-Catholic, hardcore racial antisemites, for example, Gerald L. K. Smith, Gerald Winrod, and William Dudley Pelley, than into the behavioral pattern of Catholic antisemites.[64]

Coughlin, born in Ontario in 1891, was ordained a priest in 1916 in St. Basil's Church in Toronto after some years of theological and philosophical studies. Shortly after his ordination, following some teaching and service at Kalamazoo, Michigan, he was assigned to St. Leo's Church in Detroit. It was a substantial congregation of about ten thousand. Two years later, Coughlin moved to Royal Oak, a growing suburban Detroit community feeding on the rising automobile industry but also a stronghold of the Ku Klux Klan. Coughlin built his church, which he named "The Shrine of the Flower," as an "oasis in the desert of religious bigotry."[65]

Coughlin's fame—or, rather, his notoriety—grew, not because of parish duties but as a result of his venture into radio broadcasting in 1926. His early religious messages were appreciated by both Catholics and non-Catholics. But by 1930, his tone altered; it became aggressive and confrontational as his verbal attacks on Bolsheviks and Socialists mounted. His listeners approved and increased in numbers. Soon his slashing attacks were aimed at big corporations, economic predators, and government. He had a talent for alienating one class of people from another and of fostering hatred.[66] His ecclesiastical superiors believed his radio preaching nationally, famous by 1932, followed in the footsteps of Jesus Christ, Pope Leo XIII, and Pope Pius XI.[67]

Claiming in 1934 a desire to protect the rights of the small property owner against the greed and power of big business, Coughlin formed the National Union for Social Justice (NUSJ). In announcing the formation of the NUSJ during his regular Sunday broadcast, Coughlin assured his listeners that the organization was open to individuals of all races and creeds, including Christians and Jews. At first a supporter of President Franklin D. Roosevelt and his New Deal program, Coughlin broke with FDR in the campaign of 1936. Instead, Coughlin and his NUSJ offered their endorsement to Congressman William Lemke of North Dakota as a third-party candidate under the Union Party label for the 1936 presidential election. The third party was also endorsed by one of the leading antisemites in the United States, Gerald L. K. Smith.[68]

Indeed, Coughlin's weekly newspaper, *Social Justice*, which was published first during the campaign in 1936 and lasted six years, was filled with hostile comments about Jews, as were his radio addresses during this time. He became increasingly obsessed with antisemitic rumors about Jewish international conspiracies. He had first imbibed his fantasies about Jewish designs during his early theological studies when he was befriended and influenced by clerical anti-Dreyfusards and antisemites.[69]

By 1937, Coughlin's Christianity had become increasingly infused with anti-Judaism. In June 1937, he wrote in *Social Justice:* "We are pro-Christ 1000 percent. We are for his principles and for his teachings 1000 percent. If the doctrines or the practices of the . . . Jews are not in harmony with Christ's doctrines, 1000 percent we are anti, even though the enemies wish to call it so. Really, we are pro-Christ."[70]

By 1938, *Social Justice* increased in quantity and intensity of its anti-Jewish material. Each week it included a section from the notorious fabrication *Protocols of the Elders of Zion.* The Jew, Coughlin wrote at this time, "*will not escape* persecution even in nations which hitherto have shown friendliness to him."[71] It is difficult to determine precisely why Coughlin's hatred of Jews rose to fever pitch by 1938. His biographer suggests that he believed that if he exploited "the Jewish problem," it would increase his popularity as it increased Adolf Hitler's in Germany.[72] What is clear, however, is that, like other Jew-haters, Coughlin began to associate "Jewish Wall Street bankers" with the economic decline of the 1930s. Rothschild, the famous banker, was his frequent target. Coughlin also believed that the Bolshevik Revolution was engineered by Jews and that it was financed by Jewish bankers. He reasoned that through such tactics, Jews could more easily control the world.[73] Once this frightening scenario was ostensibly uncovered by Coughlin, his tirades against the Jews increased in ferocity.

However, most ominously from the perspective of that time, by the end of the decade, Mary Christine Athans notes, Coughlin moved more deeply into the camp of hard-core racial antisemitism. Increasingly, he began to attribute what he believed to be the anti-Christian beliefs and behaviors of Jews to the influence of Satan. Throughout this time, Coughlin's greatest fear was the spread of Communism, for which he held the Jews responsible.[74] Not surprisingly, therefore, Coughlin considered the Nazi dictatorship an important antidote to the Jewish Communist conspiracy. He noted: "It should never be forgotten that the Rome-Berlin axis is the great political rampart against the spread of Communism. As such, the Rome-Berlin axis is serving Christendom in a peculiarly important manner."[75]

Neither did Coughlin shy away from advocating violence against Jews and Communists. "Meet Force with Force as a last resort," Coughlin advised his Christian listeners and readers. One of his associates told a group of Coughlin's young followers to be prepared "to go into the streets." They would be offered instruction "in the use of 'walking sticks' to protect themselves." Because of such threats, early in 1940, the Federal Bureau of Investigation arrested seventeen of Coughlin's adherents.[76]

The degree of influence Coughlin had upon American Catholics is not easy to measure. Catholic observers claim that it was slight. But Coughlin had millions of listeners and readers, most of whom were probably Catholic.[77] It was a numerical minority, to be sure, but some of these were members of the Catholic hierarchy and took his message with some seriousness.[78] Most of his support, however, according to the sociologist Father Andrew M. Greeley, came from the Irish and German working class, a group hit particularly hard by the Depression. They were also groups most susceptible to antisemitic propaganda. It was a hostility that was easily reinforced by priests and bishops who had an abiding fear of Socialism and Communism.[79] What is significant, however, as Dinnerstein has observed, is that Coughlin's hateful radio addresses were submitted before they were aired to his ecclesiastical supervisors, who failed to censor them. Forty-five radio stations in the United States were broadcasting his Sunday afternoon programs, and thirty-five million Americans were listening to them. When Coughlin lectured in Cleveland, Ohio, in 1936, a crowd of twenty-five thousand gave him a resounding ovation.[80]

There was a small but important segment of American Catholic intellectuals who did not believe that Coughlin's anti-Jewish accusations incarnated the best Christian values. A few Catholics refused to remain silent and in 1939 formed the Committee of Catholics for Human Rights. Prominent clerics such as Monsignor John A. Ryan of the Catholic University of America and the Reverend Charles Miltner of the University of Notre Dame were associated with it.[81] A few of the diocesan newspapers throughout the United States were critical of Coughlin's vitriolic attacks on Jews. Yet the degree and consistency of this clerical opposition is not clear.[82]

In this regard, *Commonweal* was among the most consistent in its expression of annoyance with Coughlin's rantings and his "emotionally intoxicated followers." The magazine opened its pages to clerics who wished to voice anti-Coughlin opinions.[83] Its editors rejected the radio priest's hostile comments about Jews, especially his decision to print and circulate the *Protocols of the Elders of Zion* in 1938. Because of it, the editors of *Commonweal* certified Coughlin with the dubious distinction of being the leading American antisemite, a great comfort to Adolf Hitler, and an encouragement to Hitler's nefarious designs.[84] They warned Coughlin and his Jew-hating followers to realize that their activities represented only one side of a coin "on whose reverse is inscribed, 'no Popery.'"[85]

George N. Shuster, one of the most outspoken of the handful of Catholic critics of antisemitism, was particularly repelled by Coughlin's distribution of the vicious *Protocols,* a document which suggested that Jews, who were responsible for the Russian revolution, were now planning to dominate the world.[86] Shuster tried to disabuse his Catholic coreligionists enamored by Coughlin rhetoric of the illogic and unlikelihood of his ominous predictions, but his arguments, it appears, fell on deaf ears.[87]

Like Shuster, John A. Ryan, the well-known liberal priest and professor at the Catholic University of America, was deeply distressed by Coughlin's rhetoric. What rankled Ryan in the late fall of 1938 was Coughlin's outrageous assertions that Jews, because of their behavior, had brought down upon their own heads the horrors of Kristallnacht (the night of shattered glass), when Germans ravaged the Jewish community, destroying synagogues and private businesses, and attacking innocent people.[88] For Jews, the event marks the beginning of the *Shoah.* On December 30, 1938, Ryan wrote: "It would seem that the enormous cruelties inflicted upon the Jewish people in Germany . . . ought to move every Christian heart to pity, ought to prevent any Christian from saying anything which would make their lot harder to bear. These considerations involve Jews everywhere, even those Jews who are our fellow citizens in the United States." It was a plea directed toward Coughlin. Ryan also had a message for American Catholics: "It has been urged that Catholics in particular ought to refrain from encouraging this campaign of anti-Semitism for fear that the same method and the same psychology will be used against them when the next anti-Catholic movement gets underway. . . . From every point of view Catholics should refrain from fostering by speech or by silence anti-Semitism in the United States."[89]

It was a noble plea, as were the sympathetic statements uttered by Shuster during this most difficult era. But the question which persists is, Why should American Roman Catholics refrain from listening to or even expressing antisemitic statements? Was it because, as Ryan warned, Catholics too might become targets of public hostility? The reason sounds pragmatic but morally lame. Clearly, as long as even compassionate observers refrained from wrestling with or even thinking about the theological roots of Christian hostility toward Jews, the underlying problem would continue to fester. Shuster's conviction that only with the strengthening of Christianity would the problem of antisemitism be solved was misplaced. His belief that "Christianity is still the deepest, the most beautiful, the most abiding of the forces which make up the life of mankind"[90] was hardly the solution for the age-old problem which was rapidly approaching its culminating horror.

By *Commonweal*'s own admission, Ryan's remonstrance fell on deaf ears. The editors noted that the message of antisemitism was not only distributed through Coughlin's communications but repeated and endorsed by some of America's largest circulating diocesan newspapers, such as the "incorrigible Brooklyn *Tablet* and other weeklies." These were busy disseminating vulgarities about Jews to American Catholics.[91]

Despite the few lonely voices of Shuster, Ryan, and others, Jews had good reason to wonder about their security in America. Coughlin and his supporters made it clear that Nazi hatred had found a niche in the Catholic community. Jewish organizations were well aware of the tenuousness of their relationship with the Christian community. The American Jewish Committee tracked and reported Coughlin's statements about Jews. In 1936, for example, it reported Coughlin's attack on "The Rothschilds of Wall Street," who, he alleged, controlled the American economy.[92] There was, in fact, little the American Jewish Committee and other Jewish defense organizations could do to stop Coughlin's anti-Jewish outbursts. They called on leading rabbis, such as Professor Louis Finkelstein, and leading Catholic spokespersons to voice their opinions about Coughlin publicly. The Social Action Department of the National Catholic Welfare Conference and the Catholic Laymen's League urged Coughlin to tone down his rhetoric. The latter group of Catholics faulted Coughlin "for his appeal to bigotry, hatred, violence and virulence" and called him an "'alien adventurer' whose cowardly Jew-hating and shameless use of his cloth to insult the President . . . should be repudiated."[93]

By the time Coughlin's broadcasts were silenced by his superiors in October 1940, he had added another string to his bow: isolationism. Coughlin's opposition to entering the war against Germany opened the door to further accusations of American Jews as being "interventionists."[94] This is not to imply that Coughlin's voice was unique among Catholics who demanded American neutrality in the European conflict. Even a few weeks preceding the bombing of Pearl Harbor, the American Catholic press continued to wage its own battle against involvement. Defeating Hitler was not the highest priority in American Catholic circles. Non-intervention was.[95]

It was one thing to oppose intervention. It was quite another to accuse, as Coughlin did, American Jews of secretly conspiring with Roosevelt to draw the United States into the world conflict. By early 1940, Coughlin had begun to side openly with Nazi Germany, while Great Britain became his foe. He defended Hitler's victories: Poland collapsed because of Jewish betrayal, Norway was invaded to protect it from England, the French collapse did not matter since few Catholics held government posts of prominence. Coughlin urged Roosevelt to stay out of the conflict and allow Germany to defeat England and the Soviet Union.

Even after the Japanese attack on December 7, 1941, Coughlin continued his relentless criticism of FDR and the Jews. The former he accused of encouraging the attack to bring the United States into the war, and the Jews he charged with engineering the entire conspiracy. Increasingly, he became a supporter of Hitler. He justified every one of the führer's victories. His attack on America's war effort angered public opinion. In 1942, many demanded his arrest as a traitor. On April 10, 1942, by government order, *Social Justice* ceased publication.[96]

Coughlin's demise left a legacy of bitterness in Catholic-Jewish relations, which only the crisis of the Second World War and its tragic consequences eclipsed.

5
Snatching Souls, 1900–1960

American Catholics were conscious of the precariousness of world Jewry and the intensification of antisemitism in the United States during the 1930s. They were not impervious to the revelations of the Holocaust that would follow. Such knowledge, however, did not diminish the church's persistence in its age-old practice: attempting to convert the Jews to Catholicism. This is not to suggest that Catholics pursued Jewish converts with the same zeal that existed among evangelical Protestants.[1] Witnessing to Jews had always been considered among the highest priorities of the Protestant evangelical community. Protestant aggressiveness was rarely duplicated by the American Catholic Church. Nevertheless, a desire to win Jewish souls was never absent from the minds of church leaders.

Proselytizing Jews was not a debatable issue. Throughout the history of Catholicism, though the papacy did not officially approve of the forced conversion of Jews, when that did occur, it did not always reject its results. The Council of Trent, which convened in the sixteenth century, officially recognized the importance of the conversion of Jews for the fulfillment of "Christianity's ultimate end." Proselytizing sermons, which Jews were forced to attend, were common in the late Middle Ages. The great desire to win Jewish converts continued throughout the eighteenth and nineteenth centuries when Jewish children were occasionally removed from their families, baptized, and raised as Catholics, all with papal approval.[2]

The most notorious case of Catholic abduction of the nineteenth century is known as the Mortara affair. It occurred in the summer of 1858 in the Italian city of Bologna, when a child by the name of Edgardo Mortara was abducted from his parents. The seven-year-old boy, church officials explained, now belonged to the Catholic Church, not to his parents. The explanation offered for the kidnapping was that, during an illness, the child (without the knowledge or consent of his parents) had been secretly baptized by his nurse. Since Edgardo was now a Catholic, it was allegedly forbidden, according to canon law, for him to be raised as a Jew.[3]

The Mortara affair generated wide protest in the Jewish community in the United States. Jews exerted strenuous efforts to elicit the intercession of President James Buchanan, but to no avail. Protestants saw the event as an opportunity to bolster the attractiveness of the anti-Catholic Know Nothing Party. A few Jews also drifted in the direction of American anti-Catholicism. The move was understandable since most Catholic newspapers in the United States defended the legality of the abduction of Edgardo Mortara.[4]

One does not generally think of American Roman Catholics as deeply involved in seeking converts. Catholic history in the United States, especially during the nineteenth century, suggests that the church was more concerned with expanding for its own rapidly growing population and defending itself against Protestant animosity. Yet none of this should conceal the church's passionate desire for converts. Such a pursuit was found even among the most prestigious leaders of the American church. Early in the nineteenth century, they included Fathers Isaac Thomas Hecker and Orestes Brownson. Both believed that they were called by God to work for the conversion of America to Roman Catholicism. Both were convinced that America was religiously in disarray and that only the Church of Rome could supply the spiritual guidance and unity so badly needed by its American people.[5] The conversion of America to Catholicism, as one scholar recently noted, was pursued unabatedly and was publicly espoused by American church leaders until the eve of the Second World War and even, as one will observe, during the years afterward.[6]

Hecker and Brownson, aided by an enormous European immigration, set the pace for future missionary activity in the United States. Throughout the remaining years of the nineteenth century and the early years of the twentieth century, Catholic missionaries continued to invite Protestants and Jews into the church. One missionary urged American Catholics to take a page from Protestants and, like them, engage in "street preaching." "The chief mission of the Church," he declared, "is to make known the true faith of Christ to all America, which belongs to the Catholic Church."[7] Leading prelates reminded the faithful that "when

Christ founded His Church and gave to the Apostles His Mandate, He gave them a commission truly Catholic: 'Go teach all nations.' He gave them a work which was to continue . . . until the end of time."[8]

The chief targets of Catholic missionaries during these years were Protestants of all denominations. Buoyed by the phenomenal growth of the church in the late nineteenth century, Catholics took an increased interest in missionary activity. New missionary societies were organized, and encouragement also came from Rome.[9] American bishops urged the faithful to accelerate missionary work. "'Go teach all the nations; preach the Gospel to every creature,'" thundered America's bishops in a pastoral letter, an urgent request that they periodically renewed during the age of the new immigration.[10] Despite the constant lament that missionaries were not doing nearly enough to win souls for the church, by 1926 American Roman Catholics were contributing more money for the support of missionary work than were the Catholics of European countries.[11]

◻ ◻ ◻

Jews were not neglected by American Catholic proselytizers in the nineteenth or twentieth centuries. Catholics took seriously Pope Leo XIII's admonition to the people of the world to turn to Christ at the dawn of the new century. Leo directed his words not only to "the heathens who sit in darkness" and "the cultured pagans among the civilized nations" but also to the Jews, "the ruin of Israel who would have no creeds and want no religion with exact dogmatic teaching." Those Jews, explained the pope, "reject dogma . . . deny Christianity."[12] Such admonitions were repeated by subsequent popes, Benedict XV and Pius XI, who imposed upon their bishops the task of restoring "those lost in darkness."[13]

Jewish converts were pursued even during the years when Jews were scarce. Alfred Young, a Catholic missionary, observed in 1888 that although Jews knew little about Catholicism, and many harbored a deep resentment about the faith, their conversion was necessary for their own salvation.[14] As was seen among Protestant missionaries, American Catholics displayed with an air of triumph each discovery of a Jewish convert, no matter where it occurred, or when it took place, or even if the conversion was genuine.[15] Late in the nineteenth century, a pronouncement was made by a Catholic missionary that the Jews of the United States had rejected their ancestral faith, that traditional Judaism was disintegrating as American rabbis were prodded by their congregants to dispense with traditional practices. "So what was once the church of God . . . has now fallen to the level of a mere sect."[16] Most probably, predicted the missionary, within a few years, only a small handful of Jews would be left in the United States. This decline, he observed, though tragic for the Jews, constituted a challenge for Catholicism and a blessing for Judaism. More significant, the disintegration of the Jewish faith provided Jews an unmatched opportunity to offer contrition and reparation for the sinful rejection and murder of Jesus Christ. "Then they shall be no more called forsaken."[17]

Till Van Rahden's study of Baltimore's Catholic newspapers in the years 1870–1940 documents that while on one hand, Catholics did not hesitate to refer to their Jewish neighbors as "Christ killers," on the other, they "supported Catholic missionary efforts towards them." All Catholic newspapers voiced the conviction that ultimately Jews would accept Christianity, and they "encouraged Catholic missionary efforts among Jews."[18] What is more, they gave wide publicity and expressed great joy when they received news about a Jewish conversion to Catholicism.[19]

Catholics not only welcomed Jewish converts but were delighted to employ them as missionaries to preach the Gospel to Jews. Jewish conversions were sometimes compared to the miraculous conversion of the Apostle St. Paul.[20] Early in the twentieth century, David Goldstein, a Jewish convert who was born in Boston, became what was referred to as "a Catholic outdoor lay apologist," that is, a street preacher. In 1906, he helped organize the Catholic Truth Guild, later called the Catholic Campaigners for Christ.[21] This lay society, founded in Boston, was designed to teach Catholics the persuasive art of street preaching to non-Catholics, especially Jews. Goldstein believed that if the streets of America's cities were available "for radicals of all tints," then they should be made available to Roman Catholics. Goldstein coached his missionaries on how they should instruct Jews who came to listen. "The Jews of today must realize," Goldstein wrote, "that there is no Aaronic priesthood, for there is no house of Aaron from which the true priesthood of the Old Law came. . . . In place of the Old, there is the Living Church of the Messiah; there is a new priesthood as predicted. It is the Church of Rome."[22] Goldstein and his team of lay preachers continued their efforts to convert Jews throughout the dark decades of the 1930s and 1940s, hoping to snatch Jewish souls during the time of their physical and mental humiliation.

Goldstein was an example of a converted Jew employed by the church to pursue his or her former coreligionists, a not uncommon practice during the first half of the twentieth century. Converted Jews, church officials believed, because of their Jewish background, made more congenial representatives of the church. Yet most Jewish converts had only a superficial and confused knowledge about their abandoned faith. This was acknowledged in 1924 by Rosalie Marie Levy, herself a convert and missionary. Levy, who published a study entitled *Why Jews Become Catholics,* which featured a collection of narratives by Jewish converts, concluded that most Jewish converts to Catholicism were ignorant of Judaism. Most saw Judaism as a collection of meaningless rituals.[23]

Like Goldstein, Levy displayed unusual energy and innovation in converting Jews during the years preceding World War II. She founded a missionary association first known as the Catholics of Israel, later renamed the Guild of Our Lady of Sion. Jews were invited to its meetings, held in a church in lower Manhattan in New York. Similarly, in 1938, a Catholic missionary organized monthly forums and discussions about Catholicism for Jews in Brooklyn. The objective of these forums was to gain Jewish converts. Their work, in which Levy was also involved, was publicized in a newsletter distributed to various Catholic churches throughout New York. It also extended its proselytism to hospitals throughout New York, reaching out to the sick and disabled during their most vulnerable moments. Between 1938 and 1946, the Catholic missionaries of the Brooklyn Center claimed to have successfully converted fifty Jews to Roman Catholicism.

With its large Jewish population, New York was an important focal point for missionaries. But cities in the Midwest were not excluded. For example, the Center of the Archconfraternity of Prayer for the Conversion of Israel was established in Kansas City shortly before the outbreak of the Second World War. It published and distributed the *A.P.A. Bulletin,* which discussed efforts to convert Jews. A few hundred clergymen were actively involved in its work, a number of whom ironically were also active in the National Conference (formerly "Council") of Christians and Jews (NCCJ), an early ecumenical organization designed to improve the relationship between the two faiths.[24]

▫ ▫ ▫

As suggested, the years from Kristallnacht in 1938 to the death tally of the *Shoah* in 1945 did not appreciably dampen Catholic enthusiasm for converting Jews. Catholics were yet unable to detect the moral contradiction of superimposing a spiritual death (for this is what conversion amounted to for most Jews) upon a physical one.

Jewish leaders, such as Rabbi James F. Heller, were concerned about Jews' becoming targets for Christian missionaries. Heller was aware of Jewish religious laxity in America during the few years before the outbreak of the Second World War. "For us," he told a national meeting of congregations, "Jewishness has become nothing but a social relationship. We no more know how to pray." *Commonweal* was interested in this admonition, for it substantiated the argument that missionaries were making.[25] *Commonweal*, which professed to be at this time an opponent of antisemitism, nevertheless declared, as one of its writers asserted in 1937, that "Judaism's inability to accept Him" continued to be its chief problem.[26]

The German army had already invaded Poland when the Catholic writer Hans Anscar urged that a center for the conversion of Jews be established in the United States. He wished to pattern it after a successful enterprise that had been launched in Vienna and Paris. It was called Opus Sancti Pauli and had received the approval and blessing of the newly elected Pope Pius XII.[27] Its European founder, Father John M. Oesterreicher, dispatched a representative to the United States, shortly before the fall of Paris, to lay plans for an American Center. It was in the progress of this center that Anscar was interested. Its first American headquarters was located at the Little Flower Monastery in Newton, New Jersey. A "discussion group" of Christians and Jews was also planned for New York. Initiators of Opus Sancti Pauli were hopeful that their efforts would be approved by American bishops.[28]

Catholic missionaries to the Jews during the war years were well aware of the tribulations that had befallen world Jewry. They were also familiar with the history of antisemitism. They saw the era of crisis faced by the Jews as a most propitious time to entice Jews from their traditional faith. The years of war created a mood of desperation among some Catholic missionaries. One writer reported that some children were baptized without the consent of their parents or guardians.[29] One missionary explained to the clergy that Jewish resistance to conversion was no different in 1942 than it had been at the time of Jesus; that every effort must be exerted to overcome this resistance, for, if successful, conversion would hasten the Second Coming. Monsignor Thomas J. McDonnell of the Society for the Propagation of the Faith advised church officials in 1941 to pursue the harassed Jewish refugees who were homeless and friendless, for they were excellent candidates for conversion.[30] Caught between laxity and religious indifference at home and destruction abroad, Jews, it appeared to those who pursued them, had little to lose by moving into the church.

In Europe, where it was possible, some Jews concealed their identity from the Germans. In some areas of Europe, Catholic churches offered Jews baptismal certificates and travel visas to enable them to survive the through prayers of charity and love, their very manner of demonstrating that relationship will probably be misunderstood and rejected."[46]

Even so, despite the callousness with which missionaries approached Jews and professed the religious and ecclesiastical imperatives behind their work, it should not take away from their occasional sincere denunciation of antisemitism. It was a rare occurrence to read in a 1960 issue of *America* an acknowledgement of the existence of anti-Judaism at the Passion Play in Oberammergau.[47] Increasingly in the years following the Second World War, hatred of Jews was decreed to be incompatible with Catholicism, that its practice would do more damage to the church than it would to Jews. To hate Jews, Catholics were warned by their highest authorities, would be as unthinkable for Catholics as to hate Christians.[48]

From the Jewish point of view, it was a noble sentiment, no doubt a result of the gas chambers of World War II. But when the sentiment was intertwined with a search for Jewish souls, it lost much of its potency.[49] Neither does it matter that apostasy was relatively rare. Although precise figures prior to the 1960s are difficult to obtain, there were probably at the time relatively few Jewish conversions to Catholicism, and according to Andrew M. Greeley, they were not much more extensive after that time.[50] Nevertheless, it is the theological underpinning of such efforts that is of major concern. What is implicit in such efforts is triumphalism, the suggestion that Catholicism offered to Jews in the years following Auschwitz a fulfillment, a "salvation" which they could not discover within their own ancestral faith.

□ □ □

Of all the efforts to convert Jews during the postwar years, probably the most sophisticated and clever occurred in 1953 with the launching of the Institute of Judaeo-Christian Studies. Lodged under the academic roof of Seton Hall University, first in Newark and later in South Orange, from the very beginning it assumed an air of scholarly detachment. The institute professed a genuine desire to promote a dialogue with Jews, to learn about the Jewish experience and Jewish faith, and to introduce Jews to the beauty and wisdom of Christian thought. In 1955, to further its ends, it began publishing a yearly journal, a "yearbook" which it called *The Bridge.*

The institute's work and its publication were widely acclaimed in Catholic circles as a major achievement. The Jesuit scholar Quentin Lauer wrote that "a group of men . . . moved by love for the crucified" and for the Jewish people "has united not to remove the stumbling block

German onslaught.[31] In a few cases, these Jews chose to remain in the church. Among the most celebrated apostates was the converted chief rabbi of wartime Rome, Israele Zolti. In February 1945, Rabbi Zolti stunned world Jewry by converting to Catholicism. It was a gesture, according to his biographers, prompted by gratitude to Pope Pius XII for his effort to save the Jews of Rome.[32]

Coming on the heels of the *Shoah,* the news of Rabbi Zolti's conversion caused shock and anger among American Jews. Lewis I. Newman's book *A "Chief Rabbi" of Rome Becomes a Catholic: A Study in Fright and Spite* was severely critical of Zolti's actions. Newman probably expressed what most American Jews thought about the incident. Newman's references to Zolti's behavior as "self-centered" and "unbalanced," with "little or no concern" for the Jewish community, expressed what most Jews thought of apostasy. However, Father Oesterreicher reacted with an equal measure of annoyance in his review of Newman's book in *Catholic World* in 1946. He described Newman's work as "downright abusive." Oesterreicher's harsh comments revealed his imperviousness to the character of Judaism during the postwar years.[33]

Although wartime missionaries became increasingly aware of the malignant spread of Jew-hatred and frequently warned against its practice, they also found it difficult to divest themselves of their own anti-Jewish hostility. Hans Anscar, for example, asserted in 1939 that Jewish suffering was well deserved, yet he urged Catholics not to join in the orgy of Jew hatred. "Purely out of self-interest," wrote Anscar, "we should be very careful as Catholics not to join in the chorus of anti-Semites." It would interfere with Catholic missionary efforts. "Does not every true Christian wish with St. Paul the Apostle that all Jews should be won for Christ? Do we not fail in charity when we embitter those Jews who might have been converted if we had not judged, condemned, and ostracized them?"[34] The missionary urged Catholics to be tolerant of offensive Jewish "standards of ethics" and magnanimously encouraged them to stand pat. "We must defend our faith when they attack it. But we may not retaliate . . . even if they should attack us . . . [but] we must protect ourselves from the bad influence of Jews."[35]

Missionaries frequently explained to their readers the horror that had befallen Jews, from the time of the Golden Calf to the destruction of their temple to their present difficulties. All of these resulted from their sinful behavior, a punishment for disobedience to God's desire. "By their refusal to come into His outstretched arms, so long as that is not done," wrote David Goldstein in 1942, "I feel assured that Antisemitism will thrive."[36]

If proselytizing activity was any measure of Catholic attitude toward Jews during World War II, then the years of the Warsaw ghetto and Auschwitz produced little enhancement in the relationship of the two faith communities.

□ □ □

One might have thought that in the decade or so following the defeat of the Axis in 1945, when the results of Germany's death camps were displayed for the world to contemplate, the church would have called for a theological reexamination of its historic relationship with the Jews. If this did occur, then it was difficult to detect, particularly in its continuing efforts to seek out conversion of the Jewish people. Shortly after the war, *America* wondered how many of the country's Catholics had given serious thought to inviting converts into the church. It suspected that only an insignificant number were assuming this religious obligation. Both from the Vatican and the American leadership came repeated reminders that the faithful had a sacred duty to share their faith with non-Catholics.[37]

One writer urged Catholics in 1946 not to overlook the Jews in these endeavors. They make fine Catholics, he reminded his readers. After all, from the founder of the Catholic Church to the first pope, Jews played a seminal role in the church. They also helped energize the faith throughout Europe in more recent years. The tragic circumstances that had forced many Jews in recent years to abandon their faith, the writer boasted, produced eight thousand Jewish converts.[38] "The conversion of Jews has primarily spiritual aspects but it also has for our Church a 'material' angle. Due to their energy, their endurance, intelligence and enthusiasm, the Catholic Jews are qualified to become the shock troops in our efforts to extend the mystical Body, to make Catholicism Catholic."[39]

One "concession," from a Catholic perspective, was granted to Jewish converts during the years following the war. Jews were informed that they would be accepted into the church, if they so desired, without giving up their identity as Jews, just as Catholics need not divest themselves from their birth heritage in order to be considered fully Catholic.[40] Catholic organizations specifically designed to offer support to Catholic Jews emerged in the United States. One which originated in France, the Institute of Notre Dame de Sion, created branches in Canada and South America as well. It sponsored lectures, discussions, and religious services especially designed for Jews, such as the Passover seder. About fifty bishops and a few hundred priests were associated with its American activ-

ities.[41] The numbers suggest the measure of the church's determination to convert Jews.

Shortly after the Second World War, the Edith Stein Guild was founded in New York to invite Jews into the church and to orient Jewish converts to the principles of Catholicism. Edith Stein had herself converted from Judaism in 1922. A writer and an intellectual, Stein entered a Carmelite convent in 1933. She became vitally interested in the conversion of Jews. Arrested by the Nazis in 1942 because she was a Jew, she died in a German gas chamber shortly afterward. The guild, which was established in her memory, was directed by the Passionist Father Thomas Berry and governed by a board of twenty persons, half of whom were Jewish converts.[42]

The idea that Judaism could be cultivated within the church was no more than a camouflage for traditional apostasy. Jews did not see it as a concession; on the contrary, they saw it as an additional insult. Catholics, however, considered this new approach progressive, as a "bridge," a link between the two faiths but one that was designed for only Jews to cross, bringing them closer to Christ. With justification, Jews viewed such Catholic "benevolence" as a form of subterfuge.

Indeed, as Arthur Gilbert, a prominent rabbi and scholar, noted in the late 1950s, Jewish suspicion of Catholics in the United States generally exceeded their suspicion of Protestants.[43] Jewish historic memory of forced conversions in the Middle Ages sabotaged any effort to persuade Jews to move away from their faith. No matter how innocuous, such efforts were disturbing to Jews. They also were upset by the church's repeated claims of its religious "fulfillment." One Catholic scholar, Charles Journet, who taught religion at Seton Hall University, South Orange, New Jersey, generated little sympathy among Jews when he explained in 1956 that Christians required Jewish conversion for their own religious fulfillment: "Israel must one day come back to its Messiah so that the nation, enlivened and enriched by its return, may of that moment enter the second stage of their conversion. As long as Israel fears and flees its reintegration into the everlasting Church, that wondrous moment is put off."[44] That Christ's return to earth was being delayed because of the slow pace of Jewish conversion was an argument that Catholic missionaries used in the postwar years.[45]

Catholic assurances to postwar Jews that their feelings toward them, even though expressed in Christian terms, were loving and sympathetic did little to ameliorate the uneasy relationship between the two groups. As Arthur Gilbert observes, "Tragically . . . even when Catholics believe that they are expressing their profoundest gratitude toward the Jew,

of the Cross, but to reveal it as the very bridge over which Israel must pass in order to enter the promise." Lauer praised the dedication of Seton Hall University and its institute for its efforts to facilitate the passage of the Old Israel into the New.[51] Or, as he more benignly expressed it somewhat later, the purpose of *The Bridge* was "not to highlight the separation of the Old from the New, but to unite both Old and New. It seeks a synthesis deeply satisfying to Israelite yearning for the Messiah and to the Christian assurance that the Messiah had already come to save the whole world."[52]

The person primarily responsible for the idea and initiation of the Institute of Judaeo-Christian Studies and *The Bridge* was soon-to-be Monsignor John M. Oesterreicher, a Jewish convert to Roman Catholicism who had been ordained a priest in 1931. Oesterreicher fled his native Vienna after the Nazi invasion of Austria in 1938. Following a short stay in France, he fled the Germans once again, went to England, and then came to the United States in 1940. The missionary techniques he brought with him to America had already been well rehearsed during the early 1930s when he lived in Vienna, in the shadow of Hitler's rise to power. It was there that he organized Opus Sancti Pauli, which, after being transported to the United States, germinated into the Institute of Judaeo-Christian Studies. In Vienna, Oesterreicher and his assistants had worked diligently to bring apostates into the church. His work was showered with praise by church leaders, including the future Pope Pius XII, then Secretary of State Cardinal Pacelli. Oesterreicher's entire Christian career was driven by a desire to convert Jews to Roman Catholicism.[53]

After arriving at Seton Hall, Oesterreicher was joined by a group of Catholic collaborators, many of whom were emerging scholars and theologians, all eager as he was to introduce Catholic ideas in an intellectually compatible way to American Jews and the remnants of world Jewry.[54] The institute's design to convert Jews was concealed by its insistence that its primary aim was to produce "scholarship." As Lauer writes, "The accent of the Institute of Judaeo-Christian Studies is definitely on scholarship. It numbers among its fellows scholars from all parts of the world, and on its advisory council some of the best Catholic scholars in the country." In an address delivered at the opening of the institute on October 7, 1953, Oesterreicher expressed the hope that the institute would blossom into a leading research center of Judaeo-Christian studies.[55]

Given the tone of Catholic-Jewish relations at this time, one could argue that it was possible that the founders of the institute believed that they could combine their interest in converting Jews with the practice of genuine scholarship. It is possible that the institute's staff could proceed with such an exercise calmly and objectively. However, the disingenuousness of such professed intentions was revealed by the explanation offered by the editors of *The Bridge* as to why they chose an intellectual and scholarly format for their yearbook; they did so because of their conviction that a cerebral approach would hold a greater appeal to Jews. As one writer put it: "The intellectual predilection of the Jews, not only in this country but throughout the world, is an established fact, and no serious *apostate* [italics mine] can neglect this aspect of the situation." What is more, the primary interest of the institute was underscored by the observation that

> at no period since the first century of the Christian era have the Jews embraced the Cross of Christ in large numbers. Nor do the collaborators of the Institute of Judaeo-Christian Studies pretend that any mass movement of conversion will result from their efforts. The aim is at once more modest and more profound than that. It is to permit Jews as Jews to be nourished from the manifold sources of Christian wisdom, and at the same time to permit Christians as Christians to drink deep of Jewish wisdom.[56]

That the conversion of the Jews was the precise purpose of *The Bridge* was acknowledged by John J. Dougherty, regent of the Judaeo-Christian Institute. Furthermore, the work of the institute and its journal received high praise from the Vatican, the American Catholic hierarchy, and leaders of the Catholic world. In this connection, Oesterreicher's words are instructive. In 1958, he wrote:

> A still deeper joy is ours because of the blessing and the loving attention given our efforts by Pope Pius XII. On the eve of the Jubilee Year 1950, when opening the Holy Door and welcoming all men to Rome, he spoke of Jews as those who sincerely though vainly look for the One Come as still to come. He saw them as men of waiting, counted them among those who adore Christ. On August first of last year . . . I was received by the Holy Father. Expressing our thanks for the inspiration we have drawn from his words of welcome that place the expectant shoulder to shoulder with the believing, and wishing to offer a token of our gratitude, I said: "Your Holiness, I beg to present to you the second volume of—" only to be interrupted gently. "Ah, *The Bridge!* I shall read it with great interest." What greater honor could come to us than to have among our readers the Pope of singular vision.[57]

When some readers of *The Bridge* wondered why the editors of a "scholarly" journal were unwilling to open their publication's pages to views about Judaism which differed from theirs, Oesterreicher responded: "We could not in conscience, that is, in the Love we bear for Christ, open our pages to a dispute on the basic tenets of our faith."[58] This would have been a perfectly acceptable explanation if the editors did not also make the concurrent claim that *The Bridge* was a journal of academic scholarship.

◻ ◻ ◻

Oesterreicher's approach to the Jews never duplicated the more zealous style of prewar missionaries but was skillfully cloaked with an air of sympathetic understanding for European Jews' recent tribulations. But when stripped of its pretensions, his message was identical to what Jews had been subjected to by missionaries of previous decades. Oesterreicher befogged his appeal with carefully crafted narratives of well-known Jewish intellectuals who escaped from a life of turmoil into Roman Catholicism. At the same time, he evinced displeasure and disappointment with those Jews who moved to the brink of the church but hesitated to take the plunge into baptism.

One year following the grand opening of the Institute of Judaeo-Christian Studies, Oesterreicher's book *Walls Are Crumbling,* with an introduction by the Catholic theologian Jacques Maritain, was published in London. The book consists of biographies of seven Jewish apostates, or near apostates, all intellectuals, writers, and philosophers who, in one degree or another, had turned to Roman Catholicism. That Oesterreicher's subjects had either perished in Hitler's death camps or suffered shattered lives because they were Jewish during the German assault makes these biographical essays particularly poignant.

Oesterreicher's message, however, is clear: Catholics suffered also during the Hitler years. More important, Oesterreicher wants his reader to believe the dubious idea that the years of pain imposed on those of Jewish ancestry during the Holocaust, whether Jewish or Catholic, will inevitably result in the shattering of the wall that has separated Jews from Catholics for almost two millennia and will hasten the conversion of the Jewish people. As Jacques Maritain expressed it in his introduction, "It was during the earthquake of monstrous persecutions, in which Jews and Christians were reunited and set out together toward Calvary, that the wall of separation began to fall." That the wall, explains Maritain, stood solidly erect for so many years was due in large part to Jewish obstinate refusal to see the truth of Christianity. It took a great catastrophe to tear it down.[59] Maritain's comment would have left Jewish readers aghast. To convert the gassing of millions of Jews into a celebration, a triumph of the Cross over Jewish "obstinacy," reached a rarely challenged height of Catholic blindness about the *Shoah*. Yet, in a sense, Maritain's remark makes a fitting introduction to *Walls Are Crumbling*.

Oesterreicher describes his work as a "book of hope." The experiences of his seven subjects, he is convinced, signify a long-awaited reverse of a two-thousand-year Jewish resistance to conversion. The message offered by the seven was one of "affirmation and hope," "a sign of a new advent."[60] Who were these seven individuals? They were the prominent European writers Henri Bergson, Edmund Husserl, Adolf Reinach, Max Scheler, Paul Landsberg, Max Picard, and Edith Stein, most of whom had left an imprint on early twentieth-century European intellectual life. These seven, none of whom had ever maintained a strong association with their respective Jewish communities, represented, according to Oesterreicher, a new potential mass movement of Jews toward Christ. He writes:

> For centuries, Jewish teachers have rejected Jesus' claim to be the Christ. . . . For centuries there has been a conspiracy of silence, so that His name was not uttered, neither in home or house of learning. Jewish unbelief and, no less, Gentile persecution built a wall which kept the Jews from Christ. But now this wall is giving way. His name is uttered. He is seen again. And this is how seven contemporary Jewish thinkers look on Him. . . . With the witness of these seven, who can doubt that the wall of separation from Christ is crumbling?[61]

▫ ▫ ▫

Oesterreicher was exceedingly pleased with his prominent Jewish converts who dared to take the plunge into Catholicism during the terrifying years of Nazi ascendance. He took satisfaction in displaying them to the world. At the same time, however, Oesterreicher could not conceal his disappointment with those Jews who were attracted to the church but who hesitated at its door, who for one reason or another were unable to tear themselves away from their religious heritage.

One such reluctant individual was the Jewish-born French writer Simone Weil. Oesterreicher found her "enigmatically" disconcerting, yet her closeness to Catholicism earned her an essay in the first volume of *The Bridge* in 1955. Although in 1938 at the age of twenty-nine, Oesterreicher tells us, Weil contemplated baptism, at the last moment she drew back and decided to remain with the "uncommitted," that is, her Jewish people. Oesterreicher denounced her decision as unacceptable. She should have offered the church, an institution she had grown so close to, her full commitment. Still, writes Oesterreicher, "For the few remaining years of her life, the question of whether she should be baptized seemed never to have left her." She spent the war years first in New York and then in London, where she died prematurely before the end of the war. "[For] all her desire to suffer," writes Oesterreicher, "even to suffer like Christ, Simone Weil was not a Christian."[62] Weil disappointed Oesterreicher because, as he put it, she "evaded Christ's embrace." Christ "demanded an unconditional 'yes,'" a total commitment, which Weil was incapable of offering. Oesterreicher would not accept Weil's despair during the years of the *Shoah*; despair was not an appropriate Christian response.[63] It was an unusually cold-hearted reaction to the suffering of a Jewish woman, marginal, to be sure, but whose life nevertheless had been destroyed during the Nazi era.

Oesterreicher's disillusionment with almost-baptized Jews is reflected in the essays contributed to *The Bridge* by his colleagues. A typical case is an account of the flirtation of the European novelist Franz Werfel with Roman Catholicism. Written by the Catholic scholar Frederick G. Ellert, it followed a familiar pattern of brinksmanship, disillusionment, and disappointment. Like Weil, Werfel was drawn to the church, and his attraction was never consummated by baptism. Werfel's hesitancy to take the final step, was, as in the case of Weil, enigmatic and deeply disappointing to Ellert. Ellert sees Werfel's interest in the church as constituting a "dilemma" for the novelist. He informs the reader that although Werfel affirmed the divinity of Jesus as the Son of God, he insisted on remaining a Jew. In spite of his Christian affirmation, Werfel would not accept conversion as a personal option. Neither did he believe that it should be a choice for any Jew.

Born in France in 1890, Werfel spent most of his productive years in Vienna, where his life was detached from the Jewish community. Like Oesterreicher, he also fled Austria to France when the Germans arrived in 1938. With the Nazi invasion of France two years later, he escaped to the United States and settled in California, where he died in 1945. Werfel, Ellert writes, concluded pessimistically that because of their rejection of Christ, Jews would never be able to escape their tragic history. They would be forever trapped, doomed to suffer eternally because of this rejection. There was no escape; they were destined to remain Jews until the end of time.[64] Werfel himself, Ellert informs us, was caught in this dilemma, tied on the one hand to his Judaic roots and driven on the other toward the Church of Rome and its doctrines. The church, Werfel believed as he viewed the chaos that engulfed him, was the last true hope for civilization, an antidote for the gross materialism of Western society. While the Holocaust was sweeping over the Jews of Europe,

Werfel adhered to his conviction "of the healing power of Christ's teachings." Neither did he ever deny that Jesus was the true Messiah for Jews as well as Christians and that some day Jews would be united with Jesus. Yet, for all these convictions, Werfel could not convince himself that conversion to Catholicism was an appropriate step for him.[65]

Reading Ellert's account examining Werfel's life, Oesterreicher could not accept the novelist's "no." On October 27, 1942, Werfel had written to Archbishop Joseph P. Rummel of New Orleans about his reluctance to convert. Rummel was also distressed at Werfel's behavior. In his letter to the archbishop, Werfel explained why despite his devotion to the church he continued to remain outside its walls:

> "I am, as stated in the foreword of *The Song of Bernadette,* a Jew by origin and have never been baptized. On the other hand, I wish to profess here before you and the world that, as is evident from the major part of my work, I have been decisively influenced and molded by the spiritual forces of Christianity and the Catholic Church. I see in the Catholic Church the purest power and emanation sent by God to this earth to right the evil of materialism and atheism, and to bring revelation to the poor souls of mankind."

Having affirmed his religious convictions to the Archbishop, Werfel proceeded to enumerate the reasons for his reluctance to join the church:

> "The first: Israel is going through the hour of its most inexorable persecution. I could not bring myself to sneak out of the ranks of the persecuted in this hour. My second answer follows from the first: Conversion brings certain advantages to the Jew. This was especially so in Europe. I did not wish to create the shadow of a doubt that I wanted to gain such advantages.
>
> "The third answer is the most important, concerning my own soul. Israel belongs, theologically, as the vessel of revelation and salvation, among the Christians . . . and even the Church, which calls itself the New Israel, has, in the course of history and in the present times, in their practical policy, not always shown full justice to the Old Israel. As long as there are anti-Semitic Christians (and even priests like Father Coughlin, preaching hatred and yet not excommunicated), the converted Jew must feel embarrassed by cutting a not altogether pleasant figure.
>
> "I have endeavored to say the whole truth and hope Your Excellency will not resent my frankness."[66]

Werfel's rejection of baptism was rooted in secular, not religious, arguments. As Ellert observes, Werfel's refusal to join the Catholic Church did not imply that he doubted the truth of the Incarnation.[67] Oesterreicher, however, did not find Werfel's explanation satisfactory. He demanded Werfel's entire soul for the church. He did not find Werfel's reasoning acceptable but indeed "un-Christian."[68]

◻ ◻ ◻

Oesterreicher's associates at the Institute of Judaeo-Christian Studies and other contributors to its yearbook shared in the desire to win Jewish souls for the church. One striking example is the case of the scholar and associate editor of *The Bridge,* Father Edward H. Flannery. In these early years following the *Shoah,* Flannery, who had studied theology in Paris, made no secret of his desire to win Jews over to Christianity. Shades of his aspiration can be detected in his 1955 report of the Finaly case, an event which had generated international headlines during the postwar years.

The case involved two little Jewish boys, ages one and two, whose parents were deported from France in 1944 by the German Gestapo and exterminated. Before their deportation, the parents entrusted their two children to a Catholic orphanage. The parents indicated to the Catholic officials their desire that the boys not be baptized and be permitted to remain Jewish. Shortly after, the boys were transferred to the school of Notre Dame de Sion and later, in order to keep the two children out of the reach of the Gestapo, to the municipal *crèche,* both institutions in Grenoble. There they were received by the director, Mademoiselle Antoinette Brun, who agreed to hide the boys among the other children. The heroism of these Catholic officials on behalf of the two Jewish boys cannot be gainsaid. The laws against harboring Jews were extremely harsh. The nuns who hid these children endangered their own lives and, if discovered, would have been tortured and killed.

The Finaly boys, as they were known, remained at the *crèche* until the end of the war. Meanwhile, Brun became attached to the children and in 1948 had them baptized, contrary to the last wishes of their parents. What is more, when Brun received persistent inquiries about the boys from their relatives, she refused to respond or release the boys.[69] The children's relatives brought the issue to the French courts, where they sued for the return of the boys. Like the Dreyfus and Mortara cases, the Finaly affair divided public opinion, Roman Catholics generally insisting that the boys, now Catholics, remain under church guardianship. Finally, in 1954, after protracted legal altercations, French church authorities, under the order of the Court, reluctantly agreed to release the boys to their Jewish relatives, who took the children to Israel, where the relatives were then residing.[70]

In his account of the Finaly case, Flannery displays a distinct ambivalence about the decision of the court and the church's compliance with it. He appears indifferent to the ethical implications of legitimizing the conversion of the two Jewish children, contrary to the desire of their parents, both of whom died at Auschwitz, depriving their children of a Jewish life. To Flannery, morality was not at all an issue in the Finaly affair. The crux of the matter was the validity of the baptism. According to Flannery, the baptism was "valid," although he acknowledges, somewhat hesitantly, that contemporary opinion rejects the church's right to baptize a child against the will of the parents, which would be a violation of "natural justice."[71]

To this ambivalence, Flannery adds an even more disconcerting observation in his concluding remarks. It might appear to the casual observer, he notes, that in the conflict between the "rights of the Church" and those of the Finaly children the church had lost out. Not so, argues Flannery. He finds reason to believe that the conflict had not resulted in a total loss for the church. If the church had lost in the courts of law, it gained in the courts of God. Since the Finaly boys had been baptized into the church, there was no need to despair about their salvation. "If grace does its work even in an unbaptized soul in a world which knows nothing of Christ, may it not work also in the baptized soul of boys who have had some training in Christian living? Is it not possible that Christ will triumph in the soul even though they are removed from the Church's motherly care? For the ways of God are inscrutable. . . . God will turn injury into blessing."[72] At least in his own mind, Flannery's victory was complete. He had skillfully snatched the souls of two Jewish children from the flames of Auschwitz.

❏ ❏ ❏

Flannery did not deny his hope for a Jewish conversion in his report on the proceedings of the Second Assembly of the World Council of Churches (the world organization of Protestant churches), which convened in Evanston, Illinois, in the summer of 1954. Flannery was particularly interested in the debates of its most turbulent session on August 24, which voted 195 to 150 "to strike from a statement on 'Christ—the hope of the World' any reference to Israel's part in Christian hope." The vote represented the will of 1,242 delegates, representing 162 Protestant denominations from 42 countries. The debate and ensuing vote concerned the issue of whether to include Jews in this "hope." The question created a great storm on the floor of the assembly.[73]

The defeat of the motion was especially bitter for the Committee on the Christian Approach to the Jews, a branch of the International Missionary Council of the World Council of Churches, and its supporters, who were eager to receive the assembly's endorsement for their evan-gelical work among the Jews. Interestingly, opposition to evangelizing the Jews came not out of any concern for Jewish sensibility but out of recognition of the desires of the impassioned prelates from the Middle East. To include the Jews in the prayers and hopes of the assembly, the delegates were told, would aggravate the conditions of Christians liv-ing in Arab countries. Because of the Middle Eastern prelates' resent-ment toward the recently established state of Israel, the delegates were informed, any gesture that would create an impression of friendliness toward Jews would be counterproductive. The earnest pleas of the Mid-dle Easterners succeeded in swaying most of the delegates, including the American representatives, to vote against the resolution. Nevertheless, a number of delegates from Europe, who had seen the results of Hitler's wrath against the Jews, detected in the debates a new form of antisemit-ism masquerading as anti-Zionism.[74]

Flannery's position fell sharply on the side of the minority, that is, those delegates who wished to include Israel on the side of Christian "hope" for their future conversion. After observing the assembly's debate and the defeat of the resolution, Flannery commented: "A Catholic gather-ing would have decided the issue on a biblical and theological basis; that the 'mystery' of Israel would take precedence over political, social and practical considerations. . . . Though not a defined dogma, the doctrine of Israel's final return to the Christ is theologically certain, for it is most firmly anchored in the sources of the Catholic faith. It is the promise of the New Testament as it is the teaching of tradition."[75] Clearly, the need to convert the Jews to Christianity continued to be a prominent consid-eration in the decade and a half following the revelations of the Holo-caust. The events that transpired during the Second World War might have altered sentiments and attitudes of Christians toward Jews, but the theological foundations of the church remained unshaken.

6

Postwar Ambivalence, 1945–60

Revelations from Auschwitz did not encourage in any fundamental way a change in the relationship between Catholics and Jews. The theological ramparts, which had for so many years blocked religious understanding between them, remained impregnable. Nevertheless, Germany's gas chambers produced a shock sufficient enough to generate some minor alteration in attitude and behavior on the part of Catholics toward Jews during the decade and a half following the Second World War.[1]

According to students of American antisemitism, a distinct decline of hostility toward Jews became evident in American society. Ideological and racial antisemitic groups so prominent during the prewar years were increasingly relegated to the lunatic fringes of American life. No doubt the improved economic and social environment during the postwar years must be included in the calculus of the antisemitic decline.[2] In this connection, Leonard Dinnerstein writes: "A remarkable metamorphosis occurred in the United States in the two decades following the end of World War II. After more than half a century of increasing animosity toward the Jews, antisemitism in the United States suddenly began to decline."[3]

Employment, housing, education, and professional opportunities improved for Jews. According to one poll, in 1940, 25 percent of the respondents said that they would prefer not to live next to a Jewish neighbor, while only 3 percent so responded in 1962. Similarly, in the same years, those who would hesitate to employ a Jew decreased from 43 percent to 3 percent. Social barriers were being lowered for Jews.[4]

Jewish anxiety about antisemitism decreased during the post–World

War II years. As Seymour Martin Lipset and Earl Raab have recently observed, political events which in the prewar decades generated public suspicion about Jews and their alleged Communist international connections did not target Jews even at the height of the fears of the cold war. Wisconsin's Republican demagogue Senator Joseph McCarthy, for example, left Jews out of his fearful equation. For four years, between 1950 and 1954, McCarthy raved about Communists' boring into the highest levels of America's government, conspiring to destroy it. He did so at a time when Americans saw the Soviet Union and the expansion of international Communism as the greatest threat to Christian civilization. But he never attacked Jews.[5]

As Patrick Allitt reminds us, the 1950s witnessed the maturation of an identifiable group of politically conservative Catholic intellectuals. To expose and counteract the thrust of the spread of Communism was a mission they all shared. They saw in the cold war "an eschatological struggle in which Christian Western . . . civilization confronted its demonic nemesis."[6] As we have seen, Soviet fears had in the previous decade produced antisemitic charges. Not so in the 1950s, when Jews were rarely linked in the public mind with the "Red menace." While antisemitism continued to exist on the fringes of society, it did not infect mainstream post–World War II America.[7]

Roman Catholic charges of Communism against Jews also decreased. One Catholic wrote in 1946 that there was nothing in Judaism and its teachings that would incline Jews toward Communism. Indeed, believing Jews were persecuted in the Soviet Union. Communism, said the writer, "is contrary to what we might be tempted to call the Jewish spirit."[8] Such remarks from a member of a church that considered the spread of Communism the chief evil of the postwar world were no light matter.

▫ ▫ ▫

Post–World War II Jewish writers acknowledged the altered attitude toward Jews displayed by the American Catholic Church. The tragic fate of Europe's Jews and the emergence of the new state of Israel were among the factors said to be responsible for this alteration. In an unprecedented fashion, representatives of the American Jewish Committee met with Catholics and Protestants in 1947 to discuss, among other matters, the need to examine religious textbooks for passages that were prejudicial to Jews.[9] It was an important step toward reducing anti-Jewish attitudes.

For the first time, Jews spoke out more openly about their perception of Roman Catholics. This too was not an issue which had been frequently examined in previous decades. Arthur Gilbert, a rabbi and director of the National Department of Inter-religious Cooperation of the Anti-Defamation League of B'nai B'rith, was deeply involved in improving Catholic-Jewish relations during the years after the Second World War. His remarks to Catholics in 1958 about Jewish concerns are instructive. Gilbert concluded that American Jews considered that Roman Catholics harbored a greater degree of hostility toward them than did the members of various Protestant denominations. Gilbert was convinced that the tension between the faiths stemmed from the theology and the religious practices of American Catholics. Jews believed, declared Gilbert, that Christian teachings in parochial schools and in sermons engendered antisemitism. Moreover, some American rabbis and Jewish leaders suspected as much and began to express this opinion publicly.[10] Gilbert urged Catholic educators to examine the consequences of their teaching and if necessary to alter it. "Unfortunately," he added, "every year offers evidence from within the Catholic press . . . to support this Jewish view that Catholics are taught to hate Jews on religious grounds." Catholic children, he declared, were subjected to misinformation about Judaism and the Jewish people.[11] Again, in an uncommon request, Gilbert urged the church leaders to present the account of the Passion in such a manner that the Jew would not stand out as the archvillain of the Christ story. His next request, indeed almost a plea, was that Catholics cease to pray for the conversion and salvation of the Jews. Jews, he explained, do not want or need the prayers of Catholics. He regretted that a number of leading American prelates and priests continued to believe and act otherwise.[12]

A large section of American Jewry was also troubled by the Catholic position on the role of religion in public education as well as its stance on government support for parochial education. Indeed, many Jews suspected (incorrectly) that American Catholics had little regard for the principle of separation of church and state. But Catholic spokespersons did not believe that without a dose of religion, moral values could be inculcated. For bitter historic reasons, however, most Jews believed differently.[13]

Not all Jews joined in the general opposition to including a measure of religion in public education. Orthodox Jews saw the Catholic request for public support for parochial schools as an opportunity to elicit financial support for Jewish parochial schools and the growing postwar day school movement. A few non-Orthodox Jews, such as the theologian Will Herberg, saw government support for religious learning as a positive idea. Herberg argued in 1957 that with America's divisiveness in matters of faith, not the public school but the parochial school should serve as the inculcator of religious values. And it behooved the government to grant the schools support for such endeavors.[14] In general, Jews rejected Herberg's views. Neither did they find value in Catholic demands to include prayers in public education. But their different views in these matters added to the postwar tensions between the two communities.[15]

Some Christian thinkers believed that in these matters, Jews were joining the forces of anti-Catholicism. The prominent Catholic theologian John Courtney Murray wrote in 1960 that "there is the ancient resentment of the Jew, who has for centuries been dependent for his existence on the good will, often not forthcoming, of a Christian community. Now in America, when he has acquired social power, his distrust of the Christian community leads him to align himself with the secularizing forces whose dominance, he thinks, will allow him a security he has never known."[16]

To some degree, Murray's assertion was valid. Its tone, however, appeared to belittle such Jewish concerns in post-Holocaust America. Jews, who numbered about 4.5 million by World War II, continued to view the Catholic tenfold numerical preponderance as a Christian force which even in America had to be guarded against. It is, therefore, understandable why Arthur Gilbert underscored the need for the modern democratic state to remain religiously neutral; he believed that was especially necessary for Jews who had had a long history of struggle with sectarian institutions. Public schools especially, he declared, must refrain from invoking religious instruction and sectarian symbols for the protection of the educational needs of non-Christians.[17]

Following the war, some Jewish leaders challenged the appropriateness of venerated and oft-repeated liturgical expressions that were seen to be insulting to Jewish sensibilities. A chief example of this was Leon Bloy's citation in 1947 of the phrases *pro perfides Judaeis* and *Judaica perfidia*. Both phrases occur in the Good Friday bidding prayers of the Roman rites. The editor of *America* informed his Jewish critic that the language is not as bad as it sounds, that *perfidia* is a reference to Jewish "unbelief" in Christ's salvation and should not be translated as "perfidious."[18]

In the same year, the missionary priest John M. Oesterreicher wrote in *Theological Studies* that the Good Friday prayer has never intended to call the Jews "wicked." What it does is "lament Israel's disbelief in Christ." The liturgy asks Christians to pray for the Jews, so that "the veil may be lifted from their hearts" that they may "learn to know Jesus."[19] The Catholic theologian Kathryn Sullivan also joined in the effort to convince American Jews of the benign character of the Latin phrase. Like other Catholic writers, Sullivan could not comprehend why an "intercessory prayer," one designed "for the . . . return of those separated from the Church's unity, for the turning to Christ of the children of Israel," could be found distasteful to Jews.[20]

Clearly, by the late 1950s, Catholic scholars had failed to grasp the antipathy in the Jewish community toward invoking prayers on their behalf, irrespective of how harmless the language might appear to Catholics. Jews saw such prayers as insulting, distasteful, and abhorrent. Yet such frank discussions between Catholics and Jews about religious differences had not been frequently heard in the two decades before World War II. It was not often that one was able to listen to a prominent young Jewish scholar such as Arthur A. Cohen voice irritation with Catholics who evinced interest in Jews and Judaism at an interfaith meeting. "The condescension of Christianity toward the House of Israel and the faith of the Jews perhaps more than all else is deeply offensive," he remarked in 1958. "Whether Israel is conceived of as an arrested child or aged father matters little, for the image of solicitude marks the attitude of the modern church."[21] Such remarks were harsh, and they suggest that there was still a considerable gulf between the two faiths.[22]

▫ ▫ ▫

None of the openness between Jews and Christians should be taken to mean that antisemitism had disappeared from American society.[23] Although it was being increasingly moved to the fringes, antisemitism was still alive and well. As Leonard Dinnerstein observed, "Fifty-seven antisemitic groups still existed in the United States in 1950." Jews were conscious of intolerance toward them throughout the decade of the 1950s. Much of it, unlike that of the 1930s, was reflected in teenage vandalism and violence. However, some of it bespoke a deeper measure of Christian anti-Judaism mixed with a large quantity of Jewish stereotypical images—Jews are all wealthy, greedy, dishonest, and cowardly.[24]

Shortly after the war ended, leaders of the American church urged the United States to admit as many of Europe's displaced persons (D.P.s) as possible. *America* estimated in 1946 that the D.P.s numbered close to one million people. No doubt, some of these were Jewish survivors of Hitler's death camps, but they were not singled out by Catholic leaders.[25] At the same time, Catholic spokespersons struck out at nativist "drum beaters" who demanded that America's door remain closed to all refugees.[26] Catholic objections, however, made no mention of the special needs of Jewish survivors.

One of the most flagrant examples of Catholic coolness to the needs of Jewish survivors is evident in an essay written by William J. Gibbons in the October 19, 1946, issue of *America* on the subject of Europe's D.P.s. In the course of his discussion of "survivors of concentration camps," he glosses over in a mere sentence the entire subject of Jewish survivors. The bulk of his discussion is devoted to non-Jewish survivors and their wartime misfortunes. Not a word is found on the subject of "death camps," "gas chambers," or a "final solution."[27] What is more, when Jewish investigators, such as David Nausbaum of the *New York Post,* contended in 1948 that among the non-Jewish D.P.s were found many war criminals who collaborated with Germany in its efforts to exterminate the Jews, the allegation was shrugged off by the editors of *America.*[28]

The destruction of six million European Jews was not a topic frequently discussed in Catholic periodicals, although a select group of American Catholics did recognize the enormity of the tragedy. The members of this group acknowledged the German Catholics' apathy in the face of their nation's crimes.[29] But as a rule, they were not representative of American Catholic postwar interests. Americans in general, and even Jews, were, in the years immediately following the war, too overwhelmed by the *Shoah,* an event which had yet no name, to grasp fully what had just transpired. What became increasingly clear, however, was that during the catastrophe, the Jews had little Christian support or even sympathy. Robert F. Drinan, a prominent Jesuit professor of law at Georgetown University, has acknowledged that "the reaction of the Christian community to the Holocaust can generally be described as mild, vague, and belated. While there are notable exceptions to the general ineffectiveness of the Church to effect its concern over rising antisemitism, it failed in any significant way to provide political or moral leadership to combat the antisemitic designs of Hitler's Germany."[30]

American Catholics sometimes resented the allegation that their German coreligionists were complicit with Hitler's crimes. They preferred to argue that German Catholics (who constituted 40 percent of the Reich's population) had little choice but to goosestep in line with Nazi orders.[31] After all, as one writer put it at the end of the war, in 1945, "I wonder how many of those who criticize the German people for ignorance or docility or condemn them for passive complicity would have raised their voices against the government in this country had they known that death or torture were the penalties."[32] No doubt the morbid query had merit. But what is equally disturbing about some of these postwar discussions of German "atrocities" is that the horrors experienced by Jews were hardly, if at all, noticed. The price paid for Hitler's work, it appeared, was paid by "humanity," the German people, the church, and its faithful.[33]

Writing about the Nazi era twenty-five years later, in 1962, the Jesuit scholar J. Franklin Ewing is even at that late date unable to acknowledge fully the *Shoah*. He is unable even to utter the word "Jew." He writes that "the real 'gods' of the Nazis—atheism, racism and statism—still live on, in other and more naked and deadly forms. The church, with the sureness and perception of its divine inspiration, knows these enemies."[34]

A Jewish reader might ask: What "more naked and deadly forms" of evil than the "final solution" hovered on the American scene in 1962? Was it Soviet Communism? For a Jesuit priest to recall the greatest Jewish catastrophe within Christian civilization as little more than a warning against "racism," "statism," and "atheism" makes one question the church's sensibilities.

◻ ◻ ◻

One might legitimately wonder if the church's dread of atheistic Communism dampened Pope Pius XII's zeal to move aggressively to oppose Hitler's war against the Jews. Such perceived insensitivity also accounts for the suspicion that most American Jewish leaders and Holocaust scholars displayed toward the wartime record of resistance toward Nazism shown by Pius XII. Pius XII has been credited by many Catholics and even some Jews with saving hundreds of thousands of Jews. He did so, it has been alleged, by working quietly through his nuncios, bishops, and lesser church officials. Considering the treacherous conditions under Nazi rule, his actions were heroic.

Nevertheless, most Jews and some Catholics argue that Pius XII did little more than what was expected of a bishop of Rome. But he failed to measure up to what is expected of a truly great religious and moral leader. His silence in the face of mass extermination of Jews which took place at his very doorstep was deafening. He appeared to be fearful of offending the Nazis. Regretfully, his actions reinforced, even inspired, Christian passivity in the face of the evil which pervaded Europe. Such apathy on the part of the "Vicar of Christ," a leading historian of European events recently observed, was an outgrowth of the church's hope to win Hitler's cooperation in the war against Soviet Communism, a threat which the pope saw as more serious than the issue of Jewish survival.[35]

The controversy over Pius XII's behavior was ignited with the staging of Rolf Hochhuth's drama *The Deputy* in 1963. Among other things, it accused the pope of moral cowardice and indifference to the fate of

Europe's Jews. Catholics, as well as a number of Jewish scholars, challenged the historical accuracy of Hochhuth's play.[36] Indeed, the controversy of Pius XII's behavior during the Second World War in respect to the Final Solution continues until this very day. Meanwhile, since the pope's motivation and behavior will remain matters of debate, we could profit by the conclusions of Robert S. Wistrich:

> There seems little doubt, that, as late as 1943, Pius XII hoped for a German victory against the Russians, his assumption being that Roman Catholicism would have a place in "The New Order" of the Nazis but stood no chance of one under Soviet Communism. . . . What is undeniable is the paucity of moral courage displayed by the Vatican when it came to the fate of the Jews.
>
> Would it have made a difference if Pius XII *had* taken a firm stand? Any answer is necessarily speculative. . . . Catholics constituted over 40 percent of the population of the greater German Reich. . . . What would have been the effect had Pius XII issued an unequivocal public denunciation of the Nazi war against the Jews, or instructed Catholics not to carry out "criminal orders" or excommunicated the devoutly Catholic leaders . . . or even Hitler himself? Perhaps very little. If nothing else, however, such actions would certainly have curbed some of the craven behavior of the German bishops. . . . Indeed, the inaction of the Church hierarchy highlights, by stark contrast, the physical and moral heroism of those ordinary Catholics (and Protestants) who hid, rescued, or saved Jews at great personal risk.[37]

◻ ◻ ◻

The ambivalence about Nazism displayed on the highest level of the church was also evident in the United States. Some American Catholics did not believe that Nazism constituted a terribly serious threat to the church or Christianity in general. Revelations of Nazism's true danger were slow in coming. By the end of the Second World War, Catholic leaders pleaded with Americans to refrain from punishing Germany and its citizens, although Catholic leaders did not oppose placing Nazi leaders suspected of war crimes on trial at Nuremberg.[38] Yet, *America,* as did other Catholic periodicals, debated the "morality" and "legality" of such a tribunal. Some Catholic writers questioned the validity a court could assume when there were representatives from the Soviet Union, a totalitarian state, which was "widely charged with committing the *identical crimes* [italics mine]." Despite such reservations, *America* believed a trial would have value.[39] This kind of debate, coupled with Catholic insistence on treating gently Germans in general, must have sounded insensitive to Jewish ears.

By the end of the war, Catholic writers and leaders began calling for a "Christian peace," a "Pax Christiana" as Bishop James A. Ryan termed it.[40] Considering the price that world Jewry paid, it was an irresponsible designation. Americans were urged by the Catholic journalist Ferdinand Hermens to deal justly with the German population, to differentiate them from their leaders, who were solely responsible for the tragic war. The German people, Americans were informed, were first to suffer "every single one of the crimes committed by the Nazis in the occupied countries."[41]

The tendency was to picture the German people as innocent of any desire to make war or commit evil. The German people were portrayed as "martyrs." These decent Germans were able to "do nothing to prevent the Gestapo from liquidating the Jews as a race."[42] In the months that followed, Hermens continued to entreat Americans to deal fairly with the defeated Germany, urging that the victors refrain from punishing Germany but reconstruct it instead. Such action would prevent the winners from feeling guilty later.[43] Most revealing, however, was Hermens's suggestive hint that Germany should be kept strong so that it would serve as a counterweight against the growing power of the Soviet Union.[44] Such thinking was realistic and in accordance with the church's concerns. Even so, not one word was uttered about the "reconstruction" of German education and the need to eradicate the racial antisemitism that had been allowed to poison German society.

The Catholic request not to deal harshly with the defeated Germans became a favorite refrain. In June 1945, for example, James McCawley, a well-known Catholic writer, defended the vast Catholic population of Germany: "Are we to assume . . . that all of the 13,000,000 Catholics were guilty of Nazi excesses, that all of the Catholic clergy can be blamed for the horrors of the Hitler regime?" German bishops and priests who risked their lives were among the most heroic opponents of Hitler, wrote McCawley in 1945. "The record of Catholic opposition to Hitler in Germany is a long one," McCawley declared to his Catholic readers.[45] Although there were some notable acts of heroism, the myth of a large Catholic resistance has by now been pretty well demolished by Holocaust scholars.[46]

To absolve German Catholics and the German Catholic Church from complicity in the Third Reich's sins was a troubling theme. Yet in the process, they rarely, if at all, singled out the magnitude of the tragedy that had befallen Germany's and Europe's Jews. Catholic writers found it exceedingly difficult to condemn the Germans after the war. As one writer put it, the church "praises, but does not condemn with certain-ty."[47] It was not the kind of sentiment that Jewish survivors of the gas chambers would have appreciated.

▫ ▫ ▫

Supplied with a false refugee passport through the good offices of a Franciscan monk, the notorious Gestapo chief Adolf Eichmann fled to Buenos Aires in 1950. Eichmann had been the chief administrator of the Final Solution. His task was to assemble Jews for extermination. Together with other war criminals in the 1950s, he lived under the protection of the Argentinian government until his abduction by members of the Shin Bet, a branch of Israel's secret service, in May 1960. The Israeli agents flew him to Israel where he was put on trial in Jerusalem. In Israel, Eichmann was charged, among other things, with "crimes against the Jewish people" and "crimes against humanity." His lengthy trial began, after an eight-month investigation, on April 11, 1961. Following an appeal to the Israeli Supreme Court, Eichmann was found guilty on all charges and sentenced to death on December 15, 1961.[48]

Few events in the fifteen years following the Second World War brought into sharper relief the horror unleashed by the German government upon the Jews than did Eichmann's testimony and the proceedings of his trial. More than anything else, the event reminded the world of the depth of inhumanity to which civilized society could sink. It offered an opportunity to reflect upon the ultimate consequences of antisemitism.[49] In this light, the ambiguity of prominent American Catholic voices is surprising. The highly respected Jesuit weekly *America,* whose editors followed the trial in Jerusalem carefully, seemed uneasy about the jurisdiction of an Israeli court over Adolf Eichmann.[50] The editors were also concerned that the Eichmann proceedings might present all Germans in a poor light and that a charge of "collective guilt" might be leveled against all of them.[51]

In this connection, it is instructive to note Arthur Gilbert's comments voiced in a published dialogue with Father Walter M. Abbott, feature editor of *America.* Gilbert, actively involved in the improvement of Jewish-Christian relations, told Abbott of his disappointment at the response of American Catholic leaders and publications to the procedure and outcome of the Eichmann trial. The Jewish community, Gilbert declared, was appalled by the criticism leveled at Israel's tactics in apprehending the Nazi killer and at the Israeli court's decision to impose the death penalty. The state of Israel, according to the Christian press, should have risen to a higher level of behavior, one befitting the ideals of the postwar era.[52] Gilbert wondered why the Catholic press never questioned the legitimacy and morality of Argentina's willingness to provide a haven for Nazi war criminals or why the issue of the death penalty was raised with such passion at this particular time, when it was imposed by an Israeli court.

In addition, Gilbert pointed out that most Catholic commentators on the Eichmann event did not attend the proceedings of the trial nor read its transcripts. Most important, their focus was rarely upon the significant and deeper implications of the trial. Never was the question raised, What did the trial tell the civilized world about antisemitism in Western civilization? Gilbert wondered what inspired only a minute minority of some Catholics to resist Hitler, and why the vast majority were not so motivated. He additionally inquired what this said about Christianity, about religion, and about humanity. American Jews would have preferred that such questions be discussed in Catholic circles rather than arguments about the legitimacy of Eichmann's abduction, the legality of the trial, and Eichmann's execution. The members of the Jewish community in America, explained Gilbert, "wanted an emphatic reaction from their neighbors, a statement of responsibility and brotherhood from the Christian."[53] In short, Gilbert had hoped that the Eichmann affair would have provided an opportunity for American Catholics to reevaluate their relationship to the Jewish people and to acknowledge their responsibility in the events that made an Eichmann possible. The trial presented the American church with a challenge to which it failed to respond adequately.[54]

This failure is evident in the reaction of America's editors to Gilbert's comments. The editors were deeply disillusioned with what they saw as Gilbert's implied suggestion that all Christians were to be found in the "same box" with Eichmann. They rejected what they believed to be the Jewish notion that all Christians were even remotely responsible for Eichmann's deeds. Eichmann's evil, the editors asserted, should not be considered as a failure of "Christian moral conscience."[55] America refused to acknowledge that Christianity's complicity with Eichmann's crimes was not the issue but rather its anti-Judaic theological foundations that supported the evil which he committed. No lesson of value could be gleaned from the Eichmann trial, they believed. There was hostility in the Catholic response:

> In the first place, this was no Nuremberg trial. It lacked the authority, the universality, the solemnity of the great Judgement passed by the Allies in 1946. It was highly colored by the political interests of the Israeli state. . . . The proceedings were given an exclusively Jewish character. Eichmann was presented as an enemy of the Jewish people, to be tried by a Jewish Court,

on the basis of Jewish (or, rather, Israeli) law, punishment to be exacted by Jewish hands. Hitler's dastardly offenses were thereby deprived of a general character as crimes against our common humanity. The Jerusalem trial exhibited a certain *racism-in-reverse* [italics mine], which was in strange contrast to the avowed purposes of the proceedings.[56]

If any serious thinking about the *Shoah* was engendered by the Eichmann affair, it was not evident in this response. One might also wonder about the degree to which the Catholic reaction was colored by the location of the trial—the new state of Israel.

◻ ◻ ◻

American Catholic insensitivity to the meaning and implication of the Holocaust was matched by Catholic indifference to Judaism's second momentous event of the 1940s: the birth of the state of Israel in 1948. These two occurrences were coupled in the Jewish mind not as cause and effect, nor as the latter being compensation for the former, but as a symbol of death and rebirth.

It was a difficult journey for those Jews who brought about the birth of the Jewish state. The state of Israel was launched in the midst of the Second World War by leaders of the Yishuv and the Jewish Agency. It was at that time concluded that Jewish survival demanded such a move. It meant that Jews would fight on two fronts: with their English allies to defeat the Nazis on the one hand, and against England to open the Yishuv to Jewish immigration. The latter constituted a move to which England fiercely objected. Following World War II, a war of terror was launched by the Yishuv against Great Britain and its mandatory government. A war-weary world watched the Jewish struggle against British resistance to build a sovereign nation in the wake of the *Shoah*.

Throughout the crisis, Great Britain, not wishing to alienate the Arab world or endanger its access to oil supplies, maintained its severe restrictions on Jewish immigration into Palestine, a policy which it had formulated before the war in the White Paper of 1939. Like other Christian nations, Great Britain was not sufficiently moved by postwar Holocaust revelations to alter its behavior toward Jews or Jewish refugees.[57]

American Jews were particularly concerned with the 50,000 to 100,000 Jewish D.P.s left homeless in Europe in 1945. Their former homes and communities were either destroyed or occupied by their erstwhile neighbors, who, in any case, did not welcome a Jewish return. Neither did the D.P.s care to return to the bosom of their persecutors. Zionists exerted every effort to transport as many of the D.P.s as possible into Palestine. With Great Britain's refusal to open the doors to them and the hesitancy of even the United States to admit more than a few thousand Jews, the creation of a Jewish state became all the more imperative. Not surprisingly, illegal immigration of Jews into Palestine mounted. Jews repeatedly ran the British blockade, sometimes with tragic consequences when ships were sunk and refugees drowned in the waters of the Mediterranean. Acts of terror against the British authorities also increased in intensity, as the potential settlers desperately tried to claim their homeland.

Tired of war and terror, by 1947, with the mandatory government on the verge of collapse, Great Britain in desperation flung the entire issue into the lap of the newly created United Nations. Here the problem of Palestine was placed in the hands of a Special Committee on Palestine (UNSCOP). UNSCOP's report, issued in November 1947, recommended a partition of Palestine between Arabs and Jews and the internationalization of Jerusalem. This entire plan angered the Arab world. When Israel proclaimed its independence on May 14, 1948, six Arab states attacked the fledgling Jewish state, attempting to snuff out its existence. Prevailing over its enemies, the infant state took its first steps into a new era in the history of the Jewish people.[58]

The cool reception accorded by church officials to the Jewish struggle for national sovereignty was reminiscent of their reception of the Balfour Declaration three decades earlier. Robert F. Drinan was both surprised and disappointed. "Having witnessed the Holocaust," he wrote in 1977, he would have expected that the Church "would lend some affirmative acquiescence to the idea of a homeland to which the twelve million surviving Jews in the world, if they so desired, might emigrate." Drinan wondered why "the Christian mind has never allowed itself to feel the same human concern for Jewish suffering that it has felt for Christian."[59]

Catholic opposition to acceptance of a Jewish state differed little in 1948 from that shown the early Zionist movement. The very notion that the Jewish people would be converting the Holy Land into their own sovereign territory was hardly an acceptable notion, even in the post-Holocaust era. The security of the religious edifices under Jewish control was a major Catholic concern, as was the fear that the establishment of a Jewish state might open a door to Soviet infiltration of the Middle East and involve the United States in armed conflict.[60] Nevertheless, Catholic reluctance to endorse a Jewish homeland was not a position shared by the American public or, for that matter, by Congress, which resolved shortly before the end of the war "that the United States shall use its good offices and take appropriate measures to the end that the door of Palestine shall be opened for free entry of Jews in that country, and that there shall be full opportunity for colonization so that the Jewish people may ultimately reconstruct Palestine as a free and democratic Jewish commonwealth."[61] When World War II ended, President Harry Truman called on Great Britain to open its doors to Palestine and allow 100,000 Jewish refugees to enter. In these efforts, American Catholics offered little support, rejecting a necessity for a Jewish state. *Commonweal,* usually more understanding of Jewish needs, nevertheless noted that "we are . . . suspicious of Zionist nationalism and we cannot withhold our sympathy from the natives of Palestine who however shortsightedly seem to prefer to keep their country for their own use. Americans, of all people, can with the least grace criticize others for attempts to restrict immigration."[62]

Writing in *America* in May 1946, William J. Gibbons, a frequent contributor, warned Jews that the tactics used by Zionists represented an extreme form of nationalism reminiscent of what Europe had recently endured. Neither a large Jewish immigration to Palestine nor the creation of a Jewish state was an acceptable option for Jews. Gibbons advised the refugees to return to their respective countries which they had inhabited before the war.[63]

As independence approached following the completion of UNSCOP's report in 1947, and as violence intensified during the last days of the mandate, *America* predicted that the Zionists "would be judged harshly" by history and that world Jewish opinion would repudiate their violent behavior. The editors were critical of Arab intransigence, which blocked a possible resolution to the Palestine problem. *America* recommended that a revised mandatory government be created for Palestine. Such thoughts were typical among many American Catholics in 1947.[64] Catholic leaders shuddered at the thought that even a part of Palestine would be offered to the Jews. They considered the Holy Land hallowed religious ground, the birthplace of the Catholic Church. Jews had forfeited their home; they had abandoned it and consequently lost their rights to it.

As Zionists prepared for independence, the American Catholic press warned that such an event would result in a bloody Arab retaliation, which would once again draw the United States into combat. *Catholic World,* in a piece which underscored the slight impact of the *Shoah* on Catholic sensibilities, declared as follows:

> No one will doubt that a powerful force behind America's entrance into the war was compassion for the persecuted Jews of Germany. . . . The

American government was under the pressure of a powerful Jewish lob-
by. . . . They sharpened the talons of the American Eagle to fly him against
the European Cormorant that gorged the Star of David. . . . She has rescued the Jews from the Nazis only to find that she will have to save them
again. . . . Is the Star of David to become another star in the American flag?[65]

Even the small handful of Jews who opposed the Zionists' national aspirations, members of the recently formed American Council for Judaism, were probably appalled at the hostile tone of the Catholic writer.

On May 14, 1948, the day that the modern Jewish state was founded, the semi-official Vatican newspaper *L'Osservatore Romano* expressed
the Vatican view of the historic event clearly: "Modern Zionism is not
the true heir of Biblical Israel, but a secular state . . . therefore, the Holy
Land and its sacred sites belong to Christianity, the True Israel!"[66] Additionally, as the new state was encircled and attacked by the surrounding Arab armies, according to the Israeli historian and diplomat Pinchas
Lapide, the Vatican did not conceal the fact that its sympathies lay with
the invading Arabs. As the war for Israel's survival proceeded, one leading Catholic writer accused the Jews of employing germ warfare against
the Arabs.[67]

There was resentment in American Catholic circles at the support the
United States offered Israel by being the first major power to recognize
Israel's independence. In July 1948, *Catholic World* editorialized as follows: "The unseemly haste with which our Department of State officially
acknowledged the 'Republic' of Israel shows that once we have gone for
international meddling, we shall play the game as all others have done
with cold-blooded disregard of ethical principles."[68] The editors of *Catholic World* accused the United States of forfeiting its right to claim world
moral leadership. In this regard, it "is finished unless America is converted, does penance, suffers, makes reparations, and so regains divine
grace." Catholic abuse was also showered upon Great Britain for initi-
ating the crisis of the Middle East by issuing the Balfour Declaration.
President Harry Truman was singled out for hypocrisy in recognizing
Israel at "breakneck speed" to gain, *Catholic World* said, the Jewish vote.
The Catholic editors were puzzled why the United States supported the
creation of a Jewish homeland and ignored the needs of Christian homelands for the people of Eastern Europe now under the domination of the
Soviet Union.[69]

The assault on the new state did not conceal occasional eschatological glimpses of the return of the Jews to Zion. Catholics speculated, as
did Protestants, about the religious meaning of the Jewish return. Some
wondered if it signified the approach of the Second Coming. Others

asked if the Jews might rebuild their temple. More significant, there were those who anticipated a concomitant conversion of Jews to Christianity. And there were still others who urged Jews to do just that, as soon as possible, to fulfill their destiny as was foretold in Christian Scripture.[70] In all this, it was rare to detect a Christian insight as to what Jewish attachment to a state of Israel, reborn, added to the enhancement of Jews' self-respect, confidence, and religious rebirth. It was no small thing for Jews to regain a home, lost but not forgotten for almost two thousand years.

But this kind of religio-nationalistic thinking represented to some Catholics a particularism which they found difficult to fathom. Even the choice of the name "Israel" for the new state represented an aggrandizement of a universal designation. As one writer observed in *Commonweal,*

> As Catholics, Israel's arrogation of a universal name for so local a habitation must distress us. . . . Israel, for every Christian, is the whole redeemed world, and all peoples, since the Incarnation, are equally chosen in fulfillment of the prophecies to be heirs to the glory. Despite our sympathy for Israel and Jew, we must not forget that to think of the Law and the Prophets as historically given only to their physical descendents, is a minimizing and a belittling of the greatest fact in history.[71]

It was quite obvious to American Jews in 1948 that their rejoicing at the rebirth of their sovereign homeland was not shared by their Catholic neighbors.

◻ ◻ ◻

Catholic ambivalence about the birth of Israel may be partially explained by the difficulty the church had in uniting what it saw as the holy with the mundane. A Vatican official explained this by noting in 1950 that in respect to Jerusalem, no degree of modern, scientific, or cultural advance would enhance the value of the Holy City for the church. Only those experiences or edifices which encompassed deep religious meaning or embodied Christian sanctity could add to the importance that Jerusalem held for the Church of Rome.[72] Unlike Jews, Catholics did not seek to settle or develop the Holy Land. Roman Catholics already were dominant and resided in a host of countries—Spain, France, Poland, Italy, Brazil, and Argentina, to name but a few—that could be considered Catholic homelands. Jews enjoyed no such national or cultural advantage before the establishment of Israel. This is not to suggest that Jews did not also view their newly established home as the religious center of

Judaism that it had been considered by many for three thousand years. Their "return" was to the birthplace of their faith and history as a people.

At the same time, the Jewish settlers in Israel never lost sight of the universal significance that the religious territory on which their new state was established held for Christianity. One of the first acts of the newly established government was to include on its highest level a cabinet post designated Minister of Religious Affairs. As an indication of the government's appreciation of the role of Christianity in Israel, its first minister of religious affairs, Yehudah ben Maimon, founded a periodical through his ministry, *Christian News from Israel.* It was the earliest ecumenical effort extended by the new state to world Catholicism.[73] And it signified the official recognition that the Israeli government accorded the Christian faith in the Holy Land.

The church, on the other hand, showed little appreciation of the significance of Israel for its Jewish inhabitants. Foremost in the thinking of church leaders and the Holy See was not the people of Israel but the safety of the holy sites in Jerusalem, Bethlehem, and other places in Israel. The principle issue and major concern was how these holy places would be dealt with by Jewish hands.[74] Even before the state was proclaimed, the church believed that the best solution for the safety of the holy places lay in the internationalization of the city of Jerusalem and its Bethlehem suburbs.[75] It preferred that the territory be placed under United Nations control. Subsequent events in the Middle East dictated otherwise. Both Israel and the kingdom of Jordan, which after 1949 divided the city of Jerusalem between them, with the western portion going to Israel and the eastern—containing most of the holy sites—to Jordan, rejected the concept of internationalization. Nevertheless, it was an idea to which the Vatican held firmly for a few more years.

In 1949, Pope Pius XII made his views clear about the internationalization of Jerusalem in his encyclical *Redemptores Nostre,* in which he urged Catholics to seek their respective governments' cooperation in this matter. "The time has come," proclaimed the pope, "when Jerusalem and its vicinity should be accorded and legally guaranteed an international status. . . . Use every legitimate means to persuade the rulers of nations . . . to accord to Jerusalem and its surroundings a juridical status. . . . Encourage the faithful committed to your charge to be ever more concerned about conditions in Palestine and have them make their lawful requests known, positively and unequivocally, to the rulers of nations."[76]

The pope's request encouraged a strong response from the American hierarchy and the American Catholic press.[77] Francis Cardinal Spellman of New York, for example, voiced great concern about the future of

Catholic rights in the Holy Land. Christians, he declared, were just as much an indigenous people of Palestine as were Jews. When war erupted in Israel in 1948, Spellman prayed primarily that the holy places in Jerusalem might be spared. Spellman also notified Chaim Weitzman, the first president of Israel, of his hope that the new state consider internationalization of Jerusalem as stipulated by the United Nations' partition plan of November 1947. Spellman did not conceal his disappointment at the refusal of both Israel and Jordan to comply with the U.N. partition plan. It was an issue that the cardinal continued to debate for many years.[78]

On December 13, 1949, the prime minister of Israel, David Ben-Gurion, announced to the Israeli Knesset (Parliament) that "for the State of Israel there is, has been, and always will be one capital only, Jerusalem, the Eternal. So it was 3000 years ago and so it will be, we believe, until the end of time."[79] Ben-Gurion's declaration stunned the Catholic world, including the American hierarchy. *America's* editor pronounced the prime minister's statement "a case of aggression" against world opinion. He approved a suggestion that there might be a need to "rescue" the holy city from the grasp of Israel.[80] The editorial bespoke a note of desperation. The problem was that in the early years of Israel's emergence, Jerusalem was viewed by the church as belonging if not to mankind then at least to the three universal faiths: Judaism, Christianity, and Islam. For the church, Jerusalem transcended the trappings of national sovereignty. Rather, Jerusalem signified a unique "universal" sovereignty. However, the Israeli government and the Jewish people categorically rejected this kind of reasoning. By their so doing, an uneasy truce prevailed throughout the 1950s between the church and the Israeli government.

Because of what Catholics saw as Israel's obstinacy in refusing to accede to the internationalization of Jerusalem, one writer depicted the Jewish state as being at war not only with its Arab neighbors but also with the Universal Church. At the same time, Arabs were seen by Catholic writers as more cooperative, more willing to work with the church. Writing in *Catholic World,* an American traveler to "Palestine," no doubt to show his sympathy for the Arab cause, refrained from employing the term "Israel." He saw no resolution to the conflict of the Near East except for Israel to remove its embassy from Jerusalem and move it back to Tel Aviv and for the Jews of Israel to convert to Christianity.[81]

Within a few years, the church would come to recognize that the security of its holy places was assured under Israeli control. Accordingly, the anti-Israeli rhetoric of the American hierarchy subsided. Yet one cannot cease to wonder what role was played by the deep religious underpinnings of the church's views of the Jews during this decade and a half of commotion. One is left to speculate why the conflict over the internationalization of Jerusalem produced such hostile rhetoric toward the Jews and their efforts to restore their homeland—an island of safety following Europe's catastrophe. At least in respect to the state of Israel, the underlying theology of the church seemed hardly dented by the fateful events of World War II.

7

Revolt of the Bishops, 1960–75

By the early 1960s, the American Catholic Church was the largest Christian denomination in the United States. By any standard of measurement, its growth was impressive. The church officially claimed in 1962 nearly 44 million adherents, 146 dioceses supported by nearly 57,000 priests and almost 18,000 parishes. By 1960, as a Catholic historian recently observed, American Catholics "had come of age."[1] Increasingly accepted by their Protestant neighbors, Catholics felt at home in America. They were proud and secure in their faith, all the more so as a Roman Catholic, John F. Kennedy, in an unprecedented victory became president of the United States.

Yet, although more prosperous and economically comfortable than ever, the American church, griped some Catholic observers, had not matched its astounding progress with intellectual achievements. There were those who contended that the church was suffering from a strain of anti-intellectualism.[2] Some were concerned that the church's concessions to modernity might require compromises which could prove threatening to its very integrity.[3] However, as a part of a Universal Church with religious directions emanating from the papal throne, the American Catholic Church was at this very moment about to embark upon an earth-shattering theological reassessment which would alter radically its view of itself and the world around it.

It is rare in religious history for a great ecclesiastical establishment, such as the Church of Rome, to acknowledge publicly its need to review and reevaluate long-held cherished beliefs and practices. Yet this revolutionary event occurred during the four sessions of the Second Vatican

Council (which came to be known also as Vatican II), convened in the years 1962–65. More than many of their European colleagues, American bishops, archbishops, and cardinals welcomed these changes, viewed them as arriving at a most propitious time, and were eager to implement them. Looking back, one cannot help but rank the achievement, at least with respect to Jewish-Catholic relations, as one of the most remarkable in the long centuries of Christian history. As one observer put it in 1964, "We are witnessing something that has been all but unknown in the almost 2000 years of Christianity."[4]

When Pope John XXIII (1958–63) convened the council in September 1962, he had already reached the venerable age of eighty-one. Few expected him to undertake such a daunting responsibility.[5] As it was, because of failing health, the pope lived to participate in only its first session, in 1962. But it was John's inspiring leadership, brief as it was, that gave the council a sense of purpose and direction. Most important, the council's work altered, perhaps irrevocably, the relationship of Christians and Jews.

The improvement of this relationship, however, was initially not the dominating concern behind the pope's decision to call together a Vatican council. This is not to say that John XXIII was unaware of and uninterested in the events that had recently transpired. As Angelo Cardinal Roncalli he had spent the war years in the Vatican's diplomatic service in Bulgaria, Turkey, and France; he was also patriarch of Venice. In all these capacities, he exerted heroic efforts to prevent Jews from being transported to death camps. While serving as papal nuncio in Istanbul, the future pope offered baptismal certificates to many Jews in order to prevent their deportation.[6] In 1960, as pope, as he thought about the need to convene a Vatican council, he had the Universal Church on his mind. Pope John's quest was for a spiritual renewal of the church. He hoped to achieve unity in the Christian world. He sought to modernize the church so that it could speak more intelligibly to all faiths.[7]

Jews, well aware of the new pope's attitude toward them, were keenly interested in his work. Pinchas Lapide recalled meeting Cardinal Roncalli in 1956, when he was cardinal patriarch of Venice, two years before his elevation to the papal office. What struck Lapide most was the great respect that the cardinal patriarch evinced for Judaism and his profound concern about the Jewish suffering during the *Shoah*. The patriarch was well aware of and acknowledged with sorrow the awful hardships imposed upon the Jews by the Christian world. As Lapide reports, the pope said, "Across the centuries our brother Abel has lain in the blood which we drew. . . . Forgive us for crucifying thee a second time . . . for we know not what we did." Lapide concluded that John's greatness as pope was manifested through his actions, which showed that, however sincere, contrition was not sufficient.[8]

Unlike the prelates who preceded him, Pope John maintained friendly although unofficial contacts with the leaders of the state of Israel. Jewish leaders were well aware of the aid he had offered numerous Jews during World War II. He also maintained a warm relationship with the leaders of the American Jewish community, with whom he had met shortly after he assumed the papal office. In 1960, an American Jewish delegation visiting Rome presented Pope John with a Torah scroll as a token of appreciation for the Jewish lives he had saved during the *Shoah*.[9]

An indication of John's sensitivity toward Jews occurred in 1959. He ordered that the phrase "unbelieving Jews," employed in the Good Friday service, be completely removed, both in its Latin and vernacular forms.[10] When a few weeks later, a group of bishops celebrating the Good Friday service in Rome, which Pope John attended, ignored his directive and recited the old text, the pope quietly halted the service and requested that it be repeated properly. The event served notice to all Catholics of his seriousness about this matter. In the following months, the new Catholic leader deleted other phrases and passages offensive to Jews from a number of other prayers.[11]

These alterations suggest that the new pope had no desire to serve as a mere caretaker of the Church of Rome. From the very beginning of his reign, he showed deep consciousness of the diverse problems that this church faced. And as early as 1959, he had concluded that the only way the church could grapple with its numerous challenges was to call an ecumenical council. Calling a council was not a usual occurrence. The last such event had taken place in 1869 and the one prior to that, the Council of Trent, in 1562. The rarity of such occurrences underlines the importance that the problems of the church held for Pope John, not the least of which was to make the church more relevant to the world and to strive for Christian unity.[12] Although John did not initially plan to establish a new relationship between the church and the Jewish people, it was precisely in that area, according to a Catholic scholar, that the Vatican scored one of its most lasting achievements.[13]

The council's genesis, according to one intimate observer, was due to the pope's original idea and its implementation by his trusted associate Augustin Cardinal Bea. Bea, the seventy-eight-year-old retired rector of the Biblical Institute of Rome, was appointed by Pope John on June 5, 1960, to the Secretariat for Promoting Christian Unity. Bea was also appointed its president, thus holding a key position for drafting and implementing council decisions.[14] The church's relationship with the Jewish people was not an issue at this point. But it would shortly become an important one. This occurred when the pope met in a private audience with the French Jewish historian Jules Isaac on June 13, 1960.[15]

◦ ◦ ◦

The problem which Jules Isaac grappled with remains one of the most disturbing of the twentieth century. How could Germany and its European collaborators, steeped in a Christian tradition, unleash the Final Solution? As one of the leading historians of his generation, Isaac employed his skills in a search of early Christian sources, looking for a clue that might explain the origins of Christian hatred of the Jewish people. The result was a series of books which both shocked and enlightened the Christian world.

Isaac was not a product of a religious home. He considered himself an agnostic, a typical characteristic of French Jews whose roots were deeply embedded in Gaul. Unlike his father, who was a professional soldier, Jules Isaac chose an academic career. His books were widely acclaimed, and his world history text was widely used in French secondary schools and colleges. In 1936, he was appointed by the French government to the highest academic post in France: inspector general of education for the entire country.[16] With the arrival of the Nazis in France, Isaac was deprived of his post. Increasingly, and for the first time in his life, the persecution of the Jews began to dominate his mind. He began to ponder the causes of antisemitism. As his studies deepened, he concluded that the roots of Jew hatred, no matter what form it eventually took, could be traced to Christian teaching. Otherwise, he asked, how could one explain the Christian apathy in the face of Jewish extermination?

The issues he dealt with became tragically personal when in 1943, while Isaac was away from home, his wife and most of his family were seized by German agents and deported to a death camp.[17] While hiding from the Nazis, Isaac continued his studies of antisemitism. Because of his tragic loss, the work became intensely meaningful, a "sacred mission." In 1947, he published *Jesus and Israel*. In this widely acclaimed work, Isaac documented the misrepresentations about Judaism which had entered into interpretations of early Christian scriptures and the distortions that had brought painful consequences to the Jewish people. When its English translation appeared in 1971, the American Catholic scholar Edward Flannery characterized it as having "revolutionary implications for Christianity," saying that it was the most potent "exposure of Christian anti-Judaism written by Christian or Jew."[18] Isaac also met at this time with groups of Jews and Catholics further to explain his findings and show how to include them in Christian education.[19]

Other influential books by Isaac followed. In 1956, Isaac's *Origins of Antisemitism* appeared. Here Isaac argued that Christianity made pagan anti-Judaism far more virulent than it had been in classical times. Isaac's writings, according to a Catholic authority on Jewish-Catholic relations, inspired the revision of religious textbooks. Such revisions, under the direction of the B'nai B'rith Anti-Defamation League and the American Jewish Committee (AJC) working with Catholic educators, were in fact undertaken during the late 1950s as a direct result of Isaac's findings. Particularly significant was Isaac's *The Teaching of Contempt*, which appeared in 1962. Yet none of these scholarly efforts fully satisfied Isaac. He sought more immediate practical results of his findings. It was this intense desire to eradicate anti-Judaism that drove Isaac to seek an audience with Pope John XXIII in June 1960.[20]

It was an open and friendly conversation which Isaac held with the pope. Isaac accused the church fathers of laying the foundations of antisemitism: the Catholic liturgy and its linguistic anti-Judaism and the church teachings throughout the ages. Isaac told the pope that "a voice from the summit could show the good path by solemnly condemning the teaching of contempt, as, in essence, anti-Christian."[21] Finally, at the conclusion of the audience, Isaac suggested that the pope appoint a committee within the planned Vatican council to study the issue of Christian antisemitism. The pope replied, "I have been thinking of that ever since you began to speak."[22]

Before Isaac departed, the pope asked him to contact Cardinal Bea, who would be requested to pursue the matter further. Isaac met with Bea on June 15, 1960. Three months later, Pope John charged Bea with the responsibility of preparing a declaration dealing with the Jewish people. According to Thomas F. Stransky, an American priest who helped draft the declaration on the Jews, neither Cardinal Bea nor Pope John anticipated the complexities which awaited the council in its efforts to produce an acceptable draft of the declaration. It was not a simple matter to please the more than twenty-four hundred bishops and hundreds of other dignitaries who gathered in Rome for the first session of the Second Vatican Council in 1962.[23]

But that the issue of Christian-Jewish relations was at all included on the agenda was in no small part due to the efforts of Jules Isaac. In 1977, a prominent American prelate noted that "on June 13, 1960, Pope John XXIII received in audience a Jewish historian named Jules Isaac. The conversation lasted only twenty-five minutes, yet it began one of the most profound renewals of Church teaching and practice in a 2000-year-long history."[24]

□   □   □

Under Cardinal Bea's direction, a committee was convened months before the opening session of the Second Vatican Council. Its charge was to prepare a draft of a "Declaration on the Jews" or, as it was to be known shortly, *Nostra Aetate,* No. 4. The committee's desire was to arrive at an acceptable draft, one that could be approved by a majority of the council fathers. It turned out to be one of the most complicated tasks experienced by the Second Vatican Council. The difficulty was its finding a draft that was theologically and politically acceptable.[25]

It was a daunting task to convince twenty-four hundred bishops to assent to a revolutionary idea, one for which they were hardly prepared. To grapple with concepts of religious freedom, Christian unity, and liturgical reform was difficult enough; but to alter deeply embedded views about Jews and Judaism was truly formidable, especially when such alterations were intertwined with Christian antisemitism, complicated by Christian-Arab hostility.[26] The final document, therefore, which was eventually approved by the Second Vatican Council on October 28, 1965, "did not," as Rabbi Daniel F. Polish recalls, "spring like Athena from the brow of the Council Fathers." There was a complex process of deliberation and even political maneuvering involved in the creation of *Nostra Aetate,* No. 4.[27]

Consequently, as is seen in any political process, the language of the final version of the declaration represented a series of compromises which enabled *Nostra Aetate,* No. 4, to be accepted by the bishops of the council. Yet, despite its weaknesses, and there were many—there was no mention of the Holocaust or the significance of the state of Israel, for example—it represented an important beginning of a genuine revolution. Even a quick reading manifested the declaration's unprecedented character. The council decided after lengthy discussion to include the "Declaration on the Jews" as the fourth section of *Nostra Aetate,* also referred to as the Declaration on the Relation of the Church to Non-Christian Religions. The church's relationship to Buddhism and Islam constitutes part of *Nostra Aetate,* although the most substantive portion of the document is relegated to the church and the Jews.

Section 4 of *Nostra Aetate,* the less than two-page part which concerns itself with the Jews, declares the following in the opening paragraph:

"She [the Catholic Church] is mindful . . . that the apostles, the pillars on which the Church stands, are of Jewish descent, as are many of the most early disciples who proclaimed the Gospel of the Christ to the world."[28] The acknowledgment was rarely concealed by the church, but neither was it usually so boldly underscored. What is more, it explained that even though the Jews did not accept the divinity of Christ at the time of his appearance, God did "not take back the gifts He bestowed on the choice He made."[29] This statement was not one that was generally part of Christian teaching. On the contrary, the popularly held view was that God had withdrawn "the choice He made" of the Jewish people as his chosen ones.

The assertion was followed by the request that Catholics and Jews engage in joint study and dialogue. The importance of this recommendation was to be amplified in the following years. The original injunction read as follows: "Since Christians and Jews have such a common spiritual heritage, this sacred Council wishes to encourage and further mutual understanding and appreciation. This can be obtained, especially, by way of Biblical and theological enquiry and through friendly discussions."[30] For Catholics and Jews to undertake joint study of biblical and theological questions was an unusual recommendation, one heretofore generally frowned upon by the Catholic Church. Neither was it a practice of which traditional Jews would ordinarily have approved.

One of the most significant and far-reaching assertions of *Nostra Aetate,* No. 4, was the church's outright rejection of the charge of deicide, which had caused Jews countless tragedies. Although the statement on the subject continued to leave some issues unresolved, it was, nevertheless, a sharp reversal of the church's position. The declaration read: "Even though the Jewish authorities and those who followed their lead pressed for the death of Christ . . . neither all Jews indiscriminately at that time, nor Jews today, can be charged with crimes committed during His Passion."[31] It was not an absolute reversal of the age-old calumny: Jewish "leaders" and their "followers" were not let off blamelessly; by church standards, however, the statement crossed traditional frontiers. Most important, it erased the ancient accusation of Jewish collective guilt for the Christian Savior's execution. This had been a horrendous charge, one that stained Christian civilization: a principle root for centuries of antisemitism.

The deicide statement was immediately followed by the reminder that the New Israel had not displaced the Old Israel in the eyes of God: "It is true that the Church is the new people of God. Yet the Jews should not be spoken of as rejected or accursed. . . . Consequently, all must take care, lest in catechizing or in preaching the Word of God, they teach anything which is not in accord with the truth of the Gospel message."[32] This admonition has done more to reform Catholic teaching than any other Vatican request. Catholics were also told that "remembering . . . her [the Catholic Church's] common heritage with the Jews and moved not by any political consideration, but solely by the religious motivation of Christian charity, she deplores all hatred, persecutions, displays of antisemitism leveled at any time or from any source against the Jews."[33]

Nostra Aetate, No. 4, represented a blueprint for a radical transformation of the Catholic relationship to the Jews. Its significance was not that it was a final word but that it initiated further study and a series of documents, statements, and interreligious activities designed to transform forever the relationship of Catholics and Jews.

◻ ◻ ◻

These events possessed no intrinsic political advantage for the church. From a political perspective, the church had little to gain by improving its relations with the Jewish people. On the contrary, the Arab world, for example, with its hundreds of thousands of Christians, not to speak of the millions of Muslims, was far from elated by the Vatican revolution. The church's efforts during the Second Vatican Council were motivated by a deep religious desire, a need to revise its direction and renew itself in relation to the Jewish people. Neither was *Nostra Aetate,* No. 4, adopted by Vatican II for the benefit of the Jewish people. It was designed as a call for religious renewal for the Catholic faithful, for all those who were motivated by a need to strengthen the church.

Since *Nostra Aetate,* No. 4, was only a beginning in offering new relations with the Jews, every effort was made in the years following 1965 to implement its statements and strengthen the church's ties of understanding with the Jewish people. Occasional meetings were held in Rome, to which American Jewish leaders were invited. In 1969, for example, the bishops of the Secretariat for Promoting Christian Unity were convened. In this instance, the bishops evaluated the progress made in Catholic-Jewish understanding since 1965. They emphasized the importance that such progress had for the renewal of the church and its need to learn more about the Jewish tradition in both biblical and postbiblical times. "It is from the Jewish tradition," they declared, "that it [the Catholic Church] draws not only its formulas, its images, its setting, but even the marrow of its concepts."[34]

To reinforce its efforts and to implement the principles expressed in

Nostra Aetate, No. 4, throughout the Catholic world, Pope Paul VI (1963–78), John's successor, appointed on October 22, 1974, the Commission for Religious Relations with the Jews, with Johannes Cardinal Willebrands, a leading member of the Curia, as its president. Shortly after the commission's creation, Willebrands announced the publication of what became one of the most important documents since *Nostra Aetate,* No. 4: "Guidelines and Suggestions for Implementing the Conciliar Declaration *Nostra Aetate* (No. 4)."[35]

This eight-page document, much longer than the 1965 declaration, filled many gaps, elaborated many points, and introduced new subjects. Less theological than pragmatic, explained Willebrands, the guidelines were designed to facilitate local churches in their efforts to reform their traditional relationships with Jews and their understanding of Judaism. Besides expressing a strong condemnation of antisemitism in any form, the guidelines urge that every effort be made on the part of Catholics to "dialogue" with Jews so that each could learn more about the other. "To tell the truth, such relations as these between Jew and Christian have scarcely ever risen above the level of monologue. From now on, real dialogue must be established," declared the document. What is more, Catholics were warned about utilizing the dialogue as a vehicle to convert Jews to Catholicism.[36] The caveat constituted a long step away from previous practices, which had embittered Jews about "dialoguing" with Roman Catholics.

Moreover, the guidelines stressed the need for Catholics to reverse the traditional teaching embedded in liturgy. On the contrary, the document urged that the new stress be placed upon "the existing links between the Christian liturgy and the Jewish." Such an exercise would underscore the continuing viability of Jewish religious practice. It would eradicate notions of displacement of the Old Israel by the New. When examining Jewish liturgical writing, the guidelines warned against the temptation to distort its meaning to the detriment of the Jewish people. Likewise, in biblical studies, sermons, and homilies, Jews were never to be pictured in an unfavorable light.[37]

The guidelines were clear in pronouncing the demise of the theology of displacement. "The history of Judaism did not end with the destruction of Jerusalem but rather went on to develop a religious tradition . . . rich in religious values," read the document.[38] In the light of the history of the Catholic Church, the affirmation of the viability of Judaism was no small matter. It corrected a long-held, distorted notion of the Jewish people and strongly encouraged the Universal Church to include the new view in its religious teaching.

▫ ▫ ▫

Daniel F. Polish put it well when he noted that the "Declaration on the Jews" was not an unprepared-for happening. Besides the complex process of deliberations and political maneuvering, "the Jewish community played an important role" in shaping the final statement that was so important to them. This occurred even though Jews or Jewish organizations were not officially invited to the sessions of Vatican II. They were granted the status of neither official observers nor even guests, a courtesy extended to other non-Catholics.[39] Still, not all Jews were unhappy at this lack of hospitality.

According to Judith Hershcopf, who analyzed the progress of the council's proceedings for the *American Jewish Yearbook,* whether Jews were invited to the council or not was not a major concern in the Jewish community. Although some Jews, such as Arthur Gilbert of the B'nai B'rith Anti-Defamation League, were disappointed to be excluded, others were altogether opposed to being invited. After all, the council was a Christian gathering, primarily interested in Christian unity and wrestling with specific Catholic problems, both theological and practical. Jewish attendance at such discussions might well be out of place. When Nahum Goldmann of the World Jewish Congress announced that Hayyim Wardi, an Israeli government official, would attend the council sessions as an unofficial observer, the Rabbinical Council of America expressed grave reservations. Arab governments also protested, arguing that Jews were seeking political involvement in a religious meeting, although they did not object to their own representation. The Wardi incident generated confusion on the part of some council members who also questioned whether Jewish representation constituted political or religious involvement. This fear, which was also seized upon by anti-Jewish elements in the council, scuttled not only the Wardi mission but also the issue of inviting unofficial Jewish observers.[40]

Nevertheless, from the very origin of the Second Vatican Council, prominent American Jews and leaders of Jewish organizations, although not official guests, established a process of regular communication with Cardinal Bea and his commission, which was responsible for fashioning a statement on the Jews. Jules Isaac, as has been seen, was the first of these individuals to establish such a practice. Spokesmen of the World Jewish Congress and of B'nai B'rith, two of the most prominent American Jewish organizations with branches throughout the world, maintained a constant communication with council leaders. They submitted to the secretariat a joint memorandum on the subject of antisemitism.

Also particularly active was the American Jewish Committee, which presented to the council leaders its findings on negative Jewish images found in Catholic religious textbooks and liturgy.[41]

Abraham Joshua Heschel, the prominent Jewish theologian and professor at the Jewish Theological Seminary of New York, was, like Jules Isaac, present at the council whenever the occasion called for it, communicating with council leaders before the entire body convened. When asked why he became involved in Vatican II, Heschel replied, "The issues at stake were profoundly theological. To refuse contact with Christian theologians, to my mind, was barbarous. There is a great expectation among Christians today that Judaism has something unique to offer." Heschel, therefore, working tirelessly "to the point of exhaustion," became involved with Vatican II.[42] During the council's preparatory stages, Heschel acted as a consultant to the American Jewish Committee and other Jewish agencies. In 1962, Heschel requested of Cardinal Bea that the council in its declaration repudiate the deicide charge against the Jews. When Cardinal Bea visited the United States in 1963, Heschel chaired a meeting between him and a group of Jewish leaders.[43]

In 1963, Heschel became concerned when he realized that efforts were being made to introduce the issue of conversion of the Jews into a revised version of the text of the "Declaration on the Jews." Heschel wrote to Bea about his concerns, strongly condemning the new version of *Nostra Aetate,* No. 4. He met with Pope Paul VI over this matter on the eve of Yom Kippur, September 14, 1964. Such a meeting at such a time stands as evidence of Heschel's deep concerns about the outcome of the inclusion of the statement.[44] Few American religious leaders were better able than Heschel to articulate Jewish concerns to Pope Paul VI. According to a Jewish observer, Heschel is credited with the changing of "thinking of . . . many of the Council Fathers and affecting the final outcome of the declaration."[45] Of all the American rabbinical scholars and writers, Abraham Joshua Heschel was the best known and most respected in the American Catholic community.

Another Jewish individual whose work influenced the council's deliberations was Joseph Lichten of the B'nai B'rith's Anti-Defamation League. Lichten also spent considerable time in Rome, distributing memos to the council fathers about Christian antisemitism in Catholic teaching. Lichten calculated results of sociological surveys which indicated that the majority of American Catholics continued to believe that all the Jews shared in the guilt of Christ's crucifixion and that nearly half believed that Jews would never be forgiven for this sin.[46] Lichten explained to American Catholics shortly before the opening of the third session of

Vatican II why a strongly worded statement on behalf of the Jews was so important. He offered these reasons:

> First, we are persuaded that anti-Semitism is partly rooted in Christian traditions.
>
> Second, we know that our sufferings are too often looked upon, even today, as God's righteous punishment for the alleged guilt of the Jewish people for the death of Christ.
>
> Third: We see our beliefs and our solidarity as a people used against us, persistently and harmfully to exclude us not only from the respect of other religious groups, but also from civil and social benefits.[47]

None of this is to suggest that Jews, uninvited, insinuated themselves into the work of the council. On the contrary, Cardinal Bea and his staff welcomed suggestions from Jewish leaders. Bea was eager to fashion a declaration which, although designed for Catholics, Jews would also be comfortable with, and he turned to Jewish organizations for help.[48] Unofficially, when needed, Jewish advice was solicited. Jewish views were sought by the secretariat from Reform, Conservative, and Orthodox authorities. There was considerable Catholic confusion about Jewish thinking on theological matters. This was not surprising, given the long history of Catholicism's misconceptions of Judaism.

In presenting their opinions about Jewish-Christian relations, Jewish organizations, such as the World Jewish Congress, B'nai B'rith, and the American Jewish Committee, had to tread cautiously. These major organizations, although created by Jews in the United States, maintained world Jewish interests and spoke for Jews internationally. Although they generally agreed on most fundamental principles, they did not agree on all matters. Tempers of the leaders, especially of those who held a more traditional religious view, became particularly fragile in 1964. For a while during the council debates of the third session, it seemed that the declaration would be so altered that it might be entirely emasculated. A number of Jewish groups talked of abandoning all efforts to deal with the council; other Jewish leaders blamed each other for not exerting enough effort on behalf of Jewish interests. Officers of the Central Conference of American Rabbis and the Rabbinical Council of America urged American Jews to abandon their work on behalf of the declaration, arguing that the issue was a Christian problem, not a Jewish one. Orthodox rabbis were especially incensed about what they saw as undignified behavior by secular and lay Jewish groups on behalf of a declaration. Not all Jews agreed with the religious objectives of the council. Orthodox rabbis were cautious and skeptical about the ultimate purpose of a

Catholic declaration. Jewish views were varied, and many agreed-upon suggestions offered to the council fathers had to be cast in a fashion acceptable to multiple Jewish opinions.[49] Despite these diverse sentiments and occasional outbursts, however, the prevailing view in the American Jewish community was that a strong declaration was necessary.[50]

Few organizations recognized more keenly the revolutionary potential in the work of Vatican II in improving Jewish-Catholic relations than did the American Jewish Committee. It worked diligently throughout the years of the Vatican council to advance that objective. AJC representatives had met with Christian leaders in previous years, sensing that the time was ripe for the germination of new views toward Jews. They recognized too that a great pope had assumed the bishopric of Rome at this propitious time. They appreciated his willingness to promulgate a thorough examination of the church's traditional views.[51]

As early as the end of the Second World War, the AJC had collaborated with Catholic Church officials to improve Christian views of Jews and Judaism. In its Paris office, the AJC staff had worked closely with Jules Isaac in efforts to combat Christian antisemitism. The staff drafted a memorandum of recommendations to Pope John XXIII. Even before the Second Vatican Council convened, the AJC forwarded inquiries to church officials about the doctrinal bases for the charge of deicide, and it was assured that there was no doctrinal basis for "collective guilt." Shortly after the war, the AJC urged Pius XII to employ his influence in halting Polish pogroms against returning Jews, survivors of the *Shoah*. Five years later, the AJC received the pope's assurance that he would urge nations to open their doors to Jewish survivors of Nazism.

The AJC's efforts to examine Catholic and Protestant instructional materials and texts which revealed anti-Jewish bias were long standing and viewed by the church as authoritative. Many of these studies were conducted by leading Catholic and Protestant scholars.[52] Even before Vatican II convened, the AJC staff had acted as consultants for Catholic preparation of religious school textbooks. The examination included at least one major study of the treatment of Christians in Jewish teaching material, undertaken by Dropsie College for Hebrew and Cognate Learning in Philadelphia.[53]

These are but a handful of examples which suggest the vast experience the AJC brought with it to Vatican II. Not surprisingly, during the preparatory phase of the Vatican council, the AJC was requested by the church authorities to submit a well-researched statement, documenting the existence of anti-Judaism in Catholic teaching and liturgical writings. The AJC was also asked to make suggestions to improve Jewish-Catholic relations.[54] During the council's sessions, the AJC officials held a number of discussions with Cardinal Bea. The viewpoints aired at these meetings regarding anti-Judaism in Catholic teaching and liturgy were extremely valuable for the preparation of the final statement. The AJC was the only American Jewish organization invited to address a committee of Vatican II.[55]

The final draft of *Nostra Aetate,* No. 4, was approved by the council by a majority of 2,221 in favor to 188 opposed. What passed—a revised and somewhat weakened version, more pleasing to conservative Catholics and Arab bishops and Muslims than to Jews—was not the version that the AJC and other Jewish organizations would have liked to see adopted. An earlier draft, which had absolved all Jews, *including* their leaders, from the crime of deicide and which the AJC and other Jewish groups would have preferred, was rejected. The rejection was a concession to conservative Catholic theologians as well as to archbishops and Muslims, who saw the former draft as a political concession to Israel. Neither was the term "deicide" maintained in the final draft, although it was in the earlier version and eliminated for the same reasons of compromise, according to Cardinal Bea.[56]

There was evidence of antisemitism in the Second Vatican Council. It represented a small number of bigots who objected to any favorable declaration about Jews. They saw such a move as a Jewish attempt to weaken the church. Neither were Arab prelates willing to support a favorable statement. They were subjected to enormous pressure from Arab governments. It took great courage to resist such pressure, although a few did. In any case, these individuals represented a small minority of bishops who hovered on the fringes of the council. The most significant opposition to a strongly worded statement on the Jews came from the small group of conservative Catholics—not all antisemites—who objected to any form of change, who looked skeptically on John XXIII's efforts to lead the church out of the thirteenth century. But they, too, failed to prevail.

Despite its mild disappointment, the AJC saw the adoption of the declaration as a singular achievement, an opening of a door to a new relationship between Catholics and Jews. Arthur Gilbert, a close observer of Vatican II, noted in 1968 that "however inadequate, theologically, the statements may have seemed from a Jewish perspective, there is no gainsaying their profound contribution to a more open atmosphere in the relations between Jews and Christians."[57] Even before the guidelines were issued in 1974, Rabbi Gilbert and other Jewish leaders recognized the great potential embedded in *Nostra Aetate,* No. 4.

◻ ◻ ◻

American Jews were not alone in their interest in achieving a strong declaration. Catholic editors and prominent American prelates also fought strenuously to attain that goal. While showing annoyance at Jewish defenders of the Israeli procedures against Adolf Eichmann, the editors of *America,* for example, voiced concern in 1964 about efforts of some council fathers to deprive the statement of "those qualities of clarity and prophetic vision" endorsed by Pope John XXIII. They noted that the Boston *Pilot* (which, in the recent past, had indicated little sympathy for Jewish difficulties) had warned the council against producing a revised and "watered-down" statement.[58]

Even before the final declaration was adopted, the editors of *America* urged the removal of antisemitic suggestions from Catholic textbooks. Young, impressionable minds, they wrote, are easily affected by messages of hate. They hoped, therefore, that the council's final statement on the Jews would offer "authoritative and constructive guidance," so that antisemitic teachings, still present in Catholic texts, would be eradicated. American Jesuits were not happy with all the Jewish demands. They recognized that theological differences would remain. But some Jews, complained *America,* would accept nothing less than the "rewriting of the New Testament," and the journal foresaw that the Passion story would continue to divide the two faith communities. "By the same token, the Vatican Council cannot legitimately be asked to betray its own theology," the editors of *America* declared. But such religious divisions, they believed, nevertheless should not stand in the way of a renewed relationship of Catholics with the Jews.[59]

To suggest that *Nostra Aetate,* No. 4, when it was approved in October 1965, offered "absolution" to the Jews for the crime of deicide was a complete distortion and misrepresentation of the declaration, said an *America* editorial: "Rather, it is a document addressed to Catholics, exhorting them to root out any misconceptions about Jewish guilt for Christ's death—false views about Jews that cause them to undergo discrimination and suffering."[60]

Such sentiments were also voiced by the editors of *Catholic World.* John B. Sheerin, its editor, though pleased with the final passage of *Nostra Aetate,* No. 4, was struck by the "vicious" antisemitic voices which came from various parts of Europe, directed at the council's efforts to reverse Christian beliefs and attitudes. One hateful missive dispatched to each of the bishops that Sheerin singled out declared that *Nostra Aetate,* No. 4, was an "abominable condemnation of Jesus." Sheerin declared himself happy that "all that dirty water has gone over the dam and the Catholic mood is one of relief and satisfaction," while "the Church has made an act of contrition for immemorial injustice to the Jews." Sheerin designated at least a few of the 250 bishops who voted against the final statement as probably "antisemites."[61] This editorial utterance represented a striking revision of attitudes expressed by Catholic editors even a short time earlier. The transformation, inspired by the meetings of the Second Vatican Council, did not escape the attention of *Catholic World* when it stated that it "is no easy thing for a great Church to make an act of contrition for its sins of the past. But it is not enough to atone for the past." The church must also alter its future behavior toward the Jewish people. Catholics were advised to familiarize themselves with the traditional and religious thought of the Jews. *Catholic World* editors hoped, too, that the Jews, for their part, would "not remain aloof" from their Catholic neighbors: "They must help us to see Judaism from the inside. . . . The age of the sword, the pogrom, the ghetto has gone forever—at least that is our sincerest hope."[62]

The Jewish organizational desire for a declaration shorn of all hints of Jewish conversion while laying bare the dangerous implications of deicide received some of its strongest support both outside the council and within it from American Catholic Church leaders. More than many non-American council participants, American prelates brought with them a tradition of democratic values, not always appreciated or understood by their foreign coreligionists. American church leaders were eager to inject ideas of religious freedom and American concepts of the separation of church and state—concepts which, they argued, were not incompatible with Catholic doctrines in discussions of church renewal. The well-known Jesuit scholar and theologian John Courtney Murray, for example, was the principle author of the "Declaration on Religious Freedom," which was adopted by the council on December 7, 1965.[63]

Although Francis Cardinal Spellman of New York was reprimanded by the church during the 1950s for his views on reform, he nevertheless was instrumental in bringing Murray into the council as an advisor on questions of religious liberty, religious freedom, and church and state.[64] In 1964, Cardinal Spellman also urged the council fathers to produce an unequivocal declaration on the Jews. He heard that during the spring and summer of 1964, a small group of council members wanted to weaken the control that Bea had over the secretariat. Reports also circulated that a revised and weaker version of the declaration was being prepared, one which advocated the hope that the Jews be converted to Christianity.[65] American bishops as well as American Jews turned for support to

Spellman, the dean of the American hierarchy and archbishop of New York. On April 30, 1964, Spellman assured a Jewish gathering that it was imperative for the Universal Church to reverse its long-held positions on the Jews. It was an impressive address from a leading prelate, widely reported and discussed, including in Rome.[66]

Like Cardinal Spellman, most American bishops encouraged the adoption of a strong declaration. Concerned about a weakened statement, 170 of the 246 American bishops met in Rome in September 1964 and agreed that they would press for a stronger "Declaration on the Jews."[67] During the Second Vatican Council debates, Joseph Cardinal Ritter of St. Louis argued that the declaration should "speak more fully and explicitly" about "the religious patrimony which the Jewish people and the Christian people . . . share." He warned that the statement must make clear to Christians that they were never to regard the Jews as a "rejected" or "cursed" people, "or in any way as deiciders." Auxiliary Bishop Stephen Leven of San Antonio told the delegates not to eliminate the word "deicide" from the text of the 1965 version. The text should make it clear that Jews must never be called a "deicide people." For centuries, the San Antonio bishop explained to the council, Christians had hurled the term "deicide" at the Jews. The term had often been used as a pretext for countless crimes against them. "We must tear this word out of the Christian vocabulary, so that it will never again be used against the Jews."[68]

Among the most persuasive voices was that of Richard Cardinal Cushing of Boston, who, on September 24, 1964, tried to counteract the growing efforts to dampen the intended spirit of the declaration. He urged the council to "make our statement about the Jews more positive, less timid, more charitable. . . . We must deny that the Jews are guilty of the death of our Savior. . . . All of us have seen the fruit of this kind of reasoning. In this august assembly, in this solemn moment, we must cry out."[69] Albert Cardinal Meyer of Chicago reflected similar sentiments four days later, when he told the council "that justice demands that we pay explicit attention to the enormous impact of the wrongs done through the centuries to the Jews." He argued that the charges of deicide should "be removed from all Jews, then and now. . . . The world waits and expects an absolute and irrefutable sign of our good faith in this matter of justice."[70]

Archbishop Patrick O'Boyle addressed the council on September 20, 1964. He advised the council to act with care, precision, and wisdom when making statements about Jews. He further advised the council fathers to examine the history of the Jews before making declarations about them. Neither should a statement be made which could not be clearly understood by the Jews and which was not in harmony with the aspirations of the "Jewish mind." Great care must be taken not to leave the impression that the declaration's motive was to seek the conversion of the Jews. Such an impression would defeat the true motive of the council's endeavor.[71]

A few days later, Joseph Cardinal Ritter declared that he eagerly await-ed the declaration, a necessity "to repair an injustice of the centuries." In church documents and liturgy, Jews had been maligned by the Cath-olic Church, whose adherents erroneously believed that God had aban-doned the Jews. "The opportunity now presents itself today that we, gathered in an ecumenical Council, reject and repair such errors and injustices," he said.[72] Cardinal Ritter asked for an improved statement; he was not pleased with the one being discussed. He thought that it did not go far enough in expressing the appropriate sentiments. The debt owed by the church to the Jews should be more emphatically proclaimed, rather than expressed with the hesitancy evident in the current schema. A more forceful pronouncement of the church's errors committed against the Jews should also be made, he declared.[73]

Although it is difficult to determine precisely the degree of influence which America's prelates wielded during the final debates over the state-ment on the Jews, it was probably large in proportion to their numbers. At any rate, one is left to wonder what the character of *Nostra Aetate*, No. 4, would have been without American intervention. The Americans' impact was acknowledged by Monsignor George G. Higgins, a Vatican II participant and director of the social action department of the National Catholic Welfare Conference. Higgins observed that American bishops spoke more frequently, more forcefully, and more persuasively than oth-ers in favor of a stronger draft regarding Jewish issues: "Indeed, I think it could be said that it was the vigorous insistence of the American spokesmen (and of others but largely of the Americans), which made it absolutely certain that the second draft (1964) would have to be revised: that the deicide issue would have to be faced and the conversion issue would have to be clarified if not completely eliminated." In this regard, Higgins made special note of the Cardinals Meyer, Ritter, Cushing, and Archbishop O'Boyle, whose vigorous and persuasive addresses helped lead the Council to favor a revision of the draft statement on the Jews.[74]

Following the vote, Bishop Francis P. Leipzig of Baker, Oregon, chair-man of the Sub-Commission on Catholic-Jewish Relations of the United States Bishops' Ecumenical Commission, remarked at a news conference, "I am sure it [*Nostra Aetate*, No. 4] will usher in a new era of friend-

ship and cooperation with our Jewish brethren for the benefit of all men."
He acknowledged that there were imperfections in *Nostra Aetate,* No.
4, but they carried "less weight than its overall spirit."[75] *Commonweal*
believed that the declaration would be of "immeasurable help in tear-
ing the roots of antisemitism out of Christian tradition." A number of
American prelates explained that the declaration must be viewed as a
beginning, not as an end. They wished to see the statement transformed
from a "lifeless piece of paper into a living document which . . . can lit-
erally change the face of the earth." Similar sentiments were echoed by
America's diocesan press, where, typically, according to Judith Hershcopf, Catholics were urged to heed the council's comments on the Jews
and to "implement them."[76]

□ □ □

American bishops wasted little time in transferring the words of *Nostra
Aetate,* No. 4, into a meaningful reality. They considered the council
declaration unquestionably authoritative for American Catholics. "Let
us consider the teaching authority of the Church," they declared in 1967.
"Vatican II reminds us of the importance of that authority."[77] This is not
to suggest that all American bishops were overjoyed about the "Declaration on the Jews." Bishop James A. McNulty of Paterson, New Jersey, for example, referring to the work of the council, noted on one occasion: "The Bark of Peter has been picking up barnacles from the
backwash of activities by 'progressive Catholics.' Efforts to remove them
will be made in the drydock of the Council." Bishop Russell R. McVin-
ney of Providence, Rhode Island, questioned the necessity of introducing any changes at all in Catholic teaching that had stood the test of two
thousand years.[78] Perhaps American conservative bishops did not share
the extreme sentiment of some of their European colleagues, of whom
one was overheard to remark at John XXIII's funeral, "It will take for-
ty years to repair the damage he has done."[79] Among a small segment
of American conservative bishops, there was little sympathy for the
unfolding theological rebellion.

But they represented a relatively small minority. Most American prelates were eager to implement the suggestions of *Nostra Aetate,* No. 4.
In March 1967, seven years before the Vatican's "Guidelines and Suggestions" would be announced by Cardinal Willebrands, the United
States National Conference of Catholic Bishops issued its own "Guidelines for Catholic-Jewish Relations." The statement requested that
American Catholics reappraise their attitudes toward Jews and foster a

"fraternal encounter" with them to acknowledge the conflicts and tensions which had kept them apart and to endeavor to eliminate these conflicts. They further urged Catholics to develop a knowledge of Judaism through study and dialogue with Jews.[80]

To strengthen the Catholic Church's relationship with Jews, American bishops established a subcommittee of their interreligious affairs committee, a subcommittee for Catholic-Jewish relations, whose purpose would be to "encourage and assist the various dioceses of the country in their efforts to put into action at all levels of the Church the Council's directions."[81] The bishops noted that since the largest Jewish community in the world resides in the United States, Catholics have faced a particularly important responsibility to foster an improved relationship with the Jewish people. The bishops recommended that a commission be appointed in each diocese to strive toward that end; that Catholics arrange meetings with Jews designed to create improved understanding and mutual respect; and that such dialogues be conducted with the greatest sensitivity and care for the feelings of Jews. They described the concept of "dialogue" as follows: "A form of group conversation in which competent participants discuss assigned topics or themes in openness, candor, and friendship. Those not well versed in inter-religious affairs run the risk of unwittingly offending by inaccurate portrayal of each other's doctrine or way of life."[82]

The bishops also requested that each diocese examine its teaching material and expunge from it all statements which in any way distorted Judaism and its practices or its place in "salvation-history." They also urged that "cooperation be encouraged in the field of social action designed to promote public welfare and morality."[83] Finally, the American bishops, in keeping with their desire to advance the spirit of *Nostra Aetate*, No. 4, declared that educators and scholars must continue to examine those specific issues which had created distortions about Judaism and divided the two faiths, and that they should investigate the religious heritage shared by Catholics and Jews. The former would include the legacy of antisemitism and the Crucifixion story, as well as the negative view of the Pharisees and Christianity's rejection of Israel's continuing viability and election.[84] Clearly, the bishops wasted little time following Vatican II in laying the basis for a new theological foundation for the American Catholic Church. It constituted an attempt to persuade American Catholics to turn away from the long tradition of hostility which pervaded popular Catholic theology. As one writer declared, the American bishops "not only intend to fulfill the Council's mandate, but also in sensitivity to Jewish concerns they have moved far beyond it."[85]

□ □ □

In 1969, the Archdiocese of New York City was the first in the United States to comply with the bishops' request. It issued its own "Guidelines for the Advancement of Catholic-Jewish Relations in the Archdiocese of New York." Recognizing the significance of the large Jewish population in its archdiocese—2.5 million—the bishops acknowledged a "special responsibility and opportunity to engage in a program of knowledge, respect, and affection with our Jewish brothers."[86] The New York guidelines recommended the formation of diocesan committees of priests, rabbis, laymen, and laywomen to work toward the improvement of mutual understanding between the faiths. Here, too, emphasis was placed on appropriately planned sessions of dialogue in the form of "group conversation." The document urged an increasing encounter between religious leaders as well as religious organizations. With some variations, the New York guidelines reaffirmed the principles and procedures recommended by the National Conference of Catholic Bishops.[87]

In 1971, the Archdiocese of Cincinnati, the home of a large, midwestern Jewish community and the academic center of Reform Judaism, the Hebrew Union College, particularly sensitive about its relationship with its Jewish neighbors, published its own "guidelines." It was one of the first of official American Catholic statements that underscored the significance of the *Shoah* and the emergence of the state of Israel in shaping interreligious conversation. "The Nazi holocaust and the establishment of the State of Israel force us to look with compassion and candor on the magnitude of these two events," read the document.[88] It also challenged its Catholic population "to examine two thousand years of vilification and persecution which have laid the burden of proving good faith on the Church's shoulders."[89]

Such American statements suggest the seriousness with which America's prelates viewed the importance of *Nostra Aetate*, No. 4. These American statements preceded the publication and anticipated many of the themes articulated in the Vatican "Guidelines and Suggestions for Implementing *Nostra Aetate*," issued over Johannes Cardinal Willebrands's signature in 1974. The publication further inspired and energized an additional flurry of activity in the United States. Thus, in November 1975, the United States National Conference of Catholic Bishops issued a revised and larger statement on Catholic-Jewish relations. America's bishops had lost none of their enthusiasm about implementing the 1965 doctrines and teachings, but they wrote with a more mature perspective, shaped by ten years of hindsight.[90] The statement recognized that "much of the alienation between Christian and Jew found its origins in a certain anti-Judaic theology which over the centuries has led not only to social friction with Jews but often to their oppression." Like other American Catholic leaders, the bishops continued to look at *Nostra Aetate*, No. 4, as an indicator and guide for further work towards the improvement of Jewish-Catholic relations.[91]

Here also, the significance of the religious link of the Jewish people with the land of Israel, omitted in *Nostra Aetate*, No. 4, as well as in the Vatican "Guidelines and Suggestions" of 1974, was underscored as an issue that Catholics must better understand.[92] Meaningful dialogue between Christians and Jews was destined for failure without an appreciation of the Jewish longing throughout their history, expressed in their worship and national aspirations, for the land of Zion.[93] It was an acknowledgment which took a long time arriving, and its arrival created a new threshold reached by the new relationship.

The American bishops' statement inspired a host of additional "Guidelines" which were issued by various American archdioceses. One of the first of such statements came from Texas, entitled "Guidelines of Archdiocese Galveston-Houston, 1975." It reflected many of the thoughts expressed by American bishops, but in some respects went even beyond them. It was one of the most thorough and well-crafted statements of contemporary American archdioceses. After reviewing the intensity of antisemitism throughout the world, it declared, "Catholics should be educated to develop a sharp sensitivity to remarks, policies, and practices which are anti-Semitic." These guidelines also but with greater elaboration recalled the horrors of the Holocaust, following that with a supportive comment about the state of Israel. The document made this affirmation despite the large number of Arab people who live in the Galveston-Houston area. It read in part: "While we have in our own diocesan family many Catholics of Arab descent, we should also become very sensitive to the religious and historic Jewish longing for a nation and a land of their own, a longing reinforced by the tragedy of the Holocaust. We recognize the right of the State of Israel to exist along with other nations of the Middle East."[94] It was a bold statement in the light of both the Vatican's and American bishops' timidity in dealing with the politically sensitive subject of Jewish sovereignty.

In a forthright fashion, the Galveston-Houston guidelines warned the faithful against the temptation of negatively juxtaposing the "Old" and "New" Testaments: "The Old Testament and the Jewish tradition founded upon it must not be set against the New Testament in such a way that the former seems to constitute a religion of only justice, fear, and legalism with no appeal to the love of God and neighbor."[95] Here, too, was a correction of an idea long embedded in the Christian theology of contempt. Even more significant was the caveat that "Catholics should all avoid all language or impressions which would imply that we hold all the Jewish people collectively, whether past or present, responsible for the death of Jesus."[96] It was a warning frequently reaffirmed, and for good reason, in American Catholic guidelines. A tone of contrition was heard in the Galveston-Houston document where the authors state: "We ask forgiveness of our Jewish brothers and sisters if in the past or present we have consciously or unconsciously contributed to anti-Semitism in the world by attributing to them the guilt for the crucifixion of Jesus."[97]

In the following years, potent statements were also issued by the dioceses of Detroit, Cleveland, Trenton, and elsewhere. Each of these statements established "Guidelines" of a renewed relationship between Catholics and Jews in their respective dioceses. While reasserting the spirit of other previously produced statements, each added a unique element more fitting to its own community.[98] The Diocese of Cleveland urged its parishioners to learn about the horrors of the Holocaust before conversing with Jews. The "Guidelines" of the Archdiocese of Detroit instructed Catholics to acquire knowledge about the basic religious traditions of Judaism and explained that the ingathering of the Jews into Israel as well as their former dispersion should be viewed as historical rather than theological events. Every attempt should be made to understand these matters from a Jewish perspective. One must remember, however, as Michael B. McGarry reminds his readers, that these statements represented a Christian understanding of Jewish issues. They were not fashioned through a dialogue with Jews.[99]

Together, all of these guidelines described a genuine desire on the part of American Catholic leadership to follow the spirit evinced by *Nostra Aetate*, No. 4, and to implement its suggestions. One could say that the church's bishops were leading a rebellion against the theology of contempt, which for centuries had poisoned its relationship with the Jews. As Rabbi A. James Rudin, a leading activist in interreligious affairs, expressed it: "Even though we will continue to hold different theological beliefs, and though we may differ on certain contemporary issues and questions, *Nostra Aetate* has freed Catholics and Jews from the tight chains of the past. We can now move together to higher grounds. This generation has the rare opportunity to chart the course of Christian-Jewish relations for the next century, and beyond."[100]

8

The Age of Dialogue, 1965–2000

An old term "dialogue" took on a new meaning as it resurfaced following the Second Vatican Council in 1965. It stood for serious religious
conversation between faiths, or, more precisely, between Catholics and
Jews. Most important, such a dialogue was designed not to win arguments but to sharpen participants' insight into each other's beliefs, to
enhance mutual wisdom about each other's religious behavior. At least,
this was the ennobling directive that Catholic Church leaders carried
away from *Nostra Aetate*, No. 4.

This is not to suggest that serious religious conversations between
Christians and Jews had not occurred before Vatican II. Indeed, with the
founding of the National Council (later, "Conference") of Christians and
Jews (NCCJ) during the 1920s, it became increasingly common for such
conversations to take place. Various programs were launched at this time
to improve the relationships between Catholics and Jews. Emphasis was
laid on the common ethical message found in the teachings of Catholics
and Jews despite their profound differences.[1]

One of the NCCJ's most innovative programs was inaugurated in 1935
when 685 prominent Americans met at Williams College for a seminar
billed as "An American Adventure in Promoting, Understanding, and
Community Cooperation." In the following years, other seminars took
place. Such interfaith gatherings sponsored by the NCCJ were, according to David Hyatt, former president of the organization, "groundbreak-
ing" in their efforts to eliminate interreligious prejudice and enhance
religious cooperation.[2] Despite all this, we know from the records of the
time that these efforts to abolish tensions between Christians and Jews

were not very effective, since the theological foundations of antisemitism remained undisturbed.

On the eve of the Second Vatican Council in December 1962, the Union of American Hebrew Congregations (UAHC) and the Central Conference of American Rabbis (CCAR), groups representing American Liberal Judaism, created the Commission on Interfaith Activities to dialogue and create understanding between Jews and Christians. At this time, the UAHC was the only Jewish organization which maintained a full-time department of interreligious affairs; it was under the direction of Rabbi Balfour Brickner. By 1970, it provided a reliable contact for American Jews in an ongoing dialogue with the Holy See.[3] In subsequent years, under Brickner's successor, Annette Daum, the Department of Inter-religious Affairs maintained close contact with the National Conference of American Bishops. Leaders of the UAHC met with Pope John Paul II in Rome on a number of occasions. In 1990, Alexander Schindler, head of the Reform movement, asked the pope to have *Nostra Aetate* translated into the vernacular throughout the world. Eugene J. Fisher of the National Conference of Catholic Bishops' Secretariat for Ecumenical and Inter-religious Affairs remarked that "the impact of the UAHC has been profound and, indeed, essential for the advances that have been made in Catholic-Jewish relations since the Second Vatican Council."[4] Efforts on the part of the NCCJ to convene well-structured conversations between Catholics and Jews did not achieve success until January 1965. As a result of the heated debates over the "Declaration on the Jews" during the third of the four sessions of the Second Vatican Council, which were riddled with antisemitic comments, a group of American Catholic leaders and theologians organized, according to a Jewish participant, "the first formal theological conversations with Jewish scholars."[5]

Arthur Gilbert, a Reform rabbi and participant in this colloquy, notes that much of the effort to convene the conference was that of the American Benedictine Order. Gilbert writes about their achievement as follows: "This was to be a historic theological encounter on the relations of American Jews and Catholics. Representatives from each group were invited to discuss together basic issues of religion in a spirit of mutual esteem, eschewing any polemic intent to demonstrate error in the other's most cherished faith commitment."[6]

Twenty-six scholars, historians, theologians, and community leaders met at the end of January 1965 at St. Vincent's Archabbey in Latrobe, Pennsylvania, for one week. As one Benedictine priest put it, the experience was "an icebreaker which plowed into an indistinct frozen mass and at last upturned and set free huge pieces of material which later can be charted and explored."[7] Both Catholic and Jewish participants in the historic meeting realized at its conclusion how little each of the two religious groups knew about the other. What is more, in the process each of the participants learned more about his own faith. They each left with a sharpened sense of the self. As Gilbert concludes, even before the promulgation of *Nostra Aetate,* "Vatican Council II seemed already to have worked its magic. Rarely had Jews and Catholics been able to discuss matters of faith together in such an atmosphere of acceptance and mutual respect."[8]

Moreover, of primary significance were the enormous increases of dialogue between Catholics and Jews that were prompted by the conference of January 1965 and *Nostra Aetate.* Such experiences inspired in the church a desire to pursue further such conversation with Jews and to learn more about their faith and religious practices. American Catholics generally found Jewish leaders of all groups willing to cooperate. In 1966, a number of American Jesuit seminarians met with Jews at Woodstock College in Maryland. There they listened to such rabbis as Jacob B. Agus of Baltimore, a philosopher; Monford Harris of Chicago; and Marc H. Tanenbaum, a spokesman for the AJC. Tanenbaum talked about theological differences between the two faiths, the difficulty of bridging them, and the necessity of dialogue.[9]

Indeed, in the following years, Jewish organizations, such as the B'nai B'rith Anti-Defamation League and the AJC, initiated dialogues on a variety of topics, including those of social interest, such as the issues of church-state, antisemitism, education, and religious teaching material. Recognizing these developments, Richard Cardinal Cushing of Boston stated to a Catholic gathering "that the Jewish-Christian dialogue was ecumenism's most 'dramatic gain.'"[10]

Not all dialogues between Catholics and Jews were characterized by conversations between learned scholars and theologians. Throughout the decades following the Second Vatican Council, such activities included groups of intelligent laypersons who met to examine each other's views on a variety of religious and social matters, for example, a state of Israel, the *Shoah,* liturgy, education, public support for religious schools, and abortion. Such dialogues occurred in churches and synagogues throughout the United States.[11]

The multiplicity of such meetings can be seen in the pages of the *Journal of Ecumenical Studies,* a journal which began publication shortly after the Second Vatican Council as a scholarly response to the recommendations of *Nostra Aetate.* It customarily listed many of the interfaith encounters occurring throughout the United States and the rest of the world. The numbers of such meetings are staggering.[12]

The interest in dialogue continued unabated throughout the remaining years of the twentieth century. Catholic and Jewish theologians sought every opportunity to exchange religious ideas. The *Journal of Ecumenical Studies* frequently opened its pages to such conversations. One 1997 issue, for example, featured a symposium in honor of Marc H. Tanenbaum, one of the leading Jewish activists in the dialogue movement, who had died in 1992. Entitled "Inter-religious Dialogue: Stretching the Boundaries," it gathered in its pages a cross section of Christians and Jews eager to scale further the uncharted heights of dialogue.[13] This avid interest on the part of some Catholic and Jewish scholars in exchanging ideas about infrequently discussed theological subjects can also be seen with the establishment in 1997 of the Center for Christian-Jewish Understanding in Fairfield, Connecticut. Strongly supported by Reform Rabbi Jack Bemporad and William Cardinal Keeler of Baltimore, the new center was designed to explore Christian and Jewish views on a variety of theological themes which the founders saw as yet unresolved.[14]

◻ ◻ ◻

Dialogues on religious matters between Catholics and Jews, occurring in either oral or written fashion, were necessary in order to advance the revolution launched by *Nostra Aetate*. Religious leaders soon learned that the success of such engagement was dependent upon certain rules of comportment on the part of the participants. In general, a dialogue was expected to be free of contentiousness, hidden agendas, or displays of triumphalism.[15] To see this, one need only examine a pre–Vatican II issue of *The Bridge*. Published with erudite articles claiming to be designed to conduct a "dialogue" with the Jews, the journal stood as an example of how difficult it was to abide by such rules of engagement.[16] A few years following the Second Vatican Council, Edward H. Flannery, formerly on the editorial board of *The Bridge,* now philosophically transformed, had become executive secretary of the Secretariat for Catholic-Jewish Relations of the National Conference of Catholic Bishops and one of the leading proponents of dialogue with Jews.[17] Flannery worked closely with Marc H. Tanenbaum in shaping a meaningful structure for Catholic-Jewish dialogue. Throughout his long career as a member of the secretariat, Flannery addressed hundreds of synagogue groups on the subject of Jewish-Christian relations. He carried away from these conversations with Jews a deeper knowledge and a heightened sensitivity about their views and anxieties about the new relationship. It was knowledge, he recalled in later years, that could not be learned "from books."[18]

Flannery was pleased with the enthusiasm that dialogue engendered among a select group of Catholics and Jews, but he was disappointed that the emphasis of this experience was limited to the goal of "understanding" each other. Dialogue, complained Flannery, emphasized too strongly the "intellectual." "Should not the ultimate and pressing goal of our efforts," asked Flannery, "be not just the mutual understanding of Judaism and Christianity, but actual reconciliation of the Christian and Jewish people?"[19] Flannery was concerned that an intellectual elite of both faiths might dominate the dialogue.

Moreover, Flannery's experience convinced him that both Jews and Catholics approached the dialogue prepared to discuss with each other different subject matters. While Catholics leaned toward the theological, Jews were drawn more to issues of intergroup relations and historical subjects. In dialoguing with Jews, Flannery said, Catholics must realize that high on the list of Jewish preferences for discussion were the subjects of antisemitism, the Holocaust, and the state of Israel. Such themes should not displace theological and biblical issues, whose importance would remain central as underscored by *Nostra Aetate*, No. 4.[20] Flannery suggested to Catholics that if their desire was to achieve reconciliation, it would be appropriate for them to adopt the Jewish agenda: "As Christians we approach our brothers and sisters in dialogue burdened with a heavy historical debt. Jews know better than Christians what the damages are. . . . What is the Jewish agenda? It has mostly to do with history and human relations." Flannery went on with his instructions to Catholics. He wrote that Jewish interests

> center on three major concerns: Antisemitism, the Holocaust, and the State of Israel. For Jews these are life-and-death issues. The important point here is that they are the issues upon which a full, mutual Jewish-Christian understanding and reconciliation largely depend. They are issues, moreover, that should trouble the Christian conscience, yet it is in them that we often find indifference, misunderstandings, and doubts among the Christian populace. To make them a Christian concern, then, is not a matter of going the "second mile" or *noblesse oblige* but of simple justice.[21]

All this means is that for Catholics to converse with Jews on a meaningful level, Flannery insisted that they come to grips with the Jewish historical past. For Flannery reminded his listeners that Jews best recall the page which Christians have torn from their history books. And since Jews remain unaware of the Christian ignorance of the Jewish past, they are all the more stunned at Christianity's indifference toward them. Reconciliation through dialogue cannot take place as long as Christian ignorance of the Jewish past remains intact, he suggested.[22] Flannery's remarks underscored the long road he had traveled since the days of his association with *The Bridge*.

Eugene J. Fisher, scholar and leading supporter of dialogue, added his own insights on the subject. A successful dialogue must be approached with honesty, he declared, with no ulterior motives. Its setting must assume the very opposite of the threatening ambience of a "medieval disputation." Catholics, Fisher advised, must strive to know Jews as they understand themselves. Fisher explained: "The rubric of respect for the validity, on its own terms, of the religious heritage of the other tradition is a basic characteristic of dialogue, properly so called. It enables the partners to enter into a relationship free of the bitterness from the past and to move toward a cooperative future in such areas as education, social action and recitation of the religious contribution of the other."[23]

Fisher cautioned Catholics to listen carefully to the words uttered during dialogue. Used carelessly by Christians, words might mean different things to their Jewish partners. He offered the term "Messiah" as a prime example of such a word. Likewise, terms which are acceptable to Christians, such as "B.C." and "A.D." or "Old Testament" and "New Testament," possess different connotations, usually negative ones, for Jews.[24]

Most significant, Fisher noted, the church needs the dialogue to better understand itself. It needs to dialogue, not with the biblical Jews, but with the postbiblical Jews whom for centuries it has ignored. Fisher's emphasis upon the importance of postbiblical Jewish history in Catholic-Jewish dialogue stresses the church's acknowledgment of the continuing viability of Judaism. It constitutes a clear rejection of the theology of displacement, a key plank in the foundation of the theology of contempt. For Fisher and other Catholic proponents of dialogue, the encounter is a primary tool for furthering the unfolding revolution. As Fisher wrote, "It can be safely said that to join in the process of dialogue is to join one of the most exciting and perhaps far reaching experiments ever in the history of humanity. No two religious communities have had a more tragic history than ours. No two have a more unique historical or present set of spiritual links. To the extent that we, each in our own ways, believe in the validity of our own traditions, to that extent we must each grapple with ways of relating to the validity of the other."[25]

□ □ □

The American Jewish view of how to conduct a dialogue did not vary appreciably from that of American Catholics, although it did emphasize different issues. Following the conclusion of the Second Vatican Council, the AJC advised Jews interested in participating in dialogue to avoid debating with their partners but to accept them in "the fullness of their differences."[26] To the AJC, a major purpose of dialogue was to enable its participants to dispel ignorance about each other's religious beliefs, institutions, and practices. Jews, the AJC declared, were as ill-informed about Catholicism as Catholics were about Judaism. Better knowledge about each other could reduce conflict between the two faiths.[27]

The AJC was particularly cautious about planning and organizing the dialogue. Its guidelines stressed such matters as the choice of partners, their numbers and experience, topics, and preparation for the experience.[28] One Jewish authority cautioned that every effort must be exerted to avoid "offering religious or historic proofs," although in some cases, he admitted, this would require great restraint. The promotion of Jewish-Christian understanding was considered by the AJC too vital a matter to be sullied by a dialogue of polemics. A dialogue, Jews were cautioned, was never to become a debate, which demanded winners and losers. Rather, it was to be designed for enhancement of insight and understanding.[29]

The AJC and other Jewish organizations were eager to join in dialogue with Catholics. Arthur Gilbert believed that Jews should strive to go beyond conversing with Christians but should also include in their dialogues those of other religions.[30] Gilbert placed biblical, historical, and more recent events of the Jewish past high on the list for discussion. He was concerned about the depth of misunderstanding which prevailed among Catholics about Jews. In this connection, he wrote: "The Catholics, on their part, found it difficult to understand what it is that makes a Jew who denied his faith and religion still a Jew and in which way such a Jew is to be considered a part of Israel."[31] At the same time, Gilbert reminded Jews of the difficulty for Catholics to give up their eschatological hope for the conversion of the world. Neither could they easily divest themselves of their hope for the salvation of the Jews. But such differences that each faith group brought to the table, according to Gilbert, should constitute no major obstacle to the practice of dialogue.[32] On the contrary, Gilbert declared, "We must cherish that which binds us together even as we affirm our sectarian convictions."[33]

In the weeks following the Second Vatican Council, not all Jewish writers approached the dialogue with the same sanguine attitude as Gilbert did. One writer, Ben Zion Bokser, for example, suspected that for the unwary, the dialogue could prove to be a cover for conversion. He concluded, therefore, that the experience of the dialogue should be reserved for those who had attained the appropriate measure of wisdom and knowledge about Judaism.[34] Bokser's prescription for Jewish engagement with Catholics was understandable during the early days of the postconciliar era. But his advice was harsher than what was seen among the more liberal-minded Jews.[35] On the contrary, as Henry Siegman informed a meeting of the Liaison Committee of the Vatican Secretariat on Religious Relations with the Jews, which met with a group of Jews in 1978, the new relationship enabled the Jews "to shed their own peculiar kind of triumphalism, the defensive triumphalism of the persecuted and the abused and to relate in a more open and creative way to the world about it."[36] At the same time, Siegman acknowledged the difficulty a Christian experienced in avoiding the temptation to witness to Jews during a dialogue. Jews, however, he declared, must claim the right to insist that no proselytizing take place during dialogue; indeed, witnessing to Jews should be completely abolished from the interfaith experience. Yet, he believed, "witnessing is a legitimate religious enterprise, as long as it respects fully the freedom of conscience of people of other faiths, and as long as that enterprise is insulated from considerations of political and other forms of coercion."[37] It was an extreme suggestion: an issue of deep Jewish concern, voiced frequently even by Jews interested in advancing the dialogue.

Despite such obstacles and fears of ultimate motives, according to Daniel F. Polish, the dialogue serves as a tool which enabled Christians to uproot erroneous notions about Jews from their dogma. Although a supporter of dialogue, unlike other Jewish proponents of that experience, Polish asserted, as did Flannery, that Jews come to dialogue for different reasons than do Christians:

> We are not drawn to it from the same theological necessity. Jews do not need to have an understanding of Christian faith to comprehend their own. Nor is a study of Christianity necessary to relate us to our own past. Our motivations are more historical. We come to the dialogue as recipients of hatred and of its consequences. We may have some intellectual curiosity to learn what it was that caused all this suffering to befall us. But we have a more intense interest in helping Christians understand those destructive forces in their own tradition and keeping them from being unleashed again.[38]

Furthermore, Polish, as well as other Jewish promoters of dialogue, was convinced that dialogue with Jews could not succeed unless American Catholics reacted more sensitively to the Jewish attachment to the state of Israel and the deep religious meaning that the land possesses for them. Catholics must comprehend that the security of the Jewish state, seen against the background of the *Shoah,* is no light matter. Jewish writers recognized that Catholic indifference to the issue of Jewish nationalism could easily signal Jewish "withdrawal" from participation in the dialogue.[39]

Like Polish, Leon Klenicki, a rabbi and director of the Department of Jewish-Catholic Relations of the Anti-Defamation League (ADL) of B'nai B'rith as well as its primary link with the Vatican, wished the dialogue to succeed. Concurrently, Klenicki recognized that for Jews to participate in an appropriate frame of mind was no simple matter. Two thousand years of memory of Christian hostility lingered in the Jewish mind. Nevertheless, it was important for Jews to strive to envision the other's faith commitment as part of "God's special design." Klenicki and other Jewish writers admitted that such theological assertions about Christianity were "not normative statements of the synagogue." But if dialogue were to offer any promise, the attempt to understand Christianity would be "not an invitation to conversion or syncretism, but to understand and recognize Christianity as the other, in faith, as a person of God. Christianity and Judaism in the present reality of dialogue and encounter require mutual understanding and recognition."[40]

Quite understandably, Terry A. Bookman, a rabbi and theologian interested in Catholic Jewish dialogue, characterized the dialogue as far more than an interreligious discussion but as a "holy conversation,"[41] one that demands a measure of religious faith in its outcome.

◻ ◻ ◻

Many rabbis and Jewish academics believed that the pursuance of interfaith dialogue was a social, communal, and religious responsibility. They were found in the Reform, Conservative, and, to a more limited degree, Orthodox movements. Their congregations found this rabbinical role acceptable. Some of the most enthusiastic voices belonged to professional activists, whose lives were also intertwined with Jewish defense and other agencies and their bureaucracies.

An outstanding example of the latter group was Marc H. Tanenbaum. One of the best-known rabbis in the United States, Tanenbaum was designated by the *New York Times* as "the father of modern Christian-Jewish dialogue in America." He labored tirelessly from the end of the Second Vatican Council until his death to create better understanding between Christians and Jews. He had many friends in the Roman Catholic community, where he was highly respected. Tanenbaum's close association with the Roman Catholic leadership occasionally created suspicion in some Jewish circles about his activities.[42]

Educated as a Conservative rabbi at the Jewish Theological Seminary, where he studied with the prominent Jewish theologian Abraham Joshua Heschel, Tanenbaum was propelled by forces similar to those which moved Jules Isaac. Like Isaac, Tanenbaum was from the very beginning of his rabbinical career deeply puzzled by how the Christian faith, steeped in the gospel of love, could succumb to the hatred of Jews. Tanenbaum was one of the first professionals in the field of Jewish-Christian relations. He served as executive vice president of the Synagogue Council of America and, beginning in 1960, as director of interreligious affairs of the AJC. He was an observer at the Second Vatican Council and "according to his recollection the only rabbi to attend." He was also a chairman of the International Jewish Committee for Inter-religious Consultations, which represents Judaism in talks with the Vatican.[43] A scholar, writer, and radio commentator, Tanenbaum represented a major voice in American Jewish organized life on behalf of the advancement of Jewish-Catholic relations through dialogue.

In these endeavors, he was not alone. Leon Klenicki was another leading professional advocate in the field of dialogue. Like Jules Isaac, Marc Tanenbaum, and other concerned Jews, he wondered why the sight of a crucifix made him uneasy. He wrote: "I see it every time I leave the synagogue. On Saturday morning after services, while going home, it is there waiting for me, challenging me. It is the cross of a nearby church. Why does it disturb me? The sanctity of the day is marred by an image projecting memories of the past, memories transmitted by generations, by my parents. They are images of contempt for my people." Yet these deep-seated feelings did not dampen Klenicki's enthusiasm for the ultimate outcome of dialogue.[44]

Klenicki believed that Jews, as a religious people, should make the effort to meet face-to-face with another religious community which had claimed a "covenantal relationship" with God for two thousand years. In this connection, he urged Jews to examine *Nostra Aetate*, No. 4: "The Vatican II text needs fulsome consideration, over and over."[45] Klenicki viewed the work of Vatican II as marking a critical turning point for Jews as well as Roman Catholics. The event, he declared, marked a "unique moment" and must be seized by both Jews and Catholics. He declared that both faiths "lived in a new time," an unprecedented "creative moment." "We are challenged by a prophetic call that will change our spiritual vocabulary."[46]

Klenicki recognized the difficulty in surmounting two thousand years of prejudice on both sides that such change would entail. He admitted the popular theology of contempt would be difficult for Catholics to overcome. Klenicki wrote, "We Jews have to surmount two thousand years of memories that haunt us."[47] Klenicki's affirmation of the need for dialogue was striking. It reflected conviction and optimism and acknowledgment of the revolutionary potential of *Nostra Aetate* for all faiths. It was the kind of optimism duplicated in the utterances of other important voices in the Jewish community. Robert Gordis, Conservative rabbi and for many years editor of *Judaism,* a journal sponsored by the American Jewish Congress, remarked in 1986, "Twentieth century religion, particularly in America, has developed one attribute without parallel in all previous history—the birth and growth of the interfaith movement."[48]

Abraham J. Peck, an archivist associated for many years with the American Jewish Archives at the Hebrew Union College in Cincinnati, also was haunted by the question which moved Jules Isaac and was a leading supporter of dialogue with Catholics. Although not as hopeful as Klenicki, Peck saw the important results that could come from interfaith conversations. Peck acknowledged that mutual enrichment for both faiths could result from such conversations. He accepted this but not at the cost of "denuding" Judaism of its theological uniqueness or at the price of relativism.[49]

Still, there were those who believed that Jews should not only accept dialogue with the other but welcome it. At least, this was the suggestion of Elliot N. Dorff, a Conservative rabbi, philosopher, and provost of the University of Judaism in Los Angeles. The linkage here, according to Dorff, was with the Jewish acceptance of pluralism. "Commitment to pluralism for Jews," wrote Dorff, "should be motivated not only by the reality of historical change . . . but also by Jewish theology." By *pluralism,* Dorff meant that one's partner's ideas, though different from one's own, might also be spiritually and ethically valid. It is a concept, he argued, embedded in rabbinic literature.[50] What is more, according to Dorff, "Everyone's quest for religious truth is aided by discussion with others, for different views force all concerned to evaluate and refine their positions." A degree of humility, because of desire to learn more, would propel one into religious discussion. For Dorff, therefore, dialogue with Catholics was a perfectly valid exercise for Jews.[51]

In general, Jewish religious scholars acknowledged the mutual benefits that would be derived through probing conversations with Catholics. They believed that despite traditional differences, great values would grow from such interreligious discussions. The biblical scholar Samuel Sandmel, long associated with the Jewish Institute of Religion, a Reform seminary in Cincinnati, wrote at the close of the Second Vatican Council: "When we read each other's books on Scripture . . . we engage in a common, religious task, and insofar as we are able to enlighten ourselves and each other, inevitably our own understanding is deepened, our horizons broadened."[52]

In this connection, one can also hear the measure of gratification and admiration that another prominent Reform rabbi and editor of the popular *Sh'ma,* Eugene B. Borowitz, expressed at the sight of non-Jews who grappled with the intricacies of Jewish rabbinical literature. He was touched by the courage and wisdom that they brought to their efforts to try to understand the meaning of the Jewish tradition.[53] Such voices as those of Sandmel and Borowitz and others helped draw American Jews deeper into dialogue. But how far and to what depths can Jews and Catholics probe each other's most sacred beliefs and emerge with a genuine knowledge of the other? It was an unanswered question which both faiths shared.

9

Pitfalls of Dialogue

For most prelates and priests, participation in dialogue presented no serious religious problem. Unlike Jewish writers and rabbis, as in the case of Elliot N. Dorff, who sought and found halakic (Jewish legal) acceptance of pluralism and dialogue with non-Jews, Roman Catholics were supported in their endeavors by *Nostra Aetate,* No. 4. Indeed, from the point of view of the new Catholic doctrine, Catholics were expected to speak to Jews and learn about their religious heritage. Theological discussion about dialogue was designed to refine its process, guide its direction, and assess its progress, not to challenge or reject the need for it. The dialogue experience carried the weight of papal authority.

Dialogue with Jews was understood to be a religious experience, a "holy conversation," and Jews were to be accorded their proper place in sacred history. As one writer stated, "To hold that Jews are today, as in biblical times, a chosen people is thus to uphold God's faithfulness to the biblical promise." The concept, Catholics were informed, constituted church dogma.[1]

It was a slow process for Catholics to reverse their many centuries of thinking otherwise suddenly to accept Judaism as a valid religious expression, as acceptable as their own faith in the eyes of God. This change did not happen overnight.[2] Catholic scholars recognized that a fruitful dialogue could result if Catholics developed a well-thought-out theology of Jewish-Christian relations, based upon the principles of *Nostra Aetate,* No. 4. Such a theology, as one Catholic scholar put it in 1980, would grow out of a sound knowledge of Judaism and its relationship with Christianity, "a theology which could no longer be the cause of, furnish an alibi for, cliches about Judaism."[3]

Even as late as 1980, it was a suggestion difficult to consummate fully. But an acknowledgment of its validity was imperative for successful dialogue. What is more, a Christian theology of Judaism "without knowledge and consideration of Jewish theology was unthinkable," wrote the Catholic theologian Clemens Thoma. This knowledge was imperative for Christians, according to Thoma, if they were to avoid superficiality and error in dialogue. Thoma was disappointed in contemporary dialogue precisely because its participants were uneducated. "A great deal of today's so-called Christian-Jewish dialogue is nothing but confused mental gesticulation," which was bound to fail, he said.[4] Increasingly, explained Thoma, the Christian churches became aware "that they must refer themselves to Judaism in questions of origin. There is a great deal in Christianity which is Jewish." Christians must recognize that they can never sever themselves from Judaism.[5]

One of the leading Catholic theologians, John T. Pawlikowski, extended further the underlying requirements of dialogue. The books on interreligious strife, Pawlikowski was convinced, would not be closed until a satisfactory theology of pluralism was fashioned by Catholics as well as Jews. Mere notions of religious toleration or religious liberty were not enough.[6] Pawlikowski offered some bold suggestions: "A theology of religious pluralism," he wrote, "might allow us to say we have more than others: but never could it permit us to say we have a hold on all religious insights."[7]

The inspiration granted to Catholics by *Nostra Aetate*, No. 4, led them toward uncharted waters. It was not long before the issue of the state of Israel and its importance for Jewish religious identity, unmentioned in the Vatican declaration, became a major theological issue. Catholics were not prepared to tangle with what to them was a puzzling intertwining of land and faith. The editors of the *Journal of Ecumenical Studies*, however, believed that Catholics should have little difficulty in grasping the Jewish coupling: "Christians who do not separate religion and politics or culture should readily understand why they must not impose upon Jewish-Christian dialogue a distinction between religion and politics that for most Jews has no ground in the history and theory of their own existence."[8] The issue of Jewish nationalism was but one instance of the growing theological complexities which faced the American Catholics.

▢ ▢ ▢

Jews shared with Catholics the hopes about the possibilities of dialogue. But as Jews, they had special concerns, although many of these were anticipated and acknowledged sympathetically by Catholic theologians. Unlike Catholics, Jews had greater freedom of choice in the acceptance of the necessity of dialogue. They did not recognize any meaningful religious links with Christianity. Jews saw no connection between the Hebrew Bible and the Christian New Testament. Apart from the historic interweaving of the church and the Jewish people and their role as a conspicuous minority in the Christian world, many Jews were puzzled by the theological role they were now invited to play. One Jewish writer wondered at the close of the Second Vatican Council if the rush to dialogue was too intense. Perhaps more time should be required for preparation and self-reflection. At first, Jews also wondered if it was possible, now that it was the fashion to do so, to accept the religious validity of the church without denying their own faith.[9]

A precondition for dialogue, according to Mordecai Waxman, a Reform rabbi in Great Neck, New York, was the need for a Catholic reexamination and rejection of its teachings about Jews and Judaism. Neither could dialogue proceed without a Christian acknowledgment that Judaism, since Christianity separated from it, has remained an independent, autonomous religion. Consequently, declared Waxman, it does not require Christian guidance in religious matters.[10] If Jews had a theology of dialogue, it amounted to a desire for Christianity to formulate a theology of Judaism, free of any elements of contempt. Only then, they believed, could a fruitful exchange of theological and historic issues take place.

This is not to suggest that in the years following Vatican II the Jews did not recognize their own responsibilities. As Michael Signer, a Reform rabbi and a theologian of dialogue, observed, Jews could profit by and learn from discussions of Christology. Jews, he believed, needed to remain open to new "sources of spirituality." Jews could also gain by attendance at Catholic services.[11] But Signer's reaction was hardly a typically Jewish one. It was more acceptable to rabbis of the Reform movement than to the more traditional segments of American Jewry. It was also more acceptable to Jewish religious thinkers more concerned about the spread of secularism in modern American society. To exchange religious thoughts with Catholics was to such Jews a less frightening prospect than to live in a world which rendered both Judaism and Catholicism irrelevant.[12] It was an anxiety that affected persons of all faiths as the twentieth century progressed.

Not unlike Catholics in the years before Vatican II, Jews, especially the more traditionally oriented, found it difficult to accept Christians as fully equal religiously. Unlike the Christian, however, the traditional Jew believed that non-Jews could earn salvation by merely adhering to the seven commandments of the sons of Noah; that is, by living in accordance with minimal civilized moral standards. This did not imply that Jewish traditional thinkers granted full validation to Christianity, which in previous centuries they had considered partially idolatrous. But they did concede its importance as a messenger of monotheism to all nations. According to some traditional thinkers, Christianity in its own way served God by performing a holy function. In this sense, according to more recent twentieth-century scholars, Christianity has become increasingly viewed as a "true" religion.[13]

◻ ◻ ◻

Some of the most eminent Jewish theologians of the late twentieth century conceded, for the sake of the success of dialogue, the full validity of Christianity in the eyes of God. One of the most important of this group was Abraham Joshua Heschel. His assertion "that there is more than one religious path acceptable to God" provided the theological rationale that enabled Jews to converse with their Catholic neighbors.[14] One scholar called Heschel a "jewel" from heaven. "When he departed life on December 23, 1972," wrote Byron L. Sherwin, "Jewish scholarship lost one of the most erudite, original, and penetrating minds. Heschel's life was a symphony of gracious deeds, sublime thoughts and arias of ideas."[15]

Heschel was born in 1907 to a prominent Hasidic family in Poland. He escaped from Europe to the United States six weeks before the *Shoah* would have engulfed him, settling in his new-found home for a life of teaching, writing, and social action. Heschel was haunted by his past. "I am a branch plucked from the fire," he recalled in 1966, "in which my people were burned to death. I am a branch plucked from the fire of an altar of Satan on which millions of human lives were exterminated to evil's greatest glory."[16] Despite his personal past, Heschel directed no anger at the Christian world, for he saw both Christians and Jews as the heirs of the Hebrew Bible. As Heschel saw it, the Hebrew Bible had been the Nazi target. Heschel concluded that both Jews and Christians were obliged to work together to rescue the Bible from the desperate blows inflicted upon it. The events of that time had almost eliminated it from the Western world. "Is Judaism, is Christianity, ready to face the challenge?" asked Heschel.[17]

Heschel believed that despite their different religious commitments, Christians and Jews could and should meet in religious discussion. "Above all, when dogmas and forms of worship are divergent, God is the same," declared Heschel. What is more, according to Heschel, the Jew cannot afford to be indifferent to the faith of his Christian neighbor. Since Jews gave birth to Christianity, contended Heschel, they must not ignore its destiny. Each of the two faiths is indebted to the other. Jews should remember, wrote Heschel, that it was the church that brought the God of Abraham to the Gentiles. Jews must acknowledge this "with a grateful heart."[18]

Moreover, in Heschel's pluralistic view, the Kingdom of God requires a diversity of religious faiths and rituals. Nothing could be more hurtful to religious sensibility than a monolithic society with one form of devotion, one belief, one set of rituals. In a striking assertion, Heschel declared: "Human faith is never final, never an arrival, but rather an endless pilgrimage, a being on the way. We have no answers to all problems. Even some of our sacred answers are both emphatic and qualified, final and tentative, final in our own position in history, tentative—because we can only speak in the tentative language of man."[19] It was a mixture of religious humility and boldness that first caused Heschel to assert in the name of Judaism ultimate answers and a concern for the dissipation of religious values and then propelled him to dialogue with Catholics and representatives of other faiths. But Heschel was cautious about who should participate in dialogue. He did not believe that those who were "half learned" should engage in formal interfaith conversation. Such activity should be the "prerogative of the few." There is always a "danger of desecration, distortion and confusion. Syncretism is a perpetual possibility," warned Heschel in 1967. There was always the danger of "interfaith becoming a faith." Individuality must be preserved. "The problem to be faced is: How to combine loyalty to one's own tradition with reverence to different traditions?"[20]

With his characteristic wisdom, Heschel outlined the mutual responsibilities of Catholics and Jews in dialogue:

A Christian ought to ponder seriously the tremendous implications of a process begun in early Christian history. I mean the conscious or unconscious dejudaization of Christianity, affecting the church: Ways of thinking its inner life as well as its relationship to the past and present reality of Israel—the father and mother of the very being of Christianity. The children did not arise to call the mother blessed; instead they called the mother blind. . . . A Christian ought to realize that a world without Israel will be a world without the God of Israel. A Jew, on the other hand, ought to acknowledge the eminent role and part of Christianity in God's design for the redemption of all men. . . . Opposition to Christianity must be challenged by the question: What religious alternative do we envisage for the Christian world? . . . A Jew ought to ponder seriously the responsibility involved in Jewish history for having been the mother of two world religions. Does not the failure of children reflect upon their mother? . . . Should a mother ignore her child, even a wayward, rebellious one?[21]

Heschel described the problem clearly but despite its complexities, he considered the dialogue with the Christian world one of Judaism's most important challenges and obligations, one that Jews dare not ignore.

Heschel's work and thought had a profound impact on American Jewish-Christian relations. His efforts were particularly significant for Roman Catholics. No Jewish thinker grasped better the Catholic mind and heart than did this deeply committed rabbi. The respect and admiration accorded to him in Catholic circles is evidenced by the decision of the Jesuit magazine *America* to publish an entire issue about Heschel three months following his death.[22]

Few Jews were acknowledged by Roman Catholics to have had as great an influence upon their thinking. The Catholic theologian Eva Fleischner noted that Heschel opened up the riches of the Hebrew scripture to American Catholics. Heschel made Catholics aware of the danger that the Christian neglect of the Hebrew Bible could precipitate. "He saw more clearly than some Christian theologians that the battle with Marcion has not yet been won, that all too often the Hebrew bible takes second place to the New Testament."[23] Fleischner suggests further that Heschel, more than anyone else, opened for Catholics the "splendors of the Jewish tradition—of the Bible, the sabbath, Hasidism, the rich life of East European Jews prior to the destruction, the mystical meaning of Israel." Other Catholics agree that Heschel's interaction with Catholics "may have done more [than that of any other Jewish writer] to inspire an enhanced appreciation of Judaism among non-Jews."[24]

Eugene J. Fisher echoed Fleischner's sentiments concerning Heschel's impact on the Catholic-Jewish dialogue. He reiterated Heschel's reminder to Christians that the manual of Jewish existence and survival is a verification of the Holy Bible. To Fisher, Heschel's teaching was also a confirmation of the Jewish declaration of the Second Vatican Council.[25]

Most important, for Fisher and other thoughtful Catholics, Heschel served as an inspiration and guide to their own religious thinking. Catholic scholars were particularly interested in Heschel's theology. One of the most thorough and systematic studies of Heschel's religious ideas has been written by the Catholic John Merkle of the College of St. Benedict in St. Joseph, Minnesota. In another study of Heschel's thought, *The Human and the Holy,* the Jesuit scholar Donald J. Moore explains the relevance of Heschel's ideas to contemporary Roman Catholicism. Such Catholic responses as those of Merkle and Moore, according to Fisher, stand as a tribute to Heschel's openness to dialogue.[26]

From a Jewish perspective, one might say that through and because of Heschel's conversations, Catholics were better able to understand and come to appreciate a faith they had been alienated from for two thousand years. Heschel's willingness to admit that "religion was no prerequisite for sanctity" or that the purpose of different religious commitments was "mutual enrichment" endeared him to thoughtful postconciliar Catholics.[27] Heschel's theology, radical as it may sound to some ears, was not designed to relativize, syncretize, or trivialize modern faith commitments. On the contrary, its only purpose was to enhance religious commitment through interfaith dialogue.

▫ ▫ ▫

More than it did Catholics, a pragmatic urge propelled a select number of Jews toward dialogue. A desire to understand and reduce Christian hostility toward them was a major factor. Less obvious was a growing concern about the secularization of modern society and the belief that the two faiths must stand together to halt its progress. This rising tide of secularization was an uncomfortable prospect, especially among traditional Jews such as Abraham Joshua Heschel and others. "If I praise *Nostra Aetate,*" declared Elie Wiesel to a group of Catholics, "it is because I believe in the urgent necessity we have of realizing together that the planet Earth is shrinking. Together, Jews and Catholics are faced with the same perils and confronted with the same challenges. . . . In joining hands, I will not be less Jewish, nor will you be less Catholic."[28]

David Novak, a graduate of the Jewish Theological Seminary, where he studied with Abraham Joshua Heschel, and a professor of Jewish studies and then chairman of the department at the University of Toronto, is one thinker to attempt to come to terms with the problems of interfaith discussions. In his *Jewish-Christian Dialogue: A Jewish Justification* (1989), one finds a major scholarly and systematic inquiry and justification for Jewish dialogue.[29] The "revolutionary" character of the new dialogue, according to Novak, should not be taken for granted; it requires religious justification.

In seeking such justification, Novak does not diminish the thinness of the ice that each of the participants must skate upon. Triumphalism, relativism, and theological distortions may threaten the value of the exchange, according to Novak. He is especially wary about the ease with which religious syncretism could affect religious thinking. Unlike some liberal Jews, David Novak frowns upon the Christian and Jewish practice of celebrating each other's holidays, for example, Jews celebrating Christmas or Catholics celebrating the Jewish Passover. He believes that such practice can lead to and has led to conversion.[30] Most important, like many traditional thinkers, Novak insists that a dialogue can take place only within the boundaries of halaka, that is, it must be confined to the rules of the Torah. Jewish law, he explains, does not prohibit authentic dialogue with Catholics; indeed, Judaism benefits from communication with non-Jews, as long as Jews converse *as Jews* with non-Jews.[31]

Like Heschel, however, Novak recognizes that the secular culture which is overwhelming Western civilization threatens the integrity of both Judaism and Christianity. The danger of the invasion of secularism transcends the risk which dialogue poses to Jews. At this historical time, contends Novak, Jews and Catholics should be rediscovering each other. For the first time, they need each other. Novak searches halakic sources to buttress his contentions, because only after the discovery of halakic justification does he believe that dialogue can be conducted as an extension of an authentic part of Judaism.[32] Novak's approval of dialogue for Jews does not in any way facilitate the experience. The requirement that it be rooted in rabbinic sources is not always easy to achieve and may be open to interpretation and debate. Nevertheless, such difficulties should not obviate the necessity for continuing conversations between differing faiths, says Novak. Only a common front of Christians and Jews can block the progress of secularism. This is one of the chief lessons that Novak carried with him from Abraham Joshua Heschel.

However, some of Novak's concerns go beyond those of Heschel. Novak declares that "Jews should realize that the enlightenment took much more from them than it gave. It basically asked Jews to divest themselves of everything that made them unique and to become part of a new social order." This statement suggests the intensity with which Novak desires to arrest modern secularism.[33] Novak's message is clear: Catholics and Jews cannot go it alone in the modern world. Neither is the proclamation of a single-faith message sufficient. A multiple religious assault on secularism is imperative. Catholics and Jews must, therefore, speak to one another, for together they have important things to say to the world about the human condition.[34]

Novak's, Heschel's, and Wiesel's requests for a combined front of Catholics and Jews against the tidal wave of secularism was not unpopular among other Jewish thinkers. Emil Fackenheim, a Reform rabbi and a leading Jewish philosopher, for example, who was not especially enamored with dialogue, accepted this idea, according to one writer, largely because of its practical utility. Fackenheim, who became disillusioned with dialogue after seeing Catholic indifference to the fate of Israel when its survival was threatened in 1967, conceded that the threat which modernity offered to both faiths demanded participation in dialogue by both Catholics and Jews.[35] Considering the many preconditions which Novak imposes on the "holy conversation," one would surmise that he, like Fackenheim, must have some ambivalence about dialogue.

◦ ◦ ◦

Forming common intellectual bonds with Catholics in an age of declining religious values was important to some Jews. They felt that religion, be it Judaism or Christianity, had much to offer the world of the late twentieth century. Not long after the close of the Second Vatican Council, one thoughtful liberal Jewish writer, Jacob Bernard Agus, declared his belief that Jews had little choice but to begin a conversational interchange: dialogue with Christians was "inescapable." He thought that Jews and Catholics needed "to meet on the common ground of religious humanism." Such an exercise, declared Agus, "will be of the greatest service to mankind."[36]

Agus viewed the coming battle against the secular pagan demons of the Western world as an uphill one, a conflict that probably would not be completely won. In the process, explains Agus, Jews will be compelled to make concessions. "The Jewish myth of the chosen people is challenged daily in the predominant Christian society. Liberal Jews will interpret their 'chosenness' as an *example,* not as an exception. They will urge the American nation to regard itself as similarly 'chosen,' i.e., dedicated to the service of mankind."[37] Agus's reaction was not unusual among Jews taken with the prospect of dialogue during the halcyon postconciliar era. Liberal Jews, especially, were willing to bend sacred traditional concepts. In the process, however, this left the Jew and the Christian wondering: Is there a religious truth?[38]

This kind of flirtation with relativism, for the sake of sweeping out secular humanism from contemporary society, was confined not only to liberal Jews. One thinks of David Hartman, the American rabbi and philosopher, who transported his academic and religious interests to Israel. As a biblical scholar and an observer of Christian behavior, he found amusement in listening to the voices of both Christians and Jews proclaiming the ownership of religious "truth." When each of the great faiths, he observes, boasts to be the "true Israel," little but tension and hostility are bound to result. "We are all guilty of the same mistake," writes Hartman. But is it possible, he asks, that different faiths possess the same "truth"? The question should not be a religious one, says Hartman. Let philosophers grope for the answer: "I say that the story of Israel is the story of God." Each faith community reserves the right to claim the "truth." "Other people," writes Hartman, revealing his deep respect for a pluralistic world, "have their own Egypt, their own desert, their own Sinai. . . . I have no criteria as to what is not to count as a person's Egypt or Sinai or desert."[39] In 1982, Hartman told a group of Catholics that he aspired to see the day when Catholics and Jews would not love each other as Catholics and Jews but see each other only as human beings: "We are the same."[40]

◻ ◻ ◻

Growing secularism was not considered a sufficient threat to convince all Jews of the necessity for dialoguing with Catholics. There were those who continued to view the contemporary church as being as dangerous today as it had been in previous ages. Neither were some Jews impressed with the results of the actions of the Second Vatican Council and its new thrust toward pluralism.[41] Such opposition does not suggest a reflexive negation on the part of some reactionaries. Rather, it indicates that some Jews continued to hold a deep sense of traditional religious values and an attachment to a long historic memory. Christian desire for dialogue, these opposers were convinced, stemmed from a need to seduce Jews away from their ancestral faith.[42]

The hope generated by *Nostra Aetate*, No. 4, was not felt by everyone. Ben Zion Bokser put it this way in 1967: "The conventional Christian concept of the Jew and Judaism is intertwined with basic Christian doctrine whose revision cannot be expected merely for the sake of facilitating better relations with Jews. . . . The test of progress in this direction will be the extent to which Christianity comes to acknowledge the legitimacy of divers paths to God."[43] Opposition to dialogue with the Catholic community emanated chiefly from American Jewish Orthodoxy.

This is not to suggest that *all* Orthodox Jews were opposed to conversing with non-Jews about religious matters, but the supporters of dialogue were not representative. The few Orthodox or traditional Jews, those who lived by the laws of Moses or halaka, who accepted the idea of dialogue, acted in opposition to most of their traditional colleagues.

Orthodox opposers, observes David Novak, appeared oblivious to the problems of modernity and its secular culture. The Orthodox assumed that their relationship with Christians had undergone little change during the past centuries. They recognized little value in the statements on Jews issued by the recent Second Vatican Council. Such negativity varied in intensity, depending upon the degree of Orthodoxy. The strongest opponents to dialogue were the "black hats," those who dressed in eighteenth-century black attire and revered tradition.[44] Neither were elements of anti-Christian hostility absent from those traditionalists who were against dialogue. This opposition is understandable and inevitable for a group that constantly focused on past events. For them, the *Shoah* loomed large as the ultimate horror unleashed by a Christian world, a product of centuries of contempt toward Judaism.[45] Most important to Novak, the greatest failing of modern Orthodoxy's opposition to dialogue is its inability to recognize that both faith communities must unite, for they both confront the common danger: secularism. Their imperviousness to this threat, he writes, can be readily understood. Catholicism has long been identified as the enemy. "Secular humanism," a relatively new threat, has found no place in the dark history of antisemitism.[46]

Among the opponents of dialogue, Joseph B. Soloveitchik, a highly revered rabbi in the United States and head of the Rabbi Isaac Elchanan Theological Seminary of Yeshiva University, was a "modern" rabbi, whose opposition to dialogue was not as extreme as that found among other Orthodox Jews. But he was the "acknowledged intellectual leader of and spokesman for halakic Judaism." His ideas, therefore, are considered important. Though non-Jews and Jews, according to Soloveitchik, travel parallel roads, their destinies are different. They remain separate and "opposed to each other." Yet, individuals are social beings who need to interact with others. According to Soloveitchik, however, such outerdirectedness does not enter the inner recesses of human existence. Human confrontation is always characterized by a degree of ambivalence.[47]

Soloveitchik believes that the Jew is a bearer of a double "burden," the covenantal and the universal. He is concerned that modern Jews are too easily seduced to give up the double confrontation for the sake of a single one. Modern Jews prefer to think of themselves only as part of humanity, a part of civilization. Consequently, they tend to ignore their unique obligations as Jews. To Soloveitchik, Jews can only be understood as singular: "There is no identity without uniqueness." It is "absurd to speak of the commensurability of two faith communities which are individual entities." Any attempt to equate Jewish identity with another faith community, writes Soloveitchik, is "sheer absurdity." Furthermore, "standardization of practices, equalization of dogmatic certitudes, and the waving of eschatological claims spell the end of the vibrant and great faith experience of any religious community."[48]

Nevertheless, Soloveitchik does not reject the "confrontation" (i.e., dialogue) of two faiths provided each remains aware of its distinct uniqueness. At the same time, he says, this should not prevent the partners from joining in projects for the amelioration of human suffering— eradication of hunger, disease, and poverty, as well as the protection of human rights.[49] However, Soloveitchik concedes to the dialogue participants little more than a right to talk about social and cultural matters. He rejects as a subject of discussion the theological matters unique to each of the partners. "Hence, it is important that the religious or theological *logos* should not be employed as the medium of communication between two faith communities whose modes of expression are as unique as their apocalyptic experiences. The confrontation should occur not at a theological, but at a mundane human level. . . . Our common interests lie not in the realm of faith, but in that of the secular orders."[50] At the same time, Soloveitchik warns Jews not to meddle with Christian theology. They should not urge changes in Christian ritual or liturgy. These are Christian matters. It would be both impertinent and unwise for an outsider to intrude upon the most private sector of the human existential experience, namely, the way in which a faith community expresses its relationship to God.

Soloveitchik also believes that Jews "have not been authorized by our history, sanctified by the martyrdom of millions, to even hint to another faith community that we are mentally ready to revise historical attitudes, to trade favors pertaining to fundamental matters of faith, and to reconcile 'some' differences." Soloveitchik reminds his coreligionists that their relationship with the outside world has always been one of an "ambivalent character." "We come close to and simultaneously retreat from the world," he writes.[51]

Obviously, on the eve of the Second Vatican Council's declaration on the Jews, Soloveitchik greeted the prospect of dialogue with Roman Catholics with distinct coolness. His caveats were incorporated into an official statement of the Rabbinical Council of America, the leading body of Orthodoxy. The statement acknowledged satisfaction at the multiplying efforts for interfaith cooperation and growing openness among differing faiths: "The current threat of secularism and materialism and the modern atheistic negation of religion and religious values makes even more imperative a harmonious relationship among the faiths." Nevertheless, the statement urged extreme caution. "Any suggestion that the historical . . . worth of a faith community be viewed against the backdrop of another faith, and the mere hint that a revision of basic historic attitudes is anticipated . . . can only breed discord and suspicion." None of this, the statement said, precluded friendly cooperation with other faiths. It concluded with the words of the prophet Micah (4:5): "Let all the people walk, each one in the name of his god, and we shall walk in the name of our Lord, our God, forever and ever."[52]

Like Soloveitchik, the members of the rabbinical council evinced concern about their liberal colleagues' willingness to converse with Catholics and others about unique theological and historical matters of their own or their partners' faiths. They rejected any suggestion that such dialogue produced value for Judaism. But, as David Novak observes, by eliminating from discussion all issues of unique religious values, very little of significance is left to talk about, except for a secular agenda.[53]

The Orthodox opposition to dialogue was evident in the years following *Nostra Aetate*, No. 4. Henry Siegman, a rabbi who held a number of leadership roles in American Orthodox circles, also saw little in dialogue that would benefit Jews. Such exercises, he declared in 1978, were of benefit only to the Christian world. Catholics seek dialogue with Jews out of a sense of guilt: "For most, it is the 'mystery of Jewish rejection of Christianity.'" A Jew, however, "need not expose his or her inner life of faith to the Christian in dialogue."[54] More than a decade after the "Declaration on the Jews," Siegman sees little that Jews have gained from such religious interchanges. He understands the Christian desire to validate the biblical roots of their faith but fails to perceive a commensurate value for their partners. To Siegman, the differing agendas with which Jews and Catholics meet each other negates any value that can be gained from the dialogue.[55]

Actually, most Orthodox groups in the United States go much further than Soloveitchik, Siegman, and other "moderates," who view Catholics as a totally alien group with whom they prefer not to speak at all. Any conversation, the ultra-Orthodox believe, would tend to blur the distinction between the two communities. The first and primary obligation of Jews is to live in accordance with the commandments of *Torah*. To do so, Jews must "dwell apart." Since for the Orthodox this requires separation from even liberal or secular Jews, it stands to reason that dialogue with Christians would hardly be an acceptable option for the right-wing Orthodox Jew.[56]

Jacob Neusner, a prolific writer and leading scholar of rabbinic Judaism, though hardly an ultra-Orthodox thinker, nevertheless shares some of these reservations about dialoguing with non-Jews. Neusner questions the usefulness that religious conversations between Jews and Christians could possibly have. He sees the distance between New Testament and Talmudic literature as too wide to be traversed in such conversations.[57] Neither does he believe that the Hebrew Bible, venerated by the church as well, can serve any purpose as a subject for dialogue. In a published conversation with Andrew M. Greeley, Neusner expresses his views about the Bible as a subject for interfaith dialogue.[58]

Neusner makes it clear from the very beginning that he believes that religions cannot speak easily to each other. Each reads the Bible differently and derives a different meaning from it. Neusner does not rule out dialogue. Religions, he believes, can "teach" one another, but they have not yet overcome the difficulty of communicating with each other. As an example of the insurmountable difficulty of communicating with the "other," Neusner writes that one often will "find the other crazy (as did Ayatollah Khomeini and Jim Jones of Jonestown), declare the other the work of the devil (as the Ayatollah did with us), or declare the other subject to such metaphors as unclean, impure, dangerous, to be exterminated, as the Germans—Christians and ex-Christians alike—did with the Jews."[59]

Before one can dialogue with the "other," one must make sense of the other, a task which has not yet been achieved, says Neusner. He looks forward to a "theological theory" of the other. The question is, How, as a believing person, can I make sense of the outsider? Such a theory might help us discern the religious thought of the other with reference to our own values.[60] At the present moment, however, intelligent biblical dialogue cannot be conducted, according to Neusner. Catholics and Jews can say much about one another but nothing to each other; Catholics and Jews can work together, but they are not ready to dialogue with each other. "The reason is," says Neusner, "that in their very essence they are talking about different things to different people." It is not one's fault, says Neusner. It is the essence of religious faith. Neusner is not impressed that Catholicism and Judaism are rooted in the same past. His focus is on the fact that the early Christians parted roads by choosing a different faith. This event ended any meaningful communication about religious matters. Each became fundamentally different: "For the two religions, standing before God, have, in fact, nothing in common—at least, nothing in common that matters very much."[61]

With Soloveitchik, Neusner, and others on one side and Heschel and Novak on the other, it is plain that there is no single clear voice on the question of dialogue among American Jewish theologians. Would a shaking of the foundations of the theology of contempt soften opposition toward "Holy Conversations" between Jews and Catholics?

10

Uprooting Contempt

The ramparts of popular theological contempt fell slowly. The Second Vatican Council and its subsequent guidelines offered encouragement, suggestions, and inspiration for the Catholic faithful; but priests, bishops, and theologians had to advance the work that had begun with *Nostra Aetate,* No. 4, in 1965. What was required was a reformulation of popular Catholic theological thinking about Jews.

Few Catholic scholars heard the call more clearly and exerted a more profound effort in this direction than John T. Pawlikowski, the author of numerous scholarly articles and books, most of which were concerned with the changing theological relationship of Catholics and Jews in postconciliar America. A priest and for many years a professor of Catholic theology at the Catholic Theological Union in Chicago, Pawlikowski has devoted most of his clerical and professional life to redefining Christian understanding of Judaism and, in the process, eradicating religious misunderstanding that has led to antisemitism.

Pawlikowski's writing stresses the importance for Christians of viewing Jews as they understand themselves. Catholics, he believes, enrich their own lives by coming to terms with the "Jewish affirmation of life," the Jewish "sense of peoplehood and community," and the positive valuation which they give to sexuality. He also points to the close interweaving of "prayer and social actions" by Jews.[1] Pawlikowski thinks that Catholicism would not only gain by such heightened awareness of Judaism but could profit by incorporating within it Jewish values that have been lost to it. A deeper consciousness of and involvement in social is-

sues is only one manifestation of change in Catholic behavior as a result of this renewed relationship, writes Pawlikowski in 1976.[2]

To Pawlikowski, the church has received far more benefit from this
new relationship than has Judaism. It has recovered the heritage which
it left behind during the Second Temple era. This new recovery Pawlikowski calls "the re-Judaization of Christianity." The gain for Catholicism is, according to Pawlikowski, a retrieval of Jewish religious values that among others include a sense of the importance of history and
the human responsibility for the welfare of the world. He has accepted
the Jewish concept that "man is basically good."[3]

Pawlikowski elaborated upon these themes in the years that followed.
Increasingly, he has come to accept the thesis that "the most promising
theological avenue to explore is that of seeing Judaism and Christianity
as two distinctive religions, each with a unique faith despite their historic links."[4] Such words stand in sharp contrast to what the church
taught in previous centuries. What is more, writes Pawlikowski, "any
Christology that simply presents the meaning of Jesus' ministry as the
fulfillment of Jewish messianic prophecies is invalid."[5]

Throughout the 1980s, Pawlikowski sought a workable theory of Jewish-Christian relations, one that would be acceptable to both faiths. It
was a formidable task for the Catholic theologian, a goal difficult to
achieve.[6] By the mid-eighties, Pawlikowski concluded that if a new theology were to be fashioned, it would be required to acknowledge the
following: "(1) that the Christ event did not invalidate the Jewish
faith . . . ; (2) that Christianity is not superior to Judaism, nor is it the
fulfillment of Judaism as previously maintained; (3) that the Sinai is in
principle as crucial to Christian faith expression as the covenant in Christ;
(4) that Christianity needs to reincorporate dimensions from its original Jewish context."[7] This, in the light of past history, constituted a bold
attempt to uproot years of anti-Judaism in popular Catholic theology.

Furthermore, Pawlikowski has declared that "the Christ Event constitutes an authentic eschatological paradigm only for the people who
have consciously accepted it as such." As an example, Pawlikowski
writes, "The Exodus Event . . . does the same for Jewish identity that the
Christ Event does for Christianity." One does not invalidate the other.[8]
Here we see a clear rejection of previous supersessionist ideas which had
permeated the church for centuries.

Pawlikowski is convinced that a new Catholic-Jewish theology could
exist comfortably with an "ongoing stress on the unique feature of the
Christ Event." In his new theology, Pawlikowski believes that each of
the faiths can maintain its uniqueness without invalidating the unique

character of the other.[9] In short, Pawlikowski is willing to accept a new theology of Jewish-Christian relations that rejects the age-old absolutist claims of the Roman Catholic Church. He recognizes that implicit in such historic claims is the Catholic conviction of its permanent superiority to the Jewish faith. But that is precisely why Pawlikowski has underscored the necessity for a new theology.

Such an assault on the historic imperialism of the Church of Rome, an attack carried forward by Catholic theologians, was one of the byproducts of the 1965 revolution. As Gregory Baum put it in 1974, "When a church that has become culturally dominant proclaims Jesus as the one way, invalidating all other ways . . . it creates a symbolic imperialism" which no amount of love and generosity can undo.[10]

Rosemary Radford Ruether, Georgia Harkness Professor of Theology at the Garrett-Evangelical Theological Seminary in Evanston, Illinois, argued in 1974 that a new theology of Jewish-Christian relations is necessary for the church because the problem of anti-Judaism has had a seriously negative impact on the morality of Catholicism. The fault can be traced, Ruether argues, to the early church's separation from the teaching of the Jews. Its initial mistake was that it viewed the Jews as an alien people. Christians, Ruether states, will need to reverse such thinking. Many Christian textbooks will need to be discarded. Many alterations in traditional Catholic teaching will have to take place in order to eradicate the friction which exists between the two faiths.[11]

Ruether's demands on the formulation of a workable theology of Christian-Jewish relations are harsh. Few Catholic theologians have gone further. She requests that the church "must turn to what was always the other side of anti-Judaism, namely Christology." Like other Catholic thinkers of the postconciliar era, Ruether asks, "Is it possible to purge Christianity of anti-Judaism without at the same time pulling up Christian faith?"[12] A willingness to acknowledge a return to the Jewish biblical roots would, according to Ruether, help eradicate the anti-Judaism of the church. Only through a revision of Catholic education can a solution be found, according to Ruether. She advises Christians to learn the history of the Jewish people "after the time of Jesus." What is more, "Christians must accept the Oral Torah [Talmudic literature] as an authentic alternative route by which the biblical past was approached and carried on. This requires the learning of a suppressed history."[13]

Ruether's assertion reflects the inspiration of *Nostra Aetate*, No. 4. But her elaboration, though necessary, must have created discomfort among the former Second Vatican Council participants, especially in her broadside on the Christian view of its own past. She writes, for example: "For

Christians to incorporate the Jewish tradition after Jesus into their theological and historical education would involve ultimately the dismantling of the Christian concept of history and the demythologizing of the myth of the Christian Era."[14]

Pawlikowski and Ruether symbolize the desire on the part of a select group of Catholic theologians of the last quarter of the twentieth century to discover a workable theology of Jewish-Christian relations.[15] Not all reached their radical heights. But their goal was clear, like that, for example, of Eugene J. Fisher. "The question today," wrote Fisher in 1977, "is not who is to blame but where do we go from here?"[16] Fisher, as well as some Catholic prelates but unlike such theologians as Pawlikowski and Ruether, was less concerned with the formulation of a new theology of Jewish-Christian relations than with the continuation of improvement of the relationship between the two faiths. To him, alterations in the education of Catholics and the refinement of the liturgy were of primary importance so that neither would harbor anti-Jewish suggestions or any statement that could be misunderstood.[17]

Catholic acknowledgement that their beloved church was permeated with Jew-hatred did not come easily. The age-old question of how a faith that professed love of people could also disseminate hostility toward them begged for an answer. Some theologians, such as Gregory Baum, professor of religious studies at St. Michael's College at the University of Toronto, in his earliest writings refused to associate anti-Judaism with the teaching of Christianity, as did Pawlikowski and Ruether. Baum looked for sociological rather than theological explanations.[18]

For Baum, Catholicism, like any other cultural institution, is affected by ideological trends of its surrounding social and cultural environment. "The hidden power of ideology," according to Baum, has contaminated Christianity's relationship with the Jewish people. Such is the power of ideology that, unless precautions are taken, it can overpower truth. In a battle like the struggle between true and false religion, the church must liberate itself from its false ideology of anti-Judaism.[19] Baum's attempt in 1972 to uproot contempt for Judaism from Catholicism absolves the church of any direct responsibility for the old evil of antisemitism. By 1978, Baum went a step further and, without reversing his original assessment, agreed that doctrinal changes in Catholic theology would have to take place. Such changes, he believed, were authorized by the Second Vatican Council as well as the requirements of a new age.[20]

Baum sees the Catholic response to the *Shoah* as making doctrinal changes with respect to Jews imperative. Although the church, says Baum, bears no direct responsibility for the *Shoah,* its rejection of the

Jewish people imposes an indirect one: "The Church's negation of Jewish existence before God has created symbols and produced an atmosphere in which it was possible for Hitler to make the Jews a scapegoat for the ills of society."[21]

The *Shoah* notwithstanding, Baum was aware that his proposal to submit the church and its teachings to a thorough doctrinal critique was not a popular prospect among Catholic leaders. The authority to reevaluate sacred doctrines did not yet seem necessary to the church's leaders. Baum's approach was to emancipate ancient Christian texts from old interpretations; old interpretations which created fantasies about the Jews as being a non-people needed to be discarded. Such theological reevaluations, Baum argued, were needed also for the enhancement of Catholic self-understanding. Baum was concerned that Catholic theologians might shy away from facing the prospect of a radical reinterpretation of Christian mythology about Judaism. In the face of Auschwitz, however, they had little alternative.[22] No resolution of the theological tensions between the two faiths could be achieved without the dismantling of the pernicious elements of the theology of contempt.

◻ ◻ ◻

The measure of determination that the Second Vatican Council inspired can be seen by the willingness of Catholic scholars to reexamine and reinterpret doctrines long held sacred. In the few decades following *Nostra Aetate,* No. 4, all elements of what has been here designated as the theology of contempt were placed on the table—the New Testament itself, the Crucifixion, displacement theology, the role of the Pharisees, the nature of Jewish law. The purpose of such a task was to determine which religious dogma, views, and practices, if any, have generated Catholic hostility toward Jews. Catholic theologians were determined to uproot the theology of contempt during the closing decades of the twentieth century.

The writing of Jules Isaac, which had been already widely circulated before the close of Vatican II, made it evident that the Gospels and Epistles themselves would not be let off scot-free. It became evident to increasing numbers of Catholics, as it has always been to Jews, that the account of Christ's passion was told at the terrible expense of the living Jews. That the story helped to generate antisemitism was at first a difficult admission for some Catholic theologians to make.[23]

Once raised, however, the question of the culpability of the New Testament in generating hostility toward Jews had a great impact on theological inquiry and teaching. Catholic theologians, such as Bruce Vawter, who earned a doctorate in Sacred Scripture from the Pontifical Biblical Institute in Rome, admitted in 1968 that an uncritical reading of the Gospels would portray Jews in a demeaning way. From an unlearned perspective, according to Vawter, the impression is that the roots of antisemitism are found in the New Testament. Jewish hostility toward the early Christians explains in part the anti-Jewish polemic found in the Christian Scripture, he says. Vawter also observes that the term *Jew* was employed broadly in the New Testament to include the entire generation of unbelievers. Consequently, according to Vawter, "The Gospels contain unquestionable hostility toward Jews."[24] The admission, hedged with numerous caveats—the Christian Scripture was polemical, it spoke in absolutes, a quarrel between sects created the impression of an intense hostility toward Jews—was, nevertheless, a remarkable assertion that would not have been made a decade earlier by a Catholic theologian.[25]

With the publication of Rosemary Ruether's *Faith and Fratricide* in 1974, a work which had a profound influence and generated controversy among religious thinkers, the New Testament suffered its severest indictment by a Catholic theologian. To Ruether, anti-Judaism was an indigenous and significant characteristic of the Christian Scripture. It was not only Christian rejection of the temple, the Law, and other sacred elements of the Jewish biblical tradition that lay the foundations for anti-Judaism, she says. The "unbelieving Jews" were juxtaposed against the "believing Gentiles." Jewish obedience to the Torah was equated with subservience to demonic influence.[26] New Testament polemics against Jews vary in intensity throughout the Christian Scripture but reach a frightening form in the Gospel of John. Ruether writes: "For John, the 'unbelief of the Jews' points to a much deeper theological mystery. 'The Jews,' for John, are the very incarnation of the false, apostate principle of the fallen world, alienated from its true being in God. They are the type of the carnal man who knows nothing spiritually."[27] Such diatribes in sacred Christian Scripture, no doubt historically explainable, nevertheless cast a long shadow of deep suspicion on the Jewish people.

Ruether's implication of the Christian Scripture as the origin of antisemitism and her conviction that the birth of Christianity was necessarily interwoven with anti-Judaism were not greeted warmly by many Catholic writers. They did not deny that the origins of antisemitism grew out of the policies of early church history, but they preferred not to carry this as far back as the Gospels. An example of such a protest can be seen in the response to Ruether by Thomas A. Idinopulos and Roy Bowen Ward, two professors of religion at Miami University, Oxford, Ohio. They challenge Ruether's proposition that anti-Judaism is a necessary logical development out of the church's basic Christological confession. "What we discern in the evidence is that with the deicide charge the Church introduced a new, more potent weapon in its ongoing, increasingly bloody rivalry with the synagogue. It is the historical or political context of church-synagogue relations which accounts for the devolution of Christian anti-Judaism into anti-Semitism, not some fateful, inner logic of Christology itself."[28]

It was difficult for Catholics fully to acknowledge the culpability of Christian Scripture. They could not deny that bad seeds were sown, but they preferred to look at the tensions between the early Christians and the Jews as an unfortunate "family quarrel." "Perhaps it is because Christianity is so close to Judaism that the differences between the two came to be such a source of tension between us," wrote Eugene Fisher in 1977. Early Christians needed desperately to find their own identity, to differentiate themselves from their mother faith, suggested Fisher.[29] Fisher, however, categorically rejects the idea that the Gospels serve as a major source of antisemitism. Antisemitism, he writes, predated the Christian era. Neither does modern racial antisemitism have any relationship to the New Testament's view of Judaism.[30] According to Fisher, the error made by those who seek the roots of anti-Judaism in the Gospels and Epistles is that they do not read the Christian Scripture against the historical backdrop of that age.[31]

John T. Pawlikowski, like Fisher, hesitates to pronounce the New Testament guilty of disseminating antisemitism. Like Fisher, he envisions the strong language as little more than a quarrel between two groups of Jews who held different views about religious matters. Also like Fisher, Pawlikowski does not see eye-to-eye with Ruether, whose thesis has been challenged by many scholars. Apart from her assertions of damaging anti-Judaism in the Gospel of John, which scholars have found difficulty disagreeing with, Ruether has generated a hearty debate about the character of the New Testament with respect to antisemitism, even though, as Pawlikowski has noted, the question remains far from settled.[32]

As Pawlikowski puts it, the problem remains: "How is the ordinary Christian man or woman to know that the negative references to Jews should be interpreted in an historical context?"[33] Still, the very fact that thoughtful Catholic thinkers have agreed to examine their sacred scriptures as an inspiration for crimes against the Jewish people is evidence of the distance traveled since the 1965 Vatican council.

◻ ◻ ◻

To uproot contempt, the person of Jesus himself, the pre-Easter Jesus, would have to undergo rehabilitation. At the very least, Catholic teaching would have to de-emphasize the Christian Savior's separation from Judaism. The image of Jesus as an observant Jew would be more appropriate for the postconciliar era. None of this would imply a desire to sell Jesus to the Jewish people in order to convert them. Conversion was not an option any more. The purpose of re-Judaizing Jesus was to enable Catholics to learn about the compatibility of the origins of their own faith with those of Judaism.

None of this was alien to the church. The Judaism of Jesus had merely been de-emphasized, not forgotten. Catholic educators noted that a future generation of Catholics must not be taught that the Jews were the enemies of Jesus and his message. Jews should not be presented as "unbelievers." On the contrary, it was the Jewish biblical message that Jesus proclaimed.[34] In this regard, Ruether notes that if Christians "want to reaffirm the gospel without this anti-Judaic left hand, we must analyze and reconstruct the basic dualism [of the Gospel and anti-Judaism] which shaped early Christian self-understanding."[35] The tendency among traditional New Testament scholars with respect to Jesus, to divide the Jews into "good guys" (the followers of Jesus) and "bad guys" (the rejecters of Jesus), has done almost irreparable damage to Jewish-Catholic relations, according to Ruether. She asks an important question: "Is it possible to say 'Jesus is the Messiah' without, implicitly or explicitly, saying at the same time 'and the Jews be damned'?"[36] One of the great challenges of Catholics of the late twentieth century was to view Jesus, the central and most important figure of their faith, without any animosity toward Jews. The dissemination of the knowledge that the Christian faith is rooted in the Jewishness of Jesus and his apostles is seen as an approach to a solution.[37]

The Jewishness of Jesus of Nazareth is not an unfamiliar subject to Jewish scholars. Throughout the twentieth century, Jews showed a deep curiosity about the Jew who brought momentum to the gentile world. The Jewish theologian Martin Buber called him a "brother." In the early twentieth century the Jewish historian Joseph Klausner, author of a Hebrew biography of Jesus, lectured about Jesus to students at the Hebrew University in Jerusalem. More recently, the Israeli scholar Pinchas Lapide has written extensively about him. American Reform rabbis since the late nineteenth century have examined Jesus' life and teaching.[38] The importance, however, is that Catholic theologians have in recent years joined the Jews in underlining the Jewish roots of Jesus and his apostles. This has been done to reduce the misunderstanding about early Christianity and Judaism. More than ever, the church reminds its faithful of the sustenance it draws from Judaism.[39]

◙ ◙ ◙

The role of the Jews in the crucifixion of Jesus had yet to be explained. Even after *Nostra Aetate,* No. 4, the charge of deicide continued to haunt Catholic-Jewish relations. The New Testament authors' and church fathers' views of the Jews as a deicide people could not be discounted. Even the Vatican's "Declaration on the Jews" of 1965, despite its good intentions, left lingering doubts about Jewish responsibility in the killing of the Christian Savior. While collective guilt of past, present, and future generations of Jews was forever dismissed as a sinful myth by the Second Vatican Council, the responsibility of Jewish leadership in engineering the heinous act was not. The suggestion of Jewish complicity, based upon flimsy historical evidence, provided just enough of a stimulant to the warped minds of potential Jew-haters.

After all, the traditional Christian myth stated that Jesus was indicted by the Sanhedrin in Jerusalem, which condemned him to death on the charge of blasphemy, a capital crime (see Matthew 26:57–68; Mark 14:53–65; Luke 22:54–71; John 11:47–53 and 18:13–24, NSRV). Since they did not possess the power of execution, the Jewish leaders, so the story went, handed Jesus over to Pontius Pilate, the Roman official who held such power.[40] At best, one might say that the "Jewish leaders" alone are implicated in the Crucifixion account of the Christian Bible, with no mention made of Roman responsibility. In future accounts of the Passion, the "Jewish leaders" and their followers of Jesus' time remained the arch-villains of the central Christian drama. Unlettered minds would easily turn their hatred of the "Jewish leaders" into a generalized animosity toward *all* Jews. Detecting this, the historian Jules Isaac declared: "The Christian religion does not require for her own glorification corresponding disparagement of ancient Israel, of the people of the Old Testament, the people of Jesus and the Apostles, and of the first Christians."[41] Catholic theologians of the postconciliar age would confront their most implacable challenge in eradicating the remnants of evil brought about by the myth of Jewish deicide.

A spokesman for America's Catholic hierarchy, George F. Higgins, cautioned concerned Catholics in 1965 about expecting quick alterations in popular thinking. Higgins told a group of Jewish listeners that many but not all Catholics continued to accept the traditional deicide myth.[42] Most important, however, is that the leading voices of the Church of Rome were determined in the years following the Second Vatican Council to reinterpret the deicide myth, so that its faithful adherents would refrain in every way from casting accusations upon the Jews.[43] Not many Catholic students and seminarians were aware of the horrors inflicted by Catholics upon their Jewish neighbors throughout European history because of the deicide accusation. Catholic educators urged that such knowledge be included in textbooks; they saw such knowledge as part of the history that Catholics had not been taught.[44] Catholic educators were advised to teach the story of Christ's Passion in a way that would not impugn the role of the Jewish people of that time. They were urged not to teach unsubstantiated myths, inventions, or exaggerations, all at the expense of Jews. Catholics were to view the history of Jesus' time with greater objectivity and with sensitivity to the linguistic and theological nuances of the early Christian era.[45]

Rosemary Ruether is quite pointed when she declares that "we find an extraordinary need in the gospels to shift blame for the death of Jesus . . . from Roman political authority to Jewish religious authority."[46] It is this kind of distortion of Jewish culpability about which Catholics were encouraged to become aware. Indeed, such observations by Catholic theologians were inspired by *Nostra Aetate,* No. 4, and an effort was made to reduce the sting of the theology of contempt. For this reason, John T. Pawlikowski was disillusioned with the deicide statement offered by *Nostra Aetate,* No. 4. Its indictment of "the Jewish authorities and those who followed their lead [and] pressed for the death of Christ," Pawlikowski believed, left the door open for future misunderstanding. Pawlikowski had hoped that the Vatican statement would have elaborated in greater detail the findings of modern scholarship. He would have preferred that the Second Vatican Council's declaration would show that the responsibility for Jesus' execution was the work of "collaboration between the Roman government and a handful of Jewish leaders who ruled occupied Palestine for the imperial government."[47] What needed to be explained, as Catholic theologians in the United States were doing, was that the Jewish population of Palestine might have disagreed with Jesus and his religious ideas, but, like him, they saw Rome as their greater enemy. It was unthinkable that Jews would have collaborated with Romans, their occupiers and enemy, in a political execution of a Jew with whom they disagreed.[48]

Few writers have done more than Pawlikowski to explain the Crucifixion story in such a way that it would create the least damage to Catholic-Jewish relations. For the most part, Pawlikowski has succeeded, although there have been occasions when his assertions would have been categorically rejected by Jewish readers. In respect to the Crucifixion, the following illustrates points which Pawlikowski made in 1984: "In relating the story of Jesus' death, the Christian Churches need to begin stressing that the religious ideals which Jesus preached, and which he tried to implement . . . *were shared by the most creative and forward looking in the Judaism of the period* [italics mine]. It was this preaching and action that brought Jesus to Calvary."[49] It is the kind of triumphalism that Pawlikowski ordinarily avoids indulging in; in this case, however, his slip is overshadowed by his effort to advance the Catholic-Jewish relationship.

This bit of triumphalism suggests the difficulty even the most prominent of scholars have found in attempting to soften the negative impact that the Crucifixion story has had upon Jewish-Christian understanding. Official Roman Catholic publications notwithstanding (neither the 1994 *Catechism of the Catholic Church* nor the 1995 edition of *The HarperCollins Encyclopedia of Catholicism* implicates the Jews in the Crucifixion),[50] the deicide matter still awaits a definitive solution.

American Catholic scholars and prelates have made enormous strides in reinterpreting and clarifying Jesus' crucifixion. By the end of the twentieth century, many reputable biblical scholars had concluded that there was no relationship between the popular narrative of the trial and crucifixion of Jesus and the actual historical event. The conclusion includes the observation that the seventy-one members of the supreme Sanhedrin of Jerusalem would not have been convened to try Jesus. Indeed, recent New Testament scholars find little evidence of mass Jewish involvement in Jesus' execution.[51] When the work of Raymond E. Brown, the leading Catholic authority on the new interpretation of the Crucifixion, is discussed in a popular magazine, it is plain that the theology of contempt is withering.[52]

Popular Catholic thinkers, especially abroad, much to the frustration of American Catholic leaders, were reluctant to release their imaginations from the ancient tales about the villainous role that the Jews played in the Crucifixion. As an example, one need only turn to the ancient German village of Oberammergau, where in 1990 one hundred performances were given of its famous Passion Play. As noted earlier, such performances of the story of Jesus as traditionally recounted had been taking place for three centuries practically unchanged. Actors playing the parts of Jews were conspicuous in all of these performances. What is surprising is the little effect that pronouncements of the Second Vatican Council, not to mention the impact of the *Shoah,* had upon the proud German Catholics of Oberammergau. All of the historical, anthropological, linguistic, and theological work and the conclusions which had been drawn since 1965 were completely ignored by the directors of the Passion Play.[53]

Dozens of antisemitic stereotypical images of Jews and insulting comments about them pervaded the play. Jews throughout the world, including the United States, were appalled. Knowledge about the play and the antisemitic details of the performance were well known to Americans while dramatic preparation and rehearsals were going on. Even before the 1990 edition of the play opened, American Catholic leaders appointed a committee of inquiry. Included on it were such well-known writers as Gerard Sloyan of Temple University; Eugene Fisher; Leonard Swidler; and John J. Kelley, liaison for the American National Secretariat of the American Council of Catholic Bishops, joined by members of the world Jewish community. They discovered and requested that at least twenty-five antisemitic references and scenes be removed from the play.[54] Some of the most notorious included the "blood charge" found in Matthew 27:25: "His blood be upon us and upon our children!" When asked by American Catholic representatives to remove this spoken curse, the Oberammergau village elders twice voted down a proposal to remove the "blood curse" from the play text.

Just as shameful were insulting scenes depicting members of the Sanhedrin of Jerusalem: all were portrayed with horns, giving each a demonic appearance. This was also true of the depiction of Moses, whose head was bedecked with devilish horns. American Catholic leaders were able to persuade the producers of the Passion Play to remove the actors' horns; some fifty pages of changes in text were also agreed to, lessening and/or eliminating many of the lesser insults.[55]

Although the ending of the American crusade to cleanse the Oberammergau play was not completely happy, one could conclude that without the vigorous intervention of American Catholic prelates and scholars, joined by American Jewish leaders, the theology of contempt would have been left intact. As it was, some forward steps into the postconciliar era were taken. More important, because of lessons learned in 1990, the preparation of future Passion Plays might well proceed with greater concern for the relationship of the two faith communities.

□ □ □

Few terms have been more seriously misunderstood throughout Western history by Catholic writers than the designation "Pharisees." Few adjectives have been more widely used by Christians to describe an individual as sanctimonious, self-righteous, or hypocritical than "Pharisaic."[56] The word was first employed in this fashion by the authors of the synoptic gospels to describe those Jews who allegedly stood in opposition to Jesus and his message and who conspired against him. Because of such usage, it became almost impossible for Christian believers to think of the Pharisees in anything but contemptible ways. Yet, as has been noted, for the Jews of Jesus' time, their Pharisaic leaders played a most important revolutionary, creative, and heroic role. They were the largest and most significant Jewish sect during the Second Temple era (circa 200 B.C.E.–70 C.E.). Historians have credited the Pharisees with laying the foundation of Judaism by replacing the Temple cult with a regimen of prayer, study, and living in accordance with the rules of the Torah, both written and oral. The rabbis refined and elaborated halakic and ethical teachings so well that they enabled Jews to live successful religious and moral lives until the secularizing influences of the Age of Enlightenment. The Pharisees are credited with enabling Jews to survive as Jews, although stateless and surrounded by the attractive but powerful and threatening forces of Christianity and Islam.[57]

Therefore, to place the Pharisees in their proper place in history and to restore their dignity in the eyes of Christendom were important tasks for Catholic scholars also. Since myths are difficult to obliterate, the task was formidable, but a group of Catholic theologians exerted every effort to restore the reputation of the Pharisees in Catholic teaching and preaching.[58]

John T. Pawlikowski, Eugene Fisher, Claire Huchet Bishop, and Rosemary Ruether stand high on the list of those who made such attempts to reevaluate the Pharisees, with Pawlikowski's writing among the first Catholic efforts to set the Jewish record straight.[59] Pawlikowski is concerned about the damaging impact that Christian denigration of the Pharisees could have on work to improve interfaith relations as well as on the integrity of the Christian record. He is disillusioned that the creative accomplishments of the Pharisees have been ignored in Catholic studies. He underscores the high moral and ethical standards of religious behavior established by the Pharisees. The development of the synagogue as a central focus of the Jewish community is considered by Pawlikowski to be a major achievement of Pharisaic Judaism. Most significant for him is the profound influence that the radical ideas of the Pharisees had upon Jesus and his ministry.[60] Like other Catholic theologians, Pawlikowski plays down the significance of the harsh language employed in the Gospels against the Pharisees and the synagogue. On the contrary, he portrays Jesus as being very close in his religious views to those of both the Torah and synagogue.[61]

Postconciliar writers tried to tone down the disagreements between Pharisees and Jesus. They saw such a disagreement as little more than a family quarrel which was in later years blown out of proportion.[62] Pawlikowski also explains to his Catholic readers that the emergence of the rabbi during the Pharisaic era as a replacement of the temple priest was a brand-new aspect of the emerging movement. The rabbi gained acceptance by the Jewish people because of his knowledge of the Torah, not through heredity, as had been the case of the temple priesthood. An important aspect of the Pharisaic revolution was the position that knowledge of the Torah held as a vehicle for leadership in the new Jewish community.[63]

Catholic writers saw the early rabbis as the "true heirs of the prophets," who tried to translate the law into everyday use, so that the Jews could live by the moral laws of the Torah. "Every ordinary, daily human action could become sacred if it were seen, as the rabbis insisted it should be seen, as an act of worship."[64] What is more, according to Pawlikowski, "through their interpretations, or the oral *Torah*, [the rabbis] succeeded in deepening, humanizing and universalizing the older Jewish tradition."[65] Most important for Catholic writers' reinterpretation of Pharisaism was their linkage of the Pharisees to the origins of the Christian faith. As Eugene Fisher writes, "Christianity is . . . essentially Jewish in origin, and it owes much of its faith to one special branch of Judaism: the Pharisees."[66]

▢ ▢ ▢

Nostra Aetate, No. 4, was explicit in its rejection of the idea that God has withdrawn his covenant which he had made with the Jewish people. Yet such rejection flew in the face of traditional church teaching that Jewish election had been transferred to the New Israel. God's displacement of the Jews had become a major plank in the anti-Jewish teaching of the church fathers.[67] The devastating implication of displacement theology on Christian-Jewish relations throughout the two millennia of Christendom is the reason that the Second Vatican Council's new declaration caused concern among the Catholic faithful over the continuing viability of Judaism in the eyes of God.

It was an announcement that required elaboration during the decades following Vatican II. After all, the Vatican statement could not by a flick of the eyebrow obliterate the mass of patristic literature and later church writing which held that the Gentiles had displaced the sinful Jews in the eyes of heaven.[68] Following the council, Catholic theologians contended that a theology of displacement which claims that other faiths are incomplete until appropriated by Christianity is incompatible with the idea of pluralism. For instance, Christian universalism, the theologian Gregory Baum argues, does not mean any more that all people must become Christians.[69]

In a similar vein, Peter Chirico, the Jesuit scholar and professor of theology at St. Patrick's Seminary in Menlo Park, California, declared in 1970 that Catholics must recognize that Judaism's authentic revelation is ongoing, just like the Christian one. Catholics, he warned, must abandon the idea that Judaism's fulfillment can come only through Christ.[70] The continuing existence of Jews, not only as individuals but as a "corporate" body, should constitute no problem for Catholicism, according to Chirico. Jewish existence has always been and continues to be a religious fact. "Peoples and groupings such as the Jews," writes Chirico, "constitute unique revelations of God, [and] they must be respected as such by Christians."[71]

The theologian Monika Hellwig's writings support this rejection of the theology of displacement. She declares: "If every spoken and written record of God's revelation is so inescapably human and particular, deep respect and total receptivity are due equally to all testimony of God's revelation."[72]

Pope John Paul II's addresses to Jewish groups during the years of his pontificate stressed his frequent rejection of any element of supersessionism. Eugene Fisher, editor of the pope's speeches, writes that the pontiff declares "the dialogue between Catholics and Jews . . . is not a dialogue between past (Judaism) and present (Christianity) realities, as if the former had been 'superseded' or 'replaced' by the other, as certain Christian polemicists would have it." In order to prevent any notion of displacement, Pope John Paul II recommended that such terms as "Old" and "New" Testament be replaced with such words as "Hebrew Scriptures" and "Christian Scriptures." Such change, he believed, might prevent the impression that one testament superseded the other.[73] The pope's words underscore the demoralizing effect of supersessionism on interfaith relations.

◻ ◻ ◻

For Jews, the obliteration of the theological suggestion that the New Israel had displaced the "Old" had enormously important implications. For the first time, it restored in the eyes of the church the viability and integrity of Judaism in God's eyes. It accepted the Jewish people as equal partners in the world of faith. Once and for all, Judaism ceased to be seen as an incomplete religion awaiting its "fulfillment" by absorption into the New Israel. And no more was its Torah viewed as an introduction to the Christian testament. In a more practical sense, the Catholic hope for the conversion of the Jews was now unnecessary. Indeed, any effort to proselytize among Jews was now considered outmoded.

Missionary work among the Jews had been an integral function of the church for centuries. Although not a well-organized crusade in the United States, the hope of Jewish conversion was never out of sight. For the church to abandon such a goal did not come easily. Even before the closing sessions of the Second Vatican Council, American Jesuits greeted the prospect of the demise of missionary work with some trepidation.[74] It was a particularly uncomfortable transition for such societies as the Sisters of Sion, one of whose major preoccupations seemed to be the conversion of Jews. First came the *Shoah*, which decimated their Paris office, and then the Second Vatican Council and new theological teachings impressed upon them the need to alter their mission and direction.[75] Many of the Sisters of Sion were confused by the new ecclesiastical changes. Many did not see a necessity for them. A few wondered if it was still proper for them to pray for the Jews. Some felt betrayed. It was difficult suddenly to abandon a lifetime of certitude for the uncertainties of interfaith work.[76]

Indeed, the decade following Vatican II was marked by a veritable crisis for Catholic missionaries. As they perused the conciliar documents, they realized that all their protests were in vain. The coming of a new era was evident. Missions, especially to the Jews, were henceforth unacceptable. The church witnessed at this time a large exodus of priests, nuns, and brothers from evangelical work. The practice of "dialogue" and advocacy of "religious liberty" had now become church doctrine.[77] To reduce, if not eliminate, all vestiges of the theology of contempt, Jews had to be assured by the church that they were not to be objects of conversion. Even as such assurance was offered, a strong trace of ambivalence about this matter remained. Among Catholic theologians, it was no simple matter on the one hand to affirm the integrity, positive value, and viability of a non-Christian faith and on the other to work toward its conversion.[78] There was universal agreement, however, that no effort be made by Catholics to proselytize Jews while dialoguing with them. As Richard Cardinal Cushing of Boston told a gathering at the Congregation of Temple Mishkan Tefila in Chestnut Hill, Massachusetts, in October 1969, "It must not be—or even thought to be—a missionary venture, an effort at proselytism on either one side or the other."[79]

Compliance with the request to refrain from proselytizing Jews was rarely an issue. John M. Oesterreicher, whose life had for many years been absorbed in trying to attract Jews to what he saw as the truth of Christianity, made a sharp turn following the direction of the Second Vatican Council. Through the pages of *The Bridge,* of which he was editor, he wrote of the impropriety of converting Jews. In 1971, he observed that "there is in the Church today no drive, no organized effort to proselytize Jews, and none is contemplated for tomorrow."[80] Yet Oesterreicher came to the rejection of "conversionist tactics" with a degree of ambivalence. He writes, "Let me say only one more word on this point: No matter how firmly we reject any 'conversionist tactics,' we must, at the same time, love the concept of, and call to, conversion."[81]

A number of Catholic thinkers recognized that after Auschwitz, any attempt to snatch Jewish souls for the church bordered on the inhumane. At the same time, they grappled with a theological rationale to justify the abandonment of missions to the Jews. Some considered conversionary efforts sinful, as another way of blotting out Jewish existence, the completion of Hitler's work.[82] Recognizing the historic changes, the highest ecclesiastical body of the Roman Catholic Church responded with its statement, "The Decree on Missionary Activity," although it did not explicitly declare the abandonment of Catholic outreach to the Jews.[83] Such ambivalence was evident in the writings of some theologians. John T. Pawlikowski, for example, noted in 1977 that "Christianity in and by itself does not contain in their fullness all the ideas necessary for a complete understanding of man's religious dimension." In regard to Judaism, Pawlikowski's view of Christology in "no way invalidates Judaism, its covenant and its distinctiveness." What is more, according to Pawlikowski, "This new Christology will force us to re-think the idea of trying to 'convert' Jews (or any other non-Christian problem)." Yet at the same time, he is unwilling "to simply exclude the Jewish people from the missionary enterprise, if similar exclusions were not urged for the other great world religions. . . . I still believe that Christians have a responsibility to present the meaning of the Christ Event to the world, including the Jewish people. But this must be done through dialogue in which we first of all respect the faith of the non-Christian and secondly realize that in this process we too will have to be converted."[84]

Pawlikowski's observation offers a clear example of the difficulty some Christian theologians who ordinarily stood at the frontier of Jewish-

Christian relations had with the problem of an absolute rejection of the conversion of Jews. Other theologians, such as Michael B. McGarry, are more emphatic in rejecting a missionary outreach to the Jews. He explains, "After what some Christians did (and did not do) during the Holocaust, Catholics should have the courtesy to leave the Jews alone."[85] For McGarry, any attempt on the part of the church to convert the Jews constitutes an affront to God. In one of his most forthright utterances, he writes:

> God's election, given through Moses[,] does not end. . . . If Christians focus their energy on converting the Jews, they are systematically attempting to eliminate the sacrament and sign that Yahweh calls humans as community as well as individually. They may be undermining their very own belief. Furthermore, if by a convert-making enterprise Christians ever eliminate the Jews . . . as a nation faithful to the call it hears through the *Torah*, then they will obscure their own belief in God: faithfulness to election. That is, if the world sees an end to the Jewish nation, then the world may well conclude that God's election is "only for a time" until some other group obliterates it by conversion. . . . From a theological perspective . . . the Roman Catholic Church can make the Jews an exception in evangelization not because of any timidity . . . but because it believes passionately what has been revealed [about election]. . . . If the Church ever believed otherwise, then it might be cutting the very tree on whom its own branch finds life and nourishment. . . . It is a posture that comes not out of convenience, not out of embarrassment for the Holocaust, not out of a liberal Christianity. . . . rather it flows from the passionate belief that a gracious and faithful God has called the Jewish people out of love for them and as a sign of an abiding, never-to-be-broken sacrament of election.[86]

As a priest and prominent religious thinker, McGarry has gone far beyond his Catholic colleagues in formulating a religious explanation for abandoning missionary work among the Jews. Although his intent was not designed to erase an ancient annoyance for Jews, it represents an important step in uprooting remnants of the church's contempt for the unconverted Jew.

I I

A New Past

In the decades preceding the Second Vatican Council, little effort was exerted by Catholic scholars to learn either the difficulties or the achievements of the Jewish people. The impact of the Roman Catholic Church on the lives of the Jews was not viewed as a subject worthy of serious contemplation. The most prominent American Catholic historians who wrote between 1946 and 1965 made little effort to gaze beyond the church. During those years, they preferred to study the history of religious orders, diocesan histories, and episcopal biographies.[1] It goes without saying that little attention was paid to Jewish themes either domestic or international. Yet a creative and productive Jewish life, rooted in the Torah and the counsel of rabbinic interpretation while existing under the shadow of the cross, was tolerated as one of the mysteries of God.

The statement of the Vatican council as well as the various guidelines and papers which followed brought about a transformation in Catholic interest, a broadening of the horizons of its vision of history in general and the Jewish past in particular.[2] This does not mean that vast numbers of Catholic historians began doing Jewish history. But the new trend left the door ajar for those few Catholic scholars who were drawn to the problem of the church and the Jews. They included theologians as well as historians, professors, and priests. After all, the church and its hierarchy advised its members to study the history of the Jewish people with the same understanding that Jews understood it themselves. Here too was an attempt to undermine the theology of contempt and, at the same time, to permit the church to reexamine its lost identity.

The new major Catholic enthusiasm was now focused on the postbiblical era, the years in which students of the church had heretofore indicated the least amount of interest. The displacement of the Old Israel by the New had fashioned the Jews into a non-people whose activities ceased to possess meaning for the Christian world. This neglect had produced a vacuum about Jews and Judaism in the Catholic world. Consequently, in the process of creating this new history, some Catholic historians turned to their Jewish counterparts.

One of the earliest of such efforts, Frederick M. Schweitzer's *A History of the Jews since the First Century A.D.*, "owed its inception" to the cooperative support of the Archdiocese of New York and the Anti-Defamation League of B'nai B'rith. At the same time, though, Schweitzer, a professor of history at Manhattan College, admits that the project's impetus came from the inspiring words of Pope John XXIII and the pronouncements of the Second Vatican Council.[3]

Schweitzer is an early representative of a new group of Catholic historians who openly recognized the pariah status and the condition of humiliation that was meted out to Jews in the age of Catholic hegemony. This was the case, he writes, in "almost every period in the two millennia of the Jewish-Christian encounter."[4] Schweitzer believes that the time has come for Catholic historians to share the story of their encounter with the Jewish people, "one that has no pages 'torn out' and includes everything that is true and significant." This is imperative, he believes, because as Catholics and historians, Catholics approach the history of the Jews with an "immense ignorance." This, Schweitzer declares, is largely the fault of Catholic education. Regardless of its level—elementary, secondary, or university—the history of the Jewish people represents the "worst lacuna" in Catholic education. Secular education is equally guilty of this sin of omission, but, in the light of conciliar and postconciliar teaching, it is inexcusable for the church.[5]

As a Catholic, Schweitzer approaches the writing of Jewish history cautiously. He believes that until one is able to divest oneself of all prejudice, "the writing of Jewish history will be extremely difficult. It requires of the historical scholar the highest canons of accuracy and truth, proportion and completeness and objectivity. He must take infinite pains if he is not to fall into the error or oversimplification that supports—or can be used to support—some old or generates some new prejudice."[6] Schweitzer's caveat represents the uncertainty of a historian treading on terra incognita. It also underscores the distance which was to be traveled from pre–Second Vatican Council historiography.

Significantly, the Catholic historian concluded after completing his examination of the Jewish past that Jewish history should not be treated as was the account of Greek civilization. This was an error that Catholics frequently committed. Unlike its Greek counterpart, writes Schweitzer, Jewish history had a profound and continuing impact on Western civilization, one which did not culminate during the classical era. He challenges his colleagues to surmount the academic wall that has traditionally separated Western and European history from that of the Jews. Schweitzer is convinced that Jewish history has a stronger claim on the Catholic curriculum than do more popular non-Western studies: Islam, Buddhism, and Hinduism. "I cannot believe," he writes, "it is possible to make much sense of European and Western history without considerable attention to post-biblical Jewry and Judaism. Such studies are not merely auxiliary and peripheral. . . . Jewish life and thought seem like golden threads woven into the very fabric of our history and culture."[7] Catholic leaders were in agreement with historians that "the long silence between the New Testament and the Holocaust . . . must come to an end in Catholic teaching," as Eugene J. Fisher observed.[8]

Whereas the Second Vatican Council strongly influenced even those who only a few years earlier desired to rescue Jews from their displacement by the New Israel through baptism, it now affected those who were eager to reinterpret the Jewish people's history. One of the most successful of these attempts is the work of Edward H. Flannery, who studied for the priesthood in France and assisted John Oesterreicher in his work to bring about the conversion of the Jews. Flannery's *The Anguish of the Jews*, first published in 1965, stands also as a prime effort to undo the old past of the Jewish people. Flannery's focus is on the horrors that Jews suffered at the hands of Christians. A book-length examination, an indictment of the Christian world, had rarely been seen before as a product of Catholic scholarship. Like Schweitzer's work, it stands as a testimony to the long road traveled in less than a decade.

Flannery's desire was to provide the "Christian an opportunity to confront a capital sin of the Christian past, recapitulated in the present." He wanted his coreligionists to face up to their responsibility in bringing about the end of "this longest hatred of human history."[9] He hoped that such knowledge would put an end to this lamentable evil. "For the Christian," writes Flannery, "such a venture would, in most instances, be an almost total uncovering of repressed material, a painful catharsis. Only such an exorcism of the demons of the past will permit a reassessment of the quality of our Christianity and the truth of our theology and lead to that attitude of maturity and responsibility so essential to the mutual understanding and cooperation with Jews to which the Church is committed."[10]

◻ ◻ ◻

Catholic scholars encountered their most difficult hurdle when rewriting the past of the era of the New Testament. To present the role of the Jews in the time of Jesus in a positive light was one matter for Catholic scholars. It was quite another to convince lay people, teachers in elementary and secondary schools, and writers of textbooks for young students to revise their deeply embedded notions about the Jews. The most sacred period in the Catholic maturation experience was not easily subject to revision. Yet that was precisely what had to be done if a new vision of the Jewish past was to materialize in the Catholic minds, and it had to begin in the Catholic schools.

Revision of the past really had to start with Catholic educators, argued post–Vatican II scholars. "Unsavory periods in church history," wrote Claire Huchet Bishop, must be taught. Such unsavory events as the Crusades and the blood accusations against European Jews, as well as the expulsions and pogroms culminating with the *Shoah,* had to be taught with honesty. Bishop and other writers called for frankness and boldness in the new Catholic education.[11]

Catholic instruction was among the church's highest priorities. Changes required the approval of the highest ecclesiastical authorities. Religious subject matter was presented to students as church doctrine. The request of American bishops in 1973 that Catholic education include the teaching of "respect" for Jews and their tradition was consequently no idle matter to faithful Catholics.[12] The importance for Catholic officials and teachers to present the Jewish experience with accuracy to Catholic listeners was stressed in a Vatican document addressed to all churches in 1985. "Notes on the Correct Way to Present the Jews and Judaism in Preaching and Catechesis in the Roman Catholic Church" was approved by Pope John Paul II. Before the Vatican committee began its deliberations, the pope impressed upon the group the need for an accurate portrayal of Judaism and its heritage in Catholic teaching.[13]

Indeed, portraying Jews with greater sensitivity was an objective urged upon those who composed and taught from prepared material in secondary schools. In 1984, Eugene J. Fisher stated that "most of the blatant anti-Jewish canards have been eliminated from our religious education and discourse." Fisher believed that Catholic teaching materials had been revised in accordance with directives from the hierarchy. He expected even further progress, especially in material relating to the deicide and Crucifixion charges.[14] Yet Fisher also recognized the existence of unresolved problems. He admitted that "few textbooks or teachers' manuals provide the background and the history of Antisemitism or in the development of the New Testament passion narratives." Without appropriate teaching, Fisher notes, the "highly volatile" texts could be damaging. "With no background material given for teachers, one can only conclude that the cumulative influence on the student, over the years of Christian education, will in the final analysis be little different than that of the sixteenth-century catechisms."[15]

American bishops together with Jewish leaders worked hard to alter Catholic teaching material. In the 1986 document "Within Context: Guidelines for the Catechetical Presentation of Jews and Judaism in the New Testament [1986]," American bishops outlined their recommendations for teaching New Testament accounts without in any way prejudicing the relationship of Jews and Catholics. They placed great emphasis on the Jewish traditions of Christian origins and the teachings of Jesus. Likewise, the liturgical links of Judaism and Catholicism were discussed in an effort to underscore Jewish-Christian bonds. The guidelines conclude that "school texts, prayerbooks and other media should, under competent auspices, continue to be examined in order to remove not only those materials that do not accord with the content and spirit of the church's teaching, but also those that fail to show Judaism's continuing role in salvation history in a positive light."[16]

The teaching of early Christian history remained a problem throughout the final years of the twentieth century. It disturbed leaders of the American Jewish community. It was difficult, as Judith H. Banki of the American Jewish Committee observed, for Christians to divest themselves of the stereotypical images of the New Testament: Jesus vs. the Pharisees, Jews and the Crucifixion, the harshness of the "Law," Church vs. synagogue.[17] These failings, however, were due more to the inexperience of lay Catholics than they were to Catholic scholars and church leaders, who were more attuned to the voices from Rome.

◦ ◦ ◦

The first centuries of Christianity corresponded to the rabbinic or Talmudic era. The literature produced by the rabbis of this time, the Talmud, which consisted of the Mishna, Gemara, and commentaries, had been viewed by the church throughout most of European history with suspicion and disdain. Perused by Catholic scholars for blasphemies against Christ and church teachings, the tractates of this hallowed work were on occasion ordered by the church to be banished and burned. Yet these sacred and erudite works unified the Jewish people, who, although stateless, maintained their Jewish identity throughout the long centuries.

It was in the post–Vatican II era that a new look was directed toward the rabbinic age of Judaism. "To skip over the Rabbinic or Talmudic period of Jewish history," writes the Catholic historian Frederick M. Schweitzer, "would be equivalent to giving an account of Christianity that ignores the patristic age."[18] In recounting the history of the rabbinic period, Schweitzer, unlike preconciliar commentators, writes with sensitivity and understanding of the role that religious, moral, and social practice played in the lives of the Jewish people, unlike Catholics, who were more inclined to follow a code of "doctrinal purity." Such comparative analysis accorded with the new attitude toward the Jewish past recommended by church officials.[19]

In the new Catholic account of the rabbinic era, no room was allowed for displacement theology. Both faiths, as Eugene J. Fisher said, had equal claim as representatives of biblical continuity in their process of developing toward maturity.[20] But, as Fisher observes, not all misrepresentations of the rabbinic time disappeared from Catholic circles. This was particularly true of some radical feminists, who were fond of juxtaposing Jesus Christ's feminism (for which there is no documentation) against the rabbinic "sexism," which was probably no different from, if not distinctly less than, that which was present in early and especially later Christian society.[21]

At the same time, the church fathers were busily reinforcing and validating the theological foundations of Christianity. In examining their writing in this age of openness and dialogue following the Vatican council, some Catholic writers concluded that the literature of the patristic age not only reinforced Christian foundations but also strengthened Christian anti-Judaism. Indeed, an important segment of the church fathers' anti-Jewish writings—sermons, letters, polemics, plays—compiled under the general heading of *Adversos Judaeos* (against the Jews) did much to fashion Catholic hostility toward Jews for centuries to come. Some of the most vitriolic of these tracts came from the fourth century C.E. It was, as Edward Flannery observed, one of the most fateful centuries in the history of Christian-Jewish relations. The age of Constantine the Great (288–337) "was at hand," and the hegemony of the Roman Catholic Church was not far off. Theologically, it was an era of achievement and ferment. St. Jerome, St. Gregory I, St. John Chrysostom, St. Ambrose of Milan, St. Augustine of Hippo, and others made the patristic age memorable for the church. But for the Jews, the church's triumph brought a time of challenge and peril.

Nevertheless, without taking away the religious significance of the church fathers, modern Catholic writers, in accordance with post–Vatican II efforts to uproot the theology of contempt, exposed, explained, or tried to strip away the hostility toward Jews found in the patristic writings. The noted Jesuit scholar Robert F. Drinan lashed out in 1977 at those Catholics who deny that early Christian writings do contain antisemitic polemics. He was critical of those "Christians, seeking to validate their contention that the Jews by divine plan will always be persecuted."[22] Although Drinan admired "the many brilliant Christian apologists" of the patristic generation, he was compelled to admit that they "enunciated so many un-Christian, untrue, and unjustified slanders against the Jews. One seeks to exculpate these writers."[23] Even though such anti-Judaism, writes Drinan, grew out of a desire to validate a yet uncertain Christianity during its first four hundred years, it was inexcusable. He finds deplorable the patristic "ominous elaboration of the theme that a divine curse or punishment was decreed by God upon the Jews for their role in the crucifixion of Christ." Drinan notes that what Jules Isaac had called "the teaching of contempt" as epitomized in patristic writings "had finally permeated the Christian mind."[24]

Rosemary Ruether, as another example, notes that the collection of testimonies in the fourth and fifth centuries in the *Adversos Judaeos* became the stock source of those accusations cast at the Jews throughout the Middle Ages and beyond: that the Jews were blind, that they killed their prophets, that they did not understand scripture.[25] Numerous authors contributed to the anti-Jewish polemical treatises. The eight sermons against the Jews by John Chrysostom at the end of the fourth century C.E. were among the most powerful in their polemical hostility toward Jews.[26]

Ruether is explicit in her assertion that the theological status of Judaism was formulated by the writings of the church fathers between the third and seventh centuries C.E. It was not a flattering picture, but it possessed an enormous Christological influence for centuries to come. A powerful theme of patristic literature, according to Ruether's study, is the election of the Gentiles, who displace the Jews as favored in the eyes of God. To the church fathers, the "evil nature of the Jews" began during their stay in Egypt and continued to grow. They became sinners and idolaters. They led a "wild and savage life" and tried to kill Moses.[27]

This was a harsh outburst by future Christian saints. Yet there is no evidence that the rabbis responded in any formal way. As Ruether notes, the rabbis did not produce *Adversos Christianos* to refute patristic charges. There were isolated critical comments about Jewish heretics in the Talmud, but they were insignificant if compared to the hateful eruptions against the Jews by the church fathers. Generally speaking, the rabbis viewed all of Christian teaching as a heresy, not worthy of serious consideration. That Christianity was viewed by Jewish leaders first as a nuisance and later, as Christianity grew in political power, as a mortal threat, also discouraged a serious Jewish polemic. If there was any Jewish response at all, it was seen in the intensification of rabbinic teaching and religious practice and the growth of cohesiveness of the Jewish community. By the early fifth century, waves of violence against the Jews were not uncommon. According to Flannery, pogroms against Jews occurred. One mob assault in 388 C.E., led by bishops, burned down a synagogue.[28]

The denunciation of the patristic writers' view of Judaism made by Rosemary Ruether, Edward Flannery, and others stands as a striking example of the courage supplied by the Second Vatican Council to these scholars which allowed them to challenge the anti-Jewish diatribes of the church fathers. But it expressed not only Catholic disappointment with the patristic writing about Judaism. Catholics were also willing to concede a parity of achievements between rabbis and church fathers in their writing for their respective faiths. Talmudic scholarship and patristic literature were seen to follow parallel routes. Writing of the church fathers in 1971, the European scholar Friedrich Heer declares, "That terrible century, engulfed in hatred, murder, expulsion, banishment and endless denunciation was the great watershed: Judaism and Christianity are still in many ways the religions of the fourth century. The Councils of Nicaea and Constantinople and the schools of Pumbeditha and Sura [Babylonian centers of Jewish learning] left their stamp on both religions."[29]

Scholars have disagreed about the intensity of anti-Judaism which existed before the fourth century C.E. No doubt both Christians and Jews eyed each other with suspicion. There was probably deep concern about the other on both sides.[30] As Christian influence grew, Judaism became more vulnerable, and the polemical assault upon it more damaging. Drinan and other Catholic writers, open to the truth and more willing than ever to improve the church's relationship with the Jews, were agreeable to writing about it. They were not turning their backs on the patristic age. Despite the church fathers' sins against the Jews, they did not lose that hallowed place in church history. But by acknowledging the horror that they inspired against the Jews, Catholic scholars have taken

a long step in the direction of uprooting the old past and with it the
theology of contempt.

◦ ◦ ◦

It is understandable why Catholics have looked back at the Middle Ages
with admiration and affection. The one thousand or so years which
stretched from the age of Constantine in the fourth century to the Re-
naissance of the sixteenth was truly a Catholic millennium. Its Christian
values were held up as models for subsequent generations to emulate.
But that the Jews lived precariously under the sometimes cruel domination of the church and its authorities was not a subject which Catholic
scholars found fit to include in discussions of the Middle Ages. Indeed,
that Jewish communities were scattered throughout Europe during the
Catholic millennium was virtually ignored by Catholic historians.[31] In
response to new Vatican doctrines and recommendations urging Catholics to acquaint themselves with the postbiblical Jewish past, a new
attitude surfaced. A small group of Catholic scholars took a new look
at the Middle Ages.[32] As Frederick Schweitzer sadly observed: "The historian of the Jewish middle ages [is] caught up in a depressing story of
man's inhumanity to man. Try as he will to emphasize the more positive aspects—Jewish achievements in scholarship, in commercial and
financial endeavors, and moments of cordiality between Jews and Christians—they are decidedly uncharacteristic of the age, and he is confronted
rather with a reign of terror."[33]

Harry James Cargas believed that it was important for Christians to
examine the violence which throughout history they had perpetrated
upon the Jews. "It is the greatest import," he wrote in 1990, "that we
Christians know precisely how Jews react to us after persecution." In
examining the treatment of Jews in the Middle Ages, Cargas detects the
foreshadowing of Nazism in some of the early church decrees.[34]

Those scholars who restored the record of Jewish existence to the
Catholic millennium were aware that it was a task done at the expense
of the church's glory. It was a depressing revelation, as Frederick Schweitzer noted. However, it was important, Catholic writers argued, for Catholics to revise their notions of the glories of the Middle Ages. The thirteenth century, for example, which Catholics recalled as an era of
unmatched greatness, was for Jews a terrible century, riddled with violence toward them. There were moments of peacefulness and security
that Jews enjoyed in the long centuries of the Middle Ages. But they were,
according to Edward Flannery, not typical. It was rare for the medieval

Jew not to be reminded of his subordination to the church authority.[35] No effort is made by postconciliar Vatican scholars to conceal the blemishes of the Middle Ages. While admitting that the thirteenth century had enjoyed the creative output of some of the church's most profound philosophers and theologians, they recognized that it was also an era of barbaric antisemitism.

High on postconciliar scholars' lists of outbreaks against the Jews were the Crusades. Economic jealousy and religious fanaticism during the Crusades marked the beginning of a long train of horrors perpetrated against the Jews. The Crusades marked a time of pillage and forced conversions, unprecedented for the Middle Ages. Even the great Catholic theologian St. Thomas Aquinas wrote, according to one Catholic historian, "It would be licit, according to custom, to hold Jews, because of their crime, in perpetual servitude, and therefore the princes may regard the possessions of Jews as belonging to their state."[36] Such license for plundering Jews gave unprincipled Catholic ruffians an opportunity of a lifetime.

Catholic historians note that as the church reached the zenith of its power and influence in the second millennium of the Common Era, the precariousness of Jewish life increased in the same measure. In Jewish history, Edward Flannery reminds his Christian readers, it would be difficult to point to the beginnings of a more dangerous time than the year 1096, the start of the first Crusade. Jews became the first victims of the Christian armies on their way to fight against the Muslims. Jewish communities were looted and their inhabitants baptized at sword point. "To find a year more fateful in the history of Judaism than 1096," writes Flannery, "would necessitate going back a thousand years to the fall of Jerusalem or forward to the genocide of Hitler. Though often suppressed by other years in the volume of atrocities, 1096 marks the beginning of a harassment of the Jews that, in duration and intensity, was unique in Jewish history."[37] It would have been extremely rare for preconciliar Catholic historians to write so bluntly about a brutal attack upon the Jews by a Christian army in the name of the church. Schweitzer makes no effort to conceal hatred of Jews by Catholic monks who considered the Jews "Children of the Devil," or condemned them as did the "popular preachers of Crusading like Peter the Hermit and Walter the Penniless." The bloody legacy that they left behind in the name of the church would linger for nearly a thousand years.[38]

For Rosemary Ruether, "The great turning point of Jewish status in the Western Middle Ages, a turning-point itself expressive of the success of the Church's indoctrination of the popular religious hatred of the Jews, was the Crusades."[39] Ruether is quite emphatic in her observation that the pillage of the Jews did not only go unopposed by the church but was encouraged by it. Crusades "enthusiasm" was appreciated by church officials who saw more good than harm resulting from it. Ruether admits that there was a time when fanaticism also served the Church well.[40]

The results of such church indifference and encouragement are a story well known, but heretofore one that was not examined with any thoroughness by Catholic scholars. One of the most notorious chapters of this legacy, especially with its deep Christological undercurrent, was the charge of ritual murder, which has been thrown at the Jewish people throughout the centuries, even in modern times. The "blood accusation" first used in the twelfth century accused Jews of allegedly kidnapping and slaughtering Christian children to use their blood for Passover observance. It is, at first glance, a charge so barbaric that it seems incomprehensible. Yet, if placed in the context of Jewish demonization encouraged by the church leaders, it can be seen as one more example of popular willingness to believe the worst of Jews.

There were other frightening experiences that the late Middle Ages imposed upon its Jewish population. All of its Talmudic volumes were periodically burned. These public conflagrations were supposedly designed to protect the Catholic Church against pernicious and blasphemous Jewish writings. Jews were periodically accused of poisoning community water supplies and spreading plagues. Because of the danger that Jews symbolized, they were often forced to wear insignia so that they could be recognized and avoided. They were isolated (though not always against their will) in ghettos, and they were periodically expelled from various European countries. All this and more began to be written about by post–Vatican II scholars.[41]

As Edward Flannery notes, the legacy of the Middle Ages was a bitter one for the Jewish people. By the beginning of the sixteenth century, the image of the Jew in the Western world had gravely deteriorated. The theology of contempt had done its work. "The terms 'Jewish' and 'diabolical' had become all but synonymous. The deliberate unbeliever and blasphemer was now also ritual murderer and poisoner of mankind, arch-conspirator, oppressor of the poor, sorcerer and magician; in short, the agent of Satan." Even more ominously, the diabolical image was grasped and exploited by men of letters, preachers, and artists. It served as a perfect excuse to arouse mobs against a scapegoat, who could rarely be appeased by the "Christian ideal of universal love."[42]

Most regretful to the Catholic historian was the deepening and widening "unbridgeable chasm" that this age dug between the two faiths. It was in part of Christian making,[43] but Christian scholars would now share with Jews a responsibility for examining their common past. Jewish demonization not only would figure as a part of that past but would be seen as a cause of Christian history.

12

Remembering the *Shoah*

The Second Vatican Council's "Declaration on the Jews" made no mention of the term *Shoah*, or Holocaust. However, within a few years following the Vatican council, the subject became increasingly important among Catholics interested in furthering the dialogue between the two faiths. Through guidelines issued by the Vatican, American bishops explained to priests and lay people the significance that the topic of the Holocaust held for their Jewish neighbors. Without a Catholic willingness to face up to the ramifications of this event, which included the issue of Christian responsibility, it would be difficult for a fruitful dialogue to materialize.[1]

Catholics were urged to contemplate the implications of the *Shoah*, not only because of its profound implications for the Jewish world but because the *Shoah* was also a momentous event for the Christian community. It was planned and executed by individuals with a Christian education, many of whom were baptized Catholics. These included the leading architects of the Final Solution, Adolf Hitler and Adolf Eichmann, neither of whom was ever subsequently excommunicated by the Catholic Church. As Robert F. Drinan noted in 1977: "It is difficult to deny that Auschwitz . . . simply has to remind Christians at all times of the profound disorders of a Christian civilization that had allowed the Nazi philosophy to grow in its very midst."[2]

Drinan, who had earned a doctorate in theology at the Pontifical Gregorian University in Rome and become an ordained priest, was a leading voice in convincing American Catholics of the importance of thinking about the *Shoah*.[3] The unprecedented horror of the Final Solution was administered in the heart of Roman Catholic Europe with the assistance of thousands of baptized Catholics. Catholics now had to face the unpleasant question: To what degree did the popular theology of contempt open a door which made it possible for the world of Hitler and Eichmann and their supporters to proceed with their work unmolested?

The question was answered at the Second Vatican Council when Cardinal Bea recommended the adoption of the "Declaration on the Jews." He explained to the council members that the perverted ideas about Jews which had permeated modern civilization had originated with ancient Catholic tradition. The cardinal told the council that there is an ancient Catholic-Christian practice of vilifying the Jews.[4]

As Catholic historians began examining the record of Catholics' behavior during the time of German Nazism, they were not happy with what they found. Their disappointment included the record of American Catholics as well. According to the historian David J. O'Brien, one of the first Americans to reevaluate American Catholic behavior during the 1930s, major Catholic newspapers in the United States showed little sympathy toward the plight of German Jews. Writing in 1967, O'Brien also records that Germany's Catholics failed to respond adequately to the Nazi threat. Even American Jews were hated by many American Catholics, because they were known for their political and social liberalism and support of the New Deal. In Brooklyn and other cities, Catholic Nazi sympathizers physically attacked Jews, O'Brien reports.[5] Although such Catholic violence against Jews did not receive the endorsement of America's bishops, there is no record of its being discouraged by America's church hierarchy.[6] O'Brien points out that in the thirties the belief "that Communism was a greater threat than Fascism" convinced many Catholics that outspoken opponents of Germany were a threat to the church. Such fears drew many American Catholics to the ranks of Father Coughlin.[7]

How American Catholics responded to Hitler's treatment of Jews constituted a problem for some postconciliar scholars. William Francis Ryan, for example, a professor of history at John Carroll University, noted that American Catholic silence during the 1930s grew out of lack of interest in and knowledge about world events and embarrassment at the little response of the church to German barbaric behavior. Studying the response of American priests who were members of the National Catholic Welfare Conference (NCWC), the organization established by American bishops in 1922 to monitor and report on social welfare issues, Ryan concluded that the NCWC's reporting established a mood of apathy toward Jewish events abroad during the thirties. The NCWC was able

to generate such an ambience since in an inform.
tion, as an official voice of American Catholics, ·
attitudes about social and political matters. Accor·
ings, the NCWC's immobility was increased by the
toward the Axis and its silence during the Holocaust.
tion mirrors the renewed desire on the part of American
to revisit the past with all its blemishes.

□ □ □

For a number of American Catholics, European Catholics' responsibility for and collaboration with the perpetrators of the *Shoah* was an even deeper concern than American apathy. For example, Gordon C. Zahn, who holds a Ph.D. from the Catholic University of America and is the author of a number of books on the Holocaust, was most disappointed in the bland explanation given by German bishops for their behavior during the Holocaust. To Zahn, German bishops have yet to come to terms with Auschwitz.[9] Zahn, much to the discomfort of some Catholic readers, accused German bishops of being among the most active supporters of Adolf Hitler.[10] German priests, according to Zahn's research, were found at the front of the patriotic procession. As one cleric put it in one of his sermons: "Everything for Germany, and Germany for Christ!"[11] With the capitulation of the German church leadership to the Nazis, not much, according to Zahn, could be expected from the mass of lay Catholics. Any "spiritual heroism" from the faithful was out of the question.[12]

Likewise, Drinan is appalled at the passivity of the German churches in the face of the Final Solution. Neither does Drinan detect many redeeming qualities in Europe's Catholics in general. Drinan writes: "While there are notable exceptions to the general ineffectiveness of the Church to affect its concern over rising antisemitism, it failed in any significant way to provide political or moral leadership to combat the antisemitic designs of Hitler's Germany."[13]

That the church failed to offer the appropriate moral leadership during the years of Nazism was frequently noted by thoughtful Catholics of the post–Vatican II years. More ominously, they wondered what "Christianity contributed to make the Holocaust possible."[14] Rosemary Ruether detected a clear causal relationship between years of Christian teaching and the *Shoah*. Even Hitler, she noted, explained at one time that in response to Jews he was putting into effect "what Christianity had preached and practiced for two thousand years."[15]

...all Catholic historians of the postwar, Vatican II era are ready to ...m that the Jew-hatred unleashed by the Nazis was a product of racial ideas which were equally anti-Christian. It would be some comfort for some to so believe. Yet there are those—Rosemary Ruether and Edward Flannery, for example—who see Nazi hatred of Jews as a new "racist" link in the long chain of Christian antisemitism. To Flannery, the difference between Christian antisemitism and the antisemitism of the Nazis constitutes a matter of degree. Because outright extermination of the Jews did not occur in the earlier centuries, it did not absolve Christianity of the horrors of modernity.[16] The Nazis, according to Flannery, completed the unfinished work of the church. Flannery writes: "The Nazis, in short, took up at the point beyond which the Church could not go. Christianity decreed that Jews, as reprobate unbelievers, must be converted and baptized, otherwise quarantined, exiled, humiliated, but *they must not be killed*. In the Nazi design, Jews, constitutionally corrupt and corrupting and unredeemable by conversion or baptism, must be oppressed, quarantined, and, when possible, *exterminated*."[17]

Flannery, a Catholic of high standing, poses questions about the church that must be taken seriously. He wonders if Christianity does not harbor a deeply embedded "subliminal" hatred of Jews, a hatred that was shared by Hitler. It is a hatred, Flannery reminds his Catholic readers, which Hitler directed at the church and its moral message as well. Neither does Flannery deny that the darkest moments of the *Shoah* were greeted by "silence" from Pope Pius XII.[18] Flannery's viewpoint is bolstered by the findings of the Catholic scholar John Morley, who, after examining Vatican archives, concluded "that Vatican diplomacy failed the Jews during the Holocaust by not doing all that it was possible for it to do on their behalf. It also failed itself because in neglecting the needs of the Jews, and pursuing a goal of reserve rather than humanitarian concern, it betrayed the ideals that it had set for itself. The nuncios, the secretary of state, and, most of all, the Pope share the responsibility for this dual failure."[19] The indictment was harsh. Coming from a devoted member of the Catholic Church, it was also morally courageous.

Not all Catholic scholars are willing or able to cross the frontiers of traditional Catholic historiography, but there is a growing number of Catholic scholars who are determined to do so. One of the outstanding examples of such new scholarship is Harry James Cargas's *Reflections of a Post-Auschwitz Christian,* which appeared in 1989. Reading this volume, Vidal Sassoon of the Hebrew University of Jerusalem characterized Cargas as "one of the new breed of brave Christians who realize that the monstrosity of the Holocaust was a Christian Tragedy."[20] Looking back at the *Shoah,* Cargas wonders, "How are we to comprehend the enormous numbers of people who could kill enormous numbers of people?" and "What of the millions who looked and pretended to see nothing? How is it that we do not live in a world saturated in remorse?" Further, he asks, "How are we to confront coreligionists who make excuses for the Event or who deny the historical perceptions?"[21] Cargas describes himself as a post-Auschwitz Christian. He views the *Shoah* as the "greatest tragedy for Christians since the Crucifixion." The "silence" of the Christian world in the face of evil appalls him. He believes strongly that the church should have excommunicated Adolf Hitler. As a Catholic, he is disturbed that even in Nazi Germany, a Catholic who fought a duel or divorced and remarried would have been expelled from the church. Yet Hitler continued as a church member in good standing and remains so after death. Excommunication, even after his demise, might send a message to contemporary neo-Nazis and other Jew haters.[22]

Cargas does not speak for the church. He is a concerned lay Catholic who feels compelled to address it. He offers recommendations to the church with the hope it will enable it to overcome the sins of its past. These include, among others, a demand that Hitler be excommunicated, that the church admit publicly its erroneous teaching about Jews and Judaism, that the Vatican's twentieth-century histories and archives be opened to Jewish scholars, that Holocaust studies be made part of all Catholic schools' curricula.[23] Cargas believes, as do other thoughtful writers, that if Christianity is to survive, it has to eliminate all hatred from its teachings, including the Gospels. Christianity must undergo a "second reformation," so that humanity will not "shake in its boots when 'onward, Christian soldiers' is sung."[24]

One cannot read Cargas and other sensitive writers of the end of the twentieth century without noting their compelling desire to remember the Christian past and see it as a prelude to the *Shoah*. They see the *Shoah* not only as part of Jewish history, which it is, first and foremost, but also as a permanent chapter in Christian history. Admitting this importance, they feel compelled to raise questions about their own faith. How could Christians participate in such horror? Equally important, How could so many others stand by, innocently observing what was taking place? Those who resisted were so very few. Most Gentiles were "unrighteous."[25] The thoughtful ask, Is traditional Christian teaching sufficient to guard against a repetition? Can Christianity survive such an abysmal failure? These are not pleasant questions to consider, and many Catholics prefer not to raise them at all. But such denial, according to one scholar, is bound to return and haunt the church. For the Catholic Church to survive, according to Michael B. McGarry, a Paulist priest, professor at Saint Paul College, and one of the most profound of contemporary Catholic theologians, it must come to grips with its lamentable past. Any attempt to escape its history could be disastrous.[26]

Catholics who grappled with the moral issues of the *Shoah* and their faith's responsibility for helping to bring it about wondered about their Christian self-image. Some American Catholics hesitated to go as far as McGarry and Cargas, wondering how much "responsibility" they should accept for the monstrous crime that took place far away.[27] Even so, according to Eugene J. Fisher, Christians must face up to an event which took place in the midst of Christian civilization. And its chief victims were the Jews, whom the church had maligned for many centuries. Fisher points out, "In this sense, the Holocaust is a Christian, not a Jewish problem."[28] He writes:

> The issue that faces us today is not one of personal guilt for the past but of objective responsibility for the future. . . . I cannot feel personally guilty for what others may have done in another time and another place. But as a Christian who wishes to take some pride in the membership in the one body of Christ, I cannot escape a sense of responsibility concerning the use to which the teachings of my Church have . . . been put. . . . As American Christians today facing the Holocaust, we can count ourselves neither absolutely guilty nor wholly guilt free. We remain responsible for the past yet hope-filled for the future. This at least I would take to be the consensus of those scholars, both Jewish as well as Christian, most deeply involved in the dialogue.[29]

Fisher's stress on the importance for Catholics to "remember" the unspeakable events of the 1940s was urged by Vatican officials upon all Christians. Johannes Cardinal Willebrands, who was the leading Vatican voice in bringing about improved relations with Jews during the years following the Second Vatican Council, emphasized its importance. No reconciliation between the church and the Jews could be consummated if Catholics did not "remember."[30]

For the church, "remembering" did not imply that Catholics become historians or that they view the *Shoah* merely as a sad chapter in history. Willebrands believes that historical analysis ought never to turn the study of the *Shoah* into an academic exercise. It would trivialize it, he says. For the Catholic, the *Shoah* should hold deeper meanings than purely historical. It must remind the Christian of his or her responsibilities, according to the cardinal. Neither should Christians succumb to the temptation of de-Judaizing the *Shoah,* for it should always be understood as a singular Jewish tragedy, one that will remain for a long time to come as a tragic event beyond human understanding. None of this, however, declares Willebrands, should in any way discourage Catholics from studying the *Shoah* and its tragic place in Christian history.[31]

◻ ◻ ◻

While "remembering" the *Shoah* and recognizing Christendom's responsibility in the matter, to the discomfort of many Jewish thinkers, the Holy See hesitated to indict the Roman Catholic Church and its teachings as a principle culprit. It drew a subtle distinction between the Holy Body of Christ (the church) and the individuals who were part of it. In this sense, in contemplating the issue of responsibility, the Holy See did not travel as far as did even some American Catholic thinkers. This does not mean that either Pope Paul VI or especially John Paul II did not show genuine sorrow and contrition when addressing the topic of Jews who suffered during the years of the *Shoah*, "'a people whose sons and daughters were intended for total extermination.'" Standing in front of the gates of Auschwitz, as John Paul II occasionally did, he reminded his audience of the significance of "remembering."[32]

As a young priest, John Paul was a personal observer of the Nazi horror unleashed upon the Jews of Poland. He carried the experience from his early priesthood in Poland to the church's highest office in Rome. It was a painful chapter of his early years. Looking back to his childhood in Poland, John Paul recalls:

> I remember above all the Wadowich elementary school, where at least a fourth of the pupils in my class were Jewish. I could mention my friendship at school with one of them, Jerzy Kluger, a friendship that has lasted throughout my school days to the present. I can vividly remember the Jews who gathered every Saturday at the synagogue behind our school. Both groups, Catholics and Jews, were united, I presume, by the awareness that they prayed to the same God.
>
> Then came the Second World War, with its concentration camps and systematic extermination. First and foremost, the sons and daughters of the Jewish nation were condemned for no other reason than that they were Jewish. . . . Whoever lived in Poland at that time came into contact with that reality.
>
> Therefore, this was also a personal experience of mine, an experience I carry with me even today.[33]

His own people, John Paul recalled, had also suffered along with the Jews. For that reason, according to Cardinal Willebrands, "no matter where his apostolic pilgrimages bring him, the Pope takes every oppor-

tunity of meeting members of the Jewish community."[34] It was not unusual for John Paul to meet with survivors of the *Shoah* and their families, particularly on Yom Hashoa (Day of Remembrance), at Vatican
City. On April 7, 1994, for example, American Jews were involved in
making arrangements for such an event.[35]

In an apostolic letter of November 1994, John Paul, according to
Commonweal, remarked that years of Christian prejudice had deadened
Christians' ability to resist the Nazis' persecution of the Jews. Howev-
er, as he spoke to a Catholic seminar on anti-Judaism in Catholic theol-
ogy, John Paul failed to go as far as did the bishops of Germany and
Poland (and later France), who some months earlier had charged the
Roman Catholic Church with complicity in the "Holocaust." John Paul
continued to place the blame for the *Shoah* in part on centuries of "anti-
Jewish prejudice" but avoided implicating the church in the *Shoah*.[36]

A similar degree of caution is seen in John Paul's endorsement of the
long-awaited Vatican report on the behavior of the Catholic world during the *Shoah*. The sixteen-page document, entitled, "We Remember: A
Reflection on the *Shoah*," which took eleven years to produce, was issued by the Vatican on March 16, 1998. Endorsed by John Paul, it was
written under the direction of the Vatican Commission for Religious Relations with the Jews, chaired by Edward Idris Cardinal Cassidy, a Vatican diplomat and theologian. This body produced a document that,
despite some serious flaws, marked an important milestone in Catholic-Jewish relations.[37]

"We Remember" was a public acknowledgment of Catholic repentance
for the failure to deter the mass killings of Europe's Jews during World
War II. Cassidy explained that the report was designed as "a teaching
document for the world wide church"; producing it was also an act of
"repentance." The document declared in part: "In the lands where the
Nazis undertook mass deportations, the brutality which surrounded
these forced movements of helpless people should have led [the world]
to suspect the worst. Did Christians give every possible assistance to those
being persecuted, and in particular to the persecuted Jews? Many did,
but others did not."[38] The Vatican statement requested that all "Christians meditate on the catastrophe that befell the Jews." The commission's
report declared that "we deeply regret the errors and failures of those
sons and daughters of the Church." It further announced its repentance
for the failure of most Christian countries to open their doors and provide shelter and safety to Jews during the *Shoah*. It hoped that the tragedy of the *Shoah* would strengthen the bonds and mutual understanding between the two faiths.[39] John Paul appended a cover letter to the

document, addressed to Cardinal Cassidy, as president of the commission. In it, the pope asked that all Christians repent for the evils of the century for which they shared responsibility. The Holy Father hoped that the statement "We Remember" would hasten the healing process of the age, that the future would make the *Shoah* "never again possible."[40]

"We Remember" had traveled beyond frontiers of any official Vatican admission of a need to repent for past errors committed against the Jews. Yet the document had not gone the distance traveled by European bishops and a number of Catholic theologians in pointing to the church's failures during the *Shoah*. Particularly disappointing to some American observers was John Paul's reluctance to criticize Pope Pius XII's silence during the Second World War.[41]

While some American Jewish leaders were disappointed in, even annoyed at, the text of the Vatican document, there were those who recognized with appreciation the continuing efforts of the church to repair its image in the Jewish community. Judith H. Banki, a Jewish activist in the promotion of Jewish-Catholic understanding, explained to the readers of *Commonweal* that Jewish negative response reflected the understandable suspicion that American Jews have had of Catholic statements on their behalf. She recalled a similar suspicion of *Nostra Aetate*: "It was too little, too late." The declaration was criticized, at that time, and with justification, because of its "lack of contrition" and absence of any assumption of "responsibility" for the antisemitism it was decrying. Jews greeted later Vatican papers, according to Banki, who for many years spoke for the American Jewish Committee, with similar dissatisfaction. Although Vatican documents were at first seen by American Jews as "seriously flawed," their "powerful and positive consequences" caused such efforts later to be valued. They helped build a new interfaith relationship. Banki believed that such previous experience would suggest that despite its weaknesses, "We Remember" would also be seen as enhancing Catholic-Jewish understanding. Banki notes that these "reflections," addressed to 800 million Catholics, are a reminder of the danger and consequences of antisemitism. They open new opportunities for study and action.[42]

The Jewish theologian David Novak goes even further than Banki in defending the Vatican document. Unlike many other Jews, Novak de-emphasizes the appropriateness of an "apology" by the church. He writes:

Now just *who* would apologize to *whom*? If one takes a Catholic who actually participated in the Nazi atrocities against the Jews, how could such a person possibly apologize? How do you apologize to someone in whose murder you were a participant? In order to apologize, you have to make your apology to someone who is capable of accepting your apology. But those who were murdered are hardly in a position to absolve anyone. And who am I, as a Jew, who was only a potential victim of Nazi murder, to forgive someone who asks my forgiveness for what he or she did to Jews now dead? How can I exonerate somebody for what he or she did to somebody else? Wouldn't that be what Christians call "cheap grace"?[43]

Novak notes, however, that the church did, in its own way, engage in self-criticism in *Nostra Aetate,* for example, which in condemning antisemitism states that "those who so taught it are to be considered in error by the internal criteria of the teaching authority of the Church itself." "We Remember" criticizes the Catholic community even further, says Novak, by expressing its "sorrow and shame that the teaching authority of the Church did not do enough to encourage such persons to resist the evil to which they succumbed. In other words, perhaps the Church did not do a good enough job of teaching the principles of Christianity to many of her sons and daughters."[44] There is little more that the Jewish people can demand of the church at this time.

Yet others of the Jewish community, Banki's and Novak's comments notwithstanding, derived less satisfaction from the Vatican commission's statement. A group of survivors of the *Shoah* informed the New York *Jewish Week* that the document's condemnation of Christian complicity "sadly fails and even regresses." The survivors were particularly disturbed by the commission's observation that the *Shoah* was the "work of a neopagan regime. Modern antisemitism has its roots outside of Christianity."[45] Paul Ellis of the *New York Times* explained the problem succinctly when he wrote on April 22, 1998: "Last month's statement on the Holocaust fell short of expectations. Now the Pope is readying a more personal mea culpa. Only two things stand in the way: the mea and the culpa."[46]

The difficulty with the document, according to many Jews and non-Jews, was its failure to condemn Pius XII's bland behavior in the face of the murder of Europe's Jews. As one Jewish leader argued, if only Pius XII had condemned antisemitism as a sin, as John Paul had done, things could have been different. John Paul's continued hesitancy to accuse the wartime pope of sinful behavior during the *Shoah* annoyed American Jews. Ellis points to Arthur Hertzberg, a historian, rabbi, and former vice-president of the World Jewish Congress, who wondered if John Paul was more of a political manipulator, trying always to placate all sides, rather than a great religious moral leader, at least in respect to Jewish issues.[47] In this connection, Ellis reminds us, "At the end of [John Paul's] pontificate, it is Pius's actions, not [John Paul's] own, that he is being called to account for." Ellis reminds us that when "We Remember" refers to the wisdom of Pius XII's diplomacy, it fails to address what the wartime pope did not do for the Jews of Europe during World War II. Although John Paul or the commission would not have been expected to criticize the record of Pius XII, neither was the Vatican commission compelled to laud Pius's wartime record. In reality, John Paul, despite his intense desire to reconcile the two faiths, is not yet ready to apologize for the errors of the church. He prefers to impose the guilt of past behavior upon the heads of sons and daughters of the church.[48]

From a Jewish perspective, the problem of the document was compounded by its inability to recognize a historic relationship between the church's theology of contempt and modern racial antisemitism. In this connection, Robert S. Wistrich writes: "The Vatican document is by no means mistaken to argue that the ideology of the Third Reich was profoundly anti-Christian, nor is it wrong to draw a distinction between Christian and Nazi anti-Semitism. But the difference is hardly absolute. It is, rather, as Milton Himmelfarb once observed, like that between an uncomfortable fever and a lethal one—they are two variants of the same sickness."[49] Meanwhile, despite the enormous progress achieved under the pontificate of John Paul II in improving understanding between Catholics and Jews, Auschwitz's shadow continues to hover over his worthwhile intentions.

The reaction of American Catholics to "We Remember" was mixed. Eugene J. Fisher saw the statement as a major step in continuing the healing process between the two faith communities. The document, declared Fisher, represented a gesture of "repentance" on the part of the church for its behavior during the *Shoah*. Fisher explained that "We Remember" is not the last word of the church on the *Shoah*. Rather, it is a mandate for further study of the Holocaust and its historical antecedents.[50]

Fisher's benign assessment was typical of that of most establishment Catholics. It stood in sharp contrast to *Commonweal*'s denunciation in one of its editorials, entitled "Misremembered." Declared *Commonweal*, "Eleven years in the writing, 'We Remember: A Reflection on the *Shoah*' . . . will not and should not satisfy those on any side of the fortuitous debate about the Church's responsibility for anti-Semitism and possible complicity in the Nazi extermination of six million Jews. Although the sincerity of the statement's desire for genuine reconciliation between Christians and Jews cannot be second-guessed, the document as a whole is a grievous disappointment."[51] The editors sympathized with the anger of a number of Jewish readers, especially at the document's undeserved praise of Pius XII's behavior during the *Shoah*. The document, the editorial declares, will need serious revision, especially the "statement's refusal to attribute any fault or error for anti-Semitism to the Church itself." The church does not stand above its errors, declared *Commonweal*'s editors. It cannot deny its responsibility for encouraging through its teachings anti-Judaism throughout the centuries which led to pogroms, expulsions, and other horrors, they said. The church must assume responsibility for what had happened to the Jews. The editorial points out:

> However one wants to understand the relationship between the mystical and visible elements of the Church, the incontrovertible historical record attests to the fact that "The Church," and not just its members, taught erroneously, even perniciously, about Judaism and the Jews. . . . To argue that there was no connection between nearly 2000 years of church-inspired anti-Semitism and the Nazi assault on European Jewry is utterly fallacious and offensive. . . . Nazism did not spring full grown from the atheistic brow of the modern world. It had obvious roots in Europe's near and ancient Christian past.
>
> How the Church can repent or correct the manifest errors of the past if it cannot honestly admit any error at all is, to say the least, something of a problem.[52]

A number of Catholic theologians, meeting with members of the American Jewish Committee during the summer of 1998, also expressed deep disillusionment with "We Remember." For example, Richard B. McBrien of the University of Notre Dame, a former president of the Catholic Theological Society of America, remarked that Rome had failed to address its responsibility in respect to the *Shoah*. McBrien noted that the document was issued twenty years too late. McBrien also challenged Cardinal Cassidy's assertion that the Church of Rome can never be considered sinful, a theological position, according to McBrien, which was not universally accepted.[53]

"Misremembered" and McBrien's reaction stand as evidence of the advance of Catholic insistence on a new level of frankness and historical accuracy on the part of the church. Even so, such views did not receive universal support in the Catholic community. For example, *First Things*, a neo-conservative Catholic magazine, was angered at the *New York Times*'s criticism of the Vatican's documents ignoring the silence of Pius XII. The editors of *First Things* reminded the *Times* of its own deafening silence in the face of the *Shoah* and the millions of deaths perpetrated by the Soviet Union. They resented having the Catholic

Church put on trial by the *Times*. They wondered if the newspaper expected either Pius XII to declare war on Hitler or all the Catholics of
Germany to commit treason and defy Hitler's orders. *First Things* accused the *Times* of being unable to show any "humility that comes from
an awareness of sin and grace, of historical ambiguity, and/or both human frailty and grandeur—an awareness entirely missing from the self-
righteous carping of the *Times* and some other, mainly Jewish, critics."[54]

Avery Dulles, a Jesuit theologian who teaches at Fordham University
and who was appointed a cardinal in January 2001, has recognized the
difficulty some Catholics today have with their church's admitting guilt
for its sins. These Catholics hold with those theologians who see the
church as holy and sinless. The sins, they believe, lie with its members,
not with the holy body of Christ. Others contend that the church has
already admitted errors. Too many apologies, they fear, could apologize
the church out of existence.[55] Without denying the enormous strides
symbolized by the effort of "We Remember" as striking a new blow both
at antisemitism and at "holocaust deniers," some Catholics and most
Jews continue to await fuller response to the role of the church during
the *Shoah*. They continue to ask: Will John Paul bail out the "flawed
Vatican text"?[56]

□ □ □

Serious reflection on the *Shoah* was not a captivating pastime among
American Catholics. Only a handful of scholars made the *Shoah* a central focus of their lives; only a few felt compelled, as Catholics, to respond to the unspeakable event of the twentieth century.[57] Yet the Second Vatican Council inspired some select individuals to inquire about
those years during the Second World War which had transformed the
nature of civilized humanity. To be sure, the questions they raised about
the *Shoah* were not identical with those voiced in the Jewish community. While Jews, primarily as victims, wondered about God's silence, God's
justice, the character of their Christian neighbors, and the behavior of
world leadership, the Christian world brooded over the degree of its own
silence, its culpability, the theology of contempt, and the roles of sin and
evil in history.[58]

Among Catholic scholars, few did more than the theologian John T.
Pawlikowski. His writing about the Catholic response to the *Shoah* has
been more extensive than that of most of his postconciliar contempo-
raries. "Auschwitz has emerged in my mind," wrote Pawlikowski in
1981, "as the beginning of a significantly new era, one in which the

extermination of human life in a guiltless fashion becomes thinkable and technologically feasible. It opens the door to an age when dispassionate torture and murder of millions has become not just an action of a crazed despot . . . but a calculated effort to reshape humanity supported by intellectual argumentation from the best and brightest minds in a society."[59] For more than a quarter of a century, Pawlikowski has produced numerous essays in which he unfolds his thoughts about the *Shoah*. He has long been an advisor on Catholic-Jewish issues to the National Conference of Catholic Bishops, and he is a strong advocate of an honest Christian confrontation with the *Shoah*. He wants to understand what the tragic event has done to the "soul of humanity."[60]

Pawlikowski rejects the notion that the *Shoah* was an irrational eruption, an aberration executed by a madman. If that were so, explains Pawlikowski, the issue would not be as theologically significant as it is. It troubles today's thinkers precisely because the *Shoah* was planned and perpetrated by rational people, many of whose "origins lie in philosophies developed by thinkers many consider to be giants of liberal Western thought and in theological attitudes central to Christianity almost to its inception."[61] Only in part does Pawlikowski agree with the Jewish philosopher Emil Fackenheim that "it is immoral to search for meaning in the *Shoah*." But Pawlikowski also insists that evil should not be ignored. One must confront, he says, what happened to the human spirit in perpetrating or witnessing the Final Solution. Such an examination should be undertaken precisely because it was an evil but rational event rooted in Christian civilization.

Pawlikowski offers his own rational explanation for the tragedy. The failure of modern humanity occurred when it aspired to create "supermen," he writes, when civilization attempted "to develop that truly liberated epitome of universal humanity." Once freed, this "new man" was raised by the Nazis to a grotesque level, and they felt a compunction to remove from the earth through a Final Solution all those who did not conform to his pattern of superiority.[62] Pawlikowski argues that profound changes have taken place in "human consciousness." Under the impact of the new science and technology, humankind has undergone "a kind of 'Prometheus unbound.'" People have experienced a new freedom and sins of autonomy, "more than Catholic theology had previously recognized."[63]

Having identified the culprit as the "new earthliness" of humanity, what was first required to bring recovery was the discovery of a sense of a "fresh transcendence." "Modern Western thought" is identified by Pawlikowski as the delinquent who laid the foundation for the Final

Solution. Pawlikowski arrives at the sweeping judgment that "Western Liberal thought . . . is responsible for the Holocaust." It did so by breaking the tight hold the God-concept had on previous generations. It paved the way for greater human freedom and self-sufficiency without realistically addressing the potential destructive forces within humankind to pervert this freedom into the cruelty revealed by the Nazi experiment.[64] The conclusion that Pawlikowski draws from the gas chambers of Auschwitz is that humanity needs to renew its commitment to God and religion. "People once more will need to experience contact with a personal power beyond themselves, a power that heals the destructive tendencies."[65] In 1989, Pawlikowski wrote: "The basic point must be made that post-Holocaust humanity needs to rediscover a personal relationship with a God who remains a direct source of strength and influence in the conduct of human affairs."[66]

Even though Pawlikowski admits that the *Shoah* was a product of modern secular culture, he does not deny that "its architects found their targets well primed for the formulation of their recent theories."[67] The observation, however, appears as only a peripheral part of Pawlikowski's work. His stress is on the pursuance of a theological explanation for the *Shoah* that could be useful for Christians grappling with the "reality and implications" of Auschwitz. He writes: "It will prove trying for Catholics to face the challenge to the traditional Catholic notion of the Church's basic moral integrity that is represented by the Holocaust. As difficult as it may be, a new ecclesiology will have to be created. As we begin to penetrate the veil of silence that has covered the Holocaust in Catholic circles, we can begin to see more clearly some of the theological postures which made at least indirect complicity with the Nazis a possible option for Roman Catholicism."[68]

Even though Pawlikowski's analysis was designed primarily for Catholic readers, some Jews might have been uneasy with his work, as was, for example, the Jewish Holocaust survivor and novelist Elie Wiesel.[69] Yet Pawlikowski's work, which shows a tendency to universalize the *Shoah,* to alter it into a symbol of Christian tragedy, stands among that of the most profound Christian writers about the *Shoah.* While a number of Catholic scholars, such as Eugene Fisher, have recognized the danger of universalizing the *Shoah* and warned against such thinking, it is Fisher who is particularly concerned with "Holocaust courses which tend to compare and equate all human suffering with the *Shoah.*"[70] Yet even among the most prominent of scholars, there are those who have succumbed to the temptation. Most Jewish readers would feel uneasy about the comment of the Dominican priest and head of the philosophy department at Hebrew University of Jerusalem, Marcel Jacques Dubois, who wrote in 1974:

> What then can be said of the death camps and of the long agony of the Jewish people? It is a striking fact that Judaism itself in the spontaneity of its deepest resilience has answered this question. The answer contains such an unexpected presentiment of the mystery of the Cross that Christians cannot fail to notice it and to be struck by it. We have recognized the fact that for the Jewish people the suffering of Israel . . . has an exemplary value for all human suffering. . . . This fact invites the Jew to give to every suffering and every misfortune in the world a meaning drawn from his own experience.[71]

Although such a Jewish service to universal understanding might enhance Catholic self-understanding, it would leave most Jews quite cold, puzzled, even resentful. Neither would most thinking Jews be ready to accept Pawlikowski's return to transcendence as a theological preventive against future attempts to destroy the Jewish minority. Even so, Pawlikowski's and other Catholic theologians' efforts to search for understanding and draw some meaningful theological conclusions from an evil experience which has yet to be fathomed must be included on the right side of the ledger. They continue the important effort which was begun with *Nostra Aetate,* No. 4, to advance the continuing discourse between the two faiths.

□ □ □

American Jews, stunned by the European revelations, did not respond to the *Shoah* with one voice. Jewish minds had yet to comprehend with clarity the implications of the Final Solution. Throughout the remaining decades of the twentieth century, they continued to grapple with the question of meaning which hovered behind the greatest tragedy that had befallen them in two thousand years.

An increased disillusionment with the Christian world was not unusual. This is reflected, for example, in the reaction of G. David Schwartz, a writer and activist in Jewish-Christian dialogue, who as late as 1994 acknowledged that there was little interest among Jews in the Catholic religious response which occurred in the wake of the *Shoah.* Schwartz declares, "We Jews are not overly concerned about the development of Christian theology." Christian efforts at "renewal of Christian faith after the Holocaust" are not ordinarily viewed as an issue of concern by Jews.[72] Schwartz is not markedly taken with, for example, John Pawlikowski's theological pronouncements. As appreciative as he is of the well-intentioned efforts of Catholic theologians of the *Shoah,* he does not believe that Jews ought to condone the intertwining of objective analysis with the emotive. "What I do not think is beneficial," writes Schwartz, "is a mea culpa beating of the chest so loudly that it drowns out the heart beating within." Schwartz is concerned that "for Christians, the Holocaust seems to be becoming a monument and the response a monumentalization."[73]

Likewise, the Nobel Laureate Elie Wiesel feared that the enormous amount of objective scholarship devoted to the *Shoah* would tend to trivialize rather than enrich memory about the event. In a dialogue with John Cardinal O'Connor of New York in 1990, Wiesel lamented that the *Shoah* "is the most documented tragedy in recorded history."[74] Wiesel explained to Cardinal O'Connor why the *Shoah* could not be understood through more theological analysis. He said:

> If in those years it was possible for six million Jews to be killed in the twentieth century, that means something was wrong with the world. And therefore, it overlapped—the cup runneth over. The violence from there and then is still here. The hatred from there and then is still here.
>
> And so, to me, it is a mystery. What happened then is the central mystery of life, and of history. On all levels, human and psychological and theological.[75]

Few Jewish writers found much comfort in the nihilism of the radical Jewish theologian Richard L. Rubenstein. Taken aback by the revelations of the *Shoah,* Rubenstein was, for a while, repelled by Christian and even Jewish dogma. In his writings, he went far beyond the point where most Jewish theologians would dare to tread. A Conservative rabbi, Rubenstein holds a M.H.L. degree from the Jewish Theological Seminary and a Ph.D. from Harvard. Rubenstein's subsequent scholarship and his efforts to speak to both faith communities are, by his own admission, welcomed more among non-Jews. Rubenstein's assertion in 1966, quite typical of his later comments, was that a genuine relationship between Christians and Jews would not materialize if each insisted on holding tightly to his respective religious myth. The Jew, Rubenstein declared with a disturbing frankness, "must release his hold on the doctrine of the election of Israel and the *Torah* as the sole content of God's revelation to mankind," while the Christian, in turn, must de-emphasize "the decisive character of the Christ event in human history," a myth that "must be at best an error and at worst blasphemy." To hold onto these myths inflexibly, insisted Rubenstein, would obscure a meaningful dialogue between the two faiths. "Not only do the mythic contents of our religious faiths impede meaningful community, they absolutely preclude it."[76]

Yet Rubenstein's unorthodox demands concealed his general agreement with other Jewish thinkers about dialogue with the Christian community after Auschwitz: human beings, not dogmas, should be placed at the center of the interfaith encounter. "If we concentrate less on what our religious inheritances promise and [focus] on the human existence which we share through the traditions, we will achieve the superlative yet simple knowledge of who we truly are. . . . If we fail to learn the simple lesson that the community of men is possible only through the encounter of persons rather than of myths or abstractions, we will only doom future generations to repeat the horrible deeds of our time."[77]

Catholic theologians would have felt much more comfortable with the writings of Emil Fackenheim, who called to the Jewish survivors of the *Shoah* and Jews in general to return to their covenantal faith. This invitation was engendered by Fackenheim's belief that God's image had vanished during the *Shoah*. It was incumbent upon Jews, declared Fackenheim, to restore God's image by returning to Judaism. This would also, he declared, deny the tyrant Hitler a posthumous victory.[78] Fackenheim also called upon Christians to reevaluate their own religious principles which infused the theology of contempt.

Michael B. McGarry believes that if Catholicism were to renew its vision of Judaism, it must abide by Fackenheim's challenge. Fackenheim, unlike Rubenstein, did not despair—despite the *Shoah*—about the future relations of the two faith communities. There was hope, he believed, if genuine religious reforms occurred. The Christian community, though, must first accept as a pivotal point the centrality of the *Shoah* to their own faith. Moreover, they must remove from the baggage of their beliefs the concept of displacement or supersessionism. He sees this theological principle as a key element in the destructiveness of the church toward Judaism, including Christian complicity in the Nazi murders.[79] McGarry finds most telling the questions Fackenheim puts to Christianity. Fackenheim demands honest answers; he wants Christians to think with great seriousness how they imagine their Savior, Jesus of Nazareth, would have behaved had he found himself in Nazi-occupied Europe. Would he have collaborated with Nazi extermination? Would he have remained silent? Would he have fled? Would he have rescued Jewish victims? Would he have died in a gas chamber with his Jewish brethren? What impact would his behavior during the *Shoah* have had on the Christians of Europe?[80]

McGarry found one of Fackenheim's questions particularly significant for post-Holocaust Catholics. Fackenheim wonders if the Christians' sacred view that the acceptance of Christ as Savior, a belief that leads to God's atonement for human sin, could still remain doctrinally pure following the *Shoah*. Do not the unspeakable horrors of the *Shoah* require a serious rethinking of the Christian "Good News"? Could such a doctrine remain intact? Has not the time arrived for the church to behave more humbly about its certainties of salvation? Has the world really been redeemed? Or should not the church resume its waiting for redemption as the Jews do?

Perhaps it is time for Christianity to admit that the Messiah has not yet appeared, says Fackenheim. By crossing such sacred frontiers, Jews and Christians might grow even closer in religious understanding and common values.[81] In this respect, unlike G. David Schwartz, Fackenheim welcomes a Christian transformation. He urges the church to grow closer to Judaism by immersing itself in the Hebrew Scripture.

The bold and unusual challenges and demands which Fackenheim brings to the church are welcomed by McGarry. McGarry acknowledges their effort to promote a *tikkun haolam* (a repair of the world). Fackenheim's requests, declares McGarry, should not be ignored. In this connection, McGarry writes: "For Christians to refrain from engaging the unique assault on Christianity which the Holocaust brings is not only cowardly, it is, in the long run, suicidal. Christians and their leaders had an opportunity to speak words from their own tradition of healing, reconciliation, and humility. They missed that opportunity. Christians cannot afford to miss again."[82]

❏ ❏ ❏

Few Jewish writers have written more brilliantly about the implications of the *Shoah* than the Orthodox rabbi, accomplished historian, communal leader, and theologian Irving Greenberg. Few also have commanded more attentiveness from the Catholic community.[83] His early study "Cloud of Smoke, Pillar of Fire: Judaism, Christianity, and Modernity after the Holocaust" (1974) opened new avenues of thinking for Christians and Jews. As does Fackenheim, Greenberg sees the *Shoah* as a profound turning point in the history of both faiths. The measure which he applies to the centrality of the *Shoah* is on a level with Exodus for Jews and Easter for Christians. Yet both faiths, he complained in 1974, continue as if nothing had changed. He is surprised, since the wound of the event has cut so deeply that he wonders if a full recovery is possible.[84]

Greenberg believes that although Christians might find it easier than Jews to live as if nothing had happened to them personally, such an attitude of indifference would be "sheer self-deception." He says, "Failure to confront and account for this evil . . . would turn both religions into empty Pollyannas," a gross deception.[85] Greenberg detects an added risk which would result from human indifference: "There is no choice but to confront the Holocaust, because it happened, and because the first Holocaust is the hardest. The fact of the Holocaust makes a repetition more likely—a limit was broken, a control or awe is gone. . . . Failure to confront it makes repetition all the more likely."[86]

Still, to Greenberg, there are no simple, definitive explanations, no simple answers for what happened. There is no appropriate or intelligible response to those who turned their tormented Jewish victims into "soap and fertilizer." Greenberg warns, "Woe to those so at ease that they feel no guilt or tension. Often this is the sign of the death of the soul." In one of his most moving statements, Greenberg proclaims: "Let us offer, then, as working principle, the following: No statement, theological or otherwise, should be made that would not be credible in the presence of the burning children."[87]

None of this implies, however, that Jews should ignore or deny the *Shoah*. On the contrary, says Greenberg, they are required to remember it. Greenberg approves of Fackenheim's reminder that God's voice, audible through Auschwitz, bids Jews to abide by the Eleventh Commandment: Jews must continue to live as Jews. They are commanded not to hand Hitler a posthumous victory. That Jewish survival continues is the only feasible response which Jews could make to the *Shoah*. It is a response accepted by other traditional Jewish thinkers. Rubenstein's denial of meaning to the continuation of Judaism is categorically rejected by Greenberg. He finds Rubenstein's pagan assertions incompatible with traditional Jewish responses to the *Shoah*. Despite all that has happened, Greenberg does not agree that all hope for Judaism is closed forever. Greenberg finds Fackenheim's Eleventh Commandment far more appealing than Rubenstein's atheism.

Like Fackenheim's and Pawlikowski's pleas, Greenberg's warn against "abandoning the divine." This, he feels, is the moral imperative which grows out of the *Shoah*. He urges Jews and Christians to seek a "renewed encounter with the transcendental." Greenberg further urges Jews and Christians to resist being totally captivated by the cultural values and authority of Western civilization.[88] Moreover, Greenberg issues a call to Jews and Christians "to resist the overwhelming attractions of the secular city even at its best." Jews, like believers of other religions, need "to

stay in spiritual tension with these same forces." He writes: "The Holocaust warns us that our current values breed their own nemesis of evil
when unchecked. . . . The Holocaust suggests a fundamental skepticism
about all human movements, left and right, political and religious—even
as we participate in them."[89]

Greenberg, Fackenheim, and Pawlikowski share the conviction that
the only appropriate response to the *Shoah* is a return to the voice of a
transcendent God. However, there is a significant difference here. Unlike previous catastrophes, following which Jews found themselves sin-
gularly alone, for the first time the two faiths have searched together for
meaning amidst the moral ruins of the twentieth century. This transformation would hardly have been possible, notwithstanding the tragic
uniqueness of the *Shoah* for the Jewish people, without the inspiring
spirit which grew from the Second Vatican Council.

13
Burden and Triumph of Jewish Sovereignty, 1949–99

As in the case of the *Shoah*, the Second Vatican Council's "Declaration on the Jews" made no mention of the importance that the state of Israel held. Neither did the Vatican guidelines (1974) mention the Jewish state or the significance of the Jewish people's return to their land. The omission was not an oversight. It was a result of lingering past attitudes toward Zionism. The Catholic Church was also reluctant to alienate further Christian Arabs and Muslims in general. Both groups were openly opposed to the existence of the state of Israel. The last thing they wished to hear was further theological and political support granted to Jewish sovereignty by the Holy See. These issues, coupled with the church's continued uncertainty about its own role and the security of the religious sites in the Jewish state, added to its reluctance to speak of Israel. Moreover, and not to be discounted, there were church doctrines which had not yet fully caught up with the concept of the revival of Jewish sovereignty in the land of Israel.[1] A student of papal diplomacy concluded that "the opposition by some prelates and clergymen to the acknowledgment of the reality of the Jewish state stemmed from the fact that 'to recognize Israel is to admit a long historical, theological, and religious process which is not always in harmony with what is thought of Israel in some Vatican circles.'"[2] It took the Holy See twenty years, until 1985, to make official reference to the significance of the state of Israel and its religious and political importance to the Jewish people. This first occurred in the document referred to as the *Notes* of 1985. And even the *Notes* were cautious in their references to Israel.[3]

Cardinal Bea, who had headed the committee that drafted *Nostra*

Aetate, was disappointed at this belated acceptance of the Jewish state in Vatican circles, as were a number of American bishops. Bea was particularly distressed at the political interpretation given by some Arab bishops and others to Vatican religious references to Israel. As the theologian Anthony J. Kenny explains, "Any reference to the State of Israel was deliberately avoided by the framers of *Nostra Aetate* for political and practical reasons. The political reason was linked to the Church's Arab presence in the Middle East, the practical reason was the survival of the document itself."[4]

Significant too is that a good many of the bishops who gathered in Rome for the Second Vatican Council in 1962 knew little about Zionism and its historical roots. Judaism and its nationalist aspirations had never been part of Catholic education. It has been suggested by Kenny that even Cardinal Bea believed Zionism to be a totally "political movement." Therefore, *Nostra Aetate,* No. 4, "reflected the ignorance of its framers." A similar charge can be directed at the guidelines of 1974. It was largely due to the initiative of John Paul II that the subsequent *Notes* of 1985 and other papers focused on the Jewish state with greater seriousness. Designed primarily for those engaged in teaching and preaching, the inclusion of the *Notes* was therefore significant for Catholics.[5]

That the religious centrality of the state of Israel to Jews was absent from the deliberations of Vatican II became evident during the pilgrimage of Pope Paul VI (1963–78) to the Holy Land. Paul, who succeeded John XXIII to the papacy in 1963, decided to include a Middle Eastern visit in his travels to encourage Christian unity and to allay Muslim fears about a Jewish declaration. The pope's three-day pilgrimage took place in January 1964, between the second and third sessions of the Vatican council.[6] In the long history of the Church of Rome, Paul VI was the first pontiff ever to set foot in Jerusalem. The gesture reflected the new openness of the church to those of other faiths.[7] Jewish leaders in the United States were interested in Paul's impending visit to Jerusalem. Rabbi Joachim Prinz, president of the American Jewish Congress, said that "it would provide 'tangible recognition of the shared roots of the Jewish and Christian traditions' and show an ecumenical spirit embracing men of all faiths."[8] In honor of the pope's visit, Jordan, which had continued its state of war against Israel since Israel's declaration of independence in 1948, silenced its guns, which for sixteen years had continued to fire across the border of divided Jerusalem.

Paul was little moved by the achievements of the new Jewish state. His primary focus was on the Christian heritage of Jerusalem and the Holy Land. However, this did not preclude Pope Paul's meeting with Israel's

President Zalman Shazar and members of the Israeli cabinet. The meeting caused annoyance in Arab capitals. George Cornell, author and prominent American religion reporter for the Associated Press, joined the pope's entourage; he later recalled the striking contrast between Israel's neatly groomed landscape, lush farms, and agricultural settlements and the unkempt environment of the Jordanian-occupied sector. The contrast was not lost on the pope as he and his colorful procession crossed the border from the Jordanian-held West Bank into Israel's territory.[9]

The first meeting that Paul had upon entering the state of Israel was with President Shazar and Israeli cabinet members. It was a historic occasion since it was the first time a pope had ever met with the head of the Jewish state on Israeli soil. After a warm greeting, Shazar declared: "Surely the devastation of my people during this last generation is a bitter warning of the depths of bestiality and loss of the divine image to which ancient prejudices and racial hatreds can drag men down if a purifying spirit does not come into being while there is yet time to dam up the dangers forever." Shazar added his hope that the vision of the Jewish prophets would enhance the vision of mankind. Pope Paul replied to Shazar that "We come as pilgrims" and spoke of the common roots of the two faiths and how moved he was to set foot on the soil of their common heritage.[10] Shazar presented the pope with a gold medallion on which was engraved a map of Israel and all its holy places. It also included the words, "Love thy neighbor as thyself." In turn, the pope gave the Israeli president two silver candleholders engraved with figures of angels.[11]

Shortly before the ceremony ended, the pope was approached by one of Israel's cabinet officials, Meir Mendes, who reminded Paul VI that in 1939, when the future pope was a Vatican undersecretary of state known as Monsignor Montini, the monsignor had intervened and helped acquire appropriate papers which enabled Mendes's family to escape Nazi capture. Also noteworthy is that Pope Paul's visit to Israel elicited a sharp protest from King Hussein and the Palestinians incorporated into his kingdom who lived on the West Bank. Hussein saw the pope's visit as implanting legitimacy to the state of Israel, which Palestinians claimed as their own. Indeed, a number of Israeli observers saw Paul's visit to Israel in 1964 as a symbolic gesture just short of a formal recognition of the state.[12]

The interpretation of impending recognition was overly sanguine. *Nostra Aetate*, certified by the signature of Pope Paul VI, made no mention of the Jewish state. When Israel's president spoke of the Jewish fulfillment of the prophecy of the Jews' return to the land of Israel, the statement made little sense to Paul. The pope knew only of one fulfillment: the fulfillment of all men through belief in Christ Jesus. There is also little evidence that the pontiff was grounded in postbiblical Jewish history or recent issues of Jewish concern. Writing in *Midstream* in 1971, the Catholic theologian Friedrich Heer states that Paul VI "clings to the theology of the murdered God," that is, the theology of contempt.[13] Likewise, Daniel F. Polish, a Reform rabbi deeply involved in Jewish-Christian relations, noted that even when visiting Israel, Paul VI displayed an attitude toward Israel and its Jews that was "at best ambivalent." While in Israel, the pope said nothing about the recent history of the Jews or the "current historical reality." He made no comment about Jewish survivors and their return to the land.[14] The Church of Rome would move slowly toward the full acceptance and recognition of the Jewish state.

□ □ □

It took a short, spectacular war in June 1967, soon known as the Six-Day War, to nudge the leadership of the Catholic Church toward the realization of the important role that the state of Israel assumed in the lives of most Jews.

Little attention was at first paid by Catholics to the train of events in the Middle East which led to Israel's preemptive strike against Egypt on the morning of June 5, 1967. The crisis which led to the war grew out of years of provocation which Israel had endured from its surrounding Arab neighbors, primarily Egypt, Syria, and Jordan. The Arabs' hostility toward Israel stemmed from their inability to accept either Jewish sovereignty over land which the Palestinian Arabs claimed to be theirs or the very existence of the state of Israel in the Arab world. Also, Arab military defeats at the hands of the Jews in 1948 and 1956 had engendered a desire for revenge.[15]

Throughout the years following Israel's establishment, Arab guerrillas launched raids across Israeli borders from Jordan, Syria, and Egypt. Such attacks cost Israel numerous civilian casualties and kept its border settlements under constant military alert. Since their defeat in 1949, Israel's Arab neighbors had refused to sign a peace treaty with the Jewish state. They considered themselves, therefore, in a continuing state of war with Israel. Israel's retaliation for the border assault was likewise costly to the Arabs. During these years of guerrilla warfare, Israel received little support from the world community or the United Nations.

Bad as it was, the situation deteriorated when Gamal Abdel Nasser, military leader and president of Egypt (the United Arab Republic), took a series of steps which endangered Israel's survival. With the expectation of Soviet as well as Syrian, Jordanian, and Iraqi support, Nasser moved his army to a position threatening to Israel. On May 14, 1967, he announced that Egyptian forces were in a "state of maximum alert." Egyptian units crossed the Suez Canal into the Sinai Peninsula. At the same time, Syria, Jordan, and Iraq mobilized and surrounded Israel, further threatening its survival. Still further, on May 22, 1967, Egypt closed the Gulf of Aqaba to Israeli ships and commerce, a measure which the Israeli government viewed as an act of war. As tensions escalated, Nasser, who was confident of the support of the Soviet Union and the Arab world, called for the annihilation of the Jewish state. By the beginning of June, with Arab armies surrounding Israel's borders in readiness to attack, Israel found itself in a dangerous crisis. The government of the Jewish state saw no option but to launch a preemptive attack. A first blow, it reasoned, was imperative if Israel was to survive a simultaneous attack on all of its borders.[16]

Within a few hours after Israel's June 5 preemptive strike, the massive Egyptian air force was entirely destroyed. Not long after, in the face of Israel's citizen recruits, the surrounding Arab armies of Egypt, Jordan, Syria, and Iraq were in total disarray. By the end of a week of fighting, Israeli forces had captured the entire Sinai Peninsula; the Gaza Strip; the West Bank, which had been under Jordanian occupation; the Golan Heights, where constant attacks had been launched from Syria against Israel's northern settlements; and the Old City of Jerusalem, which contained the sacred Western Wall and other important Jewish institutions. By June 10, in just six days, Israel had refashioned its boundaries and reshaped the map of the Near East. The victory over its Arab enemies raised Israel's confidence and sense of security. But it also intensified Arab humiliation and resentment of the Jewish state.[17]

The elation in the American Jewish community produced by the Israeli victory was intensified by its sharp contrast to the deep anxiety and fear for Israel's survival in the weeks before the war. With Arab armies surrounding Israel, with Nasser raving about pushing Israel into the sea, the days prior to June 5 had appeared bleak. Was the world to witness a repetition of the German horror? Given the situation on the ground, it was not an unreasonable concern. At the time, no one could possibly foretell that the war about to erupt would end so spectacularly in only six days.

Most disconcerting to the Jews was that the church, after all that had transpired in the recent Vatican council and given its record of silence during the Second World War, remained relatively quiet during May and early June 1967. In a sense, the example of silence came from Pope Paul VI, who had just returned from the Holy Land. He was not unaware of the threats directed at Israel. He had spoken out on behalf of Christian Arabs and the security of the holy places, yet he remained quiet about a possible repetition of genocide against the Jewish people.[18]

How, then, could American Jews depend on a show of unified support or sympathy from their Catholic neighbors? A letter written on June 8, 1967, by the president of the National Conference of Catholic Bishops, John F. Dearden, talked about the need for a peaceful resolution to the Arab-Israeli conflict: "In this hour of crisis, we, the Catholic bishops of the United States, unite with the Holy Father in his fervent hope that the United Nations Organization will be successful in halting the conflict. We pray the arms will be laid down and that an honorable accord will be concluded."[19] For American Jews, such bland evenhandedness displayed by American bishops was a depressing sign of indifference. Surely, neutrality in a conflict in which one of the two parties determines to exterminate the other is immoral.

However, a few prominent American Catholic writers were quick to see their error. They were concerned about the damaging impact of Catholic silence and impartiality on the recently improved relations and ongoing dialogue with the American Jewish community. Within a few weeks following the Six-Day War, the editor of *Catholic World* expressed his concern that the Catholic-Jewish dialogue was "floundering." He detected a "disarray" in the relationship between Catholics and Jews. The reason, he explained, was the perception of "failure of Catholic clergy to speak out" on "behalf of the Jews of Israel," while they were engaged in conflict. Catholics had also been silent, the editorial stated, "when millions of Jews were being murdered in Nazi Germany." Now they were seen to be quiet when Nasser was calling for the extermination of Israel.[20]

Catholic World noted, however, that a number of leading Catholics, such as Richard Cardinal Cushing of Boston and Archbishop Paul Hallinan of Atlanta, spoke out publicly, as did the editors of *America* and *Commonweal,* who also made public protest of Nasser's attempt to choke off Israel's commerce. John B. Sheerin, editor of *Catholic World,* admitted that many American Catholics were ill prepared to sort out the complexities of the Arab-Israeli conflict, nor were they aware of the deep American Jewish attachment to the land of Israel. He did not justify their "silence," but he hoped that despite it, the Catholic-Jewish dialogue would continue to develop an important dimension between the two faith communities.[21]

A select group of Catholic writers recognized the contradiction between the recently proclaimed *Nostra Aetate,* No. 4, and the silence of
Catholics in the face of Israel's impending destruction. As one writer put
it: "The fires of Auschwitz have not succeeded in purging the violent
hatred against the Jews. A quarter of a century after Adolf Hitler . . . the
world looks on while Nasser prepares the extermination of Israel."[22]

Neither did Israel's defeat of its Arab invaders, a victory which only
exacerbated Arab hatred of the Jewish state, disappoint all American
Catholics. The Institute of Judaeo-Christian Studies of Seton Hall University, which had before the Vatican council concerned itself with Jewish conversion, issued a strongly worded statement on November 17,
1967, justifying Israel's preemptive strike and conquest of surrounding
lands. The "Statement of Conscience" was designed as an appeal to
American Christians to understand Israel's actions in the Middle East.
Israel's preemptive strike, it declared, was an act of self-defense against
Arab intention to destroy Israel. The Arab leadership was responsible
for its own catastrophe. The Arab world has no right to threaten Israel's existence, declared the institute's document. Israel's existence is ordained by international law (the United Nations) and Hebrew Scripture,
the work of its Jewish inhabitants and their blood.[23] What is more, the
Catholic institute defended Israel's refusal to withdraw from its con-
quered land. "It would be absurd to expect Israel to withdraw behind
the armistice lines of 1949 and thus, for instance, return to Syria the very
hills from which heavy guns kept Galilean Kibbutzim (Israel's collective
farms) under fire . . . to demand of Israel to move back to borders so
vulnerable as to invite invasion."[24]

Because the crisis of the Six-Day War was short and its outcome so
satisfactory, American Jews soon agreed with their Catholic neighbors
that the dialogue which had been briefly delayed should be resumed. An
important ingredient of such renewed conversation was the recognition
of the importance that the subject of Israel was now to assume. For
Catholics, the Jewish unified response to the crisis served as a wakeup
call. It was an invitation to appreciate the corporate character of American Jewry and the importance to it of the coupling of religious and secular issues. As Arthur Gilbert wrote in 1968, "Christians will be asked
to make a greater effort to know the Jew as he is today, not as the Christian sees him through the spectrum of New Testament narration."[25] The
Six-Day War added a new and necessary plank to the growing and
strengthening structure of Christian-Jewish relations. It is a relationship,
as Pawlikowski noted, which will be strengthened with Christian understanding of the bond of American Jews and the state of Israel. But he

added that this understanding did not necessarily mean that American Catholics would be called upon to endorse every government policy of the Jewish state.[26]

◦ ◦ ◦

The reuniting of Jerusalem, an event of indescribable joy for the Jewish people and the state of Israel, left in its wake unresolved questions. Jerusalem had been a thorny problem between the Holy See and the Jewish state for years before the Six-Day War. Fundamentally, according to one Catholic writer, "it was a concern for the international and interfaith" character of the city with its holy places that made the church uncomfortable about its future. Actually, this anxiety on the part of the Holy See began to decline with Israel's reunification of the city following the 1967 War. Israel's sensitivity to the integrity and its assurance of the safety of the holy places of all faiths eventually reassured the Vatican of Israel's management of the Holy City.[27]

Yet, following the Six-Day War, the National Conference of American Bishops, meeting in Washington, D.C., displayed little enthusiasm for Israel's conquest of the Old City of Jerusalem and the unification of the city. They listened to impassioned reports about the alleged diminishing Christian population of the Old City, resulting from the Jewish occupation. The Christian population had, they were told, dropped from about 25,000 to fewer than 9,000. One reporting bishop lamented that it was difficult to be a bishop in the United States, but it was terrible to be one in Jerusalem.[28]

During the spring of 1971, Archbishop Joseph Ryan of Anchorage "pleaded" with American bishops, according to one writer, to help save Christianity in the state of Israel. Ryan's lament was that Christian Arabs were leaving Jerusalem in a "stampede" of large numbers. Priests, he predicted, would soon preside over empty churches. Christianity, Ryan nostalgically observed, had been more vital when East Jerusalem was under Jordanian rule. Although it was an isolated opinion, immediately challenged as a gross exaggeration by John Oesterreicher, director of the Institute of Judaeo-Christian Studies and a seasoned traveler to the Middle East, Ryan's view was weighed seriously by some bishops in the United States.[29]

The archbishop's forecast of gloom stemmed in part from his close association with the Catholic Near East Welfare Association, an organization, according to Oesterreicher, "that has not distinguished itself by a spirit of fairness, much less of affection for the people and state of

Israel." Oesterreicher saw Ryan's report as a bundle of vast exaggerations of the flight of Christians from Jerusalem and of demographic distortion in order to discredit Israel's administration of the unified city.[30]

In the fall of 1973, the state of Israel withstood, again victoriously, a surprise attack by the combined armies of Egypt and Syria. Since the Arab assault occurred on the holiest day on the Jewish calendar, Yom Kippur (Day of Atonement), the war was called the Yom Kippur War. A few weeks later, in November 1973, America's bishops, ignoring the unprovoked surprise attack upon Israel's sovereign territory, attributed equal fault to each of the belligerents. The bishops offered a number of recommendations for a comprehensive peace in the Middle East. These included Israel's right to exist as a sovereign state with secure boundaries. They also included the right of the Palestinians to negotiate with Israel for a sovereign state of their own. The sixth recommendation of the American bishops dealt with the future of Jerusalem and read as follows: "Given recognition of the unique status of the City of Jerusalem, its religious significance which transcends the interests of any one tradition, we believe it necessary to insure access to the city through a form of *international* guarantee."[31] Jewish observers, either in Israel or the United States, would consider a request directed to a sovereign state to impose international control upon its capital contrary to international practice, even presumptuous.[32]

By the end of the twentieth century, most Jews, Israeli or American, continued to think of Jerusalem as Israel's eternal and undivided capital. This did not completely preclude negotiations for special arrangements with Palestinian Arabs, who still sought to include East Jerusalem as a "capital" for their anticipated sovereign state. This was not a popular view, but there were a growing number of Israelis who were willing to entertain it. When John Cardinal O'Connor of New York lashed out at the Israeli government in the spring of 1990 for permitting 150 Jews to take up residence in East Jerusalem, he generated enormous anger in the American Jewish community. Although O'Connor was a longtime friend of Israel and the New York Jewish community, Seymour Reich, chairman of the Conference of Presidents of major American Jewish organizations, criticized O'Connor for attacking Israeli policy in Jerusalem.[33] The incident underscored the passion that could be mounted in the American Jewish community against any suggestion to alter the status of a unified Jerusalem as Israel's capital.

Jews were not alone in their defense of a united Jerusalem under Israeli sovereignty and in their opposition to any form of internationalization. A survey of prominent American prelates, writers, academics, and theologians, conducted by the American Jewish Committee (AJC) in 1971, revealed that even at that early date, the vast majority saw no problem in maintaining the status quo in Jerusalem. They were aware of no theological problem should the Holy City remain unified under Israeli control. Most were opposed to Pope Paul VI's recommendation for internationalization of the city. The majority of Catholics surveyed, in the United States and even in Jerusalem, rejected the rumor circulated by the media that the Jewish reunification and control of East Jerusalem had caused Catholics to flee. On the contrary, many contended that conditions had improved for the church since the end of Jordanian control.[34]

The AJC determined on the basis of its survey that, when pressed, most Catholic thinkers did not approve of Paul VI's call to the College of Cardinals in 1971 for the internationalization of the entire city of Jerusalem. The AJC report pointed out that even Karl Rahner, considered in 1971 the leading Roman Catholic theologian, was puzzled by the pope's position in this matter. Rahner saw no theological problem with Jewish control of Jerusalem.[35] The National Coalition of American Nuns, one of the most important organizations of American nuns, issued a statement during its September 1971 conference, rejecting internationalization and strongly supporting Israel's right to control its unified city.[36]

A greater convergence of views between the papacy and American Catholic leaders materialized during the pontificate of John Paul II. His 1984 Good Friday apostolic letter, which described a new relationship between the Vatican and Jerusalem, was more attuned than was the writing of Paul VI to the spirit of *Nostra Aetate* and the church's need for *tshuvah* (repentance). In the letter, John Paul explained to a group of Catholics that Judaism is not a church but rather a peoplehood which requires the land of Israel for the well-being of its Jewishness. Christians need to understand the importance of the link between land and people. In a homily on October 3, 1980, John Paul had explained how the tragedy of the *Shoah* and the need for security have made this link especially significant. Although acknowledging the significance of the city of Jerusalem for Christians, John Paul recognized the unique relationship with Christians which existed between the Jewish people and the Holy City. He spoke of the deep historic and religious roots that Judaism had planted there. He referred to it as the "sign" of its peoplehood and "capital" of its nation. These remarks went further than those made by his predecessor and had a powerful impact on the American hierarchy.[37]

For years, a number of prominent Catholics had been calling for a unified Jerusalem under Israeli sovereignty. The Arab request for East

Jerusalem was called by one writer an "unparalleled impertinence."[38] The strong language by John M. Oesterreicher was directed at a group of Muslim dignitaries who sought an audience with John Paul in order to persuade him to support their demand to return East Jerusalem to Arab control. Oesterreicher also struck out at King Hussein for his efforts to win the Christian world to his side for the same purpose. Oesterreicher was amazed at the king's presumption to appoint himself the guardian of the holy places of East Jerusalem. Only a few years earlier, before the Six-Day War, King Hussein had barred Jewish worshipers from their holy places, including the Western Wall, and had permitted desecration of synagogues during his occupation. This he did despite his pledge to allow Jewish access to the city. Given the king's record and the Muslim record in general, an Islamic country cannot be entrusted with the guardianship of the Christian or Jewish holy places, declared Oesterreicher. Indeed, argued Oesterreicher, far from shaking his trust in Israel, the king's fabrications assured him even more of the virtue of Israel's control over both East and West Jerusalem. Most important, according to Oesterreicher, though Christians and Muslims both have stakes in the city, it is by right a Jewish city. Neither Christians nor Muslims have prayed through the years for the peace of the city; only the Jewish people have. Not Muslims nor Christians but only Jews kept hope alive for a return to the city.[39]

As a prominent priest, scholar, and director of the Institute of Judaeo-Christian Studies, Oesterreicher was invited in 1974 by the American Professors for Peace in the Middle East, a Zionist-oriented organization, to edit a volume of essays on Jerusalem and its significance for Jews.[40] Most of the contributions were those of Israeli scholars. The presence of Oesterreicher among them was added evidence of the support that the state of Israel was increasingly receiving from the American Catholic Church. In the case of Oesterreicher, it also represented the almost magical transformation of American Catholic sensitivity toward Jews and Judaism inspired by the Second Vatican Council.

Oesterreicher's views were supported by other associates of the Institute of Judaeo-Christian Studies. Edward Flannery emerged after the Second Vatican Council as a prominent student of Zionism and an opponent of a divided Jerusalem. In an essay in 1986, he underscored the particular meaning that the Holy City conveyed to Jews. Jerusalem's centrality is unique, he said. To Christians and Muslims, explained Flannery, the city gains an importance because of its shrines, particular events, and personages. For Jews, the entire city is holy. It is a city given to the Jewish people by God, said Flannery. It is there that the Jewish nation was born during the reign of King David. Flannery detected no equation between Israel's claim and the demands brought forth by other faiths.[41]

Even so, by the close of the twentieth century, an element of ambivalence about the status of Jerusalem still prevailed within some circles of American Catholics. Commenting on the right of the state of Israel to exclusive control over Jerusalem, the editors of *First Things,* the neo-conservative Catholic review, declared: "It may be a good idea for the U.S. to recognize Jerusalem as the capital of Israel. It is a very bad idea to argue for such a change by claiming that Jerusalem is an exclusively Jewish City, and that the attachments of Muslims and Christians to that City are, at most, of incidental importance. Jerusalem is the earthly center of the story of the world's salvation, and as such belongs to the world." The state of Israel, the editorial went on to argue, must recognize that it is merely "the guardian" of "the City that belongs to the world."[42] Clearly, *First Things* exposes a lingering uncertainty on the part of a conservative Catholic fringe about the Jewish claim to the Holy City.

◻ ◻ ◻

In 1973, American Catholic bishops meeting with Protestant leaders issued a joint report entitled, "A Statement to Our Fellow Christians." It was based on a study of "Israel: People, Land, and State." The statement was designed for distribution to Catholic, Protestant, and Jewish organizations for discussion and suggestions. The 1973 statement is important because it reflected the thinking of American Catholic leadership about the state of Israel. While it shows the long distance traveled by the church in respect to Israel since the close of the Second Vatican Council and the Six-Day War, it also reveals a continuing uncertainty and hesitancy about the nature of Zionism and importance of the land to the Jewish people. It was an uncertainty that continued to hover subliminally in Catholic-Jewish conversations.

The statement acknowledged the existence of an "indifference and hostility to the State of Israel" which "continues to exist" among Catholics. It also recognized a variety of views about the Middle East, some of which exacerbated existing Jewish-Christian relations.[43] It urged that churches impress upon their congregants the legitimacy of the Jewish state and the right of the Jewish people to enjoy an independent sovereign existence. The statement also told American Christians to grant equal consideration to Palestinian Arab national aspirations, but it stressed the judicial, moral, and religious foundations supporting the state of Israel.[44] Significantly, the report explained that because of the threatening conditions that Israel faces in its Arab neighborhood, which refuses to make peace with the Jewish state, Israel finds no choice but to rely heavily upon its military defense. It warned American Catholics not to impose upon Israel standards of political and moral behavior "real or imaginary" that they would hesitate to impose upon other sovereign nations of the world; that is, to refrain from expecting Israelis to behave as if they were biblical prophets. By so doing, Americans would be guilty of a double standard.[45]

Even so, in the years that followed, some American prelates tried to steer a narrow course between Israeli concerns and the Palestinian desires. A case in point can be seen in remarks of New York's John Cardinal O'Connor, who usually voiced balanced but favorable comments about Israel with regrets about the plight of the Palestinian "refugees." In 1992, on one of the cardinal's numerous visits to Israel, he was meticulously careful to avoid a meeting with Israel officials in their offices lest he leave the impression that the Jewish state was officially recognized diplomatically by the church.[46] Neither did he dare to set foot in West Jerusalem. In both cases, O'Connor was guided by Vatican instructions.[47]

O'Connor's "evenhandedness" left some Jews concerned about the precise position of the church. The concern was seen in 1989 when the National Conference of Catholic Bishops released a draft statement on the Middle East calling for the establishment "of a Palestinian homeland with its sovereign status recognized by Israel." These remarks stood in sharp contradiction to the stated policy of Israel or, for that matter, the United States. At the same time, American Jewish leaders applauded the bishops' concern for guarantees for Israel's right to have secure boundaries determined through direct negotiations with its Arab neighbors. Some Jewish leaders, such as Henry Siegman, executive director of the American Jewish Congress, described the fifty-page statement as "fair and balanced." Leaders of the American Jewish Committee were equally pleased, calling it "an honest and compassionate attempt to represent the various parties concerned." Indeed, the draft was reviewed favorably by seven Jewish leaders who took part in a five-hour meeting with John Cardinal O'Connor of New York, Archbishop Roger Mahoney of Los Angeles, and Archbishop William Keeler of Baltimore, the three individuals who crafted the statement.[48]

Not all Jewish groups commended the draft statement. B'nai B'rith leadership called the recommendation for a Palestinian homeland with territorial and political sovereignty "fundamentally flawed."[49] Jews, like Catholics, were not unified on how to deal with the complex issues facing Israel. Rarely, however, did such lack of consensus on the part of American Catholics call into question the need for a Jewish state. On the contrary, in American church guidelines, Israel's existence is seen as a necessity in the wake of the *Shoah* as an antidote to antisemitism and the contemporary centrality of the land as essential to Jewish religious identity.[50]

Throughout the years following the Second Vatican Council and the Six-Day War, Catholics were urged by their leaders to learn about Israel's importance to Jews. As Richard Cardinal Cushing of Boston put it in 1969: "[The state of Israel] is not just a refuge for a people the world has abused—it is for the Jews the fulfillment of prophecy, the return to the promised land, the realization of the divine covenant, the answer to the prayers of generations of the chosen people. When it is seen in this light, so much that is otherwise hidden becomes clear, so much that is incomprehensible becomes full of meaning."[51]

In the last three decades of the twentieth century, a number of priests and scholars urged Americans to recognize the importance that the state of Israel possesses for their Jewish neighbors. Robert F. Drinan rejected the notion that self-interest alone should determine the degree of support the United States should extend to Israel. Support for Israel is a moral obligation, he believes, an obligation which transcends political interests. In matters pertaining to the Jewish state, American obligations ought not necessarily to conform to international opinion or to the views of the United Nations, wrote Drinan. Neither should Arabs be supplied with lethal weapons to facilitate their malevolent designs, declared Drinan in 1977.[52] Drinan did not conceal his anger at Arab behavior toward Israel in the United Nations and toward the Arabs' economic boycott of Israel. Drinan wanted Americans to understand Israel's "agonizing situation" in which it found itself in the 1970s. He was concerned that a new generation of Americans would lose the awareness of Israel that those who were present at Israel's birth possessed.[53]

Drinan was convinced that there was in the American Catholic community, as there was in American society in general, "a religiously rooted moral consensus that sustains the unwavering promise . . . to protect the territorial integrity of Israel."[54] As a Catholic priest, Drinan urged upon Catholics a certain awareness: "Any definition of contemporary Jewish religious experience that does not provide for due comprehension and acceptance of the inextricable bonds of God, people, *Torah*, and promised land risks distortion of the essential nature of Judaism and the Jewish people."[55] Drinan's assertiveness on behalf of the Jewish state was appreciated by American Jews. They considered him a dependable ally in Congress, where he sat as a Representative until he was ordered by the Vatican to leave in 1980.[56]

There were a handful of Catholic writers who, like Drinan, shunned impartiality and aspired to enhance the appreciation of Israel in the Catholic community. Edward H. Flannery, for example, believed the subject of Israel constitutes a major "stumbling block" in Jewish-Christian relations. At best the subject has remained of peripheral interest to American Catholics. But because of its profound importance to Jews, wrote Flannery in 1986, it was imperative for Catholic apathy to be reversed. The Christian failure to look at Israel with "a full and open heart" was disappointing to Flannery. It contradicted the intentions of the Vatican guidelines and the pronouncements of America's bishops which tried to implement the suggestions of *Nostra Aetate,* No. 4.[57]

A significant handful of Catholic writers—Drinan, Flannery, and others such as Eugene Fisher and Joseph Cardinal Bernardin—found little merit in expounding an "evenhanded" position in Israel's conflict with the Arab world.[58] This was clear to Eugene Fisher, who explained in 1981 that "we in the West must learn to grapple realistically with the fact that Muslim anti-Semitism has played, and continues to play, a critical role in the Middle East conflict. We must abandon the naïve view that because the Muslim world is classified in our newspapers under the heading 'Third World,' Arabs and Palestinians can be viewed as pure innocents."[59]

□ □ □

Remembering the *Shoah* and the near disaster of the Six-Day War, coupled with Catholic silence, American Jews displayed little appreciation for critics of Israel. For religious Jews, Israel's victory and survival were seen as God's response to their past suffering. As Irving Greenberg, speaking for traditional Jews, expressed it: "When suffering had all but overwhelmed Jews and all but blocked out God's presence, the sign out of the whirlwind gave us the strength to go on, and the right to speak authentically of God's presence still."[60]

To be sure, there were some devout Jews who refused to attribute religious qualities to Zionism, a secular movement, or to attribute any significant Jewish meaning to Israel. Yet most Jews, both the devout and the secular, felt concern about the security of the state of Israel. Jews interpreted attacks upon or lack of sympathy toward the Jewish state as unfriendliness to Jews in general. As a 1995 study of American Jewish attitudes concluded: "The major impulses that have communalized most Jews around Israel have not stemmed from Zionist ideology or from religious conviction but from tribal charity and defensiveness. The defensive posture of American Jews is sustained in part by anxiety about potential anti-Semitism in America and even more by concern about the security of Israel."[61]

Catholic writers recognized that hostility toward the Jewish state was viewed by Jews as a gesture of antisemitism. Catholic leaders cautioned Catholics to avoid repeating any of the traditional anti-Zionist, insensitive statements which emanated from the preconciliar church's theology of contempt. The theologian Charlotte Klein noted the importance of Catholic thinkers to construction of a renewed theology of Israel which does not challenge the sacred link of Jews to their land.[62] Likewise, John Pawlikowski urged his coreligionists not to look upon Israel merely as a political issue when conversing with Jews.[63] Like Klein, Pawlikowski believed that Catholics must reject the old theology which relegated Jews to eternal homelessness and perpetual wandering because of their rejection of the Christian Messiah: "This tradition has been shattered by the historical events of the twentieth century." Such traditional teaching must be abandoned, writes Pawlikowski.[64] The existence and survival of the Jewish state should obliterate traditional Catholic perceptions about Jews, he says. The existence of Israel, explains the Catholic theologian, "can become a powerful tool in the general Christian theological effort to re-examine the meaning and destiny of the Jewish people. It can help us realize that God did not abrogate his covenant with Israel. The Jews are still his people, beloved and cherished. God is faithful, he does not renege on promises once made."[65]

While Catholics learn to appreciate the Jewish "mystical" attachment to the land of Israel, "It will help us overcome," Pawlikowski tells his readers, "the negative attitudes toward 'the earthly City' that have been fundamental to the Christian tradition."[66] What is more, the Jewish return should enable Catholics to expand their vision of God's work. Catholics could accommodate Zionism as an integral part of Judaism. "Zionism," wrote Anthony J. Kenny, "is an important and valid expression of a fundamental dimension of Judaism." Catholics should recognize, observed Kenny, that Zionism, secular or religious, is "*essentially a profound longing for the fullness of Jewishness.*" Kenny cautioned that "if Catholic theology could not accommodate Zionism, neither could it accommodate Judaism." Both are inseparable, according to Kenny. For it to conform with realism, the church must grant theological recognition to Zionism. Kenny's suggestion reflected the metamorphosis of the attitude toward Zionism then taking place in American Catholic thought.[67]

▫ ▫ ▫

The inseparability of Zionism from Judaism was an equation not generally disputed by American Jews except for a few isolated voices of the American Council for Judaism and some ultra-orthodox Jews such as the Satmar Hasidim.[68] At any rate, for Jews, Jewish anti-Zionism hardly contained the anti-Jewish nuances present in Christian anti-Zionism. Indeed, a few Catholic theologians came increasingly to recognize that Christian rejection of the validity of Zionism, that is, the rejection of the necessity of a Jewish state, was an explicit expression of antisemitism.

One of the first Catholic theologians to elaborate on this ominous relationship was Edward H. Flannery. In 1969, when he was executive secretary of the American Bishops' Secretariat for Catholic-Jewish Relations and author of *The Anguish of the Jews,* he wrote a pathbreaking article, "Anti-Zionism and the Christian Psyche."[69] In this article, Flannery contends that at that time many American Catholics continued to display indifference and hostility when confronted with news of Israel's emergence. The negative attitude, he believes, is "'symptomatic of the presence of determination, unconscious forces, specifically, unrecognized antipathy against the Jewish people."[70] Flannery labels this new pathology "Christian anti-Zionism." "It has much to reveal of the Christian consciousness," writes Flannery. Christian anti-Zionism was especially stark during the Six-Day War in June 1967. At this time, when the Jewish state was faced with annihilation, the American church was apathetic and silent. Flannery believes that those who so reacted could be considered antisemites, a hatred revealed by their anti-Zionism.[71] Even when focused on the state of Israel, writes Flannery, such Christian observers

> riveted [their] attention on questions of borderlines, refugees, and the like, ignoring meanwhile the persistent threat from the Arab countries to eliminate Israel.
>
> The rationale of this position is usually justified on the grounds of an anti-Zionist stance. Critics of Israel and its triumphs repeatedly remind us that they are neither anti-Jewish nor anti-Semitic, but simply anti-Zionist. . . . The anti-Zionist simply asserts: Judaism is only a religion: The Israeli state is nothing but the creature of Zionist politics.[72]

Flannery makes a distinction from Christian anti-Zionism, which he sees as more ominous than Arab anti-Zionism. Not all writers, however, accept this dichotomy. Robert Drinan, for example, remarked in 1977 that it is wrong to accept such distinctions. The argument that Arabs "are not anti-Semitic or anti-Jewish but only anti-Zionist . . . is hard to sustain in view of the presence everywhere in the Arab world of literature containing the worst slander against Jews and Judaism. The *Protocols of the Elders of Zion,* the notorious forgery fabricated in Tsarist Russia, now has more versions and editions in Arabic than in any other language."[73]

Likewise, Lillian C. Freudmann, a student of Christian antisemitism, noted in 1994 that anti-Zionism is a twentieth-century variation of traditional antisemitism. By rejecting the Jews' right to determine their own national destiny, a right accorded to other national groups, such an attitude represents a modern version of anti-Judaism.[74] Drinan also warned that "those who seek to downgrade Zionism necessarily operate on the assumption that Israel is the product not of Judaism but only of a political movement called Zionism. Every attempt to disassociate Zionism from Judaism ends up with a caricature of both."[75]

In this sense, Drinan was not as forgiving as was Flannery about designating Arab anti-Zionism as a lesser form of antisemitism. When the Arab world managed to muster two-thirds of the votes of the United Nations General Assembly, including Third World and Communist nations, in 1973 to declare Zionism a form of racism, Drinan saw this as a blatant gesture of antisemitism.[76] The equation of Zionism and racism, hammered out by Arab delegates to the UN, was eloquently challenged by the United States ambassador, Daniel Patrick Moynihan. But the United States and its friends could not prevail against Arab, Third World, and Communist opposition. As a result, the term "Zionism" was anathemized and demonized by the very body which twenty-five years earlier had offered it international legitimacy. The Israeli ambassador to the United Nations, Haim Herzog, observed on the occasion of the UN vote on Zionism/racism that the body that emerged as a defender of human rights in opposition to Nazi Germany was now repeating the hatefulness of the antisemitic myths of Adolf Hitler.

It is important, however, that the American Catholic leadership condemned the United Nations vote. Meeting in Memphis, Tennessee, shortly after the General Assembly vote, American Catholic and Protestant leaders declared in a joint statement that "to compare Zionism with racism is a calumny against the Jews and a return to the old anti-Semitism that was a scourge of mankind for centuries."[77]

Neither was the Vatican leadership pleased. Johannes Cardinal Willebrands, the chief ecumenical leader in the Vatican, was "amazed" at the UN resolution. John Cardinal Carberry of St. Louis declared that by equating Zionism with racism, the UN "had put itself on record as racist." Some months later, sixty American bishops dispatched a letter to the United Nations secretary general, Kurt Waldheim, "denouncing the

resolution as a slander against Jews everywhere." They indicated that
for Jews, Zionism is a "sacred word, a sacred concept," which "merits
the respect and understanding of all Christians."[78]

◻ ◻ ◻

Catholic opposition to Arab and Third World assaults on Zionism during the 1970s did not suggest a willingness to offer the state of Israel official recognition. Before the mid-1980s, it seemed that such a gesture was
decades away. This reluctance remained a major obstacle in Catholic-
Jewish relations. Even the Vatican *Notes,* a document which at the initiative of Pope John Paul II was drawn up to enable teachers and preachers to view authentic Judaism as part of contemporary reality rather than
a biblical idea, hesitated to speak of the state of Israel as a modern sovereign entity deserving full recognition. Neither did this 1985 document
grant religious or theological recognition to the state of Israel.[79] American Catholic leaders had little choice but to accept the Vatican position
on Israel. It did not enhance the progress of dialogue between the two
faith communities.

Vatican diplomatic recognition of the Jewish state was an important
issue for American Jewish leaders. When meeting with Vatican officials,
Jewish leaders rarely missed an opportunity to bring this issue to their
attention but were usually rebuffed or assured that recognition would materialize just as soon as certain "practical problems" had been cleared.[80]

Although no formal relations between Jerusalem and the Vatican existed, informal contacts were made. By the mid-eighties, Israel maintained an embassy in Rome which conducted affairs with the Vatican
secretariat of state, a temporary arrangement that some American prelates hoped would be sustained until a formal exchange of ambassadors
materialized. Meanwhile, when Israeli officials visited Rome, they were
treated as official state representatives. It was a positive, though informal, relationship, one reflected in John Paul's apostolic letter of April
20, 1984, in which he declared: "For the Jewish people who live in the
State of Israel and who preserve in that land such precious testimonies
of their history and their faith, we must ask for the desired security and
tranquility that is the prerogative of every nation."[81] The Apostolic letter reflected an openness toward and a religious support for the Jewish
state which went far beyond that which had been extended in previous
decades. When John Paul met with a delegation of Jewish representatives, he never failed to express his interest in Israel and its relationship
to the Jewish people.[82]

For Jews, however, such sympathetic comments from the Holy See could not compensate for the absence of a de jure recognition of the state of Israel. In 1985, the Holy See was reminded by an official of the World Jewish Congress that despite all the progress made in the past twenty years, Jews were in general agreement that "normalization of relations with all Jews includes the Jewish people who live in Israel."[83] Likewise, in their audiences with John Paul, officials of the American Jewish Committee turned repeatedly to the subject of normalization of relations with the Jewish state. They contended, as did Howard Freedman, president of the AJC, that Vatican de jure recognition would hasten Middle East peace. The gesture would dispel illusions about Israel's outcast status in the Catholic world, not to mention that such an act would be marked, as Anthony Kenny noted, by profound moral and ethical implications. Arthur Hertzberg, a high-ranking official of the World Jewish Congress, observed, as did others, that the absence of normal diplomatic relations with the state of Israel retarded the progress of dialogue.

When Jews wondered if the silence of the Holy See represented a hesitancy to loosen its hold on the old theology of contempt, they questioned also the genuineness of the warm papal utterances about the state of Israel.[84] Other Jewish leaders and journalists attributed the Vatican's refusal to grant diplomatic recognition to the Jewish state to its concern about Arab reactions to such a move and to what it saw as Israel's uncertain borders. Such political rationalizations did little to mitigate Jewish annoyance at the behavior of the Holy See, from which they had expected a better manifestation of atonement of its "past crimes" against the Jews.[85]

In 1991, in reaction to persistent rumors to the contrary, Vatican officials denied that theological barriers had prevented the church's official recognition of the Jewish state. Rather, they said, it was Israel's unresolved conflict over the West Bank territories and its Palestinian population that had delayed full normalization. The future status of the "Old City" of Jerusalem was also cited as an important unresolved issue. The obstacles against formal Vatican recognition of the state of Israel seemed formidable when early in May 1992 the Vatican surprised American and world Jewry with the sudden announcement that a special commission of Israeli diplomats and Vatican representatives was to meet to discuss the normalization of state relations. It was to be the first formal meeting held between the Holy See and the state of Israel. Anticipated progress in peace talks between Israelis and Palestinians was a major incentive in the Vatican's change of attitude. Neither did the Vatican's discussions over the future of Jerusalem proceed without its full participation. The event was a major step in the improvement of Catholic-Jewish relations.[86]

According to George Weigel, who had numerous conversations with the pope in preparation for his writing of an outstanding biography of the pontiff, the Vatican's recognition of the state of Israel did not erupt with suddenness. Weigel writes about its origins as follows:

> [In 1981] according to Jerzy Kluger, John Paul II authorized his old [Jewish] friend to initiate private, informal discussions with Israeli diplomats in Rome to clarify the issues involved in moving toward full diplomatic relations. Kluger, an Italian citizen, was also authorized by the Government of Israeli Prime Minister Menachem Begin to speak on its behalf. One immediate result of these discussions was a papal telegram of good wishes to the President of Israel on Rosh Hashana, the Jewish New Year, in October, 1981.[87]

Such was the personal diplomacy that initiated a train of events which led to the "Fundamental Agreement" of 1993.[88]

Progress of the negotiations was observed by American Jews, who periodically sought information from American prelates addressing the New York Board of Rabbis. John Cardinal O'Connor assured his listeners in the spring of 1993 that the bilateral agreement should be consummated within a year. "I'd be surprised if in a year from now," declared O'Connor, "we wouldn't all be getting ready for a big celebration."[89] Indeed, on December 30, 1993, the Holy See and the state of Israel signed a "Fundamental Agreement" which established the guidelines for full diplomatic relations between the two entities. Among other things, the signatories of the document pledged to combat antisemitism and to grant protection for Catholic shrines.[90]

George Weigel calls the "Fundamental Agreement" a "diplomatic master stroke of John Paul's pontificate and a historic turning point in Jewish-Catholic relations." That it was accomplished at all, Weigel remarks, was "due to the initiative of John Paul II." Weigel found that its success resulted from the remarkable back-channel negotiation that saved the historic agreement at a moment when it seemed about to unravel. In its turn, the Holy See felt confident that its shrines would remain secure under Israeli law, indeed more secure than such edifices had ever been under Muslim domination.[91]

Pope John Paul II was personally pleased that official ties had been finally effected between the Holy See and the state of Israel. He had been well aware of the years of frustration that the Vatican's hesitation had caused to the Jewish people. But, as the pope wrote in his autobiography, because "of the initiative of the State of Israel, it became possible to *establish diplomatic relations between the Apostolic See and Israel.*"

The pope added that "as for the recognition of the State of Israel, it is important to realize that I myself never had any doubt in that regard." The pontiff was pleased with this decision, though he knew full well how disturbing it was for Middle East prelates and Muslims to accept it. He was also aware that some Jews did not believe that the church, for theological reasons, was ready to make the step that would "require an unthinkable alteration in Church doctrine."[92]

Even while the historical bilateral agreement was being signed, not all Jews were able to erase from their memories the pain and bloodshed they had suffered at the hands of the church in past centuries. Yossi Beillin, Israel's deputy prime minister who signed the agreement on behalf of Israel, wondered if in the light of history he possessed the moral right to do so. "It is not for us to say," declared Beillin. "Can we ignore the memories of so many years? No . . . much as it is wrong to let memories tie our hands and determine our fate."[93]

In the United States, Jewish and Catholic leaders rejoiced in the event. They viewed it as a major political and religious milestone in the relationship of the two faiths. A joint statement by the National Conference of American Bishops and the Synagogue Council of America was released on December 31. The accord was called a "revolution" in the relations between the Catholic Church and the Jews.[94] American Jewish organizations were convinced that years of quiet persuasion had played a role in convincing the Holy See of the need for recognition of the state of Israel.[95] Israeli coreligionists, however, were not willing to make that concession. Diplomatic recognition, according to one Israeli journalist, "is due to one man: Pope John Paul II." Not to be overlooked, Jewish readers are reminded, is the church's commitment, as stated in the agreement's article 2, to join forces with the Jewish state to combat antisemitism in all its forms.[96]

The event, Jewish spokespersons observed, would go a long way in defusing the impression among Jews that the church was anti-Jewish and anti-Israel. One activist rabbi declared that it was bound to energize the interfaith movement and intensify dialogue between Catholics and Jews. New York's Cardinal O'Connor agreed. "Israel has always been the major topic of the dialogue," he declared. "The pact will bring about a more harmonious relationship." Leon Klenicki, director of the Anti-Defamation League's Department of Interfaith Affairs, believed that the pact would have a positive effect upon Catholic teaching about Jews.[97] Likewise, a highly placed Catholic official, Edward Idris Cardinal Cassidy, head of the Commission for Religious Relations with the Jews, remarked a few years after the event that "Jewish-Christian relations were now better than they had ever been during the 2000 years of Christianity."[98] In the same Jerusalem symposium, the Jewish speaker Mark L. Winer, a careful observer of the negotiations, characterized the normalization of Vatican-Jewish relations as an event of "great historical and theological meaning. . . . The agreement was a fulfillment of the promise of Vatican II. . . . It was the fulfillment of the papal promises of John XXIII and Paul VI. It acknowledges the eternal nature of the Jewish people's covenant with God."[99]

Not all Jews, sensing that the years ahead would unfold new challenges and tensions between the two faiths, would have gone this far. But many suspected that a frontier which had remained impassable for two thousand years had been crossed.

Conclusion:
Living with the Other

A remarkable transformation in Jewish-Catholic relations took place during the last third of the twentieth century. After centuries of being considered the chosen, biblical people who had allegedly gone terribly astray, become obsessed with the Law, crucified God's son, been humbled for their infidelities, been expelled from their land, and been displaced by the New Israel, the Jews found that the Church of Rome was revising its perceptions of them. It did so not only to improve its relationship with the Jews but to correct its own self-understanding and fulfillment. The Catholic Church admitted that its theology had engendered contempt for the Jew and that new theological interpretation and insights were required. It assumed the awesome responsibility of reversing two thousand years of pain and humiliation which it had caused the Jewish people. It was an unprecedented admission and determination by a great world religion to make amends.

Such revolutionary events did not take place in a historical vacuum. Old theological doctrines did not unravel by themselves. They were acted upon by several events. First and foremost was the work of the Second Vatican Council and the promulgation of its draft of the "Declaration on the Jews," *Nostra Aetate*, No. 4. Second, behind the innovative work of John XXIII and his large gathering of bishops loomed the black shadow of the *Shoah*. Many in that gathering were ready to accept responsibility for the European calamity. This willingness nudged the bishops into giving their task more meaning. Finally, the crisis of the new state of Israel in 1967, more than any other event, jolted the church into a realization of the importance that nationhood held for the Jewish people.

As a direct result of the Second Vatican Council and the events which surrounded it, the church would no longer speak of God's rejection of the Jewish people. Neither would comments about collective guilt for the Crucifixion be theologically acceptable. Any suggestion of Christian supersessionism or of justification of Jewish suffering or of any other form of antisemitism would no more be tolerated by the church leaders.

Important too is the profound influence that the Catholic Church has had on shaping all Christian thinking about Jews. Popular thinking as well could not escape the notions about the Jewish people that had filtered through the pulpits of the church. The demonic image of the Jew found throughout the Western world had been inherited also by secular society, by the Right and the Left, by Jew-haters of various ideological and political stripes. Such hostility toward Jews, which often germinated from church doctrines, metastasized and metamorphosed in the nineteenth century to form the bitter fruits of Nazism and Auschwitz. The church did not deliberately conceive these grotesque modern horrors, but neither could it claim a total immunity.

At the same time, the church's efforts toward renewal and revision have also had great influence on all peoples. The religious revolution of attitudes toward Jews which were inspired by Catholicism produced an impact on Protestant denominations as well. Protestant theologians such as Paul M. Van Buren, Robert McAfee Brown, A. Roy Eckardt, and Franklin H. Littell stand as evidence of the pervasiveness of the rejection of the theology of contempt.[1]

It took two thousand years to generate this theology. Through teaching, dialogue, and theological renewal, a new metamorphosis is occurring and a new theology is taking final shape.

◻ ◻ ◻

A few weeks before the end of the twentieth century, Arthur Hertzberg asked, "If relations between Jews and the Roman Catholic Church are so good, why are they so bad?" Hertzberg went on to report that "the Catholic-Jewish dialogue has deteriorated in recent months with harsh and hurtful words being hurled in both directions."[2] What was going on?

In the Vatican, high church officials were looking forward to a relationship with the Jewish people free of any sign of antisemitism.[3] The New York *Jewish Week* reported that of the twenty-two cardinals appointed by John Paul II in the spring of 1991, many, including two Americans, had maintained over the years a warm relationship with the Jewish people and were eager to strengthen the bridges between the two groups. A number had urged the church to do *teshuvah* (to repent) for its behavior during the *Shoah* and earlier had encouraged the church to hasten diplomatic recognition of the state of Israel.[4]

In addressing the graduating class of Hebrew Union College–Jewish Institute of Religion in New York in May 1998, John Cardinal O'Connor had reaffirmed his own Catholic faith with its Jewish origins to the graduates of the Reform seminary but at the same time praised *Torah* traditions of the Jewish people. "I am here to remind you of your responsibility to be good Jews," he told the gathering of prospective rabbis. In the same month, O'Connor served also as the commencement speaker at Yeshiva University, the leading Jewish Orthodox educational institution in the United States. Here, the cardinal praised the significant impact which modern Jewish Orthodoxy had upon the revival of Jewish learning after the European tragedy.[5]

Students of American antisemitism have generally agreed that any meaningful measure of antisemitism has either greatly declined or disappeared entirely from the American scene.[6] At any rate, whatever problems do linger have been attributed less to American Christianity than to anti-Jewish sentiments, sometimes disguised as anti-Zionism, among African Americans or Muslims.[7]

This is not to suggest that all differences between Catholics and Jews, theological or political, have been resolved, or ever will be. Differing points of view will prevail. What has been resolved is that differences between Catholics and Jews will no longer be contaminated by a theology of contempt. A case in point is the deep disappointment that many Jews, and some Catholics as well, expressed with the Vatican report "We Remember." The absence in that report of any direct charge of error on the part of the church and the undeserved praise showered upon Pius XII, the wartime pope, left many deeply dissatisfied.

Jews and Catholics continue, as they should, to remain on guard. Two thousand years of history are not easily wiped away. Edward H. Flannery, for example, continued to argue, despite the findings of pollsters and sociologists, that antisemitism among Catholics is far from dead, that the issue must remain high on the dialogue agenda. Flannery asks, "Would it be realistic to expect any individual, who is heir to a religious tradition, a centuries old culture . . . permeated with Judeophobia, to be free of this animosity?"[8]

Tensions between Jews and Catholics in the United States have not been all home grown. They continue to spill over from the Vatican and its behavior toward Jews. Differences between Rome and the state of Israel inevitably affect the American dialogue. For example, when Vatican officials showed annoyance at what they alleged to be Israel's lack of appreciation for their efforts to reduce antisemitism in the church, the disagreement was reflected in the United States. During the summer of 1999, according to a newspaper report, "The Reverend David Yager [of Texas], a Vatican representative, stunned a conference on antisemitism by saying that Israel's anti-Catholic attitude—not the Catholic Church's anti-Israel attitude—was preventing relations from warming." Jewish spokespersons indicated that they were not yet ready to show the kind of response the church expected. Abraham Foxman and other representatives of the Anti-Defamation League remarked that "after 2000 years of Church-sanctioned anti-Semitism it would take time for the Jews to trust the Vatican." As the church approached its millennium, it preferred to avoid such disagreements with Israel.[9] But they appeared and reappeared as ripples throughout the final years of the twentieth century.

◻ ◻ ◻

One of the most protracted and bitter events was the Auschwitz convent controversy, which occurred during the years 1984–94. It began when about a dozen Carmelite nuns decided in 1984 to establish a convent in an abandoned theater at the edge of the death camp of Auschwitz-Birkenau. In this notorious place, the nuns determined to spend their days praying for and meditating about those who died there. Here more than two million humans had been gassed and burned, 90 percent of whom were Jewish men, women, and children. Not surprisingly, the name "Auschwitz" became almost synonymous with "Shoah." Although the desire of the Carmelite nuns was to establish a center of work, prayer, and contemplation, Jews throughout the world saw the erection of a convent at the edge of an invisible graveyard of hundreds of thousands of Jews as highly offensive.[10]

Because of Jewish protests, the nuns agreed to move their center a distance away from Auschwitz by 1989, but they did not keep their promise. Isolated from the outside world, cloistered in their convent, the nuns were not attuned to external voices. Being granted a large degree of autonomy made them even less inclined to alter their decision, once made, to pray for all the victims who lost their lives in Auschwitz. The Carmelite nuns' decision not to move was also bolstered by the support they at first received from conservative Polish church leaders, who considered Auschwitz as much a Polish graveyard as a Jewish one. It was a view which initially resonated with many Polish citizens, who viewed the unfolding controversy as a nationalistic as much as a religious one.[11]

The controversy escalated. Jews—a number from the United States—demonstrated on the convent grounds where, in the summer of 1989, they clashed with Polish workingmen repairing the convent. Poles viewed the Jewish protests as an attack on Roman Catholicism. Antisemitic epithets against Jews were dredged up by some Polish prelates. At one point, the New York Orthodox rabbi Avraham Weiss climbed over the fence surrounding the convent and tried unsuccessfully to enter it in protest, while insisting that the nuns leave the convent.[12]

A number of American Catholic theologians were critical of the behavior of the Carmelite nuns. Eva Fleischner wrote in 1986: "It is surely worrying that it does not seem to have occurred to the Carmelite sisters or to local authorities to seek out Jewish feeling about the foundation. Auschwitz has become the symbol of the greatest catastrophe in Jewish history. . . . We cannot but empathize with the feelings of most of the Jewish community who find it intolerable that a large convent and cross should be erected on what they hold as a . . . memorial."[13]

Observing the altercations which occurred at Auschwitz, John Pawlikowski became deeply concerned about the impact they would have on the continuing dialogue between Catholics and Jews. Given the history of Polish and Catholic antisemitism, Pawlikowski considered it highly presumptuous for Carmelite nuns to be praying for Jewish souls. He was disappointed that the nuns had not vacated their convent in 1989 when they were scheduled to do so.[14] Although Pawlikowski recognized overreaction on the part of Weiss on one hand and the hostility of the Polish laborers on the other, he was particularly annoyed at the anti-Jewish statements of certain Polish prelates and their refusal to recognize "the basic validity of the Jewish claim." Neither did he believe that the Vatican had exerted sufficient effort to defuse the situation. "A failure of reconciliation in this dispute," observed Pawlikowski in 1989, "would be a victory for no one but the ghost of Hitler."[15]

Concern about the injury that the Auschwitz convent controversy could inflict upon the continuing dialogue was reflected in statements of American prelates, such as Joseph Cardinal Bernardin. The event, he declared, should create added incentive to instruct all students about the nature of the *Shoah*.[16] That the conversations between the two faiths should continue without disruption was foremost on Catholic minds. As one Catholic writer put it during the tense days of 1989, "We both as people of faith would have to believe that if God is in the dialogue, no human being could ever put it back to point zero."[17]

For a number of Jewish thinkers, the problem of the Auschwitz convent controversy went far beyond the preservation of the dialogue. For

Elie Wiesel, for example, the issue revolved around the unique historical character of the *Shoah*. Jewish objection to a Christian memorial at
Auschwitz is not meant to belittle the deaths of Poles and other non-Jews,
he said. Their deaths are as important as the deaths of Jews. But Auschwitz, as was the *Shoah*, was designed primarily to exterminate all the
Jews. It is that fact and no other that makes the *Shoah* a uniquely Jewish catastrophe, he declared. Any attempt, therefore, to erect a Christian convent on the invisible graves of Jews would be "wrong and offensive." Besides, according to Wiesel, "Convents should be among the
living, not the dead." What is more, prayer should not offend; it should
console. Nevertheless, Wiesel objected to the unruly tactics of Weiss and
his students who scaled the wall surrounding the convent.[18] At the same
time, like the Catholic leadership with whom he was close, Wiesel agreed
that after all was said, bridges to understanding between the two faiths
must continue to be built.[19]

This was also the position of Judith Hershcopf Banki, who for many
years worked with the American Jewish Committee to improve the relationship between the two faith communities. She was concerned that
the Auschwitz controversy would proceed to dismantle the progress that
had been achieved in the interfaith movement: "In the end, the controversy became a kind of witches' brew, threatening to boil over and poison the surrounding atmosphere."[20]

The assault on the convent by Weiss and his students, according to
Banki, did not represent a typical American Jewish reaction to the Auschwitz controversy. Banki reported that American Jews were at first not
concerned about the actions of the Carmelite nuns, and they never felt
as intensely about the issue as did a small minority. Neither did Banki
believe that the Poles intended the convent to represent an assault upon
Jewish sensibilities. Poles, she wrote, viewed Auschwitz as a symbol of
nationalistic suffering. Most Poles, like the Carmelite nuns, had little
awareness that 90 percent of the victims of Auschwitz were Jews.[21] What
was evident by 1990 was that the leading voices in both the American
Catholic and Jewish communities saw the crisis in Poland as one requir-
ing rapid reconciliation. Both Jews and Catholics agreed that the event
marked a clash of memories and visions of past suffering, not a resur-
gence of hate.

John Paul's message to the Carmelite nuns late in the summer of 1989,
urging them to move their convent to another location, helped ease tensions but did not completely eliminate them. Although a new center had
been constructed for them, by 1993 the nuns had not yet relocated. Once
again, the pope intervened with a personal letter to the Carmelites, re-

The papal knighthood which had been created by Pius IX (1846–78) and bestowed by John Paul II upon Waldheim in July 1994 was even more difficult for Americans to accept. A. M. Rosenthal of the *New York Times* wrote on August 12, "I find myself more and more sickened about what I think is one of the more callous personal decisions made by a respected world leader in years. It is contemptuous of historical reality. It is insulting to the opinions and the emotions of the living and to the memory of the dead." Yet he hoped, as astounding and despicable as the pope's behavior was, that it would not "destroy the bridges" built between the two faiths.[27] The baffling honor, other journalists and leaders of American Jewish organizations warned, could destroy the good will which had grown between the two communities.[28] The knighthood generated a protest by a United States congressman. Eliot Engel, a Democrat from New York, led a campaign resulting in a letter signed by thirty members of Congress, which was forwarded to the United States Vatican ambassador, urging the Holy See to rescind the honor given to Waldheim.[29]

Jews, like other observers, were exceedingly perplexed by the precise motives of the Vatican honor accorded an individual listed as an "unwanted alien" in the United States. They also recognized that it was an awkward gesture and somewhat embarrassing for the pope. The ceremony did not receive much attention; Pope John Paul II did not attend the July 6 event, at which a nuncio was present. The Vatican made no official announcement of the ceremony, which took place a few weeks after the Vatican and Israel had established formal diplomatic relations.[30] What the pope was up to remained an enigma to American observers. As one journalist put it, "The Pope's honor to Kurt Waldheim is part of that wall of politeness being built around the past. I do not think the Pope has any moral right to grant civil pardon and honor to the participating witnesses, to waive at least public contrition."[31]

American Jews, angry at the pope's behavior, hesitated to meet with him in Miami at a meeting scheduled to take place during a papal visit to the United States shortly after the Waldheim fiasco. John Paul hoped that it nevertheless would take place. Before he left for the United States, he met in Rome with the members of a Jewish delegation of the International Jewish Committee, talked to them about his views of the *Shoah,* and assured them of the Holy See's continued commitment to eradicating all forms of antisemitism and the continued importance of the state of Israel. The friendly and frank exchange which took place at that meeting salvaged the Miami meeting with American Jews and restored a strong degree of understanding between American Jews and the Church

questing that they move their convent to a new location.[22] The pop
second request bore fruit. The convent controversy was resolved. But
left a legacy of misunderstanding and exposed the fragility of Jewis
Catholic relations. That the dialogue survived is testimony to the dete
mination of the American Jewish and Catholic communities to procee
with the work that had begun three decades earlier.

◻ ◻ ◻

The Auschwitz crisis was paralleled by another, which in some respects
was even more troubling to Jews and non-Jews as well. It stemmed from
an audience granted by John Paul II in 1987 to Kurt Waldheim, former
secretary general of the United Nations and president of Austria. The
problem arose from recent revelations about Waldheim's past. Waldheim,
it was discovered, had concealed his involvement in atrocities against
Jews while serving as an officer in the German army during the Second
World War. Had he been honest in revealing his Nazi past, he would not
have attained his elevated position as secretary general. When confronted, Waldheim denied awareness at the time of any atrocities against Jews.
Few believed him, including the American government, which, because
of Waldheim's Nazi past, banned him from visiting the United States.

Even though Austria was a Roman Catholic country, many believed
that the pope should not have met with the Austrian president. The
audience drew protests from American Jewish groups. Referring to
Waldheim's visit to Rome, George Weigel writes that since Waldheim
"was the democratic elected head of state of a Catholic country with
whom the Holy See had full diplomatic relations, not to receive him was
a diplomatic impossibility."[23] Such a meeting does not suggest that the
Pope endorsed or approved of Waldheim's behavior toward Jews, says
Weigel. As head of the Catholic Church, the pope met with a diverse
group of political leaders, not all of them palatable. Such reasoning,
however, did not placate Jewish and some Catholic observers of the
Waldheim audience.[24] One Catholic writer dispatched an imaginary letter
to Pope John Paul II: "Why did you meet with a man who lied about
his role as a Nazi and who presided over the United Nations when it
voted to equate Zionism with racism?"[25] The puzzlement at John Paul's
behavior was widespread. Jews and some sensitive Catholics were annoyed at the pope's inconsistency. For the Holy See to condemn the *Shoah*
as the ultimate evil on the one hand and on the other to endow with
honor a former Nazi, even though he was president of a republic, was
discomfiting.[26]

of Rome.[32] That the pope had badly blundered in his involvement with Waldheim was generally conceded in the American Jewish community. But his exertions to make amends, to assure American Jews that his heart and vision had not altered, were of even greater significance.

◻ ◻ ◻

For the past thousand years, the Roman Catholic Church, by sole authority of the pope, has elevated to sainthood selected individuals deemed venerable following their deaths. Through a careful process leading to canonization, manifested by the accumulation and examination of a considerable body of evidence, a departed individual is first declared to be blessed, then beatified, and finally canonized by a papal bull, which declares an individual already residing in heaven to be a saint.[33]

The entire process has held deep religious significance for the church and its faithful members. However, Jews have generally paid little attention to this matter, because it involves the internal business of the church. The results of canonization have held no consequence for Jews and their community. What is more, it would have been unthinkable, presumptuous, even risky for Jews to intervene in the procedure, to raise any objections to the church's choice for beatification or canonization. Besides this, as the Jewish theologian David Novak observed in 1999: "While we Jews can *empathize* with Catholics who have found yet another saint . . . it is not something we can *feel* . . . with Catholics any more than we could celebrate the Eucharist with them."[34] That Jewish intervention took place in the United States at the end of the twentieth century is an astounding occurrence, virtually unheard of heretofore. For the first time, Jews raised questions publicly about the fitness of candidates for canonization. They challenged the choices of those whose lives they viewed as far from venerable, whose work had been injurious to Jewish existence.

Pope John Paul II canonized more than three hundred individuals during his reign. But on only three (or four) occasions have Jews raised serious objections to the choice for canonization recommended to or made by the church. All of these challenges took place during the final decade of the twentieth century.

The first occurred in 1991 when a group of Spanish bishops initiated the process toward beatification of Queen Isabella of Spain (1451–1504). American Jewish leaders immediately denounced her candidacy. James Rudin, national director of interreligious affairs at the American Jewish Committee, called the choice a very "'divisive issue'" that could cause repercussions in interfaith relations. He reminded Catholics that Queen Isabella was the despot responsible for the expulsion of the Jews from Spain in 1492.[35] "It is outrageous and obscene because that lady, under any set of rules, does not deserve sainthood," declared a leader of the American Sephardic (Jews of Spanish cultural heritage) community.[36] Spanish church officials timed the canonization process to coincide with the Vatican celebration of the five-hundred-year anniversary of the introduction of Catholicism to the New World. But Jews also remembered the year as the time of their ejection from Spain by Queen Isabella and her husband Ferdinand. They were expelled for no other reason than their refusal to convert to Christianity.

Marc H. Tanenbaum, who for many years was a high official of the AJC, was also appalled by the decision to beatify Queen Isabella. To Tanenbaum, the Isabella affair loomed as a serious threat to the continuous improvement of relations between Catholics and Jews. Tanenbaum could not understand how one of the most evil and brutal of women in history—one who not only expelled the large Jewish community from Spain but inspired the Inquisition and all its brutality—could be honored by the church. After recalling the nearly eight thousand Jews burned at the stake, Tanenbaum notes: "'Put plainly, Isabella is no more deserving of sainthood than was Adolf Eichmann.'"[37] One Jewish writer suggested that the Vatican convene a conference of qualified scholars to examine the historical record of Isabella before proceeding with beatification.[38]

Jewish opposition to beatification was supported by prominent voices of the American Catholic community. Eugene Fisher, director for Catholic-Jewish relations at the National Conference of Catholic Bishops, an organization which represents 350 American bishops, said: "I don't think [Isabella's] cause should be moved forward. . . . No matter what one can say about her personally, the symbolic meaning of her reign as Queen was the expulsion of the Jews, and that symbolism is too massive in Jewish history for it to do anything but an incredible amount of damage."[39]

Daniel Montalbano, director of Catholic-Jewish relations for the archdiocese of Chicago, and John Pawlikowski also added their objections. As a result, both Jews and Catholics were elated at the news that the Pontifical Council for Christian Unity unanimously passed a resolution in 1991 stating that the beatification of Isabella "contradicts current Church positions on the freedom of conscience."[40]

As a consequence of these concerns, Tanenbaum and other Jewish leaders were assured by Edward Idris Cardinal Cassidy that beatification would not proceed. This assurance resulted from a Vatican panel's recommendation, approved by John Paul II, not to continue with Isabella's beatification.[41] Rejoicing American Jewish leaders, convinced of their own persuasive arguments and the support they had received from their Catholic friends, such as Joseph Cardinal Bernardin and others, considered that they had succeeded in aborting the Spanish efforts. Tanenbaum considered it a "remarkable victory," evidence that the new Catholic-Jewish relationship was working. James A. Rudin declared after hearing the news from Rome, "This shows the vitality of our communication and that they are sensitive to the teachings of Vatican II."[42]

A Jewish observer, Jack Bemporad, director of interreligious affairs for the Synagogue Council of America, urged Jews not to read too much into their own efforts. Bemporad said that the pontifical council's resolution had less to do with Jewish objections than with Isabella's lack of suitability as a model of sanctity. Tanenbaum also urged the Vatican to clarify the reasons behind its decision so that some Catholics would not interpret it as one generated by Jewish protests.[43] Bemporad's and Tanenbaum's caveats were insightful, as can be seen in the sainthood conflicts that followed.

◻ ◻ ◻

The debate over the beatification and canonization of Edith Stein, a Jewish convert to Catholicism, did not end as successfully for the Jews. Stein took her final vows as a Carmelite nun in 1938, at a time when the first signs of doom for Europe's Jews became evident. Some weeks later, she moved to a convent in Echt, Holland, where for a while it seemed safer for a former Jew to reside. When the Nazis invaded Holland and began rounding up converted Jews, Edith Stein, now called Teresa Benedicta á Cruce, was arrested and deported to Auschwitz, where she died in a gas chamber in August 1942.[44]

According to George Weigel, John Paul II had great admiration for Edith Stein. The pope considered her a great intellectual as well as a feminist imbued with piety. Stein was proposed as a martyr for beatification in the early 1960s by the archbishop of Cologne. In 1987, with John Paul's approval, the Congregation for the Causes of Saints confirmed her candidacy for beatification. This raised serious concerns in the Jewish world. American Jewish organizational leaders and scholars contended that Edith Stein did not die as a "Christian martyr" but that she was executed because she was a Jew. She died no differently than did six million other Jews. Jews wondered if Stein's beatification represented an effort to "Christianize" the *Shoah*.

Troubling too was that to John Paul, Edith Stein's conversion did not constitute a break with Judaism.[45] In Jewish theology, however, there is no place for dual citizenship. Jews cannot adopt Christianity and also remain Jews. John Paul's statement, which would hold no religious meaning for believing Jews, read as follows: "In the extermination camp she [Edith Stein] died as a daughter of Israel 'for the Glory of the Most Holy Name' and, at the same time, as Sister Teresa Benedicta of the Cross. . . . United with our crucified Lord, she gave her life for genuine peace and for the people."[46]

In the case of Edith Stein, Jewish opposition to beatification did not prevail. In October 1998, in a colorful ceremony in the basilica of St. Peter, Pope John Paul II bestowed sainthood on Teresa Benedicta of the Cross. She became the first Jewish-born Catholic woman to be canonized.[47]

Questions continued to be raised about Edith Stein's canonization; they came not only from Jewish observers but also from Catholics. James Carroll of the *New Yorker,* for example, asked, "In canonizing Edith Stein, has the Church misrepresented her life and history?"[48] The church's argument that Edith Stein was martyred, a sacrificial lamb chosen in retaliation for the protest against Nazism launched by Dutch bishops, and that being born a Jew was not the reason for her execution makes little sense in the light of the history of the *Shoah.* There is little dispute that Edith Stein died at the hands of the Nazis for no other reason than that she had been born a Jew.[49] A Catholic himself, Carroll writes: "By elevating her death not only above her own life but above the deaths of six million Jews, the church has made Edith Stein a flashpoint instead of a bridge."[50]

Jewish critics found little to commend in the pope's decision. Criticism of Edith Stein's canonization ranged from terming it "problematic" to calling it "offensive." Abraham Foxman saw the pope's act as an attempt to Christianize the *Shoah* and to celebrate a Jewish conversion.[51] For the Jewish theologian David Novak, the apostasy of Edith Stein held far greater significance than her canonization. He finds her conversion to Catholicism, from the perspective of normative Judaism, an unacceptable act. Jews, consequently, unlike Catholics, cannot celebrate the life and death of Edith Stein. Novak notes that even the members of her family refused to attend her beatification in Cologne in 1987.

Most serious to Jews is the claim of Teresa Benedicta of the Cross to be a Jew while practicing Catholicism. Both the church and the synagogue have ruled against such a duality. Such religious syncretism is unacceptable to both faiths. "There is no universal revelation until the end of history," declares Novak, "which is why election is the doctrine of identity for both Catholics and Jews." Each faith lives by its own truths.[52]

Edith Stein's view of Christianity as a fulfillment of Judaism constitutes a form of supersessionism, one of the key components of the theology of contempt. Otherwise, asks Novak, why would she have converted? One cannot be both a faithful Jew and a faithful Catholic. "In this world one cannot be simultaneously both," Novak writes. "Since the Jewish and Catholic communities are mutually exclusive, and both Jews and Catholics derive their identities from God's covenant with their communities, no member of one community can also be a member in good standing of the other."[53]

The central issue of the Edith Stein case, as Novak has made clear, is what the canonization of an apostate says about the integrity and uniqueness of the Jewish covenant and, by implication, the Christian covenant as well.

□ □ □

Even more objectionable to American Jews than the case of Edith Stein was the Vatican desire to elevate Pope Pius XII to sainthood. Given the pontiff's questionable behavior during the years of the *Shoah*, such annoyance among Jews was hardly surprising. Officials of the Simon Wiesenthal Center, learning that the process toward beatification was soon to be completed, lodged a complaint with the Holy See in the spring of 1993. The Vatican contended that Pius XII had a record of opposition toward the Nazis and indeed had saved hundreds of thousands of Jews from the gas chambers. Such statements were met with skepticism in Jewish circles. Officials of the Simon Wiesenthal Center requested the Vatican to open its archives and allow scholars to evaluate Pius's achievements before the canonization process was moved forward. The process had begun nearly thirty years earlier, at which time Pope Paul VI had offered the proposal for consideration. But it was not until beatification was impending that both Jewish and Catholic scholars began to raise questions about the matter.[54]

The Jews were curious about the evidence accumulated during the lengthy procedure. Recalling the silence of the wartime pope in regard to the *Shoah*, a Simon Wiesenthal Center researcher requested the Vatican offer some documentary support that would justify beatification. Leon Klenicki, an official of the Anti-Defamation League, arranged a meeting in Rome in late March 1993 with an official of the Congregation for the Causes of Saints to probe this question further. This meeting and subsequent ones did not clarify the evidence upon which canonization was to be based. Archbishop Joseph Bernardin of Chicago as well as John Cardinal O'Connor of New York supported Jewish requests to open the Vatican archives in order to clarify the canonization issue of Pius XII.[55] In the request to open Vatican archives, Jews were joined by prominent Catholic prelates and scholars.[56] Only in the last few weeks of the twentieth century did their demands begin to bear fruit.[57]

The issue of Pius XII's canonization has exacerbated tensions between the two faith communities more severely than any other event of the 1990s. Edward Cardinal Cassidy, president of the Vatican's Commission for Religious Relations with the Jews, "publicly" rebuked Jewish organizations for their aggressive attitudes toward the church. The cardinal accused the International Committee for Interreligious Consultation of launching a campaign to "denigrate the Catholic Church."[58] One Jesuit priest, Kurt-Peter Gumpel, speaking to an Austrian group, described the request of the Israeli ambassador to the Holy See, Aaron Lopez, that the canonization of Pius XII be delayed fifty years as "imprudent or provocative."[59] Considering the many questions that continue to surround the life of Pius XII, the request seems reasonable to many others. But in this case, for a long while, the church remained adamant in its refusal to accede to Jewish and some Catholic requests. For Jews, because the case of Pius XII is so intimately tied to the murder of six million Jews, it has continued to be an issue of intense significance. It is one which Jews have been unable to let go, at least until new documentation buried in papal archives has been opened to independent scholarly investigation.

In this critical issue also, the Holy See has made an unprecedented concession. In mid-October 1999, Seymour D. Reich, chairman of the International Jewish Committee for Interreligious Consultation, and Edward Cardinal Cassidy, still chairman of the Vatican's Commission for Religious Relations with the Jews, announced the appointment of a team of six historians—three Jews (Robert S. Wistrich, Michael R. Marrus, and Bernard Suchecky) and three American Catholic scholars (Gerald Fogarty, Eva Fleischner, and John Morley)—to begin an impartial search of eleven volumes of Vatican documents "to determine what the Catholic Church did and did not do to save Jews during the Holocaust." Reich suggested that if further information were needed, then additional documents from the Vatican archives would probably be made available to them. It was, according to Wistrich, "'a small window' of opportunity to seek answers" to the troubling questions concerning Pope Pius XII's behavior during World War II. "'I see it as a first step,'" declared Wistrich.[60] Given the intensity of the conflict and the deep feelings it had generated, Wistrich's comment was mild. Here, too, a frontier had been crossed.

The sainthood questions of the 1990s have placed stress on but not mortally injured the revolutionary changes and accomplishments which have occurred in the relationship between Catholics and Jews since the Second Vatican Council. Moreover, these interfaith conflicts represent a maturation in this relationship. Without underestimating the seriousness of the quarrel, it can also be viewed as one which could not have occurred in previous generations.

In addition, the debate over sainthood for Edith Stein and Pius XII took place while the relationship of the church and the Jewish people was being tightened. Under the pontificate of John Paul II, antisemitism was repeatedly repudiated and eliminated from the teaching in Catholic schools and seminaries. The pope visited and preached in a synagogue in Rome in 1986; this was the first time in the history of the church that such an event had occurred. In a somewhat stumbling way, to be sure, the church assumed responsibility and asked forgiveness for its failure to speak out more forthrightly on behalf of the Jewish victims of German barbarism. Granting full diplomatic recognition to the state of Israel also put an end to Jewish doubts about the church's ability to accept the appropriateness of Jewish national sovereignty. Indeed, the entire package of popular Catholic beliefs about the Jews which had dominated the thinking of earlier generations had come to be viewed as religiously incorrect. After two thousand years, the theological foundations of Catholic anti-Judaism were seriously damaged, perhaps mortally so, during the last thirty-five years of the twentieth century.

No pope displayed more comprehension of the insidious results that the teaching of contempt had upon Christian behavior toward the Jews than did John Paul II. As the new century dawned, though aging and infirm, he continued to ask the Jewish people to forgive the Catholics for the centuries of misery that they and his beloved church had inflicted upon the Jews. On March 12, 2000, in a mass celebrating the beginning of the first Lent of the third Christian millennium, the pope stood solemnly at St. Peter's basilica and asked forgiveness for Christian intolerance toward Jews as well as others.[61] Some of his cardinals and bishops shuddered, concerned that such a display of humility might give weapons to the enemies of the church, that it would create a bad precedent, that it would weaken an already wounded institution. But the pope persisted, driven by his memory of the Nazi era. A few days later, visiting Jerusalem and standing contemplatively at Yad Vashem, Israel's Holocaust memorial museum, he again in an act of public contrition offered *teshuvah*, repentance for Catholic behavior. He named no names, he impugned no predecessors, he even hesitated to employ the term *Shoah*, although some American Jews and Catholics would have liked to have heard him do so. They had hoped for at least a mention of Pius XII. Yet in the process of asking forgiveness, John Paul went further in strengthening the relationship of Catholics and Jews than had any other pope in the history of the Catholic Church.[62]

The disagreements which remained were inevitable between two faith communities living side by side. But by the opening of the new century, American Jews and Catholics had learned to accept and respect each other's differences. Along the way, they had crossed important religious and social boundaries. Only time will tell if these boundaries had been crossed in vain.

Notes

Introduction

1. David A. Gerber, "Anti-Semitism and Jewish-Gentile Relations in American Historiography and the American Past," in *Anti-Semitism in American History*, ed. David A. Gerber (Urbana: University of Illinois Press, 1987), 6, 22.

2. Andrew M. Greeley and Peter H. Rossi, *The Denominational Society: A Sociological Approach to Religion in America* (Glenview, Ill.: Scott, Foresman, 1972), 1; Will Herberg, *Protestant-Catholic-Jew: An Essay in American Religious Sociology* (Garden City, N.Y.: Doubleday, Anchor, 1960), 37.

3. Egal Feldman, *Dual Destinies: The Jewish Encounter with Protestant America* (Urbana: University of Illinois Press, 1990), 109.

4. "Authentic Report of the Proceedings of the Rabbinical Conference Held in Pittsburgh, November 16, 17, 18, 1885," in *The Changing World of Reform Judaism: The Pittsburgh Platform in Retrospect*, ed. Walter Jacob (Pittsburgh: Rodef Shalom Congregation, 1985), 92.

5. Ibid.

6. Feldman, *Dual Destinies*, 119.

7. See, for example, *Time*, June 7, 1999, 65.

8. Joseph L. Blau, *Judaism in America: From Curiosity to the Third Faith* (Chicago: University of Chicago Press, 1976), 47, 49.

9. Henry L. Feingold, *Zion in America: The Jewish Experience from Colonial Times to the Present* (New York: Hippocrene, 1974), 191–92.

10. Leonard Dinnerstein, "The Funeral of Rabbi Jacob Joseph," in *Anti-Semitism in American History*, ed. David A. Gerber (Urbana: University of Illinois Press, 1987), 279.

11. Jeffrey S. Gurock, "From Exception to Role Model: Bernard Drachman and the Evolution of Jewish Religious Life in America, 1880–1920," *American Jewish History* 76 (June 1986): 457–68, 482, 484.

12. Robert Gordis, *Judaism in a Christian World* (New York: McGraw-Hill, 1966), 27.

13. "Growth of the Church in the United States," in *Pastoral Letters of the United States Catholic Bishops,* vol. 4, 1975–83, ed. Hugh J. Nolan (Washington, D.C.: National Conference of Catholic Bishops, United States Catholic Conference, 1983), 580; *New York Times,* May 24, 1994, 11.

14. "The Church in 1905," *Catholic Mind,* January 8, 1906, 36–37; see also Patrick Carey, *American Catholic Religious Thought* (New York: Paulist Press, 1987), 30–31.

15. Jay P. Dolan, *The American Catholic Experience: A History from Colonial Times to the Present* (Garden City, N.Y.: Doubleday, 1985), 221.

16. William Cardinal O'Connell, *Sermons and Addresses of His Eminence William Cardinal O'Connell, Archbishop of Boston,* 3 vols. (Boston: Flynn, 1911), 1:207.

17. *National Catholic Reporter,* April 11, 1999.

18. O'Connell, *Sermons,* 1:211.

19. Dolan, *American Catholic Experience,* 222–24.

20. Ibid., 313; Most Reverend John J. Wright, "Conscience and Authority: Catholic Reflections," in *Torah and Gospel: Jewish and Catholic Theology in Dialogue,* ed. Philip Scharper (New York: Sheed and Ward, 1966), 144–46, 161.

21. Dan Herr and Joel Wells, eds., *Through Other Eyes: Some Impressions of American Catholicism by Foreign Visitors from 1777 to the Present* (Westminster, Md.: Newman Press, 1965), 80–87.

22. Carey, *American Catholic Religious Thought,* 4; Andrew M. Greeley, *The Catholic Experience: An Interpretation of the History of American Catholicism* (Garden City, N.Y.: Doubleday, 1967), 182.

23. Egal Feldman, *The Dreyfus Affair and the American Conscience, 1895–1906* (Detroit: Wayne State University Press, 1981), 140.

24. Quoted in Feldman, *Dreyfus Affair,* 140.

25. Dolan, *American Catholic Experience,* 316; Greeley, *The Catholic Experience,* 157.

26. P. R. McDevitt, "The Grievous School Questions Again Discussed," *Catholic World* 53 (September 1901): 697–708; Dolan, *American Catholic Experience,* 270.

27. Katharine T. Hargrove, ed., *The Star and the Cross: Essays on Jewish-Christian Relations* (Milwaukee: Bruce, 1966), 38.

28. John Tracy Ellis, ed., *Documents of American Catholic History, 1866–1966,* vol. 2 (Wilmington, Del.: Glazier, 1987), 483–85.

Chapter 1: Theology of Contempt

1. I will be using the terms *anti-Judaism* and *antisemitism* interchangeably.

2. Jules Isaac, *The Teaching of Contempt: Christian Roots of Anti-Semitism,* trans. by Helen Weaver (New York: Holt, Rinehart and Winston, 1964; first published in French in 1962), xii.

3. Claire Huchet Bishop, *How Catholics Look at Jews: Inquiries Into Italian, Spanish and French Teaching Materials* (New York: Paulist Press, 1974), 14–15.

4. Ibid., 15.

5. Rosemary Ruether, "Anti-Semitism and Christian Theology," in *Auschwitz: Beginning of a New Era? Reflections on the Holocaust*, ed. Eva Fleischner (New York: Ktav, the Cathedral Church of St. John the Divine, Anti-Defamation League of B'nai B'rith, 1974), 84.

6. "The Passion Play at Ober-Ammergau, 1880," part 1, *Catholic World* 31 (August 1880): 664, 666.

7. "The Passion Play at Ober-Ammergau, 1880," part 2, *Catholic World* 31 (September 1880): 746.

8. Ibid., 751.

9. Ibid., 757; see also Katherine Bregy, "The Passionsspiele of 1910: An Impression," *Catholic World* 91 (October 1910): 42–50.

10. O'Connell, *Sermons*, 1:94, 2:90–92, 184–86; see also Jules Isaac, "The Crime of Deicide," in *The Star and the Cross: Essays on Jewish-Christian Relations*, ed. Katharine T. Hargrove (Milwaukee: Bruce, 1966), 136–43.

11. "New Books," *Catholic World* 107 (August 1918): 684.

12. Menahem Stern, "The Period of the Second Temple," in *A History of the Jewish People*, ed. H. H. Ben-Sasson (Cambridge, Mass.: Harvard University Press, 1976), 235–36.

13. John T. Pawlikowski, "Jews and Christians: The Contemporary Dialogue," *Quarterly Review* 4 (Winter 1984): 23–36; Eugene J. Fisher, "Research on Christian Teaching Concerning Jews and Judaism: Past Research and Present Needs," *Journal of Ecumenical Studies* 21 (Summer 1984): 421–37.

14. "Two Miraculous Conversions from Judaism," *Catholic World* 39 (August 1884): 613–21.

15. Père Suau, *The Christian Faith* (London: Burns Oates and Washbourne, 1920), 84.

16. J. P. Arendzen, "Hillel and Shamai," *Catholic World* 120 (February 1925): 627–29, 635.

17. O'Connell, *Sermons*, 1:67.

18. Rev. J. T. Durward, *Holy Land and Holy Writ* (Baraboo, Wis.: Pilgrim, 1913), 627.

19. O'Connell, *Sermons*, 2:126; see also Leon Klenicki, ed., *Toward a Theological Encounter: Jewish Understandings of Christianity* (New York: Paulist Press, 1991), 116–17.

20. Suau, *The Christian Faith*, 92.

21. Pawlikowski, "Jews and Christians," 28.

22. Jacob Bernard Agus, *Dialogue and Tradition: The Challenges of Contemporary Judeo-Christian Thought* (New York: Abelard-Schuman, 1971), 56; Dolan, *American Catholic Experience*, 226–27.

23. Rosemary Radford Ruether, *Faith and Fratricide: The Theological Roots of Anti-Semitism* (New York: Seabury Press, 1974), 228.

24. I will be using the terms *displacement* and *supersessionism* interchangeably.

25. "The Preparation of Christianity in the Six Centuries before Christ," *Catholic World* 27 (April 1878): 13; see also O'Connell, *Sermons*, 1:201.

26. Ruether, *Faith and Fratricide*, 240; "Relations of Judaism to Christianity," *Catholic World* 27 (June 1878): part II, 573.

27. See Arthur Gilbert, *The Vatican Council and the Jews* (Cleveland: World, 1968), 203.

28. "The Preparation of Christianity," 13.

29. John F. Fenton, "A Word for the Old Testament," *Catholic World* 85 (April 1907): 54.

30. Ibid., 64.

31. O'Connell, *Sermons*, 2:179-80.

32. Ruether, "Anti-Semitism and Christian Theology," 79.

Chapter 2: Medievalism and Modernity, 1890-1930

A portion of my discussion of the Dreyfus affair, which appears at the end of this chapter, was derived, with modifications, from chapter 11 of my book *The Dreyfus Affair and the American Conscience, 1895-1906* (Detroit: Wayne State University Press, 1981).

1. Pinchas E. Lapide, *The Last Three Popes and the Jews* (London: Souvenir Press, 1967), 47-48.

2. Patrick Allitt, *Catholic Intellectuals and Conservative Politics in America, 1950-1985* (Ithaca: Cornell University Press, 1993), 9-10.

3. Shuster quoted in William M. Halsey, *The Survival of American Innocence: Catholicism in an Era of Disillusionment, 1920-1940* (Notre Dame: University of Notre Dame Press, 1980), 68-70.

4. Allitt, *Catholic Intellectuals*, 51.

5. Philip Gleason, *Keeping the Faith: American Catholicism, Past and Present* (Notre Dame: University of Notre Dame Press, 1987), 11.

6. Ibid., 25, 28.

7. Abram Leon Sachar, *A History of the Jews* (1930; reprint, New York: Knopf, 1965), 186.

8. Ibid., 192-95.

9. Ibid., 191-95.

10. Ibid., 249-55.

11. Quoted in *Catholic Mind*, October 27, 1929, 399-400.

12. "The Jews of Rome: In Christian Times," *Catholic World* 29 (April 1879): 29-39.

13. See, for example, Franz Wasner, "The Popes' Veneration of the Torah," *The Bridge* 4 (1961): 284-85, 290-91.

14. Bertrand L. Conway, "Isabella of Spain," *Catholic World* 132 (January 1931): 447; see also W. F. P. Stockley, "Popes and Jewish 'Ritual Murder,'"

Catholic World 139 (July 1934): 452; and Max L. Margolis and Alexander Marx, *A History of the Jewish People* (New York: Atheneum, 1969), 380–81.

15. Vera Elfer, "The Jews in Catholic England," *Catholic World* 119 (July 1924): 439–40.

16. Ibid., 441.

17. Manuel Perez Villamil, "The Jews in Spain during the Middle Ages," *Catholic World* 55 (June 1892): 649–61.

18. Ibid., 653.

19. Ibid., 657–58, 660.

20. Ibid., 661; see also Manuel Perez Villamil, "The Jews in Early Spanish History," *Catholic World* 54 (October 1891): 86–96.

21. Manuel Perez Villamil, "The Expulsion of the Jews from Spain in the Fifteenth Century," *Catholic World* 55 (September 1892): 851.

22. Ibid., 854.

23. Ibid., 855, 857.

24. Ibid., 859.

25. Theodore Maynard, "The Mind of Spain," *Catholic World* 129 (June 1929): 260.

26. Sachar, *A History of the Jews,* 213.

27. Ibid., 214–15.

28. Ibid., 208–11.

29. "New Books," *Catholic World* 87 (May 1908): 246–47; "The Inquisition," *Catholic World* 134 (October 1931): 92.

30. A. P. Doyle, "Encyclical Letter of Leo XIII," *Catholic World* 72 (January 1901): 427.

31. Rene Fulop-Miller, *Leo XIII and Our Time* (New York: Longmans, Green, 1937), 61–63, 71.

32. Dinnerstein, "The Funeral of Rabbi Jacob Joseph," 275–301.

33. Till Van Rahden, "Beyond Ambivalence," *American Jewish History* 82 (March 1994): 7.

34. Ibid., 23–26.

35. Ibid., 28–29; for a less-biased Catholic view of the Jewish "economy," see, for example, Emily Hickey, "Some Thoughts on *The Merchant of Venice,*" *Catholic World* 105 (May 1917): 233–34.

36. Avraham Barka, *Branching Out* (New York: Holmes and Meier, 1994), 187.

37. Charles C. Starbuck, "The Jew in Europe: The Christian's Antagonist," *Catholic World* 71 (September 1900): 828–29.

38. Ibid., 831–34.

39. Ibid., 839–41.

40. Some leading Reform rabbis, such as Emil Hirsch of Chicago and Isaac M. Wise of Cincinnati, urged American Jews not to petition France on behalf of Dreyfus, contending that the Dreyfus case was not a Jewish issue. See *New York Times,* September 8, 1899; James G. Heller, *Isaac M. Wise: His Life, Work*

and Thought (Cincinnati: Union of American Hebrew Congregations, 1965), 482–83, 613–14; *Washington Post,* December 8, 1898.

41. For a review of the American reaction to the Dreyfus Affair, see my book *The Dreyfus Affair;* for a briefer summary but in French, see my "L'Affaire Dreyfus et la conscience americaine," *Revue de la Bibliothèque Nationale de France: L'Affaire Dreyfus a l'étranger* 2 (Été 1994): 4–11.

42. Boston *Pilot,* September 2, 1899.

43. *St. Louis Post-Dispatch,* January 1, 1899. See also Boston *Pilot,* September 14, 1899; *New York Journal,* February 12, 1898; and Hannah Arendt, "From the Dreyfus Affair to France Today," in *Essays on Anti-Semitism,* ed. Koppel S. Pinson (New York: Jewish Social Studies, 1946), 209.

44. *Pilot,* October 7, 1899. See also *Catholic Mirror,* September 2, September 16, 1899; *Catholic Citizen,* September 16, 1899; *Sacred Heart Review* 22 (October 7, 1899): 288.

45. Elizabeth Raymond-Barker, "The Holy See and the Jews," *Catholic World* 70 (December 1899): 394–97.

46. Quoted in Robert H. Sherard, "Dr. Nordau on the Jews and Their Fears," *American Monthly Review of Reviews* 17 (March 1898): 317.

47. According to Father John J. Tierney, archivist of the archdiocese of Baltimore, the card index to Cardinal Gibbons's correspondence does not contain any references to Jews in the years 1896–1901 (letter to the author, January 19, 1977).

48. *Pittsburgh Catholic,* January 6, January 26, September 10, 1898; January 11, February 22, March 1, July 12, August 9, 1899; *Iowa Catholic Messenger,* February 25, September 10, 1898; June 10, 1899; *Pilot,* September 10, 1898.

49. *Irish World,* September 30, 1899; *Pilot,* January 15, June 4, 1898.

50. *Pilot,* June 10, 1899; see also *Pittsburgh Catholic,* September 13, 1899; *Catholic Citizen,* September 16, 1899; *Iowa Catholic Messenger,* September 23, 1899.

51. *Catholic World* 69 (April 1899): 128.

52. "Catholic Thought and Events in Foreign Lands," *Sacred Heart Review* 21 (December 31, 1898): 6.

53. *Catholic Columbian and Record,* October 28, 1899, 4; James R. Randall, "Randall's Letter," *Catholic Columbian and Record,* January 13, 1900, 1.

54. Randall's column was featured in a number of Catholic periodicals. See his "letter" in *Catholic Columbian and Record,* January 20, 1900, 1; *Catholic Columbian and Record,* June 9, 1900, 1.

55. *St. Louis Post-Dispatch,* September 14, 1899; *Boston Evening Transcript,* September 18, 1899.

56. Quoted in Allen S. Will, *Life of Cardinal Gibbons,* vol. 2 (New York: Dutton, 1922), 797.

57. Delassus quoted in Robert F. Byrnes, *Antisemitism in Modern France* (New Brunswick, N.J.: Rutgers University Press, 1950), 303–4. The *Catholic Mirror*

of February 18, 1898, states that it is the official organ of Cardinal Gibbons. For efforts to excuse French behavior, see *Catholic Mirror,* September 9, 1899.

58. "Christianity in France," *Catholic Mind,* March 22, 1907, 45.

Chapter 3: Holy Land and Homeland, 1900–1939

1. Howard M. Sachar, *A History of Israel* (New York: Knopf, 1979), 37–38.

2. Ibid., 16–17.

3. Robert L. Wilken, *The Land Called Holy: Palestine in Christian History and Thought* (New Haven: Yale University Press, 1992), xii.

4. Ibid.; see also p. 181 for early Christian settlements in the Negev desert.

5. Ibid., xiii–xiv, 58, 62, 253–54; see also George Cornell, *Voyage of Faith: The Catholic Church in Transition* (New York: Odyssey, 1966), 116.

6. Sachar, *A History of Israel,* 5.

7. Robert D. Cross, "The Meaning of the Holy Land to American Catholics in the 19th Century," in *With Eyes toward Zion,* vol. 2, ed. Moshe Davis (New York: Praeger, 1986), 333; Feldman, *Dual Destinies, 89.*

8. Cross, "The Meaning of the Holy Land," 333.

9. Ibid., 334.

10. Ibid., 337.

11. See, for example, P. T. B., "Mount Carmel and the Carmelites," *Catholic World* 64 (February 1897): 670–85; Ethel Nast, "From Jerusalem to Nazareth on Horseback," *Catholic World* 70 (January 1900): 449–65; William H. Bergan, *Busy Thoughts of a Traveller in the Orient* (Philadelphia: n.p., 1908).

12. Review of Robert Hichens's *The Holy Land, Catholic World* 91 (December 1910): 401.

13. Eugene Vetromile, *Travels in Europe, Egypt, Arabia Petraea, Palestine and Syria,* vol. 2 (New York: Sadlier, 1871), 13; see also Godfrey Schilling, "Life at the Holy Sepulchre," *North American Review* 452 (July 1894): 77–87.

14. Vetromile, *Travels,* vol. 2, 13–14.

15. Cross, "The Meaning of the Holy Land," 336; see also "The Holy Land," *Catholic World* 4 (January 1867): 504; James Pfeiffer, *First American Catholic Pilgrims to Palestine, 1889* (Cincinnati: Press of Jos. Berning and Company, 1892), 178–83.

16. Cross, "The Meaning of the Holy Land," 336.

17. Gershom Greenberg, *The Holy Land in American Religious Thought, 1620–1948: The Symbiosis of American Religious Approaches to Scripture's Sacred Territory* (Lanham, Md.: University Press of America; Jerusalem: Avraham Harman Institute of Contemporary Jewry, 1994), 289.

18. Mary Jo Huth, "Charles Vissani, OFM, and First American Catholic Pilgrimage to the Holy Land," *Holy Land* 10 (Spring 1990): 7–9; Vetromile, *Travels,* vol. 2, 171, 188; Greenberg, *The Holy Land,* 192–93.

19. For a detailed account of the first pilgrimage, see Pfeiffer, *First American Catholic Pilgrims;* for Protestant attitudes, see Feldman, *Dual Destinies,* 89–103.

20. Vetromile, *Travels,* vol. 2, 188.

21. Ibid., 260; see also Greenberg, *The Holy Land,* 260.

22. Andrew E. Breen, *A Diary of My Life in the Holy Land* (Rochester, N.Y.: John P. Smith Printing Co., 1906), 2.

23. Ibid., 101.

24. Ibid., 331.

25. Ibid., 490–91, 501.

26. John Durward, *Sonnets of the Holy Land* (Baraboo, Wis.: Pilgrim, 1890), 5–6; Olive Risley Seward, "The Princess De La Tour D'Auvergne at Jerusalem," *Catholic World* 62 (December 1895): 350–61; R. M. Ryan, "The City of Redemption," *Catholic World* 62 (February 1896): 667–81; Charles C. Svendsen, "Easter Scenes in Jerusalem," *Catholic World* 67 (April 1898): 767–93; review of Marie Agnes Benziger, "Off to Jerusalem," *Catholic World* 84 (March 1907): 837–38.

27. Greenberg, *The Holy Land,* 291.

28. Pfeiffer, *First American Catholic Pilgrims,* 136, 139.

29. Durward, *Holy Land, Holy Writ,* 230, 612–15.

30. Durward, *Sonnets,* 22.

31. Durward, *Holy Land, Holy Writ,* 150.

32. Ibid., 166.

33. Ibid., 538.

34. Ibid., 535–39; see also Greenberg, *The Holy Land,* 301–2.

35. Bergan, *Busy Thoughts of a Traveller,* 57.

36. Breen, *A Diary of My Life,* 359.

37. Greenberg, *The Holy Land,* 300–304.

38. In addition to scattered comments by the Franciscan pilgrims noted above, see also Svendsen, "Easter Scenes," 90.

39. Theodore Herzl, *The Complete Diaries of Theodore Herzl,* ed. Raphael Patai, 5 vols. (New York: Herzl Press and Thomas Yoseloff, 1960), vol. 2, September 9 and 11, 1897, 589, 591.

40. Quoted in John T. Pawlikowski, *What Are They Saying about Christian-Jewish Relations?* (New York: Paulist Press, 1980), 2; see also Herzl, *The Complete Diaries,* vol. 4, January 26, 1904, 1608.

41. Quoted in Pawlikowski, *What Are They Saying?,* 2.

42. Herzl, *The Complete Diaries,* vol. 2, September 9, 1897, 590; and February 8, 1899, 785; vol. 4, February 4, 1904, 1609.

43. Herzl, *The Complete Diaries,* vol. 4, January 26, 1904, 1604.

44. Ibid., 1608.

45. Sachar, *A History of Israel,* 89–115; Shmuel Almog, *Nationalism and Antisemitism in Modern Europe, 1815–1945* (New York: Pergamon Press, 1990), 80–81.

46. Esther Yolles Feldblum, *The American Catholic Press and the Jewish State, 1917–1959* (New York: Ktav, 1977), 17–18.

47. John M. Oesterreicher, "The Theologian and the Land of Israel," *The Bridge* 5 (1970): 231–32.

48. Feldblum, *The American Catholic Press*, 19.

49. Ibid., 19–20; see also Sergio I. Minerbi, *The Vatican and Zionism: Conflict in the Holy Land, 1895–1925*, trans. Arnold Schwarz (New York: Oxford University Press, 1990), 119–21.

50. Feldblum, *The American Catholic Press*, 19, 22; see also Sachar, *A History of Israel*, 115.

51. Minerbi, *The Vatican and Zionism*, 18–23, 30–31.

52. Feldman, *Dual Destinies*, 101–7.

53. "Authentic Report of the Proceedings of the Rabbinical Conference Held in Pittsburgh," 108.

54. Melvin Weinman, "The Attitude of Isaac Mayer Wise toward Zionism and Palestine," *American Jewish Archives* 3 (January 1951): 4–7; Heller, *Isaac M. Wise*, 697.

55. David Philipson, *My Life as an American Jew: An Autobiography* (Cincinnati: John G. Kidd, 1941), 70, 72, 124.

56. Marc Lee Raphael, "Rabbi Jacob Voorsanger of San Francisco on Jews and Judaism: The Implications of the Pittsburgh Platform," *American Jewish Historical Quarterly* 63 (December 1973): 200, 202–3.

57. Quoted in Richard Libowitz, "Some Reactions to *Der Judenstaat* among English-speaking Jews in the United States," in *Jewish Civilization: Essays and Studies*, vol. 1, ed. Ronald A. Brauner (Philadelphia: Reconstructionist Rabbinical College, 1979), 129; see also Philipson, *My Life as an American Jew*, 136–37; Heller, *Isaac M. Wise*, 603–4; Weinman, "The Attitude of Isaac Mayer Wise toward Zionism," 9–11.

58. Libowitz, "Some Reactions," 129–30.

59. Michael A. Meyer, "American Reform Judaism and Zionism: Early Efforts at Ideological Rapprochement," *Studies in Zionism* 7 (Spring 1983): 5; Melvin I. Urofsky, *American Zionism from Herzl to the Holocaust* (Garden City, N.Y.: Anchor, 1976), 89.

60. Meyer, "American Reform Judaism and Zionism," 64.

61. Philipson, *My Life as an American Jew*, 138–39; Urofsky, *American Zionism*, 87, 90–91, 156.

62. Eugene J. Fisher, "The Holy See and the State of Israel: The Evolution of Attitudes and Policies," *Journal of Ecumenical Studies* 24 (Spring 1987): 191–209.

63. Minerbi, *The Vatican and Zionism*, 196–97; see also Lapide, *The Last Three Popes*, 91.

64. Minerbi, *The Vatican and Zionism*, 197; see also Lapide, *The Last Three Popes*, 271.

65. Minerbi, *The Vatican and Zionism*, 198.

66. "The Pope and the Zionist Jews," *Catholic Mind*, August 8, 1920, 294–95.

67. Greenberg, *The Holy Land*, 306.

68. Minerbi, *The Vatican and Zionism*, 198.

69. Greenberg, *The Holy Land,* 306.

70. Cyprien Jourdin, "Zionism in Palestine," *The Sign: A National Catholic Magazine* 1 (July 1922): 13.

71. Ibid., 16.

72. Ibid., 17, 19.

73. Carlton J. H. Hayes, "Nationalism as a Religion: A Tribal Creed," *Commonweal,* January 13, 1926, 263.

74. Fisher, "The Holy See and the State of Israel," 196.

75. "The New Jerusalem," *America,* May 30, 1936, 172.

76. I will be using the terms *Shoah* and *Holocaust* interchangeably.

77. Quoted in Greenberg, *The Holy Land,* 308.

78. See Pierre Crabites, "Palestine Problems," *Commonweal,* January 29, 1930, 301; Vincent Sheean, "The Palestine Report," *Commonweal,* April 30, 1930, 738; D. Harold Hickey, "The Palestinian Arab Cause," *Catholic World* 143 (September 1936): 684–89; Pierre Crabites, "Palestine and Zionism," *Catholic World* 146 (October 1937): 12, 16–18; Pierre Crabites, "Toward Peace in Palestine," *Catholic World* 148 (February 1939): 553–56.

Chapter 4: Darkening Horizons, 1920–40

1. See, for example, "Editorial Comment," *Catholic World* 118 (December 1923): 404–5.

2. In this connection, see Leonard Dinnerstein, "Erecting Barriers and Narrowing Opportunities (1914–1933)," in his *Antisemitism in America* (New York: Oxford University Press, 1994), 79–104.

3. Ibid., 80–81.

4. Frederick Siedenburg, "The Immigrant Problem," *Catholic Mind,* September 8, 1915, 499.

5. Francis C. Kelley, "The Church and the Immigrant," *Catholic Mind,* September 8, 1915, 475.

6. "Editorial: National Origins," *Commonweal,* April 24, 1929, 701–2.

7. Barry D. Riccio, "American Catholic Thought in the Nineteen Twenties: Frederick Joseph Kinsman and George Shuster," in *An American Church: Essays on Americanization of the Catholic Church,* ed. David J. Alvarez (Moraga, Calif.: St. Mary's College of California, 1979), 118–19.

8. George N. Shuster, *The Catholic Spirit in America* (New York: Dial Press, 1927), 221.

9. E. Boyd Barrett, "Will American Catholics Secede from Rome?," *Forum* 132 (August 1929): 94.

10. Shuster, *The Catholic Spirit,* 25.

11. "Editorial: The Ku Klux Klan," *Catholic World* 116 (January 1923): 433; "Editorial Comments," *Catholic World* 119 (August 1924): 690–97.

12. See, for example, "Editorial," *Catholic World* 116 (January 1923): 433–43; "Editorial: Who Are Americans?," *Commonweal,* April 1, 1925, 557–58; "Editorial: The Case of the Klan," *Commonweal,* November 2, 1927: 623–24;

Shuster, *The Catholic Spirit*, 110–22; E. I. Watkin, *The Catholic Centre* (New York: Sheed and Ward, 1939), 110–15.

13. H. Shelton Smith, Robert T. Handy, and Lefferts A. Loetscher, *American Christianity: An Historical Interpretation with Representative Documents* (New York: Scribner, 1960–63), 26.

14. Hadley Cantril, ed., *Public Opinion: 1935–1946* (Westport, Conn.: Greenwood, 1951), 381–87; Dinnerstein, *Antisemitism in America*, 127.

15. "Report of the Secretary of the Anti-Defamation League, 1935," in *Jews and Judaism in the United States: A Documentary History*, ed. Marc Lee Raphael (New York: Behrman House, 1983), 140; Naomi W. Cohen, *Not Free to Desist: The American Jewish Committee, 1906–1966* (Philadelphia: Jewish Publication Society of America, 1972), 200–202, 205–7.

16. Richard Breitman and Alan M. Kraut, *American Refugee Policy and European Jewry, 1933–1945* (Bloomington: Indiana University Press, 1987), 3.

17. Henry L. Feingold, *The Politics of Rescue: The Roosevelt Administration and the Holocaust, 1938–1945* (New Brunswick: Rutgers University Press, 1970), 17–18, 21; David Wyman, *The Abandonment of the Jews: Americans and the Holocaust, 1941–1945* (New York: Pantheon, 1984), 312–13.

18. Deborah E. Lipstadt, *Beyond Belief: The American Press and the Coming of the Holocaust, 1933–1945* (New York: Free Press, 1986), 92, 97, 108–11; Edward S. Shapiro, "The Approach of War: Congressional Isolationism and Anti-Semitism, 1939–1941," *American Jewish History* 74 (September 1984): 64–65.

19. Dinnerstein, *Antisemitism in America*, 126–27.

20. George Q. Flynn, *American Catholics and the Roosevelt Presidency, 1932–1936* (Lexington: University of Kentucky Press, 1968), xii.

21. John F. X. Murphy, "The Problem of International Judaism," *Catholic Mind*, October 22, 1934, 381.

22. Ibid., 385–86.

23. Ibid., 393.

24. Ibid., 396.

25. Gerald Wynne Rushton, "The Church and Jewry," *Catholic World* 145 (July 1937): 450.

26. Ibid., 455.

27. Thomas F. Doyle, "The Sin of Anti-Semitism," *Catholic World* 151 (July 1940): 433–42 (first and second quotes); Dorothy Penn, "The 'Rota' Worn by the Jew in the Middle Ages," *Catholic World* 150 (March 1940): 689 (third quote).

28. Murphy, "The Problem of International Judaism," 397.

29. William L. Newton, *Notes on the Covenant: A Study in the Theology of the Prophets* (Cleveland: Seminary Press, 1934), 179.

30. Ibid., 229.

31. Ibid., 223.

32. Watkin, *The Catholic Centre*, 141.

33. Ibid., 178.

34. "Editorial," *Commonweal,* January 1, 1930, 239; Doyle, "The Sin of Anti-Semitism," 441.

35. Edmund A. Walsh, "What Recognition of Soviet Russia Means," *Catholic Mind,* January 22, 1934, 27–32.

36. Hugh J. Nolan, ed., *Pastoral Letters of the United States Catholic Bishops,* vol. 2, 1941–61 (Washington, D.C.: National Conference of Catholic Bishops, United States Catholic Conference, 1983), 28.

37. "Pope Pius XI's Condemnations of Communism," in *Pastoral Letters of the United States Catholic Bishops,* vol. 2, 1941–61, ed. Hugh J. Nolan (Washington, D.C.: National Conference of Catholic Bishops, United States Catholic Conference, 1983), 29; Thomas Kohler, "In Praise of Little Platoons. *Quadragesimo Anno* (1931)," in *Building the Free Society: Democracy, Capitalism, and Catholic Social Teaching,* ed. George Weigel and Robert Royal (Grand Rapids, Mich.: Eerdmans; Washington, D.C.: Ethics and Public Policy Center, 1993), 31–50.

38. Carol Rittner and John K. Roth, eds., *Memory Offended: The Auschwitz Convent Controversy* (New York: Praeger, 1990), 3; Mark Arrons and John Loftus, *Unholy Trinity* (New York: St. Mark's Press, 1991), 4–11; see also Lapide, *The Last Three Popes,* 100–103.

39. Arrons and Loftus, *Unholy Trinity,* 10–11.

40. For one of the better studies of the Spanish civil war, see Allen Guttmann, *The Wound in the Heart: America and the Spanish Civil War* (Glencoe, Ill.: Free Press, 1962).

41. J. David Valaik, "Catholics, Neutrality, and the Spanish Embargo, 1937–1939," *Journal of American History* 54 (June 1967): 73–85.

42. J. David Valaik, "American Catholic Dissenters and the Spanish Civil War," *Catholic Historical Review* 53 (January 1968): 544–47, 554.

43. Guttmann, *The Wound in the Heart,* 81.

44. Ibid., 81–82, 165.

45. Quoted in Guttmann, *The Wound in the Heart,* 97.

46. Howard M. Sachar, *A History of the Jews in America* (New York: Knopf, 1992), 434; see also Henry L. Feingold, *A Time for Searching: Entering the Mainstream, 1920–1945* (Baltimore: Johns Hopkins University Press, 1992), 209.

47. See, for example, Bernard J. Monks, "Franco of Spain," *Catholic World* 147 (September 1938): 667–74.

48. Donald F. Crosby, "Boston's Catholics and the Spanish Civil War: 1936–1939," *New England Quarterly* 44 (March–December 1971): 99–100.

49. Gilbert J. Garbaghan, "The Anti-Jesuit Decree of the Spanish Republic," *Catholic Mind,* January 22, 1933, 21; "A Statement Issued by the Catholic Hierarchy of the United States to the Spanish Hierarchy, April 18, 1937," in *Pastoral Letters of the United States Catholic Bishops,* vol. 2, 1941–61, ed. Hugh

J. Nolan (Washington, D.C.: National Conference of Catholic Bishops, United States Catholic Conference, 1983), 416–18.

50. "Editorial Comment," *Catholic World* 145 (June 1937): 265; George Q. Flynn, *Roosevelt and Romanism: Catholics and American Diplomacy, 1937–1945* (Westport, Conn.: Greenwood, 1976), 36.

51. G. M. Godden, "How Communism Attacked Spain," *Catholic World* 144 (January 1937): 403–7.

52. Monks, "Franco of Spain," 668.

53. Guttmann, *The Wound in the Heart,* 42–45.

54. Ibid., 48–51.

55. Valaik, "Catholics, Neutrality, and the Spanish Embargo," 84.

56. Ibid., 95.

57. "The Great Problem in Spain," *Catholic World* 145 (June 1937): 260.

58. J. David Valaik, "In the Days before Ecumenism: American Catholics, Anti-Semitism, and the Spanish Civil War," *Journal of Church and State* 13 (Autumn 1971): 467. This article is one of the best studies of Catholic antisemitism during the Spanish civil war.

59. Ibid., 468–69.

60. Quoted in Valaik, "In the Days before Ecumenism," 470.

61. Valaik, "In the Days before Ecumenism," 470.

62. Ibid., 491–93.

63. "What Have We Learned from Spain?," *Catholic World* 149 (May 1939): 130.

64. See, for an example of Catholic antisemitism, Andrzej Kapiszewski, "Polish-Jewish Conflicts in the United States at the Beginning of World War I," *Polish American Studies* 48 (Spring 1991): 63–78.

65. Donald S. Strong, *Organized Anti-Semitism in America: The Rise of Group Prejudice during the Decade 1930–1940* (Westport, Conn.: Greenwood, 1941), 57–61.

66. Sheldon Marcus, *Father Coughlin: The Tumultuous Life of the Priest of the Little Flower* (Boston: Little, Brown, 1971), 31; Mary Christine Athans, "A New Perspective on Father Charles E. Coughlin," *Church History* 56 (June 1987): 228.

67. Marcus, *Father Coughlin,* 33, 40, 44.

68. Ibid., 71, 112–13; Athans, "A New Perspective," 228.

69. Athans, "A New Perspective," 226–27.

70. Quoted in Athans, "A New Perspective," 229.

71. Ibid.; see also Strong, *Organized Anti-Semitism in America,* 60–61.

72. Marcus, *Father Coughlin,* 229.

73. Strong, *Organized Anti-Semitism in America,* 61–64.

74. Athans, "A New Perspective," 230–34; Marcus, *Father Coughlin,* 188–89.

75. Quoted from *Social Justice* in Marcus, *Father Coughlin,* 190.

76. Quotations from Strong, *Organized Anti-Semitism in America*, 66–67.

77. According to polls, an overwhelming majority of his listeners agreed with Coughlin's message. See Cantril, *Public Opinion, 1935–1946*, 147–48.

78. See Greeley, *The Catholic Experience*, 237–40.

79. Ibid., 243–44; see also Flynn, *American Catholics and the Roosevelt Presidency*, 210–12.

80. Dinnerstein, *Antisemitism in America*, 114–15, 118–19; see also Marcus, *Father Coughlin*, 95.

81. Marcus, *Father Coughlin*, 158.

82. Flynn, *American Catholics and the Roosevelt Presidency*, 210, 214.

83. "The Ryan-Coughlin Controversy," *Commonweal*, October 22, 1936, 597–98 (quote); "Communications," *Commonweal*, November 6, 1936, 44–45.

84. "Week by Week," *Commonweal*, December 9, 1938, 169.

85. Ibid., 170.

86. George N. Shuster, "The Jew and Two Revolutions," *Commonweal*, December 30, 1938, 262.

87. Ibid., 262–63; for Shuster's attacks on antisemitism both in the United States and Germany, see George N. Shuster, *Strong Man Rules: An Interpretation of Germany Today* (New York: D. Appleton–Century, 1934); idem, "The Political Aspect of Christian-Jewish Relations," *Religion and the Modern World* (Philadelphia: University of Pennsylvania, 1941), 185–92; idem, "The Conflict among Catholics," *American Scholar* 10 (January 1941): 5–16.

88. John A. Ryan, "Anti-Semitism in the Air," *Commonweal*, December 30, 1938, 260.

89. Ibid., 262.

90. Shuster, "The Political Aspect of Christian-Jewish Relations," 192.

91. "Week by Week," 170.

92. *The American Jewish Year Book 5698*, vol. 39, ed. Harry Schneiderman (Philadelphia: Jewish Publication Society of America, 1937), 254–55.

93. Ibid., 256.

94. Walter Johnson, *The Battle against Isolation* (Chicago: University of Chicago Press, 1944), 97.

95. See, for example, John J. Carrigg, "American Catholic Press Opinion with Reference to America's Intervention in the Second World War" (M.A. thesis, Georgetown University, 1947); Philip Hughes, "War and the Catholic Tradition," *Catholic Mind*, October 22, 1939, 869–76; William F. Drummond, "Pacifism and War," *Catholic Mind*, July 8, 1940, 241–48; Editorial Comment, "Propaganda: Latest Style," *Catholic World* 153 (September 1941) 641–52; Editorial Comment, "The Fear of Fear," *Catholic World* 153 (July 1941): 385–95; Editorial Comment, "The 'Isolationist' Argument," *Catholic World* 154 (December 1941): 257–66.

96. For an excellent discussion of Coughlin's decline, see Marcus, *Father Coughlin*, 204–7.

Chapter 5: Snatching Souls, 1900–1960

1. For Protestant missions to the Jews, see Max Eisen, "Christian Missions to the Jews in North America and Great Britain," *Jewish Social Studies* 10 (January 1948): 37–40.

2. Robert G. Weisbord and Wallace P. Sillanpoa, *The Chief Rabbi, the Pope, and the Holocaust: An Era in Vatican-Jewish Relations* (New Brunswick, N.J.: Transaction, 1992), 15, 19–22.

3. Bertram Wallace Korn, *The American Reaction to the Mortara Case, 1858–1859* (Cincinnati: American Jewish Archives, 1957), 3–4; Morris U. Schappes, ed., *A Documentary History of the Jews in the United States, 1654–1875* (New York: Schocken, 1971), 385–87.

4. Korn, *American Reaction*, 78, 123, 156; Isaac Leeser, "The Mortara Case," *Philadelphia Public Ledger*, November 25, 1958, in *A Documentary History of the Jews in the United States, 1654–1875*, ed. Morris U. Schappes (New York: Schocken, 1971), 385–93; Morton Borden, *Jews, Turks, and Infidels* (Chapel Hill: University of North Carolina Press, 1984), 54–57.

5. Vincent F. Holden, *The Yankee Paul: Isaac Thomas Hecker* (Milwaukee: Bruce, 1958), 105; see also Daniel Callahan, *The Mind of the Catholic Layman* (New York: Scribner, 1963), 38; Greeley, *The Catholic Experience*, 126–27, 140–41.

6. Michael Warner, *Changing Witness: Catholic Bishops and Public Policy, 1917–1994* (Washington, D.C.: Ethics and Public Policy Center, 1995), 47–49.

7. Alfred Young, "Street Preaching," *Catholic World* 46 (January 1888): 499–504.

8. O'Connell, *Sermons*, 2:281.

9. Robert J. Schreiter, "Changes in Roman Catholic Attitudes toward Proselytism and Mission," in *Pushing the Faith: Proselytism and Civility in a Pluralistic World,* ed. Martin E. Marty and Frederick E. Greenspahn (New York: Crossroad, 1988), 94–95.

10. "Pastoral Letter Issued by the Third Plenary Council of Baltimore, December 7, 1884," in *Pastoral Letters of the United States Catholic Bishops,* vol. 1, 1792–1940, ed. Hugh J. Nolan (Washington, D.C.: National Council of Catholic Bishops, United States Catholic Conference, 1983), 238; "Pastoral Letter, Issued by the Roman Catholic Hierarchy of the United States, September 26, 1919," in *Pastoral Letters*, vol. 1, ed. Nolan, 288.

11. "Support of the Missions," *Catholic World* 122 (February 1926): 698–99.

12. Doyle, "The Encyclical Letter of Leo XIII," 427.

13. Schreiter, "Changes in Roman Catholic Attitudes," 95.

14. Young, "Street Preaching," 499–504.

15. Joseph L. O'Brien, "A Notable French Convert," *Catholic World* 101 (July 1915): 503–12.

16. "The Present State of Judaism in America," *Catholic World* 25 (June 1877): 374–75.

17. Ibid.

18. Van Rahden, "Beyond Ambivalence," 33; see also Mary C. Boys, "The Sisters of Sion: From Conversionist Stance to a Dialogical Way of Life," *Journal of Ecumenical Studies* 31 (Winter–Spring 1994): 27–48.

19. Van Rahden, "Beyond Ambivalence," 34; see also biographical sketches of David Goldstein and Rosalie Marie Levy in *American Catholic Convert Authors*, ed. David Martin (Detroit: Walter Romig, 1944), 86–87, 135.

20. See "Two Miraculous Conversions from Judaism," 613–21.

21. Goldstein, Goldstein biography, 86–87.

22. David Goldstein, "Religious Campaigning in American Streets," *Catholic World* 121 (August 1925): 645–52; see also "The Jew and Jesus," *Commonweal*, January 25, 1928, 972.

23. Eisen, "Christian Missions," 59.

24. Ibid., 56–57.

25. "Editorial," *Commonweal*, November 27, 1936, 116.

26. Gregory Feige, "In Exitu Israel," *Commonweal*, February 16, 1937, 504.

27. Hans Anscar, "Catholics and Anti-Semitism," *Catholic World* 150 (November 1939): 173.

28. Ibid.

29. Eisen, "Christian Missions," 59.

30. Ibid., 61.

31. See John F. Morley, *Vatican Diplomacy and the Jews during the Holocaust, 1939–1943* (New York: Ktav, 1980), 18–22, 45–47.

32. Weisbord and Sillanpoa, *The Chief Rabbi*, 1–3; see also Pinchas Lapide, *Israelis, Jews, and Jesus* (Garden City, N.Y.: Doubleday, 1979), 138.

33. John M. Oesterreicher, "New Books," *Catholic World* 163 (April 1946): 86–87.

34. Anscar, "Catholics and Anti-Semitism," 176.

35. Ibid., 177.

36. David Goldstein, "Comment," *Catholic World* 156 (January 1942): 428.

37. Julius Sturm, "Catholics Don't Work at Making Converts," *America*, September 17, 1955, 589–91.

38. Erik V. Kuehnelt-Leddihn, "Do Jews Make Good Catholics?," *Catholic World* 164 (December 1946): 212–16.

39. Ibid., 216.

40. Ibid., 215; see also Robert O. Stermann, "Edith Stein, Witness to Paradox," *Catholic World* 180 (March 1957): 447–50; Margaret O'Connell, "St. Paul's Own People," *Catholic World* 186 (January 1958): 285; Leon Paul, "What Is a Jewish Catholic?," *America*, October 5, 1957, 18–19.

41. Joseph McSorley, "Jew Hatred?," *Catholic World* 188 (February 1959): 397.

42. Ibid.

43. Arthur Gilbert, "Jews, Prejudice and Catholic Practice," in *American*

Catholics: A Protestant-Jewish View, ed. Philip Scharper (New York: Sheed and Ward, 1959), 159.

44. Charles Journet, "The Mysterious Destiny of Israel," *The Bridge* 2 (1956): 69.

45. See, for example, O'Connell, "St. Paul's Own People," 284–87.

46. Gilbert, "Jews, Prejudice and Catholic Practice," 171.

47. "The Passion Play," *America,* April 9, 1960, 41–42.

48. McSorley, "Jew Hatred?," 396–97.

49. Ibid., 398.

50. Greeley and Rossi, *Denominational Society,* 237, 243.

51. Quentin Lauer, "Love Links Christian with Jew," *America,* February 11, 1956, 529–30.

52. Ibid., 530.

53. Robert A. Herrera, "Institute of Judaeo-Christian Studies Celebrates Anniversary,"*Journal of Ecumenical Studies* 16 (Summer 1979): 606–8.

54. Lauer, "Love Links," 529–30.

55. Ibid., 530.

56. Ibid.; see also John M. Oesterreicher, "Introduction," *The Bridge* 3 (1958): 11–24.

57. Oesterreicher, "Introduction," 12–13.

58. John M. Oesterreicher, "Introduction," *The Bridge* 2 (1956): 101.

59. John M. Oesterreicher, *Walls Are Crumbling: Seven Jewish Philosophers Discover Christ* (London: Hollis and Carter, 1953), viii.

60. Ibid., xiii.

61. Ibid., xiv.

62. John Oesterreicher, "The Enigma of Simone Weil," *The Bridge* 1 (1955): 125–27.

63. Ibid., 133, 158.

64. Frederick C. Ellert, "Franz Werfel's Great Dilemma," *The Bridge* 4 (1961): 197–200.

65. Ibid., 204–5, 207.

66. Quoted in Ellert, "Franz Werfel's Great Dilemma," 216.

67. Ibid., 217.

68. Oesterreicher's comments appended to Ellert, "Franz Werfel's Great Dilemma," 234–35.

69. Edward H. Flannery, "The Finaly Case," *The Bridge* 1 (1955): 294.

70. Ibid., 292–95; Charlotte Klein, "From Conversion to Dialogue: I. The Sisters of Sion and the Jews," *Christian Jewish Relations* 15 (September 1982): 7.

71. Flannery, "The Finaly Case," 307–8.

72. Ibid., 314–15.

73. Edward H. Flannery, "Hope and Despair at Evanston," *The Bridge* 2 (1956): 271.

74. Ibid., 276, 280, 282.

75. Ibid., 285.

Chapter 6: Postwar Ambivalence, 1945–60

1. J. Bruce Long, ed., "Preface," *Judaism and the Christian Seminary Curriculum* (Chicago: Loyola University Press, 1966), vi.

2. Gerber, "Anti-Semitism and Jewish-Gentile Relations," 33–35.

3. Dinnerstein, *Antisemitism in America,* 150.

4. Ibid., 153–57; Seymour Martin Lipset and Earl Raab, *Jews and the New American Scene* (Cambridge, Mass.: Harvard University Press, 1995), 78.

5. Lipset and Raab, *Jews and the New American Scene,* 94–97.

6. Allitt, *Catholic Intellectuals,* 60.

7. Lipset and Raab, *Jews and the New American Scene,* 79–80.

8. Erik V. Kuehnelt-Leddihn, "Do Jews Tend toward Communism?," *Catholic World* 164 (December 1946): 107, 110; see also Hugh J. Nolan, "Introduction," in *Pastoral Letters of the United States Catholic Bishops,* vol. 2, 1941–61, ed. Hugh J. Nolan (Washington, D.C.: National Conference of Catholic Bishops, United States Catholic Conference, 1983), 1.

9. Judith Hershcopf, "The Church and the Jews: Struggle of Vatican II," *American Jewish Year Book 1965,* vol. 66, ed. Morris Fine and Milton Himmelfarb (New York: American Jewish Committee; Philadelphia: Jewish Publication Society of America, 1965), 106.

10. Gilbert, "Jews, Prejudice, and Catholic Practice," 159–62.

11. Ibid., 164–65.

12. Ibid., 167–71.

13. Robert F. Drinan, *Religion, the Courts, and Public Policy* (New York: McGraw-Hill, 1963), 65–66, 99; for an extensive discussion of legal and constitutional implications of these matters, see Naomi Cohen, *Jews in Christian America: The Pursuit of Religious Equality* (New York: Oxford University Press, 1992).

14. Arthur Gilbert, *A Jew in Christian America* (New York: Sheed and Ward, 1966), 146–47; see also Will Herberg, "Justice for Religious Schools," *America,* November 16, 1957, 190–93; "Letters about an Editorial," *America,* February 22, 1962, 774–79.

15. Robert F. Drinan, "Prayer in the Public Schools," *America,* October 17, 1959, 70–71; Bernard J. Coughlin, "Interfaith Dialogue and Church-State Issues," *America,* June 29, 1963, 900–903; see also Allitt, *Catholic Intellectuals,* 106–10; Walter M. Abbott and Robert F. Drinan, "A Bible Reader for Public Schools," *America,* October 22, 1960, 117–19.

16. John Courtney Murray, *We Hold These Truths: Catholic Reflections on the American Proposition* (New York: Sheed and Ward, 1960), 19.

17. Gilbert, "Jews, Prejudice, and Catholic Practice," 174–75, 180–81, 185; idem, *A Jew in Christian America,* 170.

18. "The Church and the Jews," *America,* March 30, 1947, 704.

19. Quotations in "The Church and the Jews," 704.

20. Kathryn Sullivan, "Pro Perfidis Judaeis," *The Bridge* 2 (1956): 214; for similar discussions of Jewish sensibilities, see, for example, Journet, "The Mysterious Destiny of Israel," 35–90.

21. Arthur A. Cohen, "The Natural and the Supernatural Jew: Two Views of the Church," in *American Catholics: A Protestant-Jewish View,* ed. Philip Scharper (New York: Sheed and Ward, 1959), 142.

22. See, for example, Albert Dondeyne, "Tolerance and Collaboration as Facts of Philosophy Assumed into Faith," in *Tolerance and the Catholic: A Symposium,* trans. George Lamb (New York: Sheed and Ward, 1955), 92–94.

23. See, for example, "Editorials," *America,* January 23, 1960, 486; *America,* May 7, 1960, 208.

24. Dinnerstein, *Antisemitism in America,* 162–65.

25. "Editorial," *America,* November 8, 1946, 144; "War and Its Aftermath," in *Pastoral Letters of the United States Catholic Bishops,* vol. 2, 1941–61, ed. Hugh J. Nolan (Washington, D.C.: National Conference of Catholic Bishops, United State Catholic Conference, 1983), 21; see also Robert F. Drinan, *Honor the Promise: America's Commitment to Israel* (Garden City, N.Y.: Doubleday, 1977), 74–75.

26. "Editorial: Relief for Refugees," *America,* January 18, 1947, 423.

27. William J. Gibbons, "Europe's Homeless," *America,* October 19, 1946, 65–66.

28. "Editorial," *America,* December 4, 1948, 228.

29. See, for example, Frances E. McMahon, *A Catholic Looks at the World* (New York: Vanguard, 1945), 26–27, 80–81.

30. Robert F. Drinan, "The Christian Response to the Holocaust," *American Academy of Political and Social Science* 450 (July 1980): 119.

31. "Correspondence," *America,* October 24, 1956, 93.

32. James McCawley, "Atrocities—World War II," *Catholic World* 161 (August 1945): 383.

33. Ibid., 378–84; Peter Van Gestel, "Priests in Dachau," *Catholic World* 161 (September 1945): 469–75; Franklin Ewing, "Twenty-five Years Ago, the Nazis . . . ," *Catholic World* 196 (November 1962): 110–17.

34. Ewing, "Twenty-five Years Ago," 117.

35. Robert S. Wistrich, "The Pope, the Church, and the Jews," *Commentary* 107 (April 1999): 25.

36. For examples of a Catholic defense of Pius XII's wartime record, see John M. Oesterreicher, "As We Await 'The Deputy,'" *America,* November 9, 1963, 570–82; Robert A. Graham, "The Latest Charges against Pius XII," *America,* May 21, 1966, 733–36; for a Catholic criticism of Pius XII, see, for example, John T. Pawlikowski, "The Holocaust and Catholic Theology: Some Reflections," *Shoah: A Review of Holocaust Studies and Commemorations* 2 (Spring–Summer 1980): 6–9; for Jewish defense of Pius XII, see, for example, Joseph L. Lichten, "A Question of Judgement: Pius XII and the Jews," in *The Star and*

the Cross: Essays on Jewish-Christian Relations, ed. Katharine T. Hargrove (Milwaukee: Bruce, 1966), 181–209; Lapide, *The Last Three Popes,* 210–11, 230–53.

37. Wistrich, "The Pope, the Church, and the Jews," 127–28.

38. "Editorial: War Criminal Trials," *Commonweal,* September 21, 1945, 539–40; "Editorial: Nuremberg," *Commonweal,* December 7, 1945, 181–82.

39. Gustav Gundlach, "Moral Estimate of the Nuremberg Trial," *America,* November 9, 1946, 149–54.

40. James A. Ryan, "Peace with Justice," *Commonweal,* June 11, 1943, 197; Ferdinand A. Hermens, "Germany and a Christian Peace," *Catholic World* 158 (February 1944): 427–34.

41. Hermens, "Germany and a Christian Peace," 428.

42. Ibid., 429.

43. Ferdinand A. Hermens, "Punishment or Reconstruction?," *Catholic World* 160 (March 1945): 491, 497.

44. Ibid., 493.

45. James McCawley, "Punish Only—The Guilty," *Catholic World* 161 (June 1945): 240, 244.

46. See, for example, Wistrich, "The Pope, the Church, and the Jews," 24–28; Friedrich Heer, *God's First Love: Christians and Jews over Two Thousand Years,* trans. Geoffrey Skelton (New York: Weybright and Talley, 1970), 299.

47. Erik V. Kuehnelt-Leddihn, "Guilty Nations?," *Catholic World* 162 (December 1945): 208.

48. Sachar, *A History of Israel,* 552–58.

49. Lapide, *The Last Three Popes,* 335.

50. "Editorial: Eichmann and His Judges," *America,* March 25, 1961, 806; "Editorial: A Hanging in Jerusalem," *America,* January 13, 1962, 457; see also "Book Review" of Gideon Hausner's "Justice in Jerusalem," *America,* July 2, 1966, 16–17.

51. "Editorial: Eichmann the German," *America,* April 22, 1961, 167.

52. Arthur Gilbert and Walter M. Abbott, "Christians Failed Jewish Hopes," *America,* March 24, 1962, 825.

53. Ibid., 826.

54. Ibid., 827; see also Gilbert, *The Vatican Council and the Jews;* for the European Catholic reaction to the Eichmann trial, see Lapide, *The Last Three Popes,* 332–34.

55. "Editorial: Eichmann the 'Christian'?," *America,* March 24, 1962, 815.

56. Ibid.

57. The history of Israel's journey toward statehood can be followed in Ian J. Bickerton and Carla L. Klausner, *A Concise History of the Arab-Israeli Conflict,* 2d ed. (Englewood Cliffs, N.J.: Prentice Hall, 1995), chapter 3, 66–86; see also Sachar, *A History of Israel,* 240–48.

58. Sachar, *A History of Israel,* 279–314.

59. Drinan, *Honor the Promise,* 55–56.

74. George G. Higgins, "Reflections on the Ecumenical Council: A Catholic View," in *Judaism and the Christian Seminary Curriculum,* ed. J. Bruce Long (Chicago: Loyola University Press, 1966), 66.

75. Quotation from Judith Hershcopf, "The Church and the Jews: Struggle at Vatican II," in *American Jewish Year Book 1966,* vol. 67 (New York: American Jewish Committee; Philadelphia: Jewish Publication Society of America, 1966), 64.

76. Ibid., 66–67.

77. Hugh J. Nolan, "The Church in Our Day," in *Pastoral Letters of the United States Catholic Bishops,* vol. 3, ed. Hugh J. Nolan (Washington, D.C.: National Conference of Catholic Bishops, United States Catholic Conference, 1983), 134.

78. Quotations from Gilbert, *The Vatican Council and the Jews,* 74, 222–23.

79. Quotation from Lapide, *The Last Three Popes,* 344; see also Allitt, *Catholic Intellectuals,* 136–38.

80. "United States Statements," in *Stepping Stones to Further Jewish-Christian Relations,* ed. Helga Croner (New York: Paulist Press, 1977), 16.

81. Ibid., 17.

82. Ibid., 18–19.

83. Ibid., 19.

84. Ibid., 20.

85. Gilbert, *The Vatican Council and the Jews,* 234.

86. "United States Statements," 21.

87. Ibid., 22–24.

88. Ibid., 28.

89. Ibid.

90. Fisher, *Faith without Prejudice,* 159–62.

91. Ibid., 162–63.

92. According to the Catholic theologian Leonard Swidler, the issue of the link of Jews to the land was included in a Vatican study paper in 1969. But for political reasons, it was not included at that time in any official publications. See Leonard Swidler, "Catholic Statements on Jews—A Revolution in Progress," *Judaism* 27 (Summer 1978): 304.

93. Fisher, *Faith without Prejudice,* 167.

94. "Guidelines of Archdiocese Galveston-Houston, 1975," in *More Stepping Stones to Jewish-Christian Relations: An Unabridged Collection of Christian Documents, 1975–1983,* ed. Helga Croner (New York: Paulist Press, 1985), 66.

95. Ibid., 67.

96. Ibid., 70.

97. Ibid.

98. For the texts of the various "Guidelines," see Croner, *More Stepping Stones,* 85–101.

99. Michael B. McGarry, *Christology after Auschwitz* (New York: Paulist Press, 1977), 28.

100. A. James Rudin, "The Dramatic Impact of *Nostra Aetate*," in *Twenty Years of Jewish-Catholic Relations*, ed. Eugene J. Fisher et al. (New York: Paulist Press, 1986), 18.

Chapter 8: The Age of Dialogue, 1965–2000

1. David Hyatt, "The Interfaith Movement," *Judaism* 27 (Summer 1978): 267, 270.

2. Ibid., 271.

3. Gary M. Bretton-Granatoor, "UAHC Advances Catholic-Jewish Relations," *Reform Judaism* 23 (Spring 1995): 38.

4. Fisher quoted in Bretton-Granatoor, "UAHC Advances Catholic-Jewish Relations," 38.

5. Gilbert, *The Vatican Council and the Jews*, 167.

6. Ibid., 168.

7. Quoted in Gilbert, *The Vatican Council and the Jews*, 168.

8. Gilbert, *The Vatican Council and the Jews*, 169.

9. Raymond A. Schroth, "Ecumenical Encounter," *America*, April 16, 1966, 552–53; see also "Something New in Ecumenism," *America*, November 5, 1966, 533; Scharper, *Torah and Gospel*.

10. Quoted in Gilbert, *The Vatican Council and the Jews*, 177.

11. For example, for the Los Angeles area, see Alfred Wolf, "A Tale of One City," *Judaism* 27 (Summer 1978): 292–98; for the Chicago area, for example, see Joseph Cardinal Bernardin, "Hyde Park—Kenwood Interfaith Council Congregation Rodfei Zedek, June 20, 1985," in *A Blessing to Each Other: Cardinal Joseph Bernardin and Jewish-Catholic Dialogues* (Chicago: Liturgy Training Publications, 1996), 55–64.

12. See, for example, "Ecumenical Events," *Journal of Ecumenical Studies* 25 (Winter 1988): 145–59, and "Ecumenical Events," *Journal of Ecumenical Studies* 35 (Summer–Fall 1998): 533–50; see also Daniel Polish, "A Jewish Perspective: This Moment in Jewish-Christian Relations," *Ecumenical Bulletin* (November–December 1980): 8–9.

13. See the *Journal of Ecumenical Studies* 34 (Summer 1997).

14. Peter Steinfels, "New Center to Address Jewish-Catholic Issues," *New York Times*, July 6, 1992, sec. A, 9.

15. See Croner, *More Stepping Stones*, 54–55; Thomas F. Stransky, "Focusing on Jewish-Christian Relations," *Origins*, June 20, 1985, 66–69.

16. By 1970, however, the editors of *The Bridge* had reversed its former attitudes of triumphalism. See, for example, "Guidelines for Catholic-Jewish Relations," *The Bridge* 5 (1970): 257–62.

17. Edward H. Flannery, "Jews and Christians: Challenges to Face Together," *Origins*, June 20, 1985, 70–74.

18. Edward H. Flannery, "Jewish-Christian Relations Focus on the Future," *Journal of Ecumenical Studies* 34 (Summer 1997): 322–23.

19. Ibid., 323.

20. Edward H. Flannery, "Seminaries, Classrooms, Pulpits, Streets: Where We Have to Go," in *Unanswered Questions: Theological Views of Jewish-Catholic Relations,* ed. Roger Brooks (Notre Dame: University of Notre Dame Press, 1988), 130.

21. Flannery, "Jewish-Christian Relations Focus on the Future," 324.

22. Ibid., 325; see also Flannery, "Jews and Christians: Challenges to Face Together," 70–74.

23. Eugene J. Fisher, "Whither Christian-Jewish Relations," *Doctrine and Life* 33 (April 1983): 226–28.

24. Ibid., 230–33.

25. Ibid., 238.

26. American Jewish Committee, *A Guide to Inter-religious Dialogue* (New York: American Jewish Committee, 1966), 6; for a more recent discussion of the structure of a dialogue, see, for example, G. David Schwartz, *A Jewish Appraisal of Dialogue: Between Talk and Theology* (Lanham, Md.: University Press of America, 1994), 35–44.

27. American Jewish Committee, *A Guide to Inter-religious Dialogue,* 7.

28. Ibid., 8–22; Schwartz, *A Jewish Appraisal of Dialogue,* 36.

29. Schwartz, *A Jewish Appraisal of Dialogue,* 36–37, 42.

30. Arthur Gilbert, "Next Steps in the Jewish-Catholic Dialogue," in *Torah and Gospel: Jewish and Catholic Theology in Dialogue,* ed. Philip Scharper (New York: Sheed and Ward, 1966), 296–97.

31. Ibid., 299.

32. Ibid., 299, 304.

33. Gilbert, *The Vatican Council and the Jews,* 234.

34. Ben Zion Bokser, *Judaism and the Christian Predicament* (New York: Knopf, 1967), 374.

35. Wolf, "A Tale of One City," 292–98.

36. Henry Siegman, "A Decade of Catholic-Jewish Relations—A Reassessment," in *Christianity and Judaism: The Deepening Dialogue,* ed. Richard W. Rousseau (Scranton, Pa.: Ridge Row Press, 1983), 255.

37. Ibid., 168–69.

38. Polish, "A Jewish Perspective," 9.

39. Ibid., 9–10; Leon Klenicki, "From Argument to Dialogue: *Nostra Aetate* Twenty-five Years Later," in *In Our Time: The Flowering of Jewish-Catholic Dialogue,* ed. Eugene J. Fisher and Leon Klenicki (New York: Paulist Press, 1990), 77–103.

40. Klenicki, "From Argument to Dialogue," 98–99.

41. Terry A. Bookman, "The Holy Conversation: Towards a Jewish Theology of Dialogue," *Journal of Ecumenical Studies* 32 (Spring 1995): 207–25. See also Norman Solomon, "Themes in Christian-Jewish Relations," in *Toward a Theological Encounter: Jewish Understandings of Christianity,* ed. Leon Klenicki (New York: Paulist Press, 1991), 16–25; Schwartz, *A Jewish Appraisal of Dialogue,* 41–44, 56.

42. Obituary of Marc H. Tanenbaum, *New York Times,* July 4, 1992.

43. Ibid.

44. Leon Klenicki, "Toward a Process of Healing: Understanding the Other as a Person of God," in *Toward a Theological Encounter: Jewish Understandings of Christianity,* ed. Leon Klenicki (New York: Paulist Press, 1991), 1.

45. Ibid., 2.

46. Ibid., 3–4; see also Solomon, "Themes in Jewish-Christian Relations," 36.

47. Klenicki, "Toward a Process of Healing," 4.

48. Robert Gordis, "The Interfaith Movement—A Multiple Vision," *Judaism* 35 (Winter 1986): 7.

49. Abraham J. Peck, "The Very Depths of Our Pain," in *Unanswered Questions: Theological Views of Jewish-Catholic Relations,* ed. Roger Brooks (Notre Dame: University of Notre Dame Press, 1988), 176, 179, 181–82, 188.

50. Elliot N. Dorff, "The Covenant as the Key: A Jewish Theology of Jewish-Christian Relations," in *Toward a Theological Encounter: Jewish Understandings of Christianity,* ed. Leon Klenicki (New York: Paulist Press, 1991), 50–51.

51. Ibid., 51–52.

52. Samuel Sandmel, "Jewish and Catholic Biblical Scholarship," in *Torah and Gospel: Jewish and Catholic Theology in Dialogue,* ed. Philip Scharper (New York: Sheed and Ward, 1966), 79.

53. Eugene B. Borowitz, *Contemporary Christologies: A Jewish Response* (New York: Paulist Press, 1980), 197–98.

Chapter 9: Pitfalls of Dialogue

1. Fisher, *Faith without Prejudice,* 91.

2. McGarry, *Christology after Auschwitz,* 58–59.

3. Clemens Thoma, *A Christian Theology of Judaism* (New York: Paulist Press, 1980), 23. The statement was first made by the Jewish scholar Jakob Petuchowski.

4. Ibid., 28–29.

5. Ibid., 174.

6. John T. Pawlikowski, "A Theology of Religious Pluralism," in *Unanswered Questions: Theological Views of Jewish-Catholic Relations,* ed. Roger Brooks (Notre Dame: University of Notre Dame Press, 1988), 157.

7. Ibid., 159.

8. Elwyn A. Smith, "The Long Road to Jewish-Christian Understanding," *Journal of Ecumenical Studies* 6 (Spring 1969): 241.

9. David Noel Freedman, "Readers' Response: An Essay on Jewish Christianity," *Journal of Ecumenical Studies* 5 (Winter 1969): 81–82; Hershel Matt, "How Shall a Believing Jew View Christianity?," in *Judaism and Christianity: The New Relationship,* vol. 4, ed. Jacob Neusner (New York: Garland, 1993), 117–21.

10. Mordecai Waxman, "The Dialogue, Touching New Bases," in *More Stepping Stones to Jewish-Christian Relations: An Unabridged Collection of Christian Documents, 1975–1983,* ed. Helga Croner (New York: Paulist Press, 1985), 25–26.

11. Michael A. Signer, "*Speculum Concilii:* Through the Mirror Brightly," in *Unanswered Questions: Theological Views of Jewish-Christian Relations,* ed. Roger Brooks (Notre Dame: University of Notre Dame Press, 1988), 110–11.

12. Polish, "A Very Small Lever," 100–111.

13. Harold Kasimow, "Heschel's Prophetic Vision of Religious Pluralism," in *No Religion Is an Island: Abraham Joshua Heschel and Interreligious Dialogue,* ed. Harold Kasimow and Byron L. Sherwin (Maryknoll, N.Y.: Orbis, 1991), 82–84.

14. Ibid., 86.

15. Harold Kasimow and Byron L. Sherwin, eds., *No Religion Is An Island: Abraham Joshua Heschel and Interreligious Dialogue* (Maryknoll, N.Y.: Orbis, 1991), xxi.

16. Abraham Joshua Heschel, "No Religion Is an Island," in *No Religion Is an Island: Abraham Joshua Heschel and Interreligious Dialogue,* ed. Harold Kasimow and Byron L. Sherwin (Maryknoll, N.Y.: Orbis, 1991), 3.

17. Ibid., 7–8.

18. Ibid., 9, 12–13.

19. Ibid., 16.

20. Abraham Joshua Heschel, "From Mission to Dialogue?," *Conservative Judaism* 21 (Spring 1967): 7.

21. Ibid., 7–8.

22. Fleischner, "Heschel's Significance," 64.

23. Ibid., 78.

24. Ibid., 79.

25. Eugene J. Fisher, "Heschel's Impact on Catholic-Jewish Relations," in *No Religion Is an Island: Abraham Joshua Heschel and Interreligious Dialogue,* ed. Harold Kasimow and Byron L. Sherwin (Maryknoll, N.Y.: Orbis, 1991), 111.

26. Ibid., 116; see also John C. Merkle, "Heschel's Attitude towards Religious Pluralism," in *No Religion Is an Island: Abraham Joshua Heschel and Interreligious Dialogue,* ed. Harold Kasimow and Byron L. Sherwin (Maryknoll, N.Y.: Orbis, 1991), 97–109.

27. Merkle, "Heschel's Attitude towards Religious Pluralism," 99.

28. Elie Wiesel, "*Nostra Aetate:* An Observer's Perspective," *Thought* 67 (December 1992): 367–68.

29. David Novak, *Jewish-Christian Dialogue: A Jewish Justification* (New York: Oxford University Press, 1989).

30. Ibid., 14, 19, 22.

31. Ibid., 23.

32. Ibid., 9, 91.

33. David Novak, "A Jewish Theological Understanding of Christianity of Our Time," in *Toward a Theological Encounter: Jewish Understandings of Christianity,* ed. Leon Klenicki (New York: Paulist Press, 1991), 94–95.

34. Ibid., 97–99.

35. Walter Jacob, "The Judeo-Christian Dialogue in the Twentieth Century: The Jewish Response," in *Toward a Theological Encounter: Jewish Understandings of Christianity,* ed. Leon Klenicki (New York: Paulist Press, 1991), 80.

36. Agus, *Dialogue and Tradition,* 28–29.

37. Ibid., 89.

38. In this connection, see Schwartz, *A Jewish Appraisal of Dialogue,* 7.

39. David Hartman, "Jews and Christians in the World of Tomorrow," *Immanuel* 6 (Spring 1976): 79–80.

40. David Hartman, "Creating Space for the Integrity of the Other," *SIDIC* 15, no. 2 (1982): 10.

41. Bokser, *Judaism and the Christian Predicament,* 26.

42. See Novak, *Jewish-Christian Dialogue,* 3–4; Long, *Judaism and the Christian Seminary Curriculum,* 147.

43. Bokser, *Judaism and the Christian Predicament,* 372; see also pp. 365–71.

44. Novak, *Jewish-Christian Dialogue,* 3–4.

45. Ibid., 4–5.

46. Ibid., 10–11.

47. Joseph B. Soloveitchik, "Confrontation," *Tradition* 6 (Spring/Summer 1964): 5, 16.

48. Ibid., 17–19.

49. Ibid., 20–21.

50. Ibid., 24.

51. Ibid., 25–26.

52. "Statement Adopted by the Rabbinical Council of America at the Mid-Winter Conference, February 3–5, 1964," appended to Soloveitchik, "Confrontation," 28–29.

53. Novak, *Jewish-Christian Dialogue,* 6–7.

54. Siegman, "A Decade of Catholic-Jewish Relations," 243.

55. Ibid., 249.

56. Michael Wyschagrad, "A Jewish View of Christianity," in *Toward a Theological Encounter: Jewish Understandings of Christianity,* ed. Leon Klenicki (New York: Paulist Press, 1991), 109.

57. Jacob Neusner, "Foreword," in *Judaism and Christianity: The New Relationship,* vol. 4, ed. Jacob Neusner (New York: Garland, 1993), viii.

58. Andrew M. Greeley and Jacob Neusner, *The Bible and Us: A Priest and a Rabbi Read Scripture Together* (New York: Warner, 1990).

59. Ibid., 261–62.

60. Ibid., 264–65.

61. Ibid., 277–78.

Chapter 10: Uprooting Contempt

1. John T. Pawlikowski, "The Contemporary Jewish-Christian Theological Dialogue Agenda," *Journal of Ecumenical Studies* 11 (Fall 1974): 614–15.

2. John T. Pawlikowski, *Sinai and Calvary: A Meeting of Two Peoples* (Beverly Hills, Calif.: Benziger, 1976), 222.

3. Ibid., 623–24.

4. Pawlikowski, "Jews and Christians," 35.

5. Ibid., 36.

6. See, for example, John T. Pawlikowski, "New Trends in Catholic Religious Thought," in *Twenty Years of Jewish-Catholic Relations,* ed. Eugene Fisher et al., 169–90.

7. Ibid., 178.

8. Ibid., 180.

9. Ibid., 183.

10. Gregory Baum, "Introduction," in Ruether, *Faith and Fratricide,* 14.

11. Ruether, *Faith and Fratricide,* 228–31.

12. Ibid., 246, 256.

13. Ibid., 257.

14. Ibid.

15. See, for example, Wendell S. Dietrich, "*Nostra Aetate:* A Typology of Theological Tendencies," in *Unanswered Questions: Theological Views of Jewish-Christian Relations,* ed. Roger Brooks (Notre Dame: University of Notre Dame Press, 1988), 70–81.

16. Fisher, *Faith without Prejudice,* 14; see also Eugene J. Fisher, "Jews and Christians: The Next Step for Theology," *Commonweal,* November 5, 1982, 588–91.

17. Eugene J. Fisher, "The Evolution of a Tradition: From *Nostra Aetate* to the 'Notes,'" *Christian-Jewish Relations* 18 (December 1985): 32–47.

18. Gregory Baum, "The Jews, Faith and Ideology," *The Ecumenist* 10 (July/August 1972): 71–76.

19. Ibid., 72–75.

20. Gregory Baum, "Catholic Dogma after Auschwitz," in *Antisemitism and the Foundations of Christianity,* ed. Alan Davies (New York: Paulist Press, 1978), 138.

21. Ibid., 139.

22. Ibid., 140–42.

23. Katharine T. Hargrove, "The Star and the Cross," in *The Star and the Cross: Essays on Jewish-Christian Relations,* ed. Katharine T. Hargrove (Milwaukee: Bruce, 1966), 308–13.

24. Bruce Vawter, "Are the Gospels Anti-Semitic?," *Journal of Ecumenical Studies* 5 (Summer 1968): 473.

25. Ibid., 485–87.

26. Ruether, *Faith and Fratricide,* 77, 84 (quote).

27. Ibid., 113.

28. Thomas A. Idinopulos and Roy Bowen Ward, "Is Christology Inherently Anti-Semitic? A Critical Review of Rosemary Ruether's *Faith and Fratricide*," *Journal of the American Academy of Religion* 45 (June 1977): 193–94.

29. Fisher, *Faith without Prejudice*, 15–16.

30. Ibid., 54.

31. Ibid., 58; see also Pawlikowski, *What Are They Saying?*, 8–17.

32. Pawlikowski, *What Are They Saying?*, 28–31; Richard A. Bondi, "John 8:39–47: Children of Abraham or of the Devil?," *Journal of Ecumenical Studies* 34 (Fall 1997): 473–98.

33. Pawlikowski, *What Are They Saying?*, 30.

34. See, for example, Franz Mussner, *Tractate on the Jews: The Significance of Judaism for Christian Faith* (Philadelphia: Fortress Press, 1989), 50–51; Bishop, *How Catholics Look at Jews*, 115.

35. Ruether, *Faith and Fratricide*, 228.

36. Ibid., 246.

37. Ibid., 250, 254–55; see also Monika K. Hellwig, "From the Jesus of Story to the Christ of Dogma," in *Antisemitism and the Foundations of Christianity*, ed. Alan Davies (New York: Paulist Press, 1979), 119, 130–33.

38. David Novak, "The Quest for the Jewish Jesus," *Modern Judaism* 8 (May 1988): 125, 123; see also Lapide, *Israelis, Jews, and Jesus*; Karl Rahner and Pinchas Lapide, *Encountering Jesus—Encountering Judaism: A Dialogue*, trans. Davis Perkins (New York: Crossroad, 1987); Arthur E. Zannoni, ed., *Jews and Christians Speak of Jesus* (Minneapolis: Fortress Press, 1994).

39. Robert Louis Wilken, "The Jews as the Christians Saw Them," *First Things* 73 (May 1997): 28–32.

40. See Isaac, "The Crime of Deicide," 136–39.

41. Ibid., 142.

42. Higgins, "Reflections on the Ecumenical Council," 61–71.

43. Bea, *The Church and the Jewish People*, 69–70, 86–88.

44. John T. Pawlikowski, *Catechetics and Prejudice: How Catholic Teaching Materials View Jews, Protestants and Racial Minorities* (New York: Paulist Press, 1973), 100–101; Bishop, *How Catholics Look at Jews*, 13–14, 18–19.

45. Pawlikowski, *Catechetics and Prejudice*, 103–4.

46. Ruether, *Faith and Fratricide*, 88.

47. Pawlikowski, *Sinai and Calvary*, 91.

48. Ibid., 96–98.

49. Pawlikowski, "Jews and Christians," 25.

50. *Catechism of the Catholic Church* (Washington, D.C.: United States Catholic Conference, 1994); Richard P. McBrien, gen. ed., *The HarperCollins Encyclopedia of Catholicism* (San Francisco: HarperCollins, 1995).

51. For one review of scholarship, see John R. Donahue, "From Crucified Messiah to Risen Christ: The Trial of Jesus Revisited," in *Jews and Christians Speak of Jesus*, ed. Arthur E. Zannoni (Minneapolis: Fortress Press, 1994), 93–121.

52. Richard N. Ostling, "Why Was Christ Crucified?," *Time*, April 4, 1994, 72–73.

53. John J. Kelley, "The Dilemma of Oberammergau," *Christian Jewish Relations* 23 (Summer 1990): 28.

54. Ibid., 29–31.

55. Ibid., 30–32; the next Oberammergau performances, including seventy-nine "regular" and twenty-five "repeat," took place May 21–October 6, 2000.

56. Bishop, *How Catholics Look at Jews,* 36; Mussner, *Tractate on the Jews,* 164.

57. In this connection, see Menahem Stern, "The Hasmonean State," in *History of the Jewish People,* ed. H. H. Ben-Sasson (Cambridge, Mass.: Harvard University Press, 1976), 234–36.

58. John T. Pawlikowski, "The Jewish-Christian Dialogue: Assessment and Future Agenda," *Conservative Judaism* 32 (Winter 1979): 39–54.

59. John T. Pawlikowski, "On Renewing the Revolution of the Pharisees: A New Approach to Theology and Politics," *Cross Currents* 20 (Fall 1970): 415–34; Fisher, *Faith without Prejudice,* 30–33.

60. Pawlikowski, "On Renewing the Revolution," 415–16, 420–21, 423–25; see also J. Massingberd Ford, "The Christian Debt to Pharisaism," *The Bridge* 5 (1970): 218–30; Bishop, *How Catholics Look at Jews,* 35–37.

61. Pawlikowski, "On Renewing the Revolution," 426–27; see also Pawlikowski, *Sinai and Calvary,* 81–85; John T. Pawlikowski, "Jesus—A Pharisee and the Christ," in *Introduction to Jewish-Christian Relations,* ed. Michael Shermis and Arthur E. Zannoni (New York: Paulist Press, 1991), 183–88.

62. Ford, "The Christian Debt," 126; Fisher, *Faith without Prejudice,* 36–39.

63. Pawlikowski, "The Contemporary Jewish-Christian Theological Dialogue Agenda," 610–11.

64. Pawlikowski, *Sinai and Calvary,* 73.

65. Ibid., 74 (quote); see also Ford, "The Christian Debt," 229–30.

66. Fisher, *Faith without Prejudice,* 53.

67. Ruether, *Faith and Fratricide,* 136–39.

68. Ibid., 177.

69. Baum, "The Jews, Faith, and Ideology," 75.

70. Peter Chirico, "Christian and Jew Today from a Christian Theological Perspective," *Journal of Ecumenical Studies* 7 (Spring 1970): 750–53.

71. Ibid., 760.

72. Monika Hellwig, "Christian Theology and the Covenant of Israel," *Journal of Ecumenical Studies* 7 (Winter 1970): 51.

73. Eugene J. Fisher, "Pope John Paul II's Pilgrimage of Reconciliation: A Commentary on the Texts," in *Pope John Paul II on Jews and Judaism, 1978–1986,* ed. Eugene J. Fisher and Leon Klenicki (Washington, D.C.: National Conference of Catholic Bishops, 1987), 10.

74. "Vatican II and Missions," *America,* October 17, 1964, 444–45.

75. Boys, "The Sisters of Sion," 38–39.

76. Ibid., 39–42.

77. Schreiter, "Changes in Roman Catholic Attitudes," 104.

78. Ibid., 106–7.

79. Richard Cardinal Cushing, "On the Dialogue and on Israel," *The Bridge* 5 (1970): 250.

80. John M. Oesterreicher, *The Rediscovery of Judaism: A Re-examination of the Conciliar Statement on the Jews* (South Orange, N.J.: Institute of Judaeo-Christian Studies, 1971), 39.

81. Ibid., 40.

82. Gregory Baum, "Rethinking the Church's Mission after Auschwitz," in *Auschwitz: Beginning of a New Era? Reflections on the Holocaust,* ed. Eva Fleischner (New York: Ktav, Cathedral Church of St. John the Divine, Anti-Defamation League of B'nai B'rith, 1974), 113.

83. Michael B. McGarry, "Contemporary Roman Catholic Understandings of Mission," in *Christian Mission—Jewish Mission,* ed. Martin A. Cohen and Helga Croner (New York: Paulist Press, 1982), 141.

84. John T. Pawlikowski, "Christ and the Jewish-Christian Dialogue," *Chicago Studies: An Archdiocesan Review* 16 (Fall 1977): 387–88.

85. McGarry, "Contemporary Roman Catholic Understandings of Mission," 141.

86. Ibid., 142–43.

Chapter 11: A New Past

1. Jay Dolan, "New Horizons in American Studies," in *An American Church: Essays on Americanization of the Catholic Church,* ed. David S. Alvarez (Moraga, Calif.: Saint Mary's College of California, 1979), 1.

2. Ibid., 3.

3. Frederick M. Schweitzer, *A History of the Jews since the First Century A.D.,* 2d ed. (New York: Macmillan, 1980), 9–13.

4. Ibid., 15; see also Willebrands, *Church and Jewish People,* 194–96.

5. Schweitzer, *A History of the Jews,* 16 (all quotes); Egal Feldman, "Jewish History and American Education," *Judaism* 21 (Fall 1972): 470–76.

6. Schweitzer, *A History of the Jews,* 20.

7. Ibid., 297–98.

8. Fisher, *Faith without Prejudice,* 146.

9. Edward H. Flannery, *The Anguish of the Jews: Twenty-Three Centuries of Antisemitism,* rev. ed. (New York: Paulist Press, 1985), 2.

10. Ibid., 3.

11. Bishop, *How Catholics Look at Jews,* 118–19.

12. "Basic Teachings for Catholic Religious Education," in *Pastoral Letters of the United States Catholic Bishops,* vol. 3, 1962–74, ed. Hugh J. Nolan (Washington, D.C.: National Conference of Catholic Bishops, United States Catholic Conference, 1983), 360–61.

13. Vatican Commission for Religious Relations with the Jews, "Notes on the

Correct Way to Present the Jews and Judaism in Preaching and Catechesis in the Roman Catholic Church [June 24, 1985]," in *In Our Time: The Flowering of Jewish-Catholic Dialogue,* ed. Eugene J. Fisher and Leon Klenicki (New York: Paulist Press, 1990), 38–50; see also "Catechetics and Judaism: 1977 Synod [From SIDIC]," in *More Stepping Stones to Jewish-Christian Relations: An Unabridged Collection of Christian Documents, 1975–1983,* ed. Helga Croner (New York: Paulist Press, 1985), 56–59.

14. Fisher, "Research on Christian Teaching," 423.

15. Ibid., 426.

16. "Within Context: Guidelines for the Catechetical Presentation of Jews and Judaism in the New Testament [1986]," in *In Our Time: The Flowering of Jewish-Catholic Dialogue,* ed. Eugene J. Fisher and Leon Klenicki (New York: Paulist Press, 1990), 73.

17. Judith H. Banki, "The Image of Jews in Christian Teaching," *Journal of Ecumenical Studies* 21 (Summer 1984): 437–51.

18. Schweitzer, *A History of the Jews,* 40.

19. Ibid., 40–42.

20. Eugene J. Fisher, ed., *Interwoven Destinies: Jews and Christians through the Ages* (New York: Paulist Press, 1993), 3.

21. Fisher, "Research on Christian Teaching," 430.

22. Drinan, *Honor the Promise,* 10; see also Flannery, *The Anguish of the Jews,* 47–65.

23. Drinan, *Honor the Promise,* 12.

24. Ibid., 15.

25. Ruether, *Faith and Fratricide,* 117–18; see also Heer, *God's First Love,* 37–38.

26. Ruether, *Faith and Fratricide,* 119.

27. Ibid., 122–23, 125–26.

28. Flannery, *The Anguish of the Jews,* 60.

29. Heer, *God's First Love,* 36.

30. Flannery, *The Anguish of the Jews,* 46.

31. Annette Daum and Eugene Fisher, *The Challenge of SHALOM for Catholics and Jews: A Dialogical Discussion Guide to the Catholic Bishops' Pastoral on Peace and War* (Cincinnati: Union of American Hebrew Congregations; Washington, D.C.: National Conference of Catholic Bishops, 1985), 29.

32. In this connection, consider the works of Harry James Cargas, Eugene J. Fisher, Edward H. Flannery, Friedrich Heer, John Pawlikowski, Rosemary Ruether, and Frederick M. Schweitzer.

33. Schweitzer, *A History of the Jews,* 69.

34. Harry James Cargas, *Shadows of Auschwitz: A Christian Response to the Holocaust* (New York: Crossroad, 1990), 9, 11, 16.

35. Flannery, *The Anguish of the Jews,* 82, 84, 88.

36. As quoted in Cargas, *Shadows of Auschwitz,* 19–20; see also Pawlikowski, *Sinai and Calvary,* 145–47.

37. Flannery, *The Anguish of the Jews*, 91.

38. Schweitzer, *A History of the Jews*, 85–86.

39. Ruether, *Faith and Fratricide*, 205.

40. Ibid., 206.

41. Flannery, *The Anguish of the Jews*, 104–9.

42. Ibid., 143.

43. Ibid., 144.

Chapter 12: Remembering the *Shoah*

1. See, for example, "Catholic-Jewish Relationship Guidelines: Diocese of Brooklyn, November 1979," in *More Stepping Stones to Jewish-Christian Relations: An Unabridged Collection of Christian Documents, 1975–1983*, ed. Helga Croner (New York: Paulist Press, 1985), 82; "Guidelines: Diocese of Cleveland, 1979," in Croner, *More Stepping Stones*, 86.

2. Drinan, *Honor the Promise*, 24.

3. Drinan, "The Christian Response to the Holocaust," 179–89.

4. Schweitzer, *A History of the Jews*, 218.

5. David J. O'Brien, "American Catholics and Anti-Semitism in the 1930's," *Catholic World* 204 (February 1967): 270–72.

6. Many American bishops were very critical of Nazism. See, for example, Warner, *Changing Witness*, 52–53.

7. O'Brien, "American Catholics and Anti-Semitism," 273–76.

8. William Francis Ryan, "American Catholics, Fascism, and Holocaust Silence," paper presented at the Silver Anniversary Annual Scholars Conference on the Holocaust and the Churches, March 7, 1994, at Brigham Young University, Provo, Utah, 1–6.

9. Gordon C. Zahn, "An Incomplete Confession," *Commonweal*, December 15, 1995, 15–16; Robert S. Wistrich, "Helping Hitler," *Commentary* 102 (July 1996): 27–31.

10. Gordon C. Zahn, "Catholic Opposition to Hitler: The Perils of Ambiguity," *Journal of Church and State* 13 (Autumn 1971): 414–15; see also "Dialogue on a Dilemma," *America*, June 9, 1962, 377–79.

11. Quoted in Zahn, "Catholic Opposition to Hitler," 417–18.

12. Zahn, "Catholic Opposition to Hitler," 424.

13. Drinan, "The Christian Response to the Holocaust," 179.

14. Eva Fleischner, "Judaism, Christianity and Modernity after the Holocaust," in *Auschwitz: Beginning of a New Era? Reflections on the Holocaust*, ed. Eva Fleischner (New York: Ktav, Cathedral Church of St. John the Divine, Anti-Defamation League of B'nai B'rith, 1974), 11.

15. Ruether, *Faith and Fratricide*, 222.

16. Flannery, *The Anguish of the Jews*, 289–91.

17. Ibid., 290.

18. Ibid., 226–27, 294–95.

19. Quoted in Flannery, *The Anguish of the Jews*, 226.

20. Vidal Sassoon, "Foreword," in Harry James Cargas, *Reflections of a Post-Auschwitz Christian* (Detroit: Wayne State University Press, 1989), 9.

21. Cargas, *Reflections of a Post-Auschwitz Christian,* 13.

22. Ibid., 15, 17, 67–69.

23. Ibid., 162–73.

24. Sassoon, "Foreword," 10.

25. David P. Gushee, *The Righteous Gentiles of the Holocaust: A Christian Interpretation* (Minneapolis: Fortress Press, 1994), 156–59; Hans Kung, *Judaism: Between Yesterday and Tomorrow* (New York: Crossroad, 1992), 261–66.

26. Michael B. McGarry, "The Holocaust: Tragedy of Christian History," in *Introduction to Jewish-Christian Relations,* ed. Michael Shermis and Arthur E. Zannoni (New York: Paulist Press, 1991), 64–75.

27. Eugene J. Fisher, "The Holocaust and Christian Responsibility," *America,* February 14, 1981, 1.

28. Ibid.

29. Ibid., 3.

30. Willebrands, *Church and Jewish People,* 129.

31. Ibid., 131–32.

32. Pope John Paul II, "Homily at Auschwitz," June 7, 1979, quoted in *Pope John Paul II on Jews and Judaism, 1978–1986,* ed. Eugene J. Fisher and Leon Klenicki (Washington, D.C.: National Conference of Catholic Bishops; New York: Anti-Defamation League of B'nai B'rith, 1987), 26–27.

33. John Paul II, "Meditation on Judaism," quoted in *Reform Judaism* 23 (Spring 1995): 35.

34. Willebrands, *Church and Jewish People,* 68.

35. New York *Jewish Week,* April 1 and 15, 1994.

36. *New York Times,* April 8, 1994, sec. A, 6; Minneapolis *Star Tribune,* May 27, 1994; see also Minneapolis *Star Tribune,* November 1, 1997.

37. For a review of the document, see the *New York Times,* March 17, 1998, 1, sec. A, 10; see also "The Catholic Church and the Holocaust," *First Things* 83 (May 1998): 39–43.

38. *New York Times,* March 17, 1998, 1.

39. Ibid., sec. A, 11–12.

40. Ibid., sec. A, 10.

41. Editorial, "The Vatican Holocaust Report," *New York Times,* March 17, 1998, sec. A, 22.

42. Judith H. Banki, "Catholics and Jews," *Commonweal,* April 24, 1998, 10–11.

43. David Novak, "Jews and Catholics: Beyond Apologies," *First Things* 89 (January 1999): 21.

44. Ibid., 23, 24.

45. New York *Jewish Week,* May 15, 1998.

46. Paul Ellis, "John Paul's Jewish Dilemma," *New York Times Magazine,* April 22, 1998, 34.

47. Ibid., 37.

48. Ibid., 39.

49. Wistrich, "The Pope, the Church, and the Jews," 24.

50. Eugene J. Fisher, "The Start of the Healing Process," *The Jerusalem Report,* April 16, 1998, 38.

51. "Misremembered," *Commonweal,* April 10, 1998, 5.

52. Ibid., 5–6.

53. Eric J. Greenberg, "Will Pope Bail Out Flawed Catholic Text?," New York *Jewish Week,* August 14, 1998.

54. "Remembering the Holocaust," *First Things* 83 (May 1998): 65.

55. Avery Dulles, "Should the Church Repent?," *First Things* 93 (December 1998): 36–41.

56. Greenberg, "Will the Pope Bail Out Flawed Vatican Text?"

57. See Pawlikowski, "The Holocaust and Catholic Theology," 6; such writers as Eva Fleischner, Gregory Baum, David Tracy, Edward Flannery, and Michael B. McGarry are among those who also focus strongly on the implications of the *Shoah.*

58. Rosemary Radford Ruether and Herman J. Ruether, *The Wrath of Jonah: The Crisis of Religious Nationalism in the Israeli-Palestinian Conflict* (San Francisco: Harper and Row, 1989), 204–5.

59. John T. Pawlikowski, "The Holocaust: Its Implications for the Church and Society Problematic," *Encounter* 42 (Spring 1981): 143.

60. Pawlikowski, "The Contemporary Jewish-Christian Theological Dialogue Agenda," 611–12.

61. Ibid., 112; see also John T. Pawlikowski, "The Holocaust as a Rational Event," *The Reconstructionist* 39 (April 1974): 7–14.

62. John T. Pawlikowski, "The Challenge of the Holocaust for Christian Theology," in *Thinking the Unthinkable: Meanings of the Holocaust,* ed. Roger S. Gottlieb (New York: Paulist Press, 1990), 240–42.

63. Pawlikowski, "The Holocaust and Catholic Theology," 6; see also Pawlikowski, "The Holocaust: Its Implications," 144.

64. Pawlikowski, "The Challenge of the Holocaust," 243.

65. Pawlikowski, "The Holocaust and Catholic Theology," 7; see also Pawlikowski, "The Holocaust: Its Implications," 143–45.

66. John T. Pawlikowski, "Toward a Theology for Religious Diversity: Perspectives from the Christian-Jewish Dialogue," *Journal of Ecumenical Studies* 26 (Winter 1989): 146.

67. Pawlikowski, "The Challenge of the Holocaust," 243–44, 252. See also Pawlikowski, "The Holocaust and Catholic Theology," 6; my conversation with Henry Feingold.

68. Pawlikowski, "The Challenge of the Holocaust," 255.

69. Letter to me from Father John T. Pawlikowski, April 1, 1995.

70. Eugene J. Fisher, "Ani Ma'amin: Directions in Holocaust Theology," *Interface* 5 (Winter 1980): 1.

71. Marcel Jacques Dubois, "Christian Reflection on the Holocaust," *SIDIC* 7, no. 2 (1974): 13.

72. Schwartz, *A Jewish Appraisal of Dialogue*, 94–95.

73. Ibid., 97–98.

74. Elie Wiesel, ed., *A Journey of Faith* (New York: Fine, 1990), 15.

75. Ibid., 69.

76. Richard L. Rubenstein, *After Auschwitz: Radical Theory and Contemporary Judaism* (Indianapolis: Bobbs Merrill, 1966), 75.

77. Ibid., 80.

78. See John T. Pawlikowski, "The Shoah: Continuing Theological Challenge for Christians," in *Contemporary Christian Religious Responses to the Shoah*, ed. Steven L. Jacobs (Lanham, Md.: University Press of America, 1993), 147.

79. Michael B. McGarry, "Emil Fackenheim and Christianity after the Holocaust," *American Journal of Theology and Philosophy* 9 (January–May 1988): 117–19, 130–35.

80. Ibid., 122.

81. Ibid., 123–26.

82. Ibid., 135.

83. Gregory Baum, "Theology after Auschwitz: A Conference Report," *The Ecumenist* 12 (July/August 1974): 65–69.

84. Irving Greenberg, "Cloud of Smoke, Pillar of Fire: Judaism, Christianity, and Modernity after the Holocaust," in *Auschwitz: Beginning of a New Era? Reflections on the Holocaust*, ed. Eva Fleischner (New York: Ktav, Cathedral Church of St. John the Divine, Anti-Defamation League of B'nai B'rith, 1974), 7–8; see also Irving Greenberg, "Religious Values after the Holocaust: A Jewish View," in *Jews and Christians after the Holocaust*, ed. Abraham J. Peck (Philadelphia: Fortress Press, 1982), 63–85.

85. Greenberg, "Cloud of Smoke, Pillar of Fire," 9; see also Irving Greenberg, "Judaism and Christianity after the Holocaust," *Journal of Ecumenical Studies* 12 (Special Issue, Fall 1975): 521–22, 525–27.

86. Greenberg, "Cloud of Smoke, Pillar of Fire," 20.

87. Ibid., 22–23.

88. Ibid., 26–27, 30–31.

89. Ibid., 39–40.

Chapter 13: Burden and Triumph of Jewish Sovereignty, 1949–99

1. George Emile Irani, *The Papacy and the Middle East: The Role of the Holy See in the Arab-Israeli Conflict, 1962–1984* (Notre Dame: University of Notre Dame Press, 1986), 16–18.

2. Ibid., 18.

3. Anthony J. Kenny, *Catholics, Jews and the State of Israel* (New York: Paulist Press, 1993), 43–44.

4. Ibid., 46.

5. Ibid., 47–49.

6. For a full report of Pope Paul's pilgrimage to the Middle East, see Cornell, *Voyage of Faith*.

7. Cornell, *Voyage of Faith*, 57–58.

8. Quoted in Cornell, *Voyage of Faith*, 63.

9. Cornell, *Voyage of Faith*, 97.

10. Quoted in Cornell, *Voyage of Faith*, 97–98.

11. Cornell, *Voyage of Faith*, 99.

12. Ibid., 97–99, 114–16.

13. Friedrich Heer, "The Catholic Church and the Jews Today," *Midstream* 17 (May 1971): 24.

14. Polish, "A Very Small Lever," 84.

15. See Ian J. Bickerton and Carla L. Klausner, *A Concise History of the Arab-Israeli Conflict* (Englewood Cliffs, N.J.: Prentice Hall, 1991), 146–56.

16. Ibid., 150–51.

17. Ibid., 152–53; for a more detailed account of the Six-Day War, consult Sachar, *A History of Israel*, 615–64.

18. Greenberg, "Cloud of Smoke, Pillar of Fire," 47.

19. "A Letter Written by the President of the National Conference of Catholic Bishops, June 8, 1967," in *Pastoral Letters of the United States Catholic Bishops*, vol. 3, 1962–74, ed. Hugh J. Nolan (Washington, D.C.: National Conference of Catholic Bishops, United States Catholic Conference, 1983), 88.

20. John B. Sheerin, "The Arab-Israeli War and Catholic-Jewish Dialogue," *Catholic World* 205 (August 1967): 260.

21. Ibid., 260–62.

22. Heer, *God's First Love*, 3.

23. John M. Oesterreicher, "A Statement of Conscience," *The Bridge* 5 (1970): 291–92.

24. Ibid., 293.

25. Gilbert, *The Vatican Council and the Jews*, 238; see also Jacob Agus, "Israel and the Jewish-Christian Dialogue," *Journal of Ecumenical Studies* 5 (Winter 1969): 18–36.

26. Pawlikowski, *Sinai and Calvary*, 190.

27. Kenny, *Catholics, Jews and the State of Israel*, 30; Edward H. Flannery, "Israel, Jerusalem and the Middle East," in *Twenty Years of Jewish-Catholic Relations*, ed. Eugene J. Fisher et al., 83–84.

28. "Introduction," in *Pastoral Letters of the United States Catholic Bishops*, vol. 3, 1962–74, ed. Hugh J. Nolan (Washington, D.C.: National Conference of Catholic Bishops, United States Catholic Conference, 1983), 223–25.

29. John Oesterreicher, "Christianity Threatened in Israel," *Midstream* 19 (January 1973): 3–4.

30. Ibid., 6, 8.

31. "Resolution Towards Peace in the Middle East: A Statement of the National Conference of Catholic Bishops, November, 1973," in *Pastoral Letters*

of the United States Catholic Bishops, vol. 3, 1962–74, ed. Hugh J. Nolan (Washington, D.C.: National Conference of Catholic Bishops, United States Catholic Conference, 1983), 389.

32. Egal Feldman, "Conflict or Consensus in Israel's Visions of Judea and Samaria," *Middle East Review* 15 (Spring–Summer, 1983): 50.

33. New York *Jewish Week,* May 18, 1990.

34. American Jewish Committee, *Christians Support Unified Jerusalem* (New York: American Jewish Committee, 1971), 1–5, 15–19.

35. Ibid., 15–19.

36. Ibid., 17.

37. Eugene J. Fisher, "The Pope and Israel," *Commonweal,* January 11, 1985, 16–17.

38. John M. Oesterreicher, "Introduction," in *Jerusalem,* ed. John M. Oesterreicher and Anne Sinai (New York: John Day Company, 1974), xv.

39. John M. Oesterreicher, "Jerusalem the Free," in *Jerusalem,* ed. John M. Oesterreicher and Anne Sinai (New York: John Day Company, 1974), 250, 254, 258–60.

40. Ibid., xv, 249–51.

41. Flannery, "Israel, Jerusalem and the Middle East," 82–83.

42. "There Is Only One Jerusalem," *First Things* 56 (October 1995): 84–85.

43. "Joint Protestant-Catholic Document," in *Stepping Stones to Further Jewish-Christian Relations,* ed. Helga Croner (New York: Paulist Press, 1977), 153.

44. Ibid., 153–54.

45. Ibid., 154.

46. New York *Jewish Week,* January 10, 1992.

47. John Cardinal O'Connor and Mayor Edward I. Koch, *His Eminence and Hizzoner: A Candid Exchange* (New York: Morrow, 1989), 18; see also Wiesel, *A Journey of Faith,* 23–25.

48. Quoted in the New York *Jewish Week,* October 20, 1989.

49. Ibid.

50. See, for example, Kenny, *Catholics, Jews and the State of Israel,* 57–60, 114–19.

51. Cushing, "On the Dialogue and on Israel," 230.

52. Drinan, *Honor the Promise,* 4, 14.

53. Ibid., 176.

54. Ibid., 193.

55. Ibid., 203.

56. New York *Jewish Week,* August 11, 1990.

57. Flannery, "Israel, Jerusalem and the Middle East," 73–74, 76–77.

58. Ibid., 78–79; see also Edward H. Flannery, "Zionism, the State of Israel and the Jewish-Christian Dialogue," *Judaism* 27 (Summer 1978): 313–17; Flannery, "Seminaries, Classrooms, Pulpits, Streets," 142–48; Siegman, "A Decade of Catholic-Jewish Relations," 250–52.

59. Eugene J. Fisher, "Anti-Semitism: A Contemporary Christian Perspective," *Judaism* 30 (Summer 1981): 278.

60. Greenberg, "Cloud of Smoke, Pillar of Fire," 41.

61. Lipset and Raab, *Jews and the New American Scene*, 136–37.

62. Charlotte Klein, "The Theological Dimensions of the State of Israel," *Journal of Ecumenical Studies* 10 (Winter 1973): 700–715.

63. John T. Pawlikowski, "The Theological Significance of the State of Israel for Christians," *Engage/Social Action* 4 (December 1976): 34.

64. Ibid., 35.

65. Ibid., 38; see also Eugene Fisher, "Christian-Jewish Dialogue: From Theology to the Classroom," *Origins*, August 27, 1981, 170.

66. Pawlikowski, "The Theological Significance of the State of Israel," 39.

67. Kenny, *Catholics, Jews and the State of Israel*, 88–89.

68. For Jewish anti-Zionism, see, for example, Wolfgang Hamburger, "The Zionizing of Reform Judaism," *Issues of the American Council for Judaism* (Fall 1998): 1–2, 7–11; for the early history of non-Orthodox Jewish anti-Zionism, see Thomas A. Kolsky, *Jews against Zionism* (Philadelphia: Temple University Press, 1990).

69. Edward H. Flannery, "Anti-Zionism and the Christian Psyche," *Journal of Ecumenical Studies* 6 (Spring 1969): 173–84.

70. Ibid., 174.

71. Ibid., 177.

72. Ibid.

73. Drinan, *Honor the Promise*, 186.

74. Lillian C. Freudmann, *Antisemitism in the New Testament* (Lanham, Md.: University Press of America, 1994), 311.

75. Drinan, *Honor the Promise*, 121.

76. Ibid., 122–30.

77. Quoted in Drinan, *Honor the Promise*, 126.

78. Ibid., 230.

79. Kenny, *Catholics, Jews and the State of Israel*, 48–50.

80. George Weigel, *Witness to Hope: The Biography of Pope John Paul II* (New York: Cliff Street Books, 1999), 549–50.

81. "Apostolic Letter of John Paul II *Redemptionis Annos*, April 28, 1984," in *John Paul II on Jews and Judaism, 1978–1986*, ed. Eugene J. Fisher and Leon Klenicki (Washington, D.C.: National Conference of Catholic Bishops; New York: Anti-Defamation League of B'nai B'rith, 1987), 56.

82. See, for example, Willebrands, *Church and Jewish People*, 65–69.

83. Kenny, *Catholics, Jews and the State of Israel*, 13.

84. Ibid., 16–20, 26.

85. Ibid., 28–29.

86. New York *Jewish Week*, August 7, 1992; January 22, 1993.

87. Weigel, *Witness to Hope*, 701.

88. Ibid.

89. New York *Jewish Week*, June 18, 1993.

90. *New York Times*, December 31, 1993, sec. A, 1, 4.

91. For the progress of negotiations which led to the final diplomatic exchange between Israel and the Holy See, see Weigel, *Witness to Hope*, 697–709. For the full text of the agreement, see *Near East Report*, January 10, 1994, 6–8.

92. His Holiness John Paul II, *Crossing the Threshold of Hope*, ed. Vittorio Messori (New York: Knopf, 1994), 100 (first and second quotes); Weigel, *Witness to Hope*, 700 (third quote).

93. Quoted in *New York Times*, December 31, 1993, sec. A, 1.

94. Ibid., sec. A, 4; see also *New York Times*, January 6, 1994, sec. A, 12; New York *Jewish Week*, January 7, 1994.

95. New York *Jewish Week*, January 21, 1994.

96. "Eminent Embrace," *The Jerusalem Report*, April 21, 1994, 18–19.

97. New York *Jewish Week*, January 7, 1994.

98. Edward Idris Cardinal Cassidy, "The Next Issues in Catholic-Jewish Relations," *Journal of Ecumenical Studies* 34 (Summer 1997): 363.

99. Mark L. Winer, "Visions for the Future: Catholic-Jewish Relations Worldwide," *Journal of Ecumenical Studies* 34 (Summer 1997): 370–71.

Conclusion

1. See, for example, Paul M. Van Buren, *Discerning the Way: A Theology of the Jewish-Christian Reality* (New York: Seabury Press, 1980); A. Roy Eckardt, *Your People, My People: The Meeting of Jews and Christians* (New York: New York Times Book Company, 1974); Franklin H. Littell, *The Church and the Body Politic* (New York: Seabury Press, 1969).

2. Arthur Hertzberg, "The Catholic-Jewish Dispute That Won't Go Away," *Reform Judaism* 28 (Winter 1999): 30.

3. Willebrands, *Church and Jewish People*, 39–40.

4. New York *Jewish Week*, June 13, 1991.

5. Ibid., May 29, 1998.

6. See Lipset and Raab, *Jews and the New American Scene*, 27–28, 47.

7. *USA Today*, April 24, 1998; New York *Jewish Week*, November 11, 1998; *Arizona Republic*, November 24, 1998; Daniel Pipes, "America's Muslims against America's Jews," *Commentary* 107 (May 1999): 32–36.

8. Flannery, "Seminaries, Classrooms, Pulpits, Streets," 139.

9. Minneapolis *Star Tribune*, July 20, 1999.

10. For a review of the Auschwitz convent controversy, I have relied primarily upon Rittner and Roth, *Memory Offended*, and Weigel, *Witness to Hope*.

11. Carol Rittner and John K. Roth, "Introduction: Memory Offended," in *Memory Offended: The Auschwitz Convent Controversy*, ed. Carol Rittner and John K. Roth (New York: Praeger, 1990), 5–6.

12. Weigel, *Witness to Hope*, 668; Rabbi Avraham Weiss, "Let the Nuns Pray

Elsewhere,' October 15, 1989," in *Memory Offended: The Auschwitz Convent Controversy*, ed. Carol Rittner and John K. Roth (New York: Praeger, 1990), 255–57.

13. Eva Fleischner, "Contemplation and Controversy," *Commonweal*, June 20, 1986, 368, 370–71.

14. John T. Pawlikowski, "A Sign of Contradiction: Pain to Jews, Shame to Catholics," *Commonweal*, September 22, 1989, 485–86.

15. Ibid., 487–88.

16. Joseph Cardinal Bernardin, "Together We Can Move Mountains: Reflections on Catholic-Jewish Relations Today," *Christian-Jewish Relations* 23 (Summer 1990): 20–21.

17. "Close Enough to Step on Toes," *Commonweal*, October 6, 1989, 526; see also Richard John Neuhaus, "Interreligious Brinksmanship," *First Things* 1 (March 1990): 67–68.

18. Elie Wiesel and Carol Rittner, "An Interview, August 29, 1989," in *Memory Offended: The Auschwitz Convent Controversy*, ed. Carol Rittner and John K. Roth (New York: Praeger, 1990), 113–16.

19. Ibid., 116.

20. Judith Hershcopf Banki, "Historical Memories in Conflict," in *Memory Offended: The Auschwitz Convent Controversy*, ed. Carol Rittner and John K. Roth (New York: Praeger, 1990), 157.

21. Ibid., 163–64.

22. Weigel, *Witness to Hope*, 669–70; New York *Jewish Week*, February 19, 1993.

23. Weigel, *Witness to Hope*, 548.

24. Ibid., 549.

25. Cargas, *Reflections of a Post-Auschwitz Christian*, 122.

26. Schwartz, *A Jewish Appraisal of Dialogue*, 115–16.

27. *New York Times*, August 12, 1994, sec. A, 15.

28. Minneapolis *Star Tribune*, July 28, 1994.

29. New York *Jewish Week*, September 7, 1994.

30. Ibid., August 5, 1994.

31. Minneapolis *Star Tribune*, August 17, 1994.

32. Weigel, *Witness to Hope*, 549.

33. McBrien, *The HarperCollins Encyclopedia of Catholicism*, 146, 218–20, 1155–57; "Becoming Saint Trickier than Going to Heaven," *National Catholic Review*, October 23, 1998.

34. David Novak, "Edith Stein, Apostate Saint," *First Things* 96 (October 1999): 17.

35. New York *Jewish Week*, January 11, 1991.

36. Quoted in New York *Jewish Week*, January 11, 1991.

37. Quoted in Louis Auster, "The Storm over Sainthood for Queen Isabella," *Midstream* 38 (June–July 1992): 23.

38. New York *Jewish Week*, February 7, 1991.

39. Quoted in New York *Jewish Week,* January 11, 1991.

40. Auster, "The Storm over Sainthood," 24.

41. Ibid.; Debra Nussbaum Cohen, "Jews Hail Vatican Stand against Sainthood for Queen Isabella," New York *Jewish Week,* March 29, 1991.

42. Auster, "The Storm over Sainthood," 24.

43. Cohen, "Jews Hail Vatican Stand."

44. Weigel, *Witness to Hope,* 539–40.

45. Ibid., 540–41.

46. Quoted in Weigel, *Witness to Hope,* 541.

47. *USA Today,* October 12, 1998, 2A; *National Catholic Reporter,* October 23, 1998; David Van Biema, "A Martyr—But Whose?," *Time,* October 10, 1998, 98–99.

48. James Carroll, "The Saint and the Holocaust," *New Yorker,* June 7, 1999, 52.

49. Ibid., 53.

50. Ibid.

51. Van Biema, "A Martyr—But Whose?," 98; New York *Jewish Week,* October 16, 1998.

52. Novak, "Edith Stein, Apostate Saint," 15–16.

53. Ibid., 17.

54. Tom Tugend, "Jewish Group Opposes Sainthood for Holocaust Pope," New York *Jewish Week,* March 12, 1993.

55. Ibid.

56. New York *Jewish Week,* December 8, 1998; Ellis, "John Paul's Jewish Dilemma," 35; New York *Jewish Week,* October 9, 1998.

57. Eric J. Greenberg, "Jews, Catholics in 'Search for Truth,'" New York *Jewish Week,* December 10, 1999.

58. Hertzberg, "The Catholic-Jewish Dispute That Won't Go Away," 30.

59. *National Catholic Reporter,* December 11, 1998.

60. Greenberg, "Jews, Catholics in 'Search for Truth'" (first quote); Gustav Niebuhr, "Panel to Study World War II Vatican," *New York Times,* December 4, 1999, sec. A, 12 (second and third quotes).

61. According to the Catholic theologian, Lorenzo Albacete, who teaches at St. Joseph's Seminary in Yonkers, New York, the papal apology was offered not only on behalf of individuals but for the Church as well. See, *New York Times,* March 13, 2000, sec. A, 1, 10.

62. David Van Biema, "Inside the Pilgrimage," *Time,* March 20, 2000, 51; Steven E. Plaut, "Pontificating," *Midstream* 56 (April 2000): 2; *New York Times,* March 25, 2000, sec. A, 11.

Selected Bibliography

Articles

Agus, Jacob. "Israel and the Jewish-Christian Dialogue." *Journal of Ecumenical Studies* 5 (Winter 1969): 18–36.

Anscar, Hans. "Catholics and Anti-Semitism." *Catholic World* 150 (November 1939): 173–78.

Arendzen, J. P. "Hillel and Shamai." *Catholic World* 120 (February 1925): 624–35.

Athans, Mary Christine. "A New Perspective on Father Charles E. Coughlin." *Church History* 56 (June 1987): 224–35.

Auster, Louis. "The Storm over Sainthood for Queen Isabella." *Midstream* 38 (June–July 1992): 23–24.

Banki, Judith H. "Catholics and Jews." *Commonweal,* April 24, 1998, 10–11.

———. "The Image of Jews in Christian Teaching." *Journal of Ecumenical Studies* 21 (Summer 1984): 437–51.

Barrett, E. Boyd. "Will American Catholics Secede from Rome?" *Forum* 132 (August 1929): 89–94.

Baum, Gregory. "Catholic Dogma after Auschwitz." In *Antisemitism and the Foundations of Christianity,* ed. Alan Davies, 137–50. New York: Paulist Press, 1978.

———. "The Jews, Faith and Ideology." *The Ecumenist* 10 (July/August 1972): 71–76.

———. "Rethinking the Church's Mission after Auschwitz." In *Auschwitz: Beginning of a New Era? Reflections on the Holocaust,* ed. Eva Fleischner, 113–28. New York: Ktav, The Cathedral Church of St. John the Divine, Anti-Defamation League of B'nai B'rith, 1974.

———. "Theology after Auschwitz: A Conference Report." *The Ecumenist* 12 (July/August 1974): 65–80.

Bernardin, Joseph Cardinal. "Together We Can Move Mountains: Reflections on Catholic-Jewish Relations Today." *Christian-Jewish Relations* 23 (Summer 1990): 19–27.

Blanchi, Eugene C. "A Talk with Cardinal Bea." *America,* August 11, 1962, 584–90.

Bookman, Terry A. "The Holy Conversation: Towards a Jewish Theology of Dialogue." *Journal of Ecumenical Studies* 32 (Spring 1995): 207–25.

Boys, Mary C. "The Sisters of Sion: From Conversionist Stance to a Dialogical Way of Life." *Journal of Ecumenical Studies* 31 (Winter–Spring 1994): 27–48.

Brégy, Katherine. "The Passionsspiele of 1910: An Impression." *Catholic World* 91 (October 1910): 42–50.

Bretton-Granatoor, Gary M. "UAHC Advances Catholic-Jewish Relations." *Reform Judaism* 23 (Spring 1995): 38.

Carroll, James. "The Saint and the Holocaust." *New Yorker,* June 7, 1999, 52–57.

Cassidy, Edward Idris Cardinal. "The Next Issues in Catholic-Jewish Relations." *Journal of Ecumenical Studies* 34 (Summer 1997): 362–69.

"The Catholic Church and the Holocaust." *First Things* 83 (May 1998): 39–43.

Chirico, Peter. "Christian and Jew Today from a Christian Theological Perspective." *Journal of Ecumenical Studies* 7 (Fall 1970): 744–62.

"Close Enough to Step on Toes." *Commonweal,* October 6, 1989, 521–26.

Cohen, Arthur A. "The Natural and the Supernatural Jew: Two Views of the Church." In *American Catholics: A Protestant-Jewish View,* ed. Philip Scharper, 126–57. New York: Sheed and Ward, 1959.

Coughlin, Bernard J. "Interfaith Dialogue and Church-State Issues." *America,* June 29, 1963, 900–903.

Crabites, Pierre. "Palestine Problems." *Commonweal,* January 29, 1930, 360–61.

———. "Palestine and Zionism." *Catholic World* 146 (October 1937): 12–18.

———. "Toward Peace in Palestine." *Catholic World* 148 (February 1939): 553–60.

Crosby, Donald F. "Boston's Catholics and the Spanish Civil War: 1936–1939." *New England Quarterly* 44 (March–December 1971): 82–100.

Cross, Robert D. "The Meaning of the Holy Land to American Catholics in the 19th Century." In *With Eyes toward Zion,* vol. 2, ed. Moshe Davis, 333–41. New York: Praeger, 1986.

Cushing, Richard Cardinal. "On the Dialogue and on Israel." *The Bridge* 5 (1970): 248–52.

"Dialogue on a Dilemma." *America,* June 9, 1962, 377–79.

Dietrich, Wendell S. "*Nostra Aetate:* A Typology of Theological Tendencies." In *Unanswered Questions: Theological Views of Jewish-Christian Relations,* ed. Roger Brooks, 70–81. Notre Dame: University of Notre Dame Press, 1988.

Dinnerstein, Leonard. "The Funeral of Rabbi Jacob Joseph." In *Anti-Semitism in American History,* ed. David A. Gerber, 275–301. Urbana: University of Illinois Press, 1987.

Donahue, John R. "From Crucified Messiah to Risen Christ: The Trial of Jesus Revisited." In *Jews and Christians Speak of Jesus,* ed. Arthur E. Zannoni, 93–121. Minneapolis: Fortress Press, 1994.

Dondeyne, Albert. "Tolerance and Collaboration as Facts of Philosophy Assumed into Faith." In *Tolerance and the Catholic: A Symposium,* translated by George Lamb, 91–94. New York: Sheed and Ward, 1955.

Dorff, Elliot N. "The Covenant as the Key: A Jewish Theology of Jewish-Christian Relations." In *Toward a Theological Encounter: Jewish Understandings of Christianity,* ed. Leon Klenicki, 43–66. New York: Paulist Press, 1991.

Doyle, A. P. "Encyclical Letter of Leo XIII." *Catholic World* 72 (January 1901): 426–27.

Doyle, Thomas F. "The Sin of Anti-Semitism." *Catholic World* 151 (July 1940): 433–42.

Drinan, Robert F. "The Christian Response to the Holocaust." *American Academy of Political and Social Science* 450 (July 1980): 179–89.

Drummond, William F. "Pacifism and War." *Catholic Mind,* July 8, 1940, 241–48.

Dubois, Marcel Jacques. "Christian Reflection on the Holocaust." *SIDIC* 7, no. 2 (1974): 4–15.

Dulles, Avery. "Should the Church Repent?" *First Things* 93 (December 1998): 36–41.

"Ecumenical Commission—Archdiocese of Detroit, 1979." *More Stepping Stones to Jewish-Christian Relations,* ed. Helga Croner, 87–91. New York: Paulist Press, 1985.

Ellert, Frederick C. "Franz Werfel's Great Dilemma." *The Bridge* 4 (1961): 197–226.

Ellis, Paul. "John Paul's Jewish Dilemma." *New York Times Magazine,* April 22, 1998, 34–39.

Ewing, Franklin. "Twenty-five Years Ago, the Nazis. . . ." *Catholic World* 196 (November 1962): 110–17.

"Father Coughlin, Al Smith and the Popular Mind." *Catholic World* 138 (March 1934): 641–51.

Feige, Gregory. "In Exitu Israel." *Commonweal,* February 16, 1937, 504–05.

Fisher, Eugene J. "Ani Ma'amin: Directions in Holocaust Theology." *Interface* 5 (Winter 1980): 1–9.

———. "Anti-Semitism: A Contemporary Christian Perspective." *Judaism* 30 (Summer 1981): 276–82.

———. "Christian-Jewish Dialogue: From Theology to the Classroom." *Origins,* August 27, 1981, 167–75.

———. "The Evolution of a Tradition: From *Nostra Aetate* to the 'Notes.'" *Christian-Jewish Relations* 18 (December 1985): 32–47.

———. "Heschel's Impact on Catholic-Jewish Relations." In *No Religion Is an Island: Abraham Joshua Heschel and Interreligious Dialogue,* ed. Harold Kasimow and Byron L. Sherwin, 110–23. Maryknoll, N.Y.: Orbis Books, 1991.

———. "The Holy See and the State of Israel: The Evolution of Attitudes and Policies." *Journal of Ecumenical Studies* 24 (Spring 1987): 191–209.

———. "Jews and Christians: The Next Step for Theology." *Commonweal,* November 5, 1982, 588–90.

———. "The Pope and Israel." *Commonweal,* January 11, 1985, 16–17.

———. "Research on Christian Teaching Concerning Jews and Judaism: Past Research and Present Needs." *Journal of Ecumenical Studies* 21 (Summer 1984): 421–37.

———. "Whither Christian-Jewish Relations." *Doctrine and Life* 33 (April 1983): 226–35.

Flannery, Edward H. "Anti-Zionism and the Christian Psyche." *Journal of Ecumenical Studies* 6 (Spring 1969): 173–84.

———. "The Finaly Case." *The Bridge* 1 (1955): 292–313.

———. "Hope and Despair at Evanston." *The Bridge* 2 (1956): 271–91.

———. "Israel, Jerusalem and the Middle East." In *Twenty Years of Jewish-Catholic Relations,* ed. Eugene J. Fisher et al., 81–86. New York: Paulist Press, 1986.

———. "Jesus, Israel and Christian Renewal." *Journal of Ecumenical Studies* 9 (Winter 1972): 74–92.

———. "Jewish-Christian Relations Focus on the Future." *Journal of Ecumenical Studies* 34 (Summer 1997): 322–25.

———. "Jews and Christians: Challenges to Face Together." *Origins,* June 20, 1985, 70–74.

———. "Seminaries, Classrooms, Pulpits, Streets: Where We Have to Go." In *Unanswered Questions: Theological Views of Jewish-Catholic Relations,* ed. Roger Brooks, 128–49. Notre Dame: University of Notre Dame Press, 1988.

———. "Zionism, The State of Israel and the Jewish Christian Dialogue." *Judaism* 27 (Summer 1978): 313–17.

Fleischner, Eva. "Contemplation and Controversy." *Commonweal,* June 20, 1986, 368, 370–71.

———. "Heschel's Significance for Jewish-Christian Relations." *Quarterly Review* 4 (Winter 1984): 64–81.

———. "Judaism, Christianity and Modernity after the Holocaust." In *Auschwitz: Beginning of a New Era? Reflections on the Holocaust,* ed. Eva Fleischner, 11–13. New York: Ktav, The Cathedral Church of St. John the Divine, Anti-Defamation League of B'nai B'rith, 1974.

Ford, J. Massingberd. "The Christian Debt to Pharisaism." *The Bridge* 5 (1970): 218–30.

Freedman, David Noel. "Readers' Response: An Essay on Jewish Christianity." *Journal of Ecumenical Studies* 5 (Winter 1969): 81–86.

Garbaghan, Gilbert J. "The Anti-Jesuit Decree of the Spanish Republic." *Catholic Mind,* January 22, 1933, 21–37.

Gibbons, William J. "Europe's Homeless." *America,* October 19, 1946, 65–66.

———. "The Lesson of Palestine." *America,* May 18, 1946, 130–32.

Gilbert, Arthur. "Jews, Prejudice and Catholic Practice." In *American Catholics: A Protestant-Jewish View,* ed. Philip Scharper, 159–90. New York: Sheed and Ward, 1959.

Gilbert, Arthur, and Walter M. Abbott. "Christians Failed Jewish Hopes." *America,* March 24, 1962, 825–28.

Goldstein, David. "Religious Campaiging in American Streets." *Catholic World* 121 (August 1925): 645–52.

Godden, G. M. "How Communism Attacked Spain." *Catholic World* 144 (January 1937): 403–07.

Gorayer, Joseph. "The Near East since the War." *Catholic World* 114 (December 1921): 319–32.

Gordis, Robert. "The Interfaith Movement—A Multiple Vision." *Judaism* 35 (Winter 1986): 7–9.

Graham, Robert A. "The Latest Charges against Pius XII." *America,* May 21, 1966, 733–36.

"The Great Problem in Spain." *Catholic World* 145 (June 1937): 260.

Greenberg, Irving. "Cloud of Smoke, Pillar of Fire: Judaism, Christianity, and Modernity After the Holocaust." In *Auschwitz: Beginning of a New Era? Reflections on the Holocaust,* ed. Eva Fleischner, 7–55. New York: Ktav, The Cathedral Church of St. John the Divine, Anti-Defamation League of B'nai B'rith, 1974.

———. "Judaism and Christianity after the Holocaust." *Journal of Ecumenical Studies* 12 (Special Issue, Fall 1975): 521–22, 525–51.

———. "Religious Values after the Holocaust: A Jewish View." In *Jews and Christians after the Holocaust,* ed. Abraham J. Peck, 63–85. Philadelphia: Fortress Press, 1982.

"Guidelines of Archdiocese Galveston-Houston, 1975." In *More Stepping Stones to Jewish-Christian Relations: An Unabridged Collection of Christian Documents, 1975–1983,* ed. Helga Croner, 65–73. New York: Paulist Press, 1985.

"Guidelines: Diocese of Cleveland, 1979." In *More Stepping Stones to Jewish-Christian Relations: An Unabridged Collection of Christian Documents, 1975–1983,* ed. Helga Croner, 85–86. New York: Paulist Press, 1985.

Gundlach, Gustav. "Moral Estimate of the Nuremberg Trial." *America,* November 9, 1946, 149–51.

Hartman, David. "Creating Space for the Integrity of the Other." *SIDIC* 15, no. 2 (1982): 5–10.

———. "Jews and Christians in the World of Tomorrow." *Immanuel* 6 (Spring 1976): 70–81.

Hayes, Carlton J. H. "Nationalism as a Religion: A Tribal Creed." *Commonweal,* January 13, 1926, 262–63.

Hebblethwaite, Peter. "John Paul XXIII." In *The Encyclopedia of Catholicism,* general editor, Richard P. McBrien, 709–10. San Francisco: HarperCollins, 1995.

Heer, Friedrich. "The Catholic Church and the Jews Today." *Midstream* 17 (May 1971): 20–31.

Hellwig, Monika. "Christian Theology and the Covenant of Israel." *Journal of Ecumenical Studies* 7 (Winter 1970): 37–51.

———. "From the Jesus of Story to the Christ of Dogma." In *Antisemitism and the Foundations of Christianity,* ed. Alan Davies, 118–36. New York: Paulist Press, 1979.

Herberg, Will. "Justice for Religious Schools." *America,* November 16, 1957, 190–93.

Hermens, Ferdinand A. "Germany and a Christian Peace." *Catholic World* 158 (February 1944): 427–34.

———. "Punishment or Reconstruction?" *Catholic World* 160 (March 1945): 491–97.

Hershcopf, Judith. "The Church and the Jews: Struggle of Vatican II." In *American Jewish Year Book 1965,* vol. 66, 99–136. New York: American Jewish Committee; Philadelphia: Jewish Publication Society of America, 1965.

———. "The Church and the Jews: Struggle of Vatican II." In *American Jewish Year Book 1966,* vol. 67, 45–75. New York: American Jewish Committee; Philadelphia: Jewish Publication Society of America, 1966.

Hertzberg, Arthur. "The Catholic-Jewish Dispute That Won't Go Away." *Reform Judaism* 28 (Winter 1999): 30–33, 90.

Heschel, Abraham Joshua. "From Mission to Dialogue." *Conservative Judaism* 21 (Spring 1967): 1–11.

———. "No Religion Is An Island." In *No Religion Is an Island: Abraham Joshua Heschel and Interreligious Dialogue,* ed. Harold Kasimow and Byron L. Sherwin, 3–22. Maryknoll, N.Y.: Orbis, 1991.

Hickey, D. Harold "The Palestinian Arab Cause." *Catholic World* 143 (September 1936): 684–89.

Higgins, George G. "Reflections on the Ecumenical Council: A Catholic View." In *Judaism and the Christian Seminary Curriculum,* ed. J. Bruce Long, 61–71. Chicago: Loyola University Press, 1966.

Hughes, Philip. "War and the Catholic Tradition." *Catholic Mind,* October 22, 1939, 869–76.

Huth, Mary Jo. "Charles Vissani, OFM, and First American Catholic Pilgrimage to the Holy Land." *Holy Land* 10 (Spring 1990): 7–25.

Hyatt, David. "The Interfaith Movement." *Judaism* 27 (Summer 1978): 267–76.

Idinopulos, Thomas A., and Roy Bowen Ward. "Is Christology Inherently Anti-Semitic? A Critical Review of Rosemary Ruether's *Faith and Fratricide.*" *Journal of the American Academy of Religion* 45 (June 1977): 193–213.

Isaac, Jules. "The Crime of Deicide." In *The Star and the Cross: Essays on Jew-*

ish-Christian Relations, ed. Katharine T. Hargrove, 136–43. Milwaukee: Bruce, 1966.

Jacob, Walter. "The Judeo-Christian Dialogue in the Twentieth Century: The Jewish Response." In *Toward a Theological Encounter: Jewish Understandings of Christianity,* ed. Leon Klenicki, 67–84. New York: Paulist Press, 1991.

Janto, Stephen A. "Christ's Native Land in 1955." *Catholic World* 182 (December 1955): 173–79.

"The Jew and Jesus." *Commonweal,* January 25, 1928, 972–73.

"Jewish Preponderance." *Catholic World* 52 (November 1890): 200–207.

Jourdin, Cyprien. "Zionism in Palestine." *The Sign: A National Catholic Magazine* 1 (July 1922): 13–19.

Journet, Charles. "The Mysterious Destiny of Israel." *The Bridge* 2 (1956): 35–90.

Kapiszewski, Andrzej. "Polish-Jewish Conflicts in the United States at the Beginning of World War I." *Polish American Studies* 48 (Spring 1991): 63–78.

Kasimow, Harold. "Heschel's Prophetic Vision of Religious Pluralism." In *No Religion Is an Island: Abraham Joshua Heschel and Interreligious Dialogue,* eds. Harold Kasimow and Byron L. Sherwin, 79–96. Maryknoll, N.Y.: Orbis, 1991.

Kelley, Francis C. "The Church and the Immigrant." *Catholic Mind,* September 8, 1915, 471–84.

Kelley, John J. "The Dilemma of Oberammergau." *Christian Jewish Relations* 23 (Summer 1990): 28–32.

Klein, Charlotte. "From Conversion to Dialogue: I. The Sisters of Sion and the Jews." *Christian Jewish Relations* 15 (September 1982): 3–30.

———. "The Theological Dimensions of the State of Israel." *Journal of Ecumenical Studies* 10 (Winter 1973): 700–715.

Klenicki, Leon. "From Argument to Dialogue: *Nostra Aetate* Twenty-five Years Later." In *In Our Time: The Flowering of Jewish-Catholic Dialogue,* ed. Eugene Fisher and Leon Klenicki, 77–103. New York: Paulist Press, 1990.

Kohler, Thomas. "In Praise of Little Platoons. *Quadragesimo Anno* (1931)." In *Building the Free Society: Democracy, Capitalism, and Catholic Social Teaching,* ed. George Weigel and Robert Royal, 31–50. Grand Rapids, Mich.: Eerdmans; and Washington, D.C.: Ethics and Public Policy Center, 1993.

Kuehnelt-Leddihn, Erik V. "Do Jews Make Good Catholics?" *Catholic World* 164 (December 1946): 212–16.

———. "Do Jews Tend toward Communism?" *Catholic World* 164 (December 1946): 107–13.

Lauer, Quentin. "Love Links Christian with Jew." *America,* February 11, 1956, 529–30.

Lichten, Joseph L. "Jules Isaac: The Teaching of Contempt." In *The Star and the Cross: Essays on Jewish-Christian Relations,* ed. Katharine T. Hargrove, 133–36. Milwaukee: Bruce, 1966.

————. "A Question of Judgement: Pius XII and the Jews." In *The Star and the Cross: Essays on Jewish-Christian Relations,* ed. Katharine T. Hargrove, 181–209. Milwaukee: Bruce, 1966.

————. "The Statement on the Jews." *Catholic World* 202 (March 1966): 357–63.

"Los Angeles Guidelines: Jewish-Catholic Dialogue, 1977." In *More Stepping Stones to Jewish-Christian Relations,* ed. Helga Croner, 74–78. New York: Paulist Press, 1985.

"The Mass Murder of Jews." *America,* June 12, 1943, 266.

Matt, Hershel. "How Shall a Believing Jew View Christianity?" In *Judaism and Christianity: A New Relationship,* ed. Jacob Neusner, 117–21, 124–27+. New York: Garland, 1993.

McCawley, James. "Atrocities—World War II." *Catholic World* 161 (August 1945): 378–84.

————. "Punish Only—The Guilty." *Catholic World* 161 (June 1945): 240–47.

McGarry, Michael B. "Contemporary Roman Catholic Understandings of Mission." In *Christian Mission—Jewish Mission,* ed. Martin A. Cohen and Helga Croner, 119–46. New York: Paulist Press, 1982.

————. "Emil Fackenheim and Christianity after the Holocaust." *American Journal of Theology and Philosophy* 9 (January–May 1988): 117–35.

————. "The Holocaust: Tragedy of Christian History." In *Introduction to Jewish-Christian Relations,* ed. Michael Shermis and Arthur E. Zannoni, 63–86. New York: Paulist Press, 1991.

McSorley, Joseph. "Jew Hatred?" *Catholic World* 188 (February 1959): 397.

Merkle, John C. "Heschel's Attitude towards Religious Pluralism." In *No Religion Is an Island: Abraham Joshua Heschel and Interreligious Dialogue,* ed. Harold Kasimow and Byron L. Sherwin, 97–109. Maryknoll, N.Y.: Orbis, 1991.

"Misremembered." *Commonweal,* April 10, 1998, 5–6.

Monks, Bernard J. "Franco of Spain." *Catholic World* 147 (September 1938): 667–74.

Murphy, John F. X. "The Problem of International Judaism." *Catholic Mind,* October 22, 1934, 381–97.

Murray, John Courtney. "The Declaration on Religious Freedom." In *Vatican II: An Interfaith Appraisal,* ed. John H. Miller, 565–76. Notre Dame: University of Notre Dame Press, 1966.

Nast, Ethel. "From Jerusalem to Nazareth on Horseback." *Catholic World* 70 (January 1900): 449–65.

Neuhaus, Richard John. "Interreligious Brinksmanship." *First Things* 1 (March 1990): 67–68.

"Neutrality? What do You Mean 'Neutrality'?" *Catholic World* 150 (November 1939): 129–37.

Novak, David. "Edith Stein, Apostate Saint." *First Things* 96 (October 1999): 15–17.

———. "A Jewish Theological Understanding of Christianity of Our Time." In *Toward a Theological Encounter: Jewish Understandings of Christianity*, ed. Leon Klenicki, 85–103. New York: Paulist Press, 1991.

———. "Jews and Catholics: Beyond Apologies." *First Things* 89 (January 1999): 20–25.

———. "The Quest for the Jewish Jesus." *Modern Judaism* 8 (May 1988): 119–38.

O'Brien, David J. "American Catholics and Anti-Semitism in the 1930's." *Catholic World* 204 (February 1967): 270–76.

O'Brien, Joseph L. "A Notable French Convert." *Catholic World* 101 (July 1915): 503–12.

O'Connell, Margaret. "St. Paul's Own People." *Catholic World* 186 (January 1958): 284–87.

Oesterreicher, John M. "As We Await 'The Deputy.'" *America*, November 9, 1963, 570–73, 576–82.

———. "Christianity Threatened in Israel." *Midstream* 19 (January 1973): 3–16.

———. "The Enigma of Simone Weil." *The Bridge* 1: (1955): 118–58.

———. "Statement of Conscience." *The Bridge* 5 (1970): 291–95.

Ostling, Richard N. "Why Was Christ Crucified?" *Time*, April 4, 1994, 72–73.

"The Passion Play." *America*, April 9, 1960, 41–42.

"The Passion Play at Ober-Ammergau, 1880." Part 1. *Catholic World* 31 (August 1880): 648–69.

"The Passion Play at Ober-Ammergau, 1880." Part 2. *Catholic World* 31 (September 1880): 736–57.

Paul, Leon. "What Is a Jewish Catholic?" *America*, October 5, 1957, 18–19.

Pawlikowski, John T. "The Challenge of the Holocaust for Christian Theology." In *Thinking the Unthinkable: Meanings of the Holocaust*, ed. Roger S. Gottlieb, 240–70. New York: Paulist Press, 1990.

———. "Christ and the Jewish-Christian Dialogue." *Chicago Studies: An Archdiocesan Review* 16 (Fall 1977): 367–89.

———. "The Contemporary Jewish-Christian Theological Dialogue Agenda." *Journal of Ecumenical Studies* 11 (Fall 1974): 599–616.

———. "The Holocaust and Catholic Theology: Some Reflections." *Shoah: A Review of Holocaust Studies and Commemorations* 2 (Spring–Summer 1980): 6–9.

———. "The Holocaust as a Rational Event." *The Reconstructionist* 39 (April 1974): 7–14.

———. "The Holocaust: Its Implications for the Church and Society Problematic." *Encounter* 42 (Spring 1981): 143–54.

———. "Jesus—A Pharisee and the Christ." In *Introduction to Jewish-Christian Relations*, ed. Michael Shermis and Arthur E. Zannoni, 174–201. New York: Paulist Press, 1991.

———. "The Jewish-Christian Dialogue: Assessment and Future Agenda." *Conservative Judaism* 32 (Winter 1979): 39–54.

———. "Jews and Christians: The Contemporary Dialogue." *Quarterly Review* 4 (Winter 1984): 23–36.

———. "New Trends in Catholic Religious Thought." In *Twenty Years of Jewish-Catholic Relations,* ed. Eugene Fisher et al., 169–90. New York: Paulist Press, 1986.

———. "On Renewing the Revolution of the Pharisees: A New Approach to Theology and Politics," *Cross Currents* 20 (Fall 1970): 415–34.

———. "The Shoah: Continuing Theological Challenge for Christians." In *Contemporary Christian Religious Responses to the Shoah,* ed. Steven L. Jacobs, 140–65. Lanham, Md.: University Press of America, 1993.

———. "A Sign of Contradiction: Pain to Jews, Shame to Catholics." *Commonweal,* September 22, 1989, 485–88.

———. "The Theological Significance of the State of Israel for Christians." *Engage/Social Action* 4 (December 1976): 34–40.

———. "A Theology of Religious Pluralism." In *Unanswered Questions: Theological Views of Jewish-Catholic Relations,* ed. Roger Brooks, 153–67. Notre Dame: University of Notre Dame Press, 1988.

———. "Toward a Theology for Religious Diversity: Perspectives from the Christian-Jewish Dialogue." *Journal of Ecumenical Studies* 26 (Winter 1989): 138–51.

Peck, Abraham J. "The Very Depths of Our Pain." In *Unanswered Questions: Theological Views of Jewish-Catholic Relations,* ed. Roger Brooks, 176–88. Notre Dame: University of Notre Dame Press, 1988.

Penn, Dorothy. "The 'Rota' Worn by the Jew in the Middle Ages." *Catholic World* 150 (March 1940): 688–90.

Pignedoli, Sergio. "The Aims of the Holy Year 1950." *Official Bulletin of Central Comity Holy Year* 1 (January 1949): 3–5.

Pipes, Daniel. "America's Muslims against America's Jews." *Commentary* 107 (May 1999): 32–36.

Polish, Daniel F. "Contemporary Jewish Attitudes to Mission and Conversion." In *Christian Mission—Jewish Mission,* ed. Martin A. Cohen and Helga Croner, 147–69. New York: Paulist Press, 1982.

———. "A Jewish Perspective: This Moment in Jewish-Christian Relations." *Ecumenical Bulletin* (November–December 1980): 8–9.

———. "A Very Small Lever Can Move the Entire World." In *Unanswered Questions: Theological Views of Jewish-Catholic Relations,* ed. Roger Brooks, 82–102. Notre Dame: University of Notre Dame Press, 1988.

P. T. B. "Mount Carmel and the Carmelites." *Catholic World* 64 (February 1897): 670–85.

Rackauskas, Constantine. "The Jerusalem Problem: A Note on Legality." *Thought* 25 (March 1950): 100–114.

Raymond-Barker, Elizabeth. "The Holy See and the Jews." *Catholic World* 70 (December 1899): 394–409.

"Report of the Secretary of the Anti-Defamation League, 1935." In *Jews and*

Judaism in the United States: A Documentary History, ed. Marc Lee Raphael, 140. New York: Behrman House, 1983.

Riccio, Barry D. "American Catholic Thought in the Nineteen Twenties: Frederick Joseph Kinsman and George Shuster." In *The American Church: Essays on Americanization of the Catholic Church,* ed. David J. Alvarez, 113–23. Moraga, Calif.: St. Mary's College of California, 1979.

Rushton, Gerald Wynne. "The Church and Jewry." *Catholic World* 145 (July 1937): 450–57.

Ryan, James A. "Peace with Justice." *Commonweal,* June 11, 1943, 196–98.

Ryan, John A. "Anti-Semitism in the Air." *Commonweal,* December 30, 1938, 260–62.

Ryan, R. M. "The City of Redemption." *Catholic World* 62 (February 1896): 667–81.

Sandmel, Samuel. "Jewish and Catholic Biblical Scholarship." In *Torah and Gospel: Jewish and Catholic Theology in Dialogue,* ed. Philip Scharper, 65–79. New York: Sheed and Ward, 1966.

Schilling, Godfrey. "Life at the Holy Sepulchre." *North American Review* 452 (July 1894): 77–87.

Schreiter, Robert J. "Changes in Roman Catholic Attitudes toward Proselytism and Mission." In *Pushing the Faith: Proselytism and Civility in a Pluralistic World,* ed. Martin E. Marty and Frederick E. Greenspahn, 93–103. New York: Crossroad, 1988.

"Seeing Waldheim." *Commonweal,* July 17, 1987, 405–06.

Sheean, Vincent. "The Palestine Report." *Commonweal,* April 30, 1930, 737–39.

Sheerin, John B. "The Arab-Israeli War and Catholic-Jewish Dialogue." *Catholic World* 205 (August 1967): 260–62.

———. "Has Interfaith a Future?" *Judaism* 27 (Summer 1978): 308–12.

Sherard, Robert H. "Dr. Nordau on the Jews and Their Fears." *American Monthly Review of Reviews* 17 (March 1898): 315–17.

Shuster, George N. "The Conflict among Catholics." *American Scholar* 10 (January 1941): 5–16.

———. "The Jew and Two Revolutions." *Commonweal,* December 30, 1938, 262–64.

———. "The Political Aspect of Christian-Jewish Relations." *Religion and the Modern World,* 185–92. Philadelphia: University of Pennsylvania Press, 1941.

Siedenburg, Frederick. "The Immigrant Problem." *Catholic Mind,* September 8, 1915, 484–500.

Siegman, Henry. "A Decade of Catholic-Jewish Relations—A Reassessment." In *Christianity and Judaism: The Deepening Dialogue,* ed. Richard W. Rousseau, 243–60. Scranton, Pa.: Ridge Row Press, 1983.

Signer, Michael A. "*Speculum Concilii:* Through the Mirror Brightly." In *Unanswered Questions: Theological Views of Jewish-Christian Relations,* ed. Roger Brooks, 105–25. Notre Dame: University of Notre Dame Press, 1988.

Smith, Elwyn A. "The Long Road to Jewish-Christian Understanding." *Journal of Ecumenical Studies* 6 (Spring 1969): 239–42.

Sobel, Ronald B. "To Angelicum Colloquium on *Nostra Aetate*, April 19, 1985." In *Pope John Paul II on Jews and Judaism, 1978–1986*, ed. Eugene J. Fisher and Leon Klenicki, 68–73. Washington, D.C., National Conference of Catholic Bishops; New York: Anti-Defamation League of B'nai B'rith, 1987.

Solomon, Norman. "Themes in Christian-Jewish Relations." In *Toward a Theological Encounter: Jewish Understandings of Christianity*, ed. Leon Klenicki, 16–42. New York: Paulist Press, 1991.

Soloveitchik, Joseph B. "Confrontation." *Tradition* 6 (Spring/Summer 1964): 5–27.

Starbuck, Charles C. "The Jew in Europe: The Christian's Antagonist." *Catholic World* 71 (September 1900): 828–41.

Stermann, Robert O. "Edith Stein, Witness to Paradox." *Catholic World* 180 (March 1957): 447–50.

Stern, Menahem. "The Period of the Second Temple." In *A History of the Jewish People*, ed. H. H. Ben-Sasson, 183–303. Cambridge, Mass.: Harvard University Press, 1976.

Stransky, Thomas F. "Focusing on Jewish-Christian Relations." *Origins*, June 20, 1985, 1, 67–70.

———. "Holy Diplomacy: Making the Impossible Possible." In *Unanswered Questions: Theological Views of Jewish-Catholic Relations*, ed. Roger Brooks, 51–69. Notre Dame: University of Notre Dame Press, 1988.

Sturm, Julius. "Catholics Don't Work at Making Converts." *America*, September 17, 1955, 589–91.

Sullivan, Kathryn. "Pro Perfidis Judaeis." *The Bridge* 2 (1956): 212–23.

Swidler, Leonard. "Catholic Statements on Jews—A Revolution in Progress." *Judaism* 27 (Summer 1978): 299–307.

"Two Miraculous Conversions from Judaism." *Catholic World* 39 (August 1884): 613–21.

Uhler, John Earle. "Is America Fair to Islam?" *Catholic World* 162 (February 1946): 396–402.

Valaik, J. David. "American Catholic Dissenters and the Spanish Civil War." *Catholic Historical Review* 53 (January 1968): 537–55.

———. "Catholics, Neutrality, and the Spanish Embargo, 1937–1939." *Journal of American History* 54 (June 1967): 73–85.

———. "In the Days before Ecumenism: American Catholics, Anti-Semitism, and the Spanish Civil War." *Journal of Church and State* 13 (Autumn 1971): 461–77.

Van Gestel, Peter. "Priests in Dachau." *Catholic World* 161 (September 1945): 469–75.

Van Rahden, Till. "Beyond Ambivalence." *American Jewish History* 82 (March 1994): 7–39.

Vatican Commission for Religious Relations with the Jews. "Notes on the Correct Way to Present the Jews and Judaism in Preaching and Catechesis in the Roman Catholic Church [June 24, 1985]." In *In Our Time: The Flowering of Jewish-Catholic Dialogue,* ed. Eugene J. Fisher and Leon Klenicki, 38–50. New York: Paulist Press, 1990.

"Vatican II and Missions." *America,* October 17, 1964, 444–45.

Vawter, Bruce. "Are the Gospels Anti-Semitic?" *Journal of Ecumenical Studies* 5 (Summer 1968): 473–87.

Villamil, Manuel Perez. "The Expulsion of the Jews from Spain in the Fifteenth Century." *Catholic World* 55 (September 1892): 851–59.

———. "The Jews in Early Spanish History." *Catholic World* 54 (October 1891): 86–96.

———. "The Jews in Early Spanish History." *Catholic World* 54 (December 1891): 360–71.

———. "The Jews in Spain during the Middle Ages." *Catholic World* 55 (June 1892): 649–61.

Walsh, Edmund A. "What Recognition of Soviet Russia Means." *Catholic Mind,* January 22, 1934, 27–32.

Wasner, Franz. "The Popes' Veneration of the Torah." *The Bridge* 4 (1961): 274–93.

Waxman, Mordecai. "The Dialogue, Touching New Bases." In *More Stepping Stones to Jewish-Christian Relations: An Unabridged Collection of Christian Documents, 1975–1983,* ed. Helga Croner, 24–31. New York: Paulist Press, 1985.

Weiss, Rabbi Avraham. "'Let the Nuns Pray Elsewhere,' October 15, 1989." In *Memory Offended: The Auschwitz Convent Controversy,* ed. Carol Rittner and John K. Roth, 255–57. New York: Praeger, 1990.

"What Have We Learned from Spain?" *Catholic World* 149 (May 1939): 130.

Wiesel, Elie. "*Nostra Aetate:* An Observer's Perspective." *Thought* 67 (December 1992): 366–70.

Wiesel, Elie, and Carol Rittner. "An Interview, August 29, 1989." In *Memory Offended: The Auschwitz Convent Controversy,* ed. Carol Rittner and John K. Roth, 113–16. New York: Praeger, 1990.

Wilken, Robert Louis. "The Jews as the Christians Saw Them." *First Things* 73 (May 1997): 28–32.

Winer, Mark L. "Visions for the Future: Catholic-Jewish Relations Worldwide." *Journal of Ecumenical Studies* 34 (Summer 1997): 369–76.

Wistrich, Robert S. "Helping Hitler." *Commentary* 102 (July 1996): 27–31.

———. "The Pope, the Church, and the Jews." *Commentary* 107 (April 1999): 22–28.

Wolf, Alfred. "A Tale of One City." *Judaism* 27 (Summer 1978): 292–98.

Wyschagrad, Michael. "A Jewish View of Christianity." In *Toward a Theological Encounter: Jewish Understandings of Christianity,* ed. Leon Klenicki, 104–19. New York: Paulist Press, 1991.

Young, Alfred. "Street Preaching." *Catholic World* 46 (January 1888): 499–504.

Yzermans, Vincent A. "Declaration on the Relationship of the Church to Non-Christian Religions: Historical Introduction." In *American Participation in the Second Vatican Council,* ed. Vincent A. Yzermans, 569–85. New York: Sheed and Ward, 1967.

———. "Declaration of the Relationship of the Church to Non-Christian Religions: Interventions." In *American Participation in the Second Vatican Council,* ed. Vincent A. Yzermans, 586–91. New York: Sheed and Ward, 1967.

Zahn, Gordon C. "Catholic Opposition to Hitler: The Perils of Ambiguity." *Journal of Church and State* 13 (Autumn 1971): 413–25.

———. "An Incomplete Confession." *Commonweal,* December 15, 1995, 15–16.

Books and Theses

Agus, Jacob Bernard. *Dialogue and Tradition: The Challenges of Contemporary Judeo-Christian Thought.* New York: Abelard-Schuman, 1971.

Alberigo, Giuseppe, and Joseph A. Komonchak, eds. *History of Vatican II.* Vol. 1. Maryknoll, N.Y.: Orbis, 1995.

Allitt, Patrick. *Catholic Intellectuals and Conservative Politics in America, 1950–1985.* Ithaca: Cornell University Press, 1993.

Alvarez, David J., ed. *An American Church: Essays on the Americanization of the Catholic Church.* Moraga, Calif.: St. Mary's College of California, 1979.

American Jewish Committee. *Christians Support Unified Jerusalem.* New York: American Jewish Committee, 1971.

———. *A Guide to Inter-religious Dialogue.* New York: American Jewish Committee, 1966.

———. *The Second Vatican's Declaration on the Jews: A Background Report.* New York: American Jewish Committee Institute of Human Relations, 1965.

Anderson, Floyd, ed. *Council Daybook, Vatican II, Session 3.* Washington, D.C.: National Catholic Welfare Conference, 1965.

Barka, Avraham. *Branching Out.* New York: Holmes and Meier, 1994.

Baum, Gregory G. *Christian Theology after Auschwitz.* London: Council of Christians and Jews, 1976.

Bea, Augustin Cardinal. *The Church and the Jewish People.* Translated by Philip Loretz. New York: Harper and Row, 1966.

Ben-Sasson, H. H., ed. *A History of the Jewish People.* Cambridge, Mass.: Harvard University Press, 1976.

Bergan, William H. *Busy Thoughts of a Traveller in the Orient.* Philadelphia: n.p., 1908.

Bickerton, Ian J., and Carla L. Klausner. *A Concise History of the Arab-Israeli Conflict.* Englewood Cliffs, N.J.: Prentice Hall, 1991; 2d ed., 1995.

Bishop, Claire Huchet. *How Catholics Look at Jews: Inquiries Into Italian, Spanish and French Teaching Materials.* Preface by Monsignor Olin J. Murdick. New York: Paulist Press, 1974.

Blau, Joseph L. *Judaism in America: From Curiosity to the Third Faith.* Chicago: University of Chicago Press, 1976.

Bokser, Ben Zion. *Judaism and the Christian Predicament.* Foreword by Frederick C. Grant. New York: Knopf, 1967.

Borowitz, Eugene B. *Contemporary Christologies: A Jewish Response.* New York: Paulist Press, 1980.

Breen, Andrew E. *A Diary of My Life in the Holy Land.* Rochester, N.Y.: John P. Smith Printing Co., 1906.

Brooks, Roger, ed. *Unanswered Questions: Theological Views of Jewish-Catholic Relations.* Notre Dame: University of Notre Dame Press, 1988.

Byrnes, Robert F. *Antisemitism in Modern France.* New Brunswick, N.J.: Rutgers University Press, 1950.

Callahan, Daniel. *The Mind of the Catholic Layman.* New York: Scribner, 1963.

Cantril, Hadley, ed. *Public Opinion: 1935–1946.* Westport, Conn.: Greenwood, 1951.

Carey, Patrick, ed. *American Catholic Religious Thought.* New York: Paulist Press, 1987.

Cargas, Harry James. *Reflections of a Post-Auschwitz Christian.* Foreword by Vidal Sassoon. Detroit: Wayne State University Press, 1989.

———. *Shadows of Auschwitz: A Christian Response to the Holocaust.* New York: Crossroad, 1990.

Carrigg, John J. "American Catholic Press Opinion with Reference to America's Intervention in the Second World War." M.A. thesis, Georgetown University, 1947.

Catechism of the Catholic Church. Washington, D.C.: United States Catholic Conference, 1994.

Cohen, Naomi. *Jews in Christian America: The Pursuit of Religious Equality.* New York: Oxford University Press, 1992.

Cornell, George. *Voyage of Faith: The Catholic Church in Transition.* New York: Odyssey, 1966.

Croner, Helga, ed. *More Stepping Stones to Jewish-Christian Relations: An Unabridged Collection of Christian Documents, 1975–1983.* New York: Paulist Press, 1985.

———. *Stepping Stones to Further Jewish-Christian Relations.* Foreword by Edward A. Synan. New York: Paulist Press, 1977.

Daum, Annette, and Eugene Fisher. *The Challenge of SHALOM for Catholics and Jews: A Dialogical Discussion Guide to the Catholic Bishops' Pastoral on Peace and War.* Cincinnati: Union of American Hebrew Congregations; Washington, D.C.: National Conference of Catholic Bishops, 1985.

Davies, Alan, ed. *Antisemitism and the Foundations of Christianity.* New York: Paulist Press, 1979.

Davis, Moshe, ed. *With Eyes Toward Zion—Vol. II.* New York: Praeger, 1986.

Dinnerstein, Leonard. *Antisemitism in America.* New York: Oxford University Press, 1994.

Dolan, Jay P. *The American Catholic Experience: A History from Colonial Times to the Present.* Garden City, N.Y.: Doubleday, 1985.

Drinan, Robert F. *Honor the Promise: America's Commitment to Israel*. Garden City, N.Y.: Doubleday, 1977.

———. *Religion, the Courts, and Public Policy*. New York: McGraw-Hill, 1963.

Durward, Rev. J. T. *Holy Land and Holy Writ*. Baraboo, Wis.: Pilgrim, 1913.

———. *Sonnets of the Holy Land*. Baraboo, Wis.: Pilgrim, 1890.

Ellis, John Tracy, ed. *Documents of American Catholic History, 1866–1966*. Vols. 1–3. Wilmington, Del.: Glazier, 1987.

Feingold, Henry L. *A Time for Searching: Entering the Mainstream, 1920–1945*. Baltimore: Johns Hopkins University Press, 1992.

Feldblum, Esther Yolles. *The American Catholic Press and the Jewish State, 1917–1959*. New York: Ktav, 1977.

Feldman, Egal. *The Dreyfus Affair and the American Conscience, 1895–1906*. Detroit: Wayne State University Press, 1981.

———. *Dual Destinies: The Jewish Encounter with Protestant America*. Urbana: University of Illinois Press, 1990.

Fine, Morris, and Milton Himmelfarb, eds. *American Jewish Year Book 1965*. Vol. 66. New York: American Jewish Committee; Philadelphia: Jewish Publication Society of America, 1965.

———. *American Jewish Year Book 1966*. Vol. 67. New York: American Jewish Committee; Philadelphia: Jewish Publication Society of America, 1966.

Fisher, Eugene J. *Faith without Prejudice*. New York: Paulist Press, 1977.

Fisher, Eugene J., ed. *Interwoven Destinies: Jews and Christians through the Ages*. New York: Paulist Press, 1993.

———. *Visions of the Other: Jewish and Christian Theologians Assess the Dialogue*. New York: Paulist Press, 1994.

Fisher, Eugene J., and Leon Klenicki, eds. *In Our Time: The Flowering of Jewish-Catholic Dialogue*. New York: Paulist Press, 1990.

———. *Pope John Paul II on Jews and Judaism, 1978–1986*. Washington, D.C.: National Conference of Catholic Bishops; New York: Anti-Defamation League of B'nai B'rith, 1987.

Fisher, Eugene J., et al., eds. *Twenty Years of Jewish-Catholic Relations*. New York: Paulist Press, 1986.

Flannery, Austin, gen. ed. *Vatican Council II: The Conciliar and Post Conciliar Documents*. Preface by John Cardinal Wright. Vol. 1. Collegeville, Minn.: Liturgical Press, 1975.

———. *Vatican Council II: More Postconciliar Documents*. Vol. 2. Collegeville, Minn.: Liturgical Press, 1982.

Flannery, Edward H. *The Anguish of the Jews: Twenty-Three Centuries of Antisemitism*. Rev. ed. New York: Paulist Press, 1985.

Fleischner, Eva, ed. *Auschwitz: Beginning of a New Era? Reflections on the Holocaust*. New York: Ktav, The Cathedral Church of St. John the Divine, Anti-Defamation League of B'nai B'rith, 1974.

Flynn, George Q. *American Catholics and the Roosevelt Presidency, 1932–1936*. Lexington: University of Kentucky Press, 1968.

Fogarty, Gerald P. *The Vatican and the American Hierarchy from 1870 to 1965.* Stuttgart: Anton Hiersemann, 1982.

Freudmann, Lillian C. *Antisemitism in the New Testament.* Lanham, Md.: University Press of America, 1994.

Fulop-Miller, Rene. *Leo XIII and Our Time.* New York: Longmans, Green, 1937.

Gannon, Robert Ignatius. *The Cardinal Spellman Story.* Garden City, N.Y.: Doubleday, 1962.

Gerber, David, ed. *Anti-Semitism in American History.* Urbana: University of Illinois Press, 1987 edition.

Gilbert, Arthur. *A Jew in Christian America.* New York: Sheed and Ward, 1966.
———. *The Vatican Council and the Jews.* Cleveland: World, 1968.

Gleason, Philip. *Keeping the Faith: American Catholicism, Past and Present.* Notre Dame: University of Notre Dame Press, 1987.

Gordis, Robert. *Judaism in a Christian World.* New York: McGraw-Hill, 1966.

Gottlieb, Roger S., ed. *Thinking the Unthinkable: Meanings of the Holocaust.* New York: Paulist Press, 1990.

Greeley, Andrew M. *The Catholic Experience: An Interpretation of the History of American Catholicism.* Garden City, N.Y.: Doubleday, 1967.

Greeley, Andrew M., and Jacob Neusner. *The Bible and Us: A Priest and a Rabbi Read Scripture Together.* New York: Warner, 1990.

Greeley, Andrew M., and Peter H. Rossi. *The Denominational Society: A Sociological Approach to Religion in America.* Glenview, Ill.: Scott, Foresman, 1972.

Greenberg, Gershom. *The Holy Land in American Religious Thought, 1620–1948: The Symbiosis of American Religious Approaches to Scripture's Sacred Territory.* Lanham, Md.: University Press of America; Jerusalem: Avraham Harman Institute of Contemporary Jewry, 1994.

Guidelines for Catholic-Jewish Relations. Washington, D.C.: Secretariat for Catholic-Jewish Relations, Bishops' Committee on Ecumenical and Interreligious Affairs, National Conference of Catholic Bishops, 1985.

Gushee, David P. *The Righteous Gentiles of the Holocaust: A Christian Interpretation.* Minneapolis: Fortress Press, 1994.

Guttmann, Allen. *The Wound in the Heart: America and the Spanish Civil War.* Glencoe, Ill.: Free Press, 1962.

Halecki, Oscar. *Eugenio Pacelli: Pope of Peace.* New York: Farrar, Straus and Young, 1951.

Halsey, William M. *The Survival of American Innocence: Catholicism in an Era of Disillusionment, 1920–1940.* Notre Dame: University of Notre Dame Press, 1980.

Hargrove, Katharine T., ed. *The Star and the Cross: Essays on Jewish-Christian Relations.* Milwaukee: Bruce, 1966.

Heer, Friedrich. *God's First Love: Christians and Jews over Two Thousand Years.* Translated by Geoffrey Skelton. New York: Weybright and Talley, 1970.

Heller, James G. *Isaac M. Wise: His Life, Work and Thought.* Cincinnati: Union of American Hebrew Congregations, 1965.

Herr, Dan, and Joel Wells, eds. *Through Other Eyes: Some Impressions of American Catholicism by Foreign Visitors from 1777 to the Present.* Westminster, Md.: Newman Press, 1965.

Herzl, Theodor. *The Complete Diaries of Theodor Herzl.* Edited by Raphael Patai. Translated by Harry Zahn. 5 vols. New York: Herzl Press and Thomas Yoseloff, 1960.

Irani, George Emile. *The Papacy and the Middle East: The Role of the Holy See in the Arab-Israeli Conflict, 1962–1984.* Notre Dame: University of Notre Dame Press, 1986.

Isaac, Jules. *The Teaching of Contempt: Christian Roots of Anti-Semitism.* Introduction by Claire Hutchet Bishop. Translated by Helen Weaver. New York: Holt, Rinehart and Winston, 1964.

Jacob, Walter, ed. *The Changing World of Reform Judaism: The Pittsburgh Platform in Retrospect.* Pittsburgh: Rodef Shalom Congregation, 1985.

John Paul II, His Holiness. *Crossing the Threshold of Hope.* Edited by Vittorio Messori. New York: Knopf, 1994.

Johnson, Walter. *The Battle against Isolation.* Chicago: University of Chicago Press, 1944.

Kasimow, Harold, and Byron L. Sherwin, eds. *No Religion Is An Island: Abraham Joshua Heschel and Interreligious Dialogue.* Maryknoll, N.Y.: Orbis, 1991.

Kenny, Anthony J. *Catholics, Jews and the State of Israel.* New York: Paulist Press, 1993.

Klein, Charlotte. *Anti-Judaism in Christian Theology.* Translated by Edward Quinn. Philadelphia: Fortress Press, 1978.

Klenicki, Leon, ed. *Toward a Theological Encounter: Jewish Understandings of Christianity.* New York: Paulist Press, 1991.

Korn, Bertram Wallace. *The American Reaction to the Mortara Case: 1858–1859.* Cincinnati: American Jewish Archives, 1957.

Lapide, Pinchas E. *The Last Three Popes and the Jews.* London: Souvenir Press, 1967.

Lipset, Seymour Martin, and Earl Raab. *Jews and the New American Scene.* Cambridge, Mass.: Harvard University Press, 1995.

Long, J. Bruce, ed. *Judaism and the Christian Seminary Curriculum.* Chicago: Loyola University Press, 1966.

Marcus, Sheldon. *Father Coughlin: The Tumultuous Life of the Priest of the Little Flower.* Boston: Little, Brown, 1971.

Margolis, Max L., and Alexander Marx. *A History of the Jewish People.* New York: Atheneum, 1969.

Martin, David, ed. *American Catholic Convert Authors.* Detroit: Walter Romig, 1944.

Marty, Martin E., and Frederick E. Greenspahn, eds. *Pushing the Faith: Proselytism and Civility in a Pluralistic World*. New York: Crossroad, 1988.

McBrien, Richard P., gen. ed. *The HarperCollins Encyclopedia of Catholicism*. San Francisco: HarperCollins, 1995.

McGarry, Michael B. *Christology after Auschwitz*. New York: Paulist Press, 1977.

McMahon, Frances E. *A Catholic Looks at the World*. New York: Vanguard, 1945.

Minerbi, Sergio I. *The Vatican and Zionism: Conflict in the Holy Land, 1895–1925*. Translated by Arnold Schwarz. New York: Oxford University Press, 1990.

Morley, John F. *Vatican Diplomacy and the Jews during the Holocaust, 1939–1943*. New York: Ktav, 1980.

Murray, John Courtney. *We Hold These Truths: Catholic Reflections on the American Proposition*. New York: Sheed and Ward, 1960.

Neusner, Jacob, ed. *Judaism and Christianity: The New Relationship*. Introduction by Jacob Neusner. Vol. 4. New York: Garland, 1993.

Newton, William L. *Notes on the Covenant: A Study In the Theology of the Prophets*. Cleveland: Seminary Press, 1934.

Nolan, Hugh J., ed. *Pastoral Letters of the United States Catholic Bishops*. Vols. 1–4. Washington, D.C.: National Conference of Catholic Bishops, United States Catholic Conference, 1983.

Novak, David. *Jewish-Christian Dialogue: A Jewish Justification*. New York: Oxford University Press, 1989.

O'Connell, William Cardinal. *Sermons and Addresses of His Eminence William Cardinal O'Connell, Archbishop of Boston*. 3 vols. Boston: Flynn, 1911.

O'Connor, John Cardinal, and Mayor Edward I. Koch. *His Eminence and Hizzoner: A Candid Exchange*. New York: Morrow, 1989.

Oesterreicher, John M. *The Rediscovery of Judaism: A Re-Examination of the Conciliar Statement on the Jews*. South Orange, N.J.: Institute of Judaeo-Christian Studies, 1971.

———. *Walls Are Crumbling: Seven Jewish Philosophers Discover Christ*. Foreword by Jacques Maritain. London: Hollis and Carter, 1953.

Oesterreicher, John M., and Anne Sinai, eds. *Jerusalem*. New York: John Day Company, 1974.

Pawlikowski, John T. *Catechetics and Prejudice: How Catholic Teaching Materials View Jews, Protestants and Racial Minorities*. New York: Paulist Press, 1973.

———. *The Challenge of the Holocaust for Christian Theology*. New York: Center for Studies on the Holocaust, Anti-Defamation League of B'nai B'rith, 1978.

———. *Sinai and Calvary: A Meeting of Two Peoples*. Beverly Hills, Calif.: Benziger, 1976.

————. *What Are They Saying about Christian-Jewish Relations?* New York: Paulist Press, 1980.

Peck, Abraham J., ed. *Jews and Christians after the Holocaust*. Foreword by Elie Wiesel. Philadelphia: Fortress Press, 1982.

Pfeiffer, James. *First American Catholic Pilgrimage to Palestine, 1889*. Cincinnati: Press of Jos. Berning and Company, 1892.

Pinson, Koppel S., ed. *Essays on Anti-Semitism*. New York: Jewish Social Studies, 1946.

Rahner, Karl, and Pinchas Lapide. *Encountering Jesus—Encountering Judaism: A Dialogue*. Translated by Davis Perkins. New York: Crossroad, 1987.

Rittner, Carol, and John K. Roth, eds. *Memory Offended: The Auschwitz Convent Controversy*. New York: Praeger, 1990.

Rousseau, Richard W., ed. *Christianity and Judaism: The Deepening Dialogue*. Scranton, Penn.: Ridge Row Press, 1983.

Rubenstein, Richard L. *After Auschwitz: Radical Theory and Contemporary Judaism*. Indianapolis: Bobbs Merrill, 1966.

Ruether, Rosemary Radford. *Faith and Fratricide: The Theological Roots of Anti-Semitism*. New York: Seabury Press, 1974.

Sachar, Abram Leon. *A History of the Jews*. 1930. Reprint, New York: Knopf, 1965.

Sachar, Howard M. *A History of Israel*. New York: Knopf, 1979.

————. *A History of the Jews in America*. New York: Knopf, 1992.

Sandmel, Samuel. *Anti-Semitism in the New Testament?* Philadelphia: Fortress Press, 1978.

Scharper, Philip, ed. *Torah and Gospel: Jewish and Catholic Theology in Dialogue*. New York: Sheed and Ward, 1966.

————. *American Catholics: A Protestant-Jewish View*. With an afterword by Gustave Weigel. New York: Sheed and Ward, 1959.

Schneiderman, Harry, ed. *The American Jewish Year Book 5698*. Vol. 39. Philadelphia: Jewish Publication Society of America, 1937.

Schwartz, G. David. *A Jewish Appraisal of Dialogue: Between Talk and Theology*. Lanham, Md.: University Press of America, 1994.

Schweitzer, Frederick M. *A History of the Jews since the First Century A.D.*, 2d ed. New York: Macmillan, 1980.

Shermis, Michael, and Arthur E. Zannoni, eds. *Introduction to Jewish-Christian Relations*. New York: Paulist Press, 1991.

Shuster, George N. *The Catholic Spirit in America*. New York: Dial Press, 1927.

————. *Strong Man Rules: An Interpretation of Germany Today*. New York: D. Appleton–Century, 1934.

Strong, Donald S. *Organized Anti-Semitism in America: The Rise of Group Prejudice during the Decade 1930–1940*. Westport, Conn.: Greenwood, 1941.

Suau, Père. *The Christian Faith*. Introduction by C. C. Martindale. London: Burns Oates and Washbourne, 1920.

Thoma, Clemens. *A Christian Theology of Judaism.* Foreword by David Flusser. Translated and edited by Helga Croner. New York: Paulist Press, 1980.

Vetromile, Eugene. *Travels in Europe, Egypt, Arabia Petraea, Palestine and Syria.* 2 vols. New York: Sadlier, 1871.

Warner, Michael. *Changing Witness: Catholic Bishops and Public Policy, 1917–1994.* Foreword by George Weigel. Washington, D.C.: Ethics and Public Policy Center; Grand Rapids, Mich.: Eerdmans, 1995.

Watkin, E. I. *The Catholic Centre.* New York: Sheed and Ward, 1939.

Weigel, George. *Catholicism and the Renewal of American Democracy.* New York: Paulist Press, 1989.

———. *Witness to Hope: The Biography of Pope John Paul II.* New York: Cliff Street Books, 1999.

Weigel, George, and Robert Royal, eds. *Building the Free Society: Democracy, Capitalism, and Catholic Social Teaching.* Grand Rapids, Mich.: Eerdmans; Washington, D.C.: Ethics and Public Policy Center, 1993.

Weisbord, Robert G., and Wallace P. Sillanpoa. *The Chief Rabbi, the Pope, and the Holocaust: An Era in Vatican-Jewish Relations.* New Brunswick, N.J.: Transaction, 1992.

Wiesel, Elie, ed. *A Journey of Faith.* Foreword by Gabe Pressman. New York: Fine, 1990.

Wilken, Robert L. *The Land Called Holy: Palestine in Christian History and Thought.* New Haven: Yale University Press, 1992.

Will, Allen S. *Life of Cardinal Gibbons.* Vol. 2. New York: Dutton, 1922.

Willebrands, Johannes Cardinal. *Church and Jewish People: New Considerations.* New York: Paulist Press, 1992.

Yzermans, Vincent A., ed. *American Participation in the Second Vatican Council.* New York: Sheed and Ward, 1967.

Zannoni, Arthur E., ed. *Jews and Christians Speak of Jesus.* Minneapolis: Fortress Press, 1994.

Index

EGAL FELDMAN is an emeritus professor of history at the University of Wisconsin at Superior where he served as the dean of the College of Letters and Science and for many years as the chairman of its Department of History. He holds a Ph.D. in history from the University of Pennsylvania. He has written four books, including *The Dreyfus Affair and the American Conscience, 1895–1906* (Detroit, 1981) and *Dual Destinies: The Jewish Encounter with Protestant America* (Urbana, 1990).

Composed in 10.5/13 Sabon
with Sabon display
by Jim Proefrock
at the University of Illinois Press
Designed by Dennis Roberts
Manufactured by Maple-Vail
Book Manufacturing Group

University of Illinois Press
1325 South Oak Street
Champaign, IL 61820-6903
www.press.uillinois.edu